ALSO BY ANDREW WILSON

Mad Girl's Love Song:
Sylvia Plath and Life Before Ted

Shadow of the Titanic:
The Extraordinary Stories of Those Who Survived

Harold Robbins:
The Man Who Invented Sex

Beautiful Shadow:
A Life of Patricia Highsmith

The Lying Tongue

ALEXANDER McQUEEN

BLOOD BENEATH THE SKIN

ANDREW WILSON

SCRIBNER

New York   London   Toronto   Sydney   New Delhi

SCRIBNER
An Imprint of Simon & Schuster, Inc.
1230 Avenue of the Americas
New York, NY 10020

First Scribner hardcover edition September 2015

SCRIBNER and design are registered trademarks of The Gale Group, Inc.,
used under license by Simon & Schuster, Inc., the publisher of this work.

For information about special discounts for bulk purchases,
please contact Simon & Schuster Special Sales at 1-866-506-1949
or business@simonandschuster.com.

The Simon & Schuster Speakers Bureau can bring authors to your live event.
For more information, or to book an event, contact the Simon & Schuster Speakers Bureau
at 1-866-248-3049 or visit our website at www.simonspeakers.com.

Manufactured in the United States of America

1   3   5   7   9   10   8   6   4   2

Library of Congress Cataloging-in-Publication Data

Wilson, Andrew, date.
Alexander McQueen : blood beneath the skin / Andrew Wilson.
pages cm
1. McQueen, Alexander, 1969–2010. 2. Fashion designers—Great Britain—Biography. I. Title.
II. Title: Blood beneath the skin. III. Title: Alexander McQueen.
TT505.M37W55 2015
746.9'2092—dc23
[B]   2015012025

ISBN 978-1-4767-7673-6
ISBN 978-1-4767-7676-7 (ebook)

CONTENTS

ALEXANDER McQUEEN

INTRODUCTION

On the morning of Monday, 20 September 2010, the steps outside St. Paul's Cathedral in London were transformed into a catwalk. From a fleet of sleek black cars emerged a procession of beautiful women, "some in homage plumes, nearly all in raven black."[1] There was Kate Moss in a black leather dress and tuxedo jacket, revealing a sliver of sun-kissed cleavage (one writer called it a "staggeringly inappropriate amount of décolletage"[2]); Naomi Campbell wore a black feather jacket and a pair of studded boots with gilt heels; Sarah Jessica Parker arrived in a fairy-tale cream dress under a black coat; and Daphne Guinness sported a pair of twelve-inch platform black boots that, at one point as she walked down the paved approach, threatened to unsteady her. Together with 1,500 or so assembled guests, they had gathered at Sir Christopher Wren's baroque church at the top of Ludgate Hill to celebrate the life of one of Britain's most lauded and notorious fashion designers. Friends and family knew him as Lee, the rest of the world as Alexander McQueen, the so-called bad boy of fashion.[3]

As they took their seats inside St. Paul's, an organist played Edward Elgar's "Nimrod" from the *Enigma Variations*. The choice of music, one of the fourteen variations on a hidden theme, was appropriate for the occasion. Elgar's missing motif, what the composer described as "its dark saying" because its "chief character is never on stage," captured the strange contrariness of the event, a memorial for a man who was physically absent, but whose ghostly presence haunted every moment of the service.

Indeed, McQueen himself was often described as an enigma. "L'Enfant terrible. Hooligan. Genius. Alexander McQueen's life makes for an intriguing story," wrote one commentator after his death. "Few understood Britain's most accomplished fashion designer, a sensitive visionary who reinvented fashion in so many ways."[4] The stylist Katy England, who worked with the designer and who attended the memorial with her husband, the pop star Bobby Gillespie, described McQueen as "quite a closed shop . . . he does isolate himself, he does cut himself off,"[5] while Trino Verkade, a trusted member of McQueen's staff, said that "Lee definitely became more introverted and, in the end, he could only handle being around very few people."[6] Although, one observer declared, McQueen would have loved the memorial service, which had, she said, "all the theatrical drama, raw human emotion, heritage, ecclesiastical splendour and beauty that characterized his catwalk shows,"[7] the designer would have been unable to sit through the series of fulsome accolades and eulogies. He might have been, in his own words, "a big-mouth east London yob"[8] and supremely confident of his abilities, but he was so fundamentally shy that at the end of each show he would only make the briefest of appearances on the catwalk before being whisked off home or to dinner with friends. "He would be amazed that he was held in such high esteem," said his sister Jacqui. "At the end he would think, 'I'm just Lee.' "[9]

The service, which began promptly at eleven o'clock—unlike so many McQueen shows that started behind schedule—opened with an address given by Reverend Canon Giles Fraser. "It was a life lived in the public gaze, but it was as vulnerable and retiring as it was glamorous," he said. Fraser, wearing one of the gold and white copes encrusted with Swarovski crystals that had been commissioned for the cathedral's three hundredth anniversary, spoke of McQueen's achievements: how he was named British Designer of the Year four times between 1996 and 2003 and International Designer of the Year in 2003, and how that same year he was made a Commander of the British Empire. "We give thanks for his creative mind, his showmanship, and for his capacity to shock." Fraser also acknowledged McQueen's strong commitment to friends, his love of animals (especially his three dogs, which he left behind), and his "challenging nature"—those who had been on the receiving end of his "sharp tongue" must have smiled to themselves when they heard that. "When he needed support and solace, he found it in his family," added Fraser, "which is why, despite the dazzle of his world, he never forgot his East End roots and how much he owed to his loved ones."[10]

That day in the cathedral McQueen's family sat apart from the celebrities and the models. Andrew Groves, one of McQueen's former boyfriends, noticed that the designer's taxi-driver father, Ronald, and his brothers and sisters seemed distinctly uncomfortable. "They felt really out of place at that event," said Groves, who in the nineties worked as a fashion designer under the name Jimmy Jumble and who is now also a fashion tutor. "To me it felt as though they didn't really understand Lee's legacy. It was like, 'what's all this about?' "[11] Alice Smith, a fashion recruitment consultant and a friend who met McQueen in 1992, was struck by the difference in footwear on the two sides of the aisle. "The memorial service was very odd, as I couldn't reconcile the family with the fashion crowd. I kept looking at their shoes—the family had very normal high street shoes—and on the other side were these fantastically expensive, ostentatious shoes."

That contrast symbolized one of the paradoxes of McQueen's life, a contradiction that the designer never fully resolved. "That was his problem," said Alice. "His family was well-behaved, they were nice people trying to live a good life and on the other side of his life was this completely bonkers world."[12] The atmosphere that day was awkward as the guests consisted of a number of cliques and groups—the supermodels, the actresses, the famous designers, the East End family, the gay friends from Old Compton Street—none of whom knew one another. "It was a weird mixture of people there and no one was interacting," said Andrew Groves. "When you go to a fashion show everyone knows where they are meant to sit. If I go to a fashion show I know, as I'm in education, that I'll be right on the back row, and I know that Anna [Wintour] will be on the front row. I know for that moment we are in the same world, but in reality we're not."[13]

After the Lord's Prayer, the congregation stood to sing "I Vow to Thee My Country," a hymn that includes two lines McQueen would have found especially poignant: "And there's another country I've heard of long ago, / Most dear to them that love her, most great to them that know." Throughout his life the designer was searching for "another country" of his own. McQueen yearned for a place, a state, an idea, a man, a dress, a dream, a drug that would transform his reality. Yet if he was addicted to anything—Lee made no secret of his seemingly insatiable appetite for cocaine—ultimately he was addicted to the lure of fantasy, the prospect that one day he might be free of his body, his memories, his regrets, his past.

It was clear that McQueen thought that love had the ultimate transformative power. "Of course, there is a dark side," said Katy England three years before her friend's death. "But there is also a truly romantic side. Lee's such a romantic character and he has these dreams. It's all about him looking for love, isn't it? It's him looking for love and his idea of love and romance, well, it's way above and beyond reality."[14]

On his upper right arm the designer had a tattoo of the words, spoken by Helena, in Shakespeare's *A Midsummer Night's Dream*, "Love looks not with the eyes, but with the mind." The quotation is key to understanding both Lee McQueen the man and Alexander McQueen the superstar designer. As Andrew Bolton, curator of *Savage Beauty*, the Metropolitan Museum of Art's 2011 exhibition of McQueen's work and the consultant curator of the Victoria and Albert Museum exhibition of the same name, stated, "In her contemplations, Helena believes that love has the power to transform something ugly into something beautiful, because love is propelled by subjective perceptions of the individual, not by objective assessments of appearance. This belief was not only shared by McQueen but also critical to his creativity."[15]

McQueen's extraordinary talent as a designer was the subject of an address given by Anna Wintour. "He was a complex and gifted young man who, as a child, liked nothing more than watching the birds from the roof of [an] east London tower block," said the editor in chief of American *Vogue*, who was wearing a black and gold embroidered McQueen coat.[16] "He has left us with an exceptional legacy, a talent that soared like the birds of his childhood above us all." During the course of his career, from his 1992 Central Saint Martins MA graduate show to his death in February 2010, McQueen had harnessed "his dreams and demons." It was no surprise to learn that McQueen's final collection, which the designer was working on at the time of his death and which Wintour described as a battle between "dark and light," became unofficially known as *Angels and Demons*.[17] Three years before his death, McQueen had told the French magazine *Numéro*, "I oscillate between life and death, happiness and sadness, good and evil."[18] "Lee combined two things, the superficiality of fashion and the sublime beauty of death," said his friend Jake Chapman, the artist. "The reason his work has resonance was the self-destruction. We were watching someone kind of crumble."[19]

Despite the black specter of depression that overshadowed his later years, McQueen had an unstoppable energy and zest for life. He was an unashamed hedonist—he adored both the finest caviar and a treat of beans and poached eggs on toast while sitting on the sofa watching *Coronation Street*. He loved Maker's Mark and Diet Coke, the sleazier end of gay pornography and a great deal of anonymous sex. So it was fitting that at the memorial service, after Anna Wintour sat down, the composer Michael Nyman came forward to play "The Heart Asks Pleasure First," from his score to Jane Campion's 1993 film, *The Piano*. The heroine of that film, Ada McGrath (played by Holly Hunter), is a mute woman who has not spoken since she was six years old and expresses herself through playing the piano. Verbal articulacy was not McQueen's strong point—"I saw him off his face at parties . . . he was completely incomprehensible, he didn't know what he was saying," said the broadcaster and writer Janet Street-Porter[20]—but his greatest eloquence could be found in the radical clothes he designed and the spectacular shows he staged. "What you see in the work is the person himself," McQueen once said. "And my heart is in my work."[21]

The jeweler Shaun Leane, whose address followed Nyman's performance, and who worked with Lee on a number of collections, said, "I watched you grow, you broke the boundaries and succeeded." He spoke of how, on a recent trip to Africa, he had looked up at the sky and asked, " 'Where are you, Lee?' As the words left my mouth, a shooting star shot across the sky—you answered me. You moved stars like you moved our lives."[22] Leane also recalls his friend's "dirty laugh, brave heart, memory like an elephant and bright blue eyes."[23]

When Leane retook his seat a collection was passed around the congregation to raise funds for the Terrence Higgins Trust, Battersea Dogs & Cats Home and Blue Cross, all charities close to McQueen's heart. The soulful voices of the London Community Gospel Choir echoed throughout the church. "Amazing grace, how sweet the sound / That saved a wretch like me! / I once was lost, but now am found; / Was blind, but now I see." McQueen's grace, the thing that gave him hope—at least in the early days—was fashion. Alice Smith remembers Lee as a young graduate with too much time on his hands when he would haunt her office in St. Martin's Lane "and pick up *Draper's Record*, which is quite a sombre [trade] publication, or at least it used to be, and he would flick through the pages going 'Fashion! Fashion! Fashion!' We would say, 'It's not Italian *Vogue*.' "[24]

After the gospel choir finished singing "Amazing Grace," Suzy Menkes, then fashion editor of the *International Herald Tribune*, took her turn and spoke of McQueen's vision. "In thinking about the McQueen legacy, I remember his bravery, his daring and his imagination," she said. "But I keep coming back to the beauty: the streamlined elegance of his tailoring, the wispy lightness of printed chiffon, the weirdness of animal and vegetable patterns that showed a designer who cared about the planet, not just Planet Fashion." She recalls the first time she met Lee, then an angry and rather fat young man in his East End studio, "ankle deep in cuts of fabric, turning his scissors savagely into the cloth he was cutting." Later, he transformed himself into a slimmer and altogether sleeker product and she remembers him "cackling with joy" as the fashion editors rushed backstage to congratulate him after a truly exceptional show. "The imagination and showmanship never drowned out his flawless tailoring, nor the subtle fluidity he learnt during his period in Paris haute couture," she said. "I had no doubt—and nor did he—that he was an artist who just happened to work with clothing and whose shows were extraordinary vaults of the imagination. And above all, that his work was deeply personal."

Menkes, who had seen every McQueen show from the beginning of his career, related the last conversation she had had with the designer after his menswear show in Milan in January earlier that year. "But bones are beautiful!" he had said, in an attempt to explain why the "tailored suits . . . wallpaper and flooring" looked like something from an ossuary, "with artistic arrangements of everyone's skeletal ending." Of course, she should not have been surprised by this latest "riff on the macabre," she said, as you could "trace harbingers of death and destruction through his extraordinary collections." Before stepping down, Menkes went on to quote something McQueen had once told her about himself; interestingly, the designer had already talked about himself in the past tense, as if he were already dead: "Anger in my work reflected angst in my personal life. What people see is me coming to terms with what I was in life. It's always about the human psyche. My work is like a biography of my own personality." Although Menkes urged the congregation to remember McQueen by the words from Keats's poem "Ode on a Grecian Urn," "Beauty is truth. Truth beauty. That is all ye know on earth—and all ye need to know," it was difficult for friends and family to forget the manner in which the forty-year-old designer had died.[25] On 11 February 2010, the day before his mother's funeral, he had committed suicide at his flat in London's Mayfair.

Murray Arthur, who was Lee's boyfriend between 1996 and 1998, felt an overwhelming sense of loss both when he heard the shocking news of McQueen's death and during the memorial service itself. "I remember I couldn't look down," he told me. "I had to keep looking up because I knew that if I looked down tears would come and I'd choke up."[26] Like many in the audience, he found the next performance, Björk's live rendition of Billie Holiday's "Gloomy Sunday," particularly difficult to endure: "Gloomy Sunday, with shadows I spend it all. / My heart and I have decided to end it all."

Dressed in a "feathery grey and brown skirt and a parchment set of wings,"[27] Björk looked like one of the hybrid creatures that so often haunted McQueen's shows, a half-woman, half-bird, a wounded Ariel singing of the dark side of the creative imagination.

The lyrics, which were originally written by László Javór, and which became known as "the Hungarian suicide song," stand as a poetic distillation of both McQueen's inner torment and the sense of despair suffered by those he left behind; in the dark hinterland following McQueen's death, many close friends and some family members experienced suicidal thoughts. "Gloomy Sunday" could also be seen as McQueen's posthumous paean to his friend and early mentor Isabella Blow, who suffered from depression and who had killed herself by drinking weed killer in May 2007. After Isabella's death, McQueen became increasingly obsessed with the idea of trying to contact his friend beyond the grave and spent hundreds of pounds on mediums and psychics in an attempt to reach her. "Lee was obsessed with the afterlife," said Archie Reed, who first met Lee in 1989, and who became his boyfriend ten years later. "I got the impression that both Issie and him were rushing towards death."[28]

The relationship between Isabella and Lee, between a high-born aristocrat with a face like a medieval saint and an overweight son of an East End taxi driver with, as Blow observed, teeth that "looked like Stonehenge," was a complex one.[29] Their friendship was bound together by their love of the metamorphosing power of fashion, its ability to mutate and transform the appearance and mind-sets of those who felt ugly, shy, strange or at odds with the world. Both of them knew that fashion was not only about the surface. "With me, metamorphosis is a bit like plastic surgery, but less drastic," McQueen said in 2007. "I try to have the same effect with my clothes. But ultimately I do this to transform mentalities more than the body."[30] In the end, fashion did not have the ability to save either of them; in fact, there are those who claim that the industry contributed to their deaths. According to McQueen, Isabella "would say that fashion killed her," but he added, "she also allowed that to happen in a lot of ways."[31] The same could be said of McQueen himself.

After the prayers, led by Philip Treacy, the Reverend Jason Rendell, Gary James McQueen, the designer's nephew, and Jonathan Akeroyd, the CEO of Alexander McQueen, the London Community Gospel Choir got to their feet once more to sing Quincy Jones's "Maybe God Is Tryin' to Tell You Something." Friends and family stood for the blessing—"Go forth into the world in peace," said the canon in residence, "hold fast that which is good; render to no one evil for evil"—at which point a lone piper, Donald Lindsay, wearing McQueen tartan, walked gracefully down the center aisle and led the congregation out of the church to the *Braveheart* pipe motif. As the crowd gathered on the steps of St. Paul's they listened as twenty more men, all dressed in tartan kilts, struck up their bagpipes. "The whole thing was just like one of his shows," said Andrew Groves. "We were cursing him, just in terms of his music choice, because he was pushing all your buttons and emotions."[32]

McQueen was an anti-intellectual and his formal education was patchy to say the least, but he had an innate ability to provoke and manipulate emotion. "I don't want to do a cocktail party, I'd rather people left my shows and vomited," he once said. "I prefer extreme reactions."[33] He certainly divided opinion. "He was one of a kind, the service was bitter-sweet, perfect," said Sarah Jessica Parker after the memorial.[34] Kate Moss said simply, "I loved him," while Shaun Leane added that McQueen "never knew quite how many people cared about him."[35] Yet it can't be denied that there were those who felt betrayed, frustrated, and angry with him; very often the same people who also loved him so deeply. "He's the one person I would probably forgive anything," said Annabelle Neilson, who together with some of his friends helped organize the service. "Maybe you forgive difficult people more."[36] He was, as he described himself, "a romantic schizophrenic," a personality often at battle with itself.[37]

Accessing his creativity was never hard for McQueen—he said he could plan a collection in the space of two days—because he used his raw and unfettered self as his subject. "My collections have always been autobiographical," he said in 2002, "a lot to do with my own sexuality and coming to terms with the person I am—it was like exorcizing my ghosts in the collections. They were to do with my childhood, the way I think about life and the way I was brought up to think about life."[38] His work can be read, in the words of Judith Thurman of the *New Yorker*, as "a form of confessional poetry." In the same essay, Thurman continues, "Therapists who treat children often use dolls' play as a tool for eliciting their stories and feelings, and one has the sense that the dolls' play of fashion was such a tool for McQueen."[39]

His life has many of the elements of a dark folktale or a mythic fable. It is the story of a shy, strange-looking boy from a poor working-class background who used his gothic imagination to transform himself into a fashion superstar—by the time of his death, at the age of forty, he had amassed a fortune of £20 million—but who along the way lost a part of his innocence. As one commentator observed, his life was a "modern-day fairy-tale infused with the darkness of a Greek tragedy."[40] It's no surprise to learn that in his posthumous collection, *Angels and Demons*, one of the pieces, an exquisite coat "tailored from lacquered gold feathers,"[41] referenced both Grinling Gibbons, who worked his sculptural magic in St. Paul's Cathedral, and the myth of Icarus, the boy whose wild aspirations drew him too close to the sun. Birds swept in and out of McQueen's brief life, from the birds of prey he used to watch from the roof of the tower block behind his childhood home, to the beautiful prints of swallows featured in his Spring/Summer 1995 collection, *The Birds*, inspired by M. C. Escher's illustrations and Hitchcock's film. Then there were the hawks and kestrels and falcons that he had learnt to handle at Hilles, Issie and her husband Detmar Blow's grand country home in Gloucestershire. "He's a wild bird and I think he makes clothes fly," said Isabella of her friend.[42]

There were others who took the metaphor one step further. "He behaves like a bird, twitchy and nervous, rarely making eye contact," said the journalist Vassi Chamberlain.[43] Easily bored and restless, McQueen sometimes behaved like someone with attention deficit disorder—he would often return from expensive exotic holidays early and, like a bird or wild animal, hated the idea of being constrained or contained. His most challenging work explored the idea of the hybrid and the mutant, the way that strands of our primitive and savage state continue to twine their way through our DNA. His favorite books were the Marquis de Sade's *The One Hundred and Twenty Days of Sodom* and Patrick Süskind's *Perfume*, works that explore transgression and the darker aspects of human existence. He injected the seemingly superficial world of fashion with classic Freudian concepts of dreams and delusions, totem and taboo, the ego and the id and civilization and its discontents. "I don't think like the average person on the street," he said. "I think quite perversely sometimes."[44] He visualized and made real the deviant and the depraved, but swathed his dark ideas in exquisite fabrics and constructed them around elegantly tailored pieces, clothes that were beautiful and, despite repeated accusations of misogyny, incredibly empowering for women. "When you see a woman wearing McQueen, there's a certain hardness to the clothes that makes her look powerful," he said. "It kind of fends people off."[45]

This book will tell the twisted fairy story of McQueen's life, from his hard east London upbringing to the hedonistic world of fashion. Those closest to McQueen—his family, friends and lovers—have spoken for the first time about the man they knew, a fragmented, insecure individual, a lost boy who battled to gain entry into a world that ultimately destroyed him.

"There's blood beneath every layer of skin," McQueen once said.[46] This biography aims to get beneath his skin to reveal the raw source of his genius and to show the links between his dark work and even darker life. "McQueen is totally unlike what one expects him to be," wrote one observer six years before his death. "He is his own wounded work of art."[47]

CHAPTER ONE

A history of "much cruelty and dark deeds."

—*Joyce McQueen*

When Lee Alexander McQueen was born, on 17 March 1969 at Lewisham Hospital in southeast London, he weighed only five pounds ten ounces. The doctors told his mother, Joyce, that his low weight could mean that he might have to be placed in an incubator, but he soon started to feed, and mother and baby returned home to the crowded family home at 43 Shifford Path, Wynell Road, Forest Hill. Although Joyce and Ron, in the words of their son Tony, "always said that he [Lee] was the only one they tried for," the birth of the youngest of their six children did nothing to soothe the tense atmosphere in the McQueen household.

"My dad had a breakdown in 1969, just as my mum gave birth," said Lee's brother Michael McQueen. "He was working too hard, a lot of hours as a lorry driver with six children, too many really."[1] His brother Tony, who was fourteen years old at the time, remembers noticing that one day his father went unnaturally quiet. "He was working seven days a week, he was hardly ever home," said Tony. "My mum got someone round and they institutionalized him. It was a difficult period for us." Joyce, in an unpublished manuscript she compiled for the family, noted that her husband spent only three weeks in Cane Hill Hospital, Coulsdon, but according to Tony, "Dad had a nervous breakdown and he went into a mental institution for two years."[2]

Cane Hill Hospital was the archetypal Victorian asylum, an enormous rambling madhouse of the popular imagination. Designed by Charles Henry Howell, it was originally known as the Third Surrey County Pauper Lunatic Asylum, so called because the county's other two institutions, Springfield and Brookwood, had reached full capacity. "Cane Hill was typical of its time, providing specialized wards for different categories of patients, with day rooms on the ground floor and dormitories and individual cells mostly on the second and third floors," wrote one historian. "Difficult patients were confined to cells and those of a more clement disposition could walk the airing grounds . . . By the 1960s, the hospital had changed little."[3] Former patients included Charlie Chaplin's mother, Hannah, and the half brothers of both Michael Caine and David Bowie, who used a drawing of the administration block on the American cover of his 1970 album *The Man Who Sold the World*.

Lee McQueen was fascinated by the idea of the asylum—he featured the iconography of the madhouse in a number of his collections, particularly *Voss* (Spring/Summer 2001)—and he would have been intrigued by the rumors about a subterranean network of tunnels near Cane Hill. Over the years it has been suggested that the series of brick-lined tunnels housed a mortuary, a secret medical testing facility and a nuclear bomb shelter. Although the truth was much more mundane—the tunnels were built as bomb shelters during the Second World War and then taken over by a company that manufactured telescopes—the network of underground chambers "became somehow connected with the institution and the obscure rusting of machinery took on sinister new overtones, driven by the superstition surrounding the complex."[4]

Years after the closure of Cane Hill, a couple were walking around the grounds of the hospital when, in the Garden House, they came across a bundle of faded yellow pages, remnants of the kind of questionnaire Ronald McQueen would have encountered while a patient at the institution. Many of the fifty-one questions, which patients were encouraged to answer with a response of "true" or "false," would have had a particular resonance if they had later been applied to Lee: "I have not lived the right kind of life," "Sometimes I feel as if I must injure myself or someone else," "I get angry sometimes," "Often I think I can't understand why I have been so cross and grouchy," "I have sometimes felt that difficulties were piling up so high that I could not overcome them," "Someone has it in for me," "It is safer to trust nobody," and "At times I have a strong urge to do something harmful or shocking."[5]

It's difficult to know the exact effect of Ronald's breakdown on his youngest son. A psychotherapist might be able to draw links between Lee's later mental health issues and his father's illness. Did Lee come to associate his birth, his very existence, with madness? Did the boy feel some level of unconscious guilt for driving his father into a psychiatric ward? There is no doubt, however, that in an effort to comfort both her infant son and herself, Joyce lavished increased levels of love on Lee and, as a result, the bond between them intensified. As a little boy, Lee had a beautiful blond head of curls, and photographs taken at the time show him to be an angelic-looking child. "He had preferential treatment from my mother but not my dad; he was a bit Neanderthal because of his hard upbringing," said Michael McQueen.[6]

When Lee was less than a year old the family moved from south London to a council house in Stratford, a district close to the dock area of east London. "I think if you're from the East End you can't get used to the south side," said Lee's sister Janet McQueen. "They say you can't move an old tree and it was like that. I think it was probably that a housing initiative came up and we had the chance of moving into a house, a new house."[7] The council house, at 11 Biggerstaff Road, was a three-story brick terraced house and although it had four bedrooms it was still a squeeze for the family. "We boys slept three to a bed in there," said Tony McQueen. "My mum would say, 'Which end would you like?' and I would say, 'The shallow end; Lee keeps pissing himself.'"[8] Family photos show that the house was a typical modern working-class home with a fitted patterned carpet,

floral sofas with wooden arms, papered walls and gilt-framed repro-
ductions of paintings by Constable. At the back of the house there
was a small paved garden with a raised fishpond and a white gate that
led out onto a grassy communal area in front of a tower block.

Ron couldn't work because of his condition, and money was in
short supply. Janet left school at fifteen and took a job in London
Bridge in the offices of a dried egg import business to help support
the family. Her brother Tony recalls how difficult it was for the family
to survive. "My mum would give me the money to go on the bus to
where Janet was working, to get her wages off her, and then I would
bring the money back to my mum and meet her and do the shopping
with her," he said. "Mum was working as well, doing cleaning in the
morning and the evening."[9]

When Ron returned from Cane Hill to the house in Stratford, he
trained to become a black-cab driver so he could work the hours that
suited him. He had, in Joyce's words, "wonderful willpower to get
better again."[10] He took up fishing and snooker and finally started to
earn a little more money. Life in 1970s Britain was, for many ordinary families like the McQueens, a rather grim affair. In 1974 there
were two general elections and the country was gripped by economic
and social unrest. Power cuts were a regular feature of daily life (a
three-day weekly limit for the commercial consumption of electricity
had been imposed), rubbish went uncollected for weeks and unemployment surged past the all-important one million mark (by 1978
it stood at 1.5 million).

Yet the work ethic was strong in the McQueen family—Ron
eventually bought the house from the council in 1982—and he
expected his sons to get steady and reliable jobs as plumbers, elec-
tricians, bricklayers or cabdrivers. The upbringing was strict, almost
Victorian. If he saw his children "getting beyond or above themselves," he would try and bring them back down to earth, quashing
their confidence in the process. "We were seen and not heard," said
Lee's sister Jacqui.[11] By the time Tony was fourteen he had traveled
all over the country with Ron in a lorry. "So my education suffered

a bit," he said. "That was me and Michael's childhood."[12] Tony left school to work as a bricklayer and Michael became a taxi driver like his father. They were born into the working classes and their father believed that any aspiration above and beyond that would not only lead to personal unhappiness and dissatisfaction but would serve as a betrayal of their roots too. Creativity in any form was frowned upon and regarded as a total waste of time; dreaming was all well and good but it would not put food on the table.

It was into this world that Lee, a sensitive, bright child with a vivid imagination, was born. From the very beginning the cherubic-looking boy strived for something more, a desire that he found he could express through the medium of clothes. When he was three he picked up a crayon lying around his sisters' bedroom and drew an image of Cinderella, "with a tiny waist and a huge gown," on a bare wall.[13] "He told me about that Cinderella drawing on the wall, I thought it was quite magical," said his friend Alice Smith, who visited the house in Biggerstaff Road a number of times. "I also remember him telling me about how one day his mum dressed him up to go out when he was little. He was wearing trousers with an anorak and they were going to the park and he said, 'Mum, I can't wear this.' She asked him why not and he replied, 'It doesn't go.'"[14] His sisters started to ask him about what they should wear to work and he soon became their "daily style consultant." "I was absorbed early on by the style of people, by how they expressed themselves through what they wear," he said.[15]

When Lee was three or four he was playing by himself at the top of the house in a bedroom that looked out towards Lund Point, a twenty-three-story tower block behind the terrace. He climbed onto a small ottoman that sat beneath the window and pushed the window wide open. Just as he was stretching out to reach through the window his sister Janet walked into the bedroom. "The window had no safety catch and he was stood on the ottoman reaching out," she said. "I thought to myself, 'No, don't say anything.' I went up behind him and grabbed him. I probably told him off because he could easily have fallen out of the window."[16] He was, by all accounts, a mischievous, spirited little boy. He stole his mother's false teeth and put them in his mouth for a joke or repeated the same trick with a piece of orange peel cut into jagged, teeth-like shapes. He would take hold of his mother's stockings and pull them over his head to frighten people. With his sisters he would go along to the local swimming club to take part in synchronized-swimming competitions. "You would hear our trainer, Sid, shouting, 'Lee—Lee McQueen?' and he would be under the water looking at us," said Jacqui. "Or he would have a hula skirt on and suddenly jump into the water. He was so funny."[17] One day, Lee did a backflip off the side of the swimming pool and hit his cheekbone, an accident that left him with a small lump.

After Lee and Joyce's deaths her treasured photograph albums were passed around between her remaining five children. Seeing images of Lee as a boy, looking bright-eyed and full of fun, was especially hard for the McQueens. Here was Lee with a swathe of white fabric around his head, his right foot wrapped in a bandage, his left eye smudged with makeup so as to give him a black eye, and a cane in one hand and a box of chocolates in the other; around his neck hangs the sign "All Because the Lady Loved Milk Tray." There are plenty more taken at similar holiday camp competitions—one of him holding a prize while staying at Pontins and another of him, when he was only three or so, dancing with a little girl the same age, his blond hair falling down the side of his head, his mouth open wide with joy. There is one of him enjoying being picked up and cuddled by a man in a panda suit and another of him looking a little more self-conscious, probably a photograph taken at junior school, trying to smile but careful to keep his mouth closed because he did not want his prominent and uneven front teeth to show. One day when Lee was a young boy he tripped off the small wall in the back garden of the house in Biggerstaff Road and hit his teeth. "He was always self-conscious about his teeth after that," said Tony.[18] "I remember he had an accident when he was younger and lost his milk teeth and the others came through damaged or twisted," said Peter Bowes, a school friend who knew him from the age of five. "So he had these buck front teeth, one of the things that would give him a reason to be humiliated and picked on. He was called 'goofy' and things like that."[19]

Lee knew that he was not like other boys from an early age, but the exact nature and source of this difference were still unclear to him. His mother picked up the fact that her youngest son was a strange mix of surface toughness and unusual vulnerabilities and did everything she could to protect him. "He was this little fat boy from the East End with bad teeth who didn't have much to offer, but he had this one special thing, this talent, and Joyce believed in him," said Alice Smith. "He told me once that she had said to him, 'Whatever you want to do, do it.' He was adored; they had a special relationship, it was a mutual adoration."[20]

When Lee was a boy he would watch in wonder as his mother unrolled an eight-foot-long scroll decorated with elaborate coats of arms. She would point out the names of long-dead ancestors on the family tree and talk about the past. Joyce was passionate about genealogy—she later taught the subject at Canning Town Adult Education Centre—and she told her young son that she suspected that the McQueen side of the family had originated from the Isle of Skye. Lee had become increasingly fascinated with the island's gothic history and his ancestors' place in it. It was on a holiday with Janet in 2007 that he first visited the small cemetery in Kilmuir—the last resting place of the Jacobite heroine Flora MacDonald—and saw a grave marked with the name Alexander McQueen; in May 2010, the designer's cremated remains were buried in the same graveyard.

Joyce spent years plotting out the family tree, but by the end of her research she had failed to find any definitive evidence linking her husband's McQueen ancestors to Skye. But, like many things in Lee's life, the romance of the idea was more alluring than the reality. Listening to his mother's tales of Scotland's brutal history, and the suffering that his ancestors endured at the hands of the English landowners, he constructed an imaginative bloodline across the centuries. One of the attractions of boyfriend Murray Arthur was the fact that he was from north of the border. "He was obsessed by Scotland, and loved the fact that I was Scottish," he said.[21] Lee's bond with Scotland grew increasingly strong over the years—it inspired collections such as *Highland Rape* (1995) and *Widows of Culloden* (2006)—and in 2004, when his mother asked him what his Scottish roots meant to him, McQueen replied, "Everything."[22]

Joyce McQueen's journey back into the past started when her husband asked her to find out about the origins of his family: "Are we Irish or Scottish?" By 1992, she had gathered her work into a manuscript that told the story of the McQueens' roots. "Researching family history can be fun, but more than this it can give us a sense of belonging and how we came to be," wrote Joyce.[23] For Lee, this was especially important as it provided him with a connection to history and opened up possibilities that allowed his imagination to fly.

Joyce noted how the earliest mention of the name McQueen on the Isle of Skye was in the fourteenth century during the reign of John MacLeod, Laird of Dunvegan Castle, a place that Lee visited later in his life. MacLeod "was a man of fiendish cruelty who on hearing that two of his daughters wanted to marry the two brothers of the MacQueen of Roag had his two daughters buried alive," wrote Joyce. "The two brothers MacQueen were flogged to death and thrown over the precipice."[24] Another story unearthed by Mrs. McQueen and passed down to her son related to another supposed ancestor, Duncan McQueen, who in 1742, together with his friend Angus Buchanan, waylaid a merchant at Rigg, where they robbed and then murdered him. After both men were caught they confessed to the crime and were sentenced to death by hanging. "The history of Skye contains much cruelty and dark deeds," wrote Joyce.[25]

In Joyce's booklet on the history of the McQueen family she reproduced a rough sketch of two "Highland peasants" wearing "the actual clothing which was discovered on skeletons who lived in the early 1700s." Detailed glimpses of historical costume, illustrating Lee's intertwined passions of history and fashion, can be found throughout his mother's manuscript. For instance, in the section on the Gallowglass sept (or clan), a cross between the Norse and Pict men who had invaded Ireland by the middle of the thirteenth century, Mrs. McQueen described how these "foreign young fighting men" were "of great stature, courage and fierce in battle" and dressed "in coats of mail to the knees and armed with battleaxes." Joyce, and in turn Lee, learnt how the Clan McQueen were said to be of Norse descent and of how they invaded Ireland and the Western Isles of Scotland. "Swean, Sweyn is certainly a Norse name as is Revan which appears among the McQueens' early history," wrote Joyce. "The Revan or Refan is Norse for raven, the black bird that is the emblem of the Danes."[26] (Later, McQueen would include references to ravens in his collections, such as *Eclect Dissect* and *The Horn of Plenty*.) It is thought that some of these early McQueens were subjects of a lord who settled in the area around Snizort on Skye, where one of the earliest effigies of a clan member can be found.

It's probable that Lee felt a certain empathy with the unnamed knights whose graves on Skeabost Island his mother wrote about in her history of the McQueens. In the booklet she included a description of one effigy, which lies to the southwest of a neglected church, as having a "bluish schist." In a sunken panel one could just make out the figure of an armed man wearing a bascinet, a camail of banded mail and a quilted coat that reached to his knees, holding a three-foot-long claymore.

Two events in Scottish history haunted McQueen's consciousness and provided him with inspiration: the Jacobite rebellion and the Battle of Culloden in 1746, both of which he believed involved his ancestors. As his mother told him, the McQueens had joined with other small clans to form a body called the Clan Chattan, which, under the leadership of the Chief Mackintosh, helped defend their families on the Isle of Skye. But then in 1528, in Joyce's words, "James V was responsible for a savage commission of fire and sword granted to his half-brother James Earl of Moray for punishing Clan Chattan for widespread discord . . . It demanded the 'utter extermination and destruction' of the clan and its supporters leaving none alive, but priest, women and bairns, the latter to be shipped across the sea to the Low Countries or Norway." Although the order was not carried out to its fullest extent, it inevitably meant a dispersal of the clan. Following the Battle of Culloden the family suffered further losses on Skye, while "those that were not killed during these battles were taken prisoner and endured great hardships," said Joyce. "By ship they were taken south of the border where they were imprisoned or transported to other countries. Many would die of disease or from their wounds before they had even arrived at their destination. Some sailed from Liverpool to the Virginias in America while others were sent to such places as the Tower of London, Newgate prison and Tilbury Fort in Essex." However, some of the clan managed to receive pardons and others, who swore allegiance to the king, were released.

Joyce never could quite work out the exact connection between the McQueens of Skye and her husband's forefathers, but she was certain that his ancestors would have suffered violence, poverty and fragmentation, a triumvirate that continued to shape the family over the course of the next couple of centuries. The more Joyce told Lee about his ancestors the more he came to identify with them, viewing them as brave outsiders who fought against a system. He would have been particularly intrigued to learn that his middle name, Alexander, had been passed down through his immediate family since the beginning of the nineteenth century when three brothers—Alexander, John and William McQueen, all stonemasons—settled in London, in the area of St. George in the East.

In 1806, Alexander, the eldest of the three brothers, married Sarah Vallas, a woman of Huguenot descent. Her heritage appealed to Lee, who was told by his mother that the "Huguenots were French protestants who flew from France after the edict of Nantes to escape persecution. Their most popular place of settlement was in Spitalfields where they worked as silk weavers high in the garret rooms near a large window which lit their looms." Alexander and Sarah went on to have five sons, one of whom, also called Alexander, particularly interested both Joyce and Lee. In the 1851 census, Alexander described himself as a mat manufacturer who lived with his wife, Ann, and daughter Ellen. "But this was not strictly true," wrote Joyce. "Alexander did not marry his wife Ann Seymour until their daughter Ellen was eighteen years old." Ten years later the couple owned a lodging house at 28–29 Dorset Street, which was, in Joyce's words, "one of the most notorious streets in the area, where few dared to stray for fear of being robbed or assaulted." This stretch of dank, crowded doss-houses, the so-called worst street in London, would forever be associated with Jack the Ripper, the unidentified serial killer who murdered at least five women in the East End of London in 1888. "It was in this environment that our ancestors lived and one can only imagine their fear and apprehension during the time these terrible murders were taking place," said Joyce.[27]

On 9 November 1888, the body of twenty-five-year-old prostitute Mary Jane Kelly, thought to be the Ripper's last victim, was discovered at 13 Millers Court, a room at the back of 26 Dorset Street. In his report, Dr. Thomas Bond, the surgeon who performed the autopsy on Kelly's body and who would later commit suicide by throwing himself from a bedroom window, described the horrific manner in which the woman had been mutilated. "The whole surface of the abdomen and thighs was removed and the abdominal cavity emptied of its viscera," he said. "The breasts were cut off, the arms mutilated by several jagged wounds and the face hacked beyond recognition of the features . . . The viscera were found in various parts . . . the uterus and kidneys with one breast under the head, the other breast by the right foot, the liver between the feet, the intestines by the right side and the spleen by the left side of the body. The flaps removed from the abdomen and thighs were on a table."[28] Lee found this kind of macabre detail fascinating and later, while studying fashion at Saint Martins, he would take the name of the serial killer as inspiration for his graduate collection.

Tragedy and horror seemed to be a constant presence in the history of the McQueens. In 1841, while a branch of the family was living in Sun Court, Leadenhall Street, a two-year-old girl, Sarah McQueen, was so terribly scalded in an accident that she died from her injuries. Forty years later, in 1880, Ellen, the daughter of Alexander McQueen, who had grown up in Dorset Street, was living with her second cousin William MacQueen and her two-year-old daughter Clara in Hoxton, east London. One day Ellen was doing her washing with her daughter at her side, but "leaving the child for a few moments she returned to find that Clara had fallen into the tub of suds and drowned," wrote Joyce. Such was the level of poverty, it was, she added, difficult for her to imagine how people survived. She consulted records that showed that, at one point in the mid-nineteenth century, twelve members of the McQueen family were living at 6 Bakers Court, Bishopsgate, a dwelling place that was subsequently knocked down to make way for Liverpool Street station. "The living conditions of these people must have been intolerable for it is known that a whole family would have to live in just one room or perhaps two if they were lucky," wrote Joyce. Of course, she added, there was no such thing as hot running water. "There was only the fire to heat water and cook food. Light was provided by candle or oil lamps . . . In those days the poor people had to go to the Poor House for treatment if they were ill."

In order to piece together the history of the family, Joyce McQueen spent hours at various libraries, including public record offices in Chancery Lane, Clerkenwell and Kew, as well as the Society of Genealogists and the Guildhall Library. Each day, after hours of work, she returned to the family in Biggerstaff Road and told them of her discoveries. Joyce brought the past to life in a way that made it so real to Lee that he thought he could almost smell it. Who were these men who went by the name of Alexander McQueen and who had died so many years before? There was, he learnt, Alexander McQueen the stonemason, born in 1847, who married an Irish girl called Jane Little, from County Cork, Ireland, whose father brought the family over to England after the great potato famine. Alexander and Jane had six children, including three daughters, Rose, Jane and another Jane, all of whom died young. This Alexander, by all accounts a rather large man, made his money by collecting the money from the stallholders of Petticoat Lane, while Jane took in washing. Towards the end of his life he laid paving stones for a living and by the time of his death in 1920 he was living at 5 William Street, in the parish of St. George in the east. "Perhaps it's worth reflecting that had his only son Alexander not survived we might not have been here today," wrote Joyce.[29]

That man, Lee's great-grandfather, was born on 19 March 1875 in Spitalfields and although he attended a charity or Sunday school he left being unable to write. At the age of twenty he was working as a bricklayer and was regarded, according to Joyce, as the "black sheep of the family." In 1897, Alexander married Annie Gray at St. John the Evangelist church in Golding Street, Stepney—"both made their mark with a cross because they could not write or spell their name," wrote Joyce. By 1907, Alexander had been forced to give up work as a bricklayer after he fell from a tall ladder, breaking his foot; after the accident he took a job as a carman working down on the docks. "Annie, like thousands of women in her day, took in washing which draped in the rooms and all along the hallway to dry," wrote Joyce, who from relatives learnt of Annie's skill as a clog dancer. Annie, a large woman, and Alexander, a short man with dark hair, had at least twelve children, but their marriage was far from happy. "She was known to have suffered violence from her husband mainly through drinking, which in those days seems to have been the normal thing to do," wrote Joyce. "She also witnessed a murder down Cable Street when a sailor was stabbed to death."[30] Three children did not live beyond infancy; a son, Walter Samuel, was injured at Dunkirk and died soon after he returned home; and another son, Henry, died at the age of twenty-eight from blood poisoning after a splinter lodged in his finger while he was playing snooker.

Alexander and Annie's second-eldest son, Samuel Frederick, Lee's grandfather, was born on 24 December 1907 in St. George in the East. He grew up to be a docker and also a presser who worked in ladies' tailoring, a skill that he passed down to both his daughter, Irene or Renee, and his grandson Lee. In November 1926, while living at 5 Crellin Street, Lee's grandfather married nineteen-year-old Grace Elizabeth Smith, a woman whose harsh upbringing resulted in a hardened character. Grace, Lee's paternal grandmother, was the illegitimate daughter of Elizabeth Mary Smith and Ernest Edmund Jenkins, who worked at a paper stall in the City of London. "Grace was a hard and strict mother, she had no love for her stepfather, it was probably the hard life she suffered as a child that made her determined to be a survivor," wrote Joyce.[31]

In May 1940, Samuel volunteered to join the Royal Engineers and later that year he was employed in the bomb disposal unit. "I think he pissed off and went into the army without her [Grace] knowing," said Michael McQueen, Lee's brother.[32] Between July 1941 and September 1942 Samuel worked in Iceland "maintaining the ships until the Americans came to take over," wrote Joyce.[33] While her husband was away at war, Grace brought up her brood of children single-handedly—"they only surfaced to breed," Lee said later.[34] "Grace kept her home and children spotless but this left very little time to demonstrate any love to her children," wrote Joyce.[35]

One day, Grace's home in the East End was hit by a bomb and she and her teenage daughter, also called Grace, were buried under a mound of rubble. When Grace was at last pulled free she saw that "part of her ear was hanging off and had to be stitched back," wrote Joyce.[36] On Samuel's return from war in November 1944, after being discharged from the army for medical reasons, the marriage deteriorated further. The couple's eight children grew up in a home poisoned by domestic violence. "My mother told me that he was a very hard man, a drunkard," said Jacqui McQueen of her paternal grandfather.[37] Michael remembers Grace, the woman he knew as "Nanny McQueen," as being "as mad as a March hare."[38] Lee confessed in an interview, talking of his father's background: "He didn't have the best mother and father himself. His dad was an alcoholic, his mother not much better."[39] When Grace was around sixty years old her marriage finally broke down and she obtained a legal separation and went to live on her own in a flat in Abbey Wood.

Grace and Samuel's eldest son, Ronald Samuel—Lee's father—was born on 19 April 1933 at 3 Raine Street and later moved with his parents to various addresses around Wapping, St. John's Hill and Artichoke Hill. Ronald attended Christian Street School in Stepney on the same street where his father worked as a tailor's presser. Ronald and his brothers and sisters were brought up Catholics and they attended St. Patrick's Church, Tower Hill, where for a time Ron served as an altar boy. During the Second World War, the boy was evacuated to Newton Abbott and taken in by the Easterbrook family; Ronald always had fond memories of his time in Devon and later spoke lovingly of Mrs. Easterbrook, "to whom he grew greatly attached."[40] No doubt he saw her as the mother he might have had: kind, loving and attentive. The return back to his real parents, Samuel and Grace, must have broken his heart. "My nan [Grace], she was pretty hard," said Tony McQueen. "I think she was quite stern with all the children and rumour has it that she hit my dad once with a milk bottle on the head. So he had a rough upbringing. His upbringing made him what he was."[41] According to Jacqui, Ron "had to take over being the breadwinner. He had three jobs and the money was taken from him. And then his mother took out her temper on him."[42]

After leaving school, Ronald worked at the British Road Service depot in Aldgate where he was in charge of looking after two horses, Bill and Daisy. It was his job to prepare them ready for work—"horses were still being used after the war as a form of transport, for coal delivery and by milkmen," wrote Joyce.[43] The creatures grew so accustomed to hearing Ronald walk into the yard each morning that they would both neigh at the sound of his approaching footsteps. When Ronald was twenty, his sister Jean introduced him to her friend, Joyce Barbara Deane, the woman he would marry. "I cannot put into words the love your father and I had for each other," Joyce wrote to her children just before she died. "He worshipped the ground I walked on."[44]

Later in life, Joyce said she had traced her own family, the Deane line, back to the Normans, but when she told Lee this he replied, "I feel more Scottish than Norman."[45] On the scroll Joyce made about her side of the family, she documented the origins of the Deane name—"a Saxon word meaning 'a clearing in a wood or valley where swine feed.'" As these clearings became inhabited by people, they in turn would call themselves "of the Deane."[46]

On the same scroll, fashioned on graph paper, Joyce painted in watercolor a number of heraldic shields relating to the family: a white cross on a red background belonging to Drue Deane, a knight of Edward I; five black stars arranged in an upturned V shape on a bright green background, signifying Sir Henry de Den, Lord of Dean, who died in 1292 in Gloucester; and a black lion, the animal's paw raised in the air in a gesture of defiance, the escutcheon of Sir John de Dene who died in the first part of the fourteenth century. The mystique surrounding these long-dead historical figures was a very long way from the reality of life at Biggerstaff Road. For Joyce and Lee the past was a way of escaping the poverty of everyday life.

Joyce's father, George Stanley, worked as a grocer's warehouseman, while her mother, Jane Olivia Chatland, grew up in a desperately poor family. Jane's father, John Archibald Chatland, could not work because he only had one leg. From a young girl Jane suffered from malnutrition and had to be admitted to Bethnal Green Infirmary at the age of one, and by the "age of five or six [she] was sent to a home in Kent by nuns because she was so thin and undernourished," recalled Joyce. Later, Joyce remembered her mother telling her that she often went to school without shoes. "Her father was a bully and made their lives miserable," wrote Joyce of her mother.[47] Jane met her husband, George, at the age of thirteen and the couple married in August 1933, at Christ Church, Hackney. Six months later, on 15 February 1934, their eldest child, Joyce Barbara, was born.

Joyce attended Teesdale Street School in Bethnal Green and at the age of five was evacuated to King's Lynn, Norfolk, where she lived with six different families, an experience she must have found deeply disturbing. During this time she also suffered a broken nose after being knocked down by a delivery bike. At the end of the war in 1945 Joyce returned to London to live with her parents at their new flat at 148 Skidmore Street, Stepney, first attending a school run by nuns off Cambridge Heath Road and then going to Hally Street School, Stepney. While still at school she worked at Woolworth's and then, after leaving Hally Street, she took a job in a solicitor's office in Moorgate. In her spare time she liked going to the cinema and enjoyed a night out at the Poplar Civic with her friend Jean McQueen. One contemporary observer noted that the Civic was a "big dance-hall and, though expensive, had a really good band, with girls from all over the East End, not the usual bunch one saw every night."[48]

One day in 1953 Jean introduced Joyce to her brother Ron, then a lorry driver. The attraction was instant and on 10 October 1953 the pair married at the Roman Catholic Church of the Guardian Angels on Mile End Road. A photograph taken at their wedding shows a handsome young couple about to cut the cake. He is wearing a dark suit, white shirt and tie, and she a simple, tailored white dress with an elaborate lace veil. On the table by their side is a spray of carnations and a lucky horseshoe.

Their first child, Janet Barbara, was born on 9 May 1954, followed by Anthony Ronald in 1955, Michael Robert in 1960, Tracy Jane in 1962, Jacqueline Mary in 1963 and then, in 1969, after a gap of six years, Lee Alexander. He grew up to be known in the household as "Blue Eyes"—not only because of the color of his eyes, but also a reference to the fact that he was the baby of the family and as such occupied a special place within the home.

At the age of five Lee enrolled at Carpenter's Road Junior School, a newly built single-story structure a couple of minutes' walk from the family home. Peter Bowes was a pupil at the same school—indeed, the two boys would remain close friends throughout junior and secondary school—and remembers his friend with fondness. "Even then he liked to draw, he would rather draw than read or write," he said. "He was in the football team in the juniors and although he joined in with everyone, there was always something about him, even at a very young age, that made him different to all of us. I wouldn't say it was to do with sexuality, it's just that he was different. He was very artistic, a bit flamboyant, a bit of a showman, and yet at the same time he could be quite shy, which is an interesting contrast. He wasn't feminine or sissy-like. He was actually someone who could look after himself."[49]

Later in life, Lee would talk about how he realized that he was gay—or "queer," as the other boys called him—when he was still a young child. He told the journalist Lynn Barber that he was six years old when he first realized that he was gay. On a family holiday to Pontins he won a "Prince of Pontins" competition, "but I wanted the boy who came second to win because I fancied him!" he said.[50] He claimed to have been at ease with his sexuality from an early age—"I was sure of myself and my sexuality and I've got nothing to hide," he said. "I went straight from my mother's womb onto the gay parade."[51] In interviews he would often call himself the "pink sheep of the family," but this was, as McQueen's former boyfriend Andrew Groves said, merely a pat quote to stop further discussion of the subject. The truth was much more complex, and disturbing.

When he was nine or ten something happened to Lee which was to have a profound effect on his later life: he started to be sexually abused by his brother-in-law, Terence Anthony Hulyer, a violent man who Janet married in 1975. Janet knew nothing about the abuse until about four years before Lee died, when he confided in her. The horrific news came as such a shock to her that Janet did not know what to say. She simply asked him whether he held it against her and he replied no, he did not. But she still felt overwhelmed by guilt and shame and despair. Why had she not been able to protect her little brother? she asked herself. After that brief conversation Lee never mentioned the abuse to Janet again and she didn't want to ask any more questions because she felt so sickened by what her first husband had done.[52]

Over the years Lee talked, sometimes obliquely, about the sexual abuse to a number of close friends and boyfriends, but he rarely went into detail about what it consisted of or for how long he had been forced to endure it. "Lee told me he had been sexually abused and that it massively affected him," recalls Rebecca Barton, who was a close friend of Lee's when he was at St. Martins.[53] "Once when we were at my flat in Green Lanes he broke down and said he had been abused," said Andrew Groves. He believes that the sexual abuse contributed to McQueen's unsettling "sense that someone was going to screw him over" and an inability to trust those close to him.[54] Once, when Lee was feeling particularly overwhelmed by a sense of darkness, he had "a real heart to heart" with his boyfriend Richard Brett "about why he went to the dark place" and he told him too about the sexual abuse, but again kept the exact details to himself. "But I got the impression that some nasty stuff had happened to him when he was a boy," said Richard.[55] Lee also confided in Isabella Blow and her husband, Detmar. "He was hurt and angry and said that it had robbed him of his innocence," said Detmar. "I thought it brought a darkness into his soul."[56]

Lee's friend BillyBoy*, whom he met in 1989, believes that the sexual abuse shaped McQueen for the rest of his life. "I got the impression that he endured it for a very long time," he said. "He was not well adjusted, he was angry, and he never had a relationship that lasted any length of time. Some of the men he had were like rough trade. I didn't trust them; they were like thieves. I didn't want them near me because they were on the make. One of his ex-boyfriends was an ex-prostitute. But he was attracted to that. He was masochistic and insecure and unhappy and had very low self-esteem, which is strange because he had a great talent and people told him that all the time. Anna Wintour and people would tell him endlessly how much they admired his work, but it was so sad because it didn't compensate for his insecurity."[57]

Janet knew Terence Hulyer was a violent man before she married him, but she was only twenty-one and desperate to leave home.

For years she suffered at his hands—once he beat her up because she took it upon herself to order a cup of tea and didn't let him speak to the waitress in the café. "I did lose two babies as a result of violence," said Janet, who went on to have two sons, Gary and Paul, with him.[58] Yet although Janet knew her husband had a bad temper, she never suspected he could be capable of hurting a young boy, let alone her brother. Lee not only had to endure sexual abuse at Hulyer's hands but he also had to watch as his elder sister got beaten senseless. "I was this young boy and I saw this man with his hands round my sister's neck," he told the journalist Susannah Frankel in 1999. "I was just standing there with her two children beside me."[59]

In his imagination, Lee began to fuse his experiences with Janet's. Both of them had suffered abuse at the hands of the same man and he felt the need to purge the stew of feelings—anger, revenge, despair, corruption, guilt and fragmentation—that he felt growing inside him. He saw his sister as the archetypal woman, vulnerable but strong, a survivor, and she became the blueprint for everything he did later. This was the woman he wanted to protect and empower through his clothes; the patina of armor that he created for her would shield her from danger. "I've seen a woman get nearly beaten to death by her husband," he said later. "I know what misogyny is! I hate this thing about fragility and making women feel naïve . . . I want people to be afraid of the women I dress."[60]

The bruised, battered and bloodied models that he sent down the catwalk wearing the most graceful and bewitching creations carried traces of both his sister and himself. Through the medium of his work he aligned himself with his sister, and with each new collection he revisited and replayed the abuse that both of them had suffered. He managed to take something ugly and, through the transformative power of his imagination, recast it as a thing of beauty. "I gave adults a lot of time in my life when I was young and some of them hurt me," he once said. "And that way I learnt even more. Let's say I turned the negative into a positive."[61] The result was intoxicating, a mutant hybrid, the product of a strange metamorphosis.

• • •

In the autumn of 1980, Lee moved from Carpenter's Road to Rokeby School, a boys' comprehensive situated off Stratford High Street. On that first day, Lee, dressed in his uniform of black trousers, black blazer and a white shirt, made his way down Biggerstaff Road to his friend Jason Meakin's house on Carpenter's Road. Then the two boys called for fellow pupils Peter Bowes and Russell Atkins and they all walked the ten minutes to school. They laughed and joked, but the bravado only covered up their anxieties at entering a large, single-sex school that had a tough reputation. Once inside the building the new boys were told to make their way to the main hall, and there they were lined up in alphabetical order "and read the riot act."[62] The boys were streamed according to their perceived ability using a system based around the letters making up the school's name, Rokeby: the most academic were placed in "R," the top set, then "O" and down to "Y." In the first year, Lee was assigned "E"; by his second year he had dropped down to "B."

From the outset, school never interested McQueen, and at the end of that first term the head of year wrote in his report, "I feel quite confident that if Lee is prepared to try to come to terms with Rokeby, he will discover that not only will he feel happier but his work will improve too. However, without this effort he is going to become increasingly unhappy."[63] His punctuality was regarded as "poor"— he missed a total of six half days during that first term—and he was thought to be too much of a chatterbox and a distraction to the other pupils. His form teacher believed that the boy was finding it "difficult to cope in a large comprehensive school."[64] In English he scored 58 percent, with a C for effort; in his geography exam 38 percent, together with a comment from the teacher urging him to settle down and "begin to act like a comprehensive pupil instead of fooling about all the time"; and in math only 23 percent, together with an observation that his "class behaviour interferes with his work." On 15 December 1980, McQueen's father Ronald, after reading the report, wrote back to Lee's form teacher, "Lee has always been too interested in everybody else instead of getting on with his own work. I have told him about this and hope he will listen. Also he is sent to school at 8:30 every morning but tells me he waits for his friend. I am very annoyed over this. Apart from this I know he likes school and will settle down as he matures."[65]

His next surviving report, which Lee brought home to his parents in March 1982, did show some signs of improvement. In math he scored 49 percent, with a B for effort; his English teacher gave him an exam result of 54 percent, and a B+ for effort; in history he came eighth in the class, with 63 percent and an A for effort. However, some teachers noted some problems with his behavior during class. The French teacher said that Lee needed "constant goading to get his attention down to his work. He too often day-dreams and enjoys chatting"; the RE tutor wrote that he was "very erratic in his work. He concentrates well at times and does very little work sometimes"; and the head of the lower school summarized the report as a "mixed bag—he has the ability but seems to choose when to apply it."[66]

There was one subject, however, which captured his imagination from the beginning: art. In his first-year exam he scored 73 percent, with a B for effort and a comment from the teacher, "Lee has done some good work in art this term," while fifteen months later his teacher gave him an A- for art. "Excellent," he wrote. "Lee has artistic ability and always works hard."[67] Lee started to read books about fashion from the age of twelve. "I followed designers' careers," he said later. "I knew Giorgio Armani was a window-dresser, Ungaro was a tailor . . . I always knew I would be something in fashion. I didn't know how big, but I always knew I'd be something."[68]

His friends noticed Lee's passion for drawing. "He just seemed to be sketching, drawing all the time," said Jason Meakin. "I never thought he would be famous, but I always remember him drawing dresses."[69] Peter Bowes recalls that in school Lee would always carry a little book around with him. Instead of listening to the teacher or doing the work assigned in a particular class Lee would bring out his sketchbook and a clutch of pencils and draw. "It was full of nutters," McQueen said later about Rokeby. "I didn't learn a thing. I just drew clothes in class."[70] One day Lee showed Peter some of his sketches, drawings of the female form. "He was drawing clothes, people, figures, he knew how the female form worked, but it was nothing rude," he said. "He lived in the art department and his work was always superb."[71]

After a morning of lessons, Lee and his friends would go to the nearby pie and mash shop, where a meal of a broken pie and potatoes would cost ten pence; the rest of the boys' diet consisted of "bread and jam and chocolate and chips."[72]

Outside school, Lee loved watching the birds that would circle around the tops of the tower blocks and he joined the Young Ornithologists Society. "It's almost like *Kes*, isn't it?" he said.[73] Later, he told a journalist that he envied birds because they were free. Free from what? "The abuse . . . mental, physical," he said, refusing to elaborate.[74] He also liked playing with the family's pet dog—a black chow, officially named Black Magic of Chang Li, rechristened Shane and described by Joyce as "gentle as a lamb."[75] When Shane died, aged around fifteen in 1983, Lee was heartbroken but soon learnt to love its replacement, Ben, a red chow with a blue tongue. According to Peter Bowes, Lee helped to buy the dog with money that he had saved from his after-school job collecting glasses at Reflections, a pub situated near the school gates. One day Lee and his school friend Russell Atkins came out of Rokeby and as they were walking past Reflections they were asked by a barman whether they would like to earn a little extra money bottling up. The boys accepted immediately as the hours—the occasional lunchtime and Saturday and Sunday mornings—and pay (around £30 a week) suited them perfectly. They were also impressed by the flash interior—all the walls were covered with giant mirrors, hence the name—and glitzy bar. "I wouldn't say there were villains in there, but it was quite a hard pub," said Russell. After a few months, the manager, Kenny, asked the new boys whether they would like to work nights, collecting glasses; Russell turned down the offer, but Lee accepted. "There were fights in there, but then there were fights everywhere," said Russell. The two boys worked there until they were sixteen, when Reflections closed down. "We went there one day to get paid to find the police there," said Russell. "Something had happened, I'm not sure what, but they told us we couldn't go in."[76]

Homework was not Lee's strong point, and he preferred messing about with his friends on the estate. He and Jason would throw stones at the caravans belonging to a group of gypsies that pitched up on a patch of industrial wasteland at the back of the estate and then run as fast as they could. They loved getting into abandoned shopping trolleys and riding them around the streets. The boys would also tie a rope from a nearby footbridge and use it as a swing; one day, when another friend, Raymond, was playing on it, Lee and Jason cut the rope and the boy came crashing down. They carried out the same trick on another boy who was playing on a swing under the railway bridge; but this time "the kid fell in the river—we were pissing ourselves," said Jason.

There used to be a petrol station on the corner of Jupp Road West and Carpenter's Road. Often the boys would tie an old wallet or purse to a length of fishing wire. Then they would place the wallet on the forecourt of the petrol station and hide. They thought it was hilarious when someone stopped to pick up the purse and they would pull it away; even more hilarious was the sight of a man or woman chasing the wallet across the ground or around the petrol pumps. "We were just terrors, making people's lives a misery," said Jason. In the run-up to Bonfire Night, Lee, Jason and their little gang would try to light the bonfires of rival gangs on nearby estates; for hours on end they would stand outside in the freezing cold guarding their own tall piles of broken pallets and waste wood.[77]

One day in 1983 their schoolboy pranks nearly got them into trouble with the police. "I stole some drink out of a drinks factory when I was about fourteen," said McQueen later when asked whether he had ever broken the law.[78] Jason recalls the incident well: a favorite game involved trespassing on the Schweppes industrial unit situated by a walkway near Abbey Lane. The boys would climb over the fence and steal into the backs of lorries, where they would enjoy a tonic water or a ginger ale. "I remember once we heard the coppers walking past and so we hid, but they found us," said Jason.[79]

Peter Bowes maintains that Lee was "quite a tough guy—he wasn't scared of people,"[80] and, despite Lee's nickname at school of "Queeny" or "Queer boy Queeny," Jason "didn't believe he was gay."[81] After school, and on weekends, Lee and Jason would go to the back of a local engineering firm situated near the River Lea. There, Lee would kiss a string of local girls—there were Sharon, Maria and Tracy, who was a dwarf. "I don't want to go into details but I know three girls who Lee kissed and cuddled," said Jason. "One of them went a bit further, not full sex. It was messing around. As far as being gay, no way—that was a big surprise."[82] One detail Peter noticed, but never commented on, was the fact that often Lee wore girls' white socks to school. He never knew whether this was because Lee had to borrow his sisters' socks due to the family's economic circumstances or whether it was a way for his friend to express an aspect of his sexuality. "And if he was alive today I would ask him," he said.[83]

A black-and-white photograph taken in Lee's third year at school shows that style or fashion did not feature prominently in the lives of the boys from Rokeby. At the end of term they were given permission to shed their uniforms and come to school in their own clothes. Most boys chose to wear parkas made from nylon, most probably the coats they wore over their blazers each day, together with nondescript shirts, sweaters and trousers. Stylistic references to pop-cultural movements such as punk or the New Romantics are noticeably absent—it's even difficult to spot one pair of jeans—and the boys look like miniature versions of their working-class fathers. Neither is there anything striking about Lee's appearance. Dressed in a functional monochrome jacket, he looks directly to the camera, with a smile on his face. Perhaps he's smiling because he knew he was going places.

Sometimes Peter and Lee would take the lift to the top of James Riley Point, one of the tower blocks on the estate, and smoke Embassy Number Ones sitting on the back staircase looking out towards Essex. There the two boys would chat about school, the estate and their futures. Lee had a sense of yearning, a desire to achieve something, but he was realistic enough to know that he was, in the eyes of his teachers at least, "just another East End oik going nowhere fast."[84] "I don't think he knew where he was going, but he wanted to do something artistic, something creative," said Peter Bowes. "But you've got to remember that we were boys on an inner London estate. We never really got opportunities. The school was a factory—get you in, keep you safe, push you out at the end and whatever you got, good luck to you."[85] Peter remembers one conversation he had with Lee about his middle name. "He was fascinated by Alexander the Great and he claimed to have found in his family a link back to him," he said. The allure of the past was working its magic on Lee; for him it would increasingly represent a place of romance and security, an escape from the harsh reality and pain in his life.

Towards the end of his time at Rokeby, Lee started to suffer from sudden attacks of frustration and anger. "I wouldn't say he was bipolar but he had his ups and downs with moods," said Peter. "He had a bit of a temper on him as well. I remember in certain lessons he would be chatting and he'd get told off. He would erupt and kick off and get thrown out or put into detention."[86]

None of his friends at school could have realized it, but Lee later claimed he was suffering yet more sexual abuse during this period, this time at the hands of a teacher. Again Lee kept the abuse to himself, only telling his sisters later in life. Years later, when Jacqui learnt of the two counts of abuse suffered by her brother everything began to make sense: the anger had to come out somehow and Lee later expressed it through his work, an opinion echoed by the Metropolitan Museum's *Savage Beauty* curator Andrew Bolton, who said, "McQueen sewed anger into his clothes."[87]

On 27 May 1985, just as Lee was preparing to sit his O levels, his brother-in-law Terence Hulyer left the house on Marlborough Road, Dagenham, that he shared with Janet and his two sons, to get a morning newspaper. As he drove down the street the thirty-five-year-old factory worker suffered a massive heart attack and lost control of the car, which careered into a nearby house. He was taken to Oldchurch Hospital, Romford, where he later died. Hulyer had been a diabetic from the age of eighteen and in those days, according to Janet, sufferers "used to take pork insulin, derived from pigs, and it furred up the arteries."[88] Lee must have felt relieved at the death of one of his abusers, but perhaps he also felt guilty; after all, he must have wished his brother-in-law dead on more than one occasion.

McQueen's puberty and sexual awakening in the eighties coincided with the rise of a virus that was widely dubbed in the media at the time "the gay plague." As a result, Lee was, in the words of *New Yorker* writer Judith Thurman, "forced to witness a primal scene that haunted the youth of his generation: sex and death in the same bed."[89] For a young imaginative gay man like Lee, the specter of AIDS was all too real. The imagery associated with the disease—from the television adverts featuring grim reapers and icebergs to the newspaper front pages showing men as thin as skeletons—sent out a seemingly ineluctable message that if you were a gay man you had a high chance of dying young. In addition to the roll call of famous faces—Rock Hudson (who died in October 1985, age 59), fashion designer Perry Ellis (1986, age 46), Liberace (1987, age 67), Robert Mapplethorpe (1989, age 42), actor Ian Charleson (1990, age 40), artist Keith Haring (1990, age 31), Freddie Mercury (1991, age 45), Anthony Perkins (1992, age 60), Rudolf Nureyev (1993, age 54), Leigh Bowery (1994, age 33), Derek Jarman (1994, age 52) and Kenny Everett (1995, age 50)—there were thousands of mostly gay young men in Britain whose lives were cut short by the disease.

"I lived through a period in the late eighties, early nineties, when there was a whole tsunami of close friends who died from AIDS," said artist and filmmaker John Maybury, who later became both a collaborator and friend of McQueen's. "I lost twenty close friends in

two or three years. Lee's generation saw this other generation deci-
mated. It was horrific beyond all imagining, but the wider society at
large chose to ignore it. These kids like Lee were beginning to create
their sexual identities at a time when this shadow, this spectre, was
hanging over them."[90]

Despite the large, bustling household on Biggerstaff Road, and
the fun that he had with his straight friends from school, for a great
chunk of his adolescence McQueen felt terribly isolated and alone.
"I didn't have any gay people to look up to," he said later. "No gay
friends."[91] Lee also had to endure the casual homophobia of his father,
a man who would come home after driving his cab around London
and joke in front of his son, "God, I nearly ran over a bloody queer
last night in Soho."[92]

Escape was uppermost in Lee's mind. By the time he left school in
June 1985, with one O level—a grade B in art; "I had to draw a stupid bowl of fruit," he said later—he had made up his mind to try and
do something with his life. His resources were limited, he knew that,
but he reasoned it was worth a try. "It's not heard of to be a fine artist
in an east London family," he said. "But I always had the mentality
that I only had one life and I was going to do what I wanted to."[93]

CHAPTER TWO

I wanted to learn everything, everything, give me everything.
—*Lee McQueen*

One of the myths surrounding McQueen is that he was a boy prodigy, a kind of Edward Scissorhands who could take a piece of fabric and, with a few manic flashes of his shears, transform it into a fabulous coat, jacket or dress. He was able to bypass the usually obligatory process of sketching out a template or pattern on paper or cardboard; instead, in the words of Mark Lee, the former president of Yves Saint Laurent and Gucci, McQueen had the ability to "just take a bolt of fabric and, in front of [your] eyes, would cut the pattern for his clothes."[1] McQueen himself was partly responsible for this perception. "I don't think you can become a good designer, or a great designer, or whatever," he said. "To me, you just are one. I think to know about colour, proportion, shape, cut, balance is part of a gene."[2]

In reality, McQueen's journey from fashion enthusiast to fashion genius took the best part of seven years. In September 1985 he enrolled at what was then West Ham Technical College in Stratford to take an evening class in art. Later, he recalled that this "meant I ended up with housewives and people who just wanted to pass the time. So it wasn't quite where I wanted to go."[3] According to his sister Janet, the course involved an element of dressmaking, and by the end of the year he had finished a number of wearable garments, some of which he had made for Janet. One skirt, a simple black tube, was "so tight it moulded itself to me and I couldn't lift my leg to get up the step," she said. "The other one came apart—he wasn't very happy when I told him that as he was a bit of a perfectionist."[4]

Around this time, Lee started to read *McDowell's Directory of Twentieth Century Fashion*, a book that he later regarded as something of a style bible. The guide, first published in 1984, is an A to Z of international fashion, with potted biographies of the twentieth century's greatest designers. In its opening chapter—titled "Clothes as a Weapon"—the author, the renowned journalist Colin McDowell, outlined the importance of fashion and its place in history. The words struck a chord with the young McQueen. "The more remote fashionable people become, the more powerful and awe-inspiring they seem to the unfashionable majority," he wrote. "In the past this meant that clothes became not only the trappings of power, but part of the exercise of power itself."[5] Lee read about the connection between fashion and the visual arts, how Dior, Chanel and Schiaparelli "were all closely involved with artists, writers and intellectuals." McDowell went on to explain why fashion is so often wrongly regarded as a somewhat frivolous discipline. The first reason, he said, was visual—unlike objects created by furniture or interior designers, a jacket or a dress "loses a great deal of its point when hanging in a wardrobe. It becomes a rounded and convincing creation only when there is a body inside it." The other reason why fashion is denigrated is because for a long time it has been seen as the "domain of women . . . as feminists see it, men have manipulated women and treated them as objects, frequently using dress as a bait and as a reward. An interest in clothing has become a symbol of suppression. The 'little woman' is bought with an expensive dress and by wearing it she feeds a man's ego. She is telling her friends, by her expensive appearance, how rich and powerful he is to be able to buy and possess such a beautifully caparisoned object."[6] McQueen made it his mission to subvert this attitude: the women who bought his clothes not only earned their own money, but by the very act of wearing McQueen they made a statement to the world that they were not passive objects, but active, and potentially dangerous, subjects.

Lee also started to experiment with photography, an art that always held an allure for him. One photograph, now in the possession of Janet, shows his nephew Gary dressed in an oversize overcoat standing next to a wall on which the McQueen boys had daubed their names in white paint.

When Janet—who had trained as a black-cab driver like her father—had to work nights, Lee would often babysit for her sons, Paul and Gary. "After my dad died he would come over and bring horror films with him to watch," said Gary, who later worked at McQueen as a menswear textile designer. "I think in the early days his work was definitely influenced by horror. He would chase us around the house and try and hunt us down and say that an old lady lived under our bed. He always had this loud, psychotic laugh. He used to do a lot of sketches as well. I remember a cabbage, a lot of monsters as well as fashion pictures. There was nudism, a lot of flesh on show even then, men and women, as well as a few feathers and birds. He liked to style us a bit as well, used to try and do things with my hair which back then was like a bird's nest. I always liked him because I have an artistic side; I was always drawing, so we had that in common. I have a darker mind than my brother—I think he used to scare Paul a bit—and so I used to appreciate his sense of humour." One day Gary transformed the headboard of his bed into a tombstone, complete with the letters *RIP*, and waited patiently stretched out with his eyes closed until his grandmother Joyce came into the room. After getting over the initial shock Joyce then gave him "a good hiding."[7]

Paul recalls how his uncle would creep up the stairs and shout, "I'm coming to get you!" Lee liked to be pampered and would pay his nephew fifty pence to massage his feet. He didn't bother with fancy lotions—"just the sweat from his feet, that was enough," he said. At this stage, Paul cannot remember Lee having many friends—"he was ostracized by his peers because of the way he was," he said.[8]

During his time at West Ham Technical College, McQueen chose some of his designs to feature in a catwalk show. Today, Janet regrets not attending that event, but "looking back none of us thought that Lee was going to become one of the greatest fashion designers of all time."[9] He also earned pocket money by working part-time in a West Ham pie and mash shop.

According to McQueen, one afternoon in 1986 he was at home in Biggerstaff Road when he saw a program on television about how the art of tailoring was in danger of dying out. There was, said the report, a shortage of apprentice tailors on Savile Row and so his mother said to him, "Why don't you go down there, give it a go?"[10] Speaking in 1997, Joyce recalled, "He always wanted to be a designer, he always has, [but] when he left school he wasn't sure what to do. Quite a few of the family were involved in tailoring so I just said to him, 'You know, why don't you go and try?'"[11] Spurred on by his mother, Lee took the tube to Bond Street and walked through the smart streets of Mayfair until he came to 30 Savile Row, the headquarters of Anderson & Sheppard. "I hardly had any qualifications when I left school, so I thought the best way to do it was to learn the construction of clothes properly and go from there," he said.[12]

Anderson & Sheppard was founded in 1906 by Peter or Per Gustaf Anderson, a protégé of Frederick Scholte, who was famous for developing the English drape for the Duke of Windsor, and the trouser cutter Sidney Horatio Sheppard. "A Scholte coat was roomy over the chest and shoulder blades, resulting in a conspicuous but graceful drape," wrote one style commentator, "the fabric not flawlessly smooth and fitted by gently descending from the collarbone in soft vertical ripples. The upper sleeves, too, were generous, allowing for a broad range of motion, but the armholes, cut high and small, held the coat in place, keeping its collar from separating from the wearer's neck when he raised his arms. The shoulders remained unpadded, left to slope along the natural lines of the wearer."

Anderson & Sheppard owed its success to Scholte's reluctance to cater to celebrity clients, "believing them to be undesirable riffraff." Customers soon included Nöel Coward, Ivor Novello, Cole Porter,

Gary Cooper, Douglas Fairbanks Jr., and Fred Astaire, who, it is said, would ask for the antique rug in the fitting room to be rolled back so he could feel what it was like to dance in his new suit. Marlene Dietrich was another famous customer—"ladies were welcome, provided they wore men's suits."[13]

That day in 1986, Lee, dressed in jeans and a baggy top and looking more than a little disheveled, walked through the heavy double doors, across the herringbone floor and into the mahogany-paneled room. The contrast between the interior of Biggerstaff Road and the inside of the tall Neoclassical building could not have been more striking, but the overpowering aroma of privilege did not intimidate him. "He wasn't a timid person," said John Hitchcock, who started working for the tailor in 1963. Lee told the besuited man standing by the long table piled high with expensive tweeds that he was interested in becoming an apprentice. A moment or so later, Norman Halsey, the head salesman and later managing director, came down to interview him. The handsome older man, with his aquiline nose and head of silver hair, was an astute judge of character, and after talking with the seventeen-year-old boy Halsey offered him a job. The position would not have been well paid and McQueen would have earned only a few thousand pounds a year, probably the equivalent of three Anderson & Sheppard suits. "It was obvious when he first came he did not know anything, he was a blank canvas," said Hitchcock, who worked as a cutter in the mid- to late eighties and who is now the company's managing director.[14]

Lee was assigned Cornelius O'Callaghan as a mentor, a man McQueen described as a "master tailor."[15] This strict Irishman, who was known by the name of Con, was regarded as one of the best makers of "coats" (Savile Row–speak for jackets) in the business. The hours were fixed—Lee was expected to arrive by 8:30 in the morning and work through until 5 p.m. On his first day he was given a thimble—which he placed on the middle finger of his right hand—a scrap of fabric and a line of thread and shown the basics of padding. "New apprentices have to practise doing this [padding] stitch, and they have to keep doing it," said John Hitchcock. "An apprentice will do thousands and thousands of these stitches and, although it becomes very boring, they have to learn. After doing that for a week, the apprentice might then move on to learn about inside padding, how to canvas the jacket, put the pockets in, and the flaps. It normally takes about two years to learn the simple tasks."[16]

Talking about his time at Anderson & Sheppard, McQueen later remembered it as being quite a romantic interlude. "It was like Dickens, sitting cross-legged on a bench and padding lapels and sewing all day—it was nice," he said. But again he felt isolated because of his sexuality. "It was a weird time for me, because at sixteen, seventeen, eighteen, I was going through the situation of coming to terms with my sexuality and I was surrounded by heterosexuals and quite a few homophobic people and every day there would be some sort of remark," he said. "Downstairs on the shop floor was quite gay but upstairs was full of people from Southend and south London, just like any other apprentice trade, full of lads being laddish. So I was trying to keep my mouth shut most of the time because I've got quite a big mouth."[17]

Everyone knew McQueen was gay, according to John Hitchcock, but it was not an issue. "There are quite a few in the trade," he said. "It certainly never bothered me. AIDS frightened people, and a lot of men did get frightened, but it was silly really because you are not what they are after. The funny thing with these people who are gay is that they get on very well with the girls. The girls don't mind one bit. They think the same. They have their effeminate ways but it doesn't matter."

Hitchcock remembers Lee coming to work every day always dressed in baggy jeans, a thick black or gray roll-neck sweater, with sometimes a checked jacket and Doc Martens. A photograph taken in the workshop at the time shows an awkward-looking Lee wearing a red shirt buttoned up to the collar and snow-washed jeans pulled tight with a belt. He was not, by all accounts, a popular member of staff.

"He came over a bit too intense for me," said Derrick Tomlinson, who was an apprentice at the same time as Lee. "He always tried to have these intense conversations with me and I wasn't really up for that. And the two girls, who worked here in the same room, they didn't get on with him either, there was a clash of personalities with them." Was his unpopularity due to the fact he was gay? "I didn't know he was gay, he never talked about it," said Derrick. "He did behave in a slightly strange way, but I didn't put it down to him being gay."

As they worked, the tailors and apprentices listened to the easy-listening music of Radio 2, but in private Lee was an avid fan of house music. "I knew nothing about house music until Lee introduced me to it," said Derrick. "At the time it was one of the new fad things, acid house, the rave scene."[18]

The goal of every new apprentice tailor is to make what is called a "forward"—a jacket that is nearly complete and ready for a first fitting on a customer. Normally, it would take between four and five years for a new person to learn the necessary skills, but McQueen did this in two. "Con taught him well," said Hitchcock. "Lee was very keen to learn and he had a natural ability."[19]

Rosemarie Bolger, a tailor with the company at that time, recalls Lee as being a quiet, nondescript boy who got on with his work. "I actually never knew Alexander McQueen, I knew this kid called Lee," she said. "He was just one of a succession of kids that didn't make it as tailors. Some people don't make it because they are not good enough at sewing, others because they lack the discipline. Lee fell into the category of those people who don't really intend to make a profession as a tailor because they want to use the training for other things. But at the time I couldn't see any difference between him and any of the other kids."[20]

If McQueen's stories of working at Anderson & Sheppard are to be believed, the young apprentice actually did leave his mark behind. "When you first start you're there for three months solid just padding lapels," he said later. "So you get bored and then you do a bit of scribbling inside the jacket, and you might scrawl an obscenity—like a sixteen-year-old does when it's bored. But it was just a passing phase. If I'd known it was going to be brought up so many times I don't think I would ever have mentioned it."[21] During a television interview with Frank Skinner he entertained the audience by expanding on the story. "I'm in Savile Row in the top of this old building with a load of old tailors and it's really boring and it just happened to be Prince Charles's jacket that I was working on at the time," he said. "And so I drew this big willy on it, like you do."[22] Another variation on the same theme was that he used a Biro to write the words "I am a cunt" inside the jacket.

Was this true? John Hitchcock said that McQueen's boss, Con, "was a strong Catholic, he went to church, and if he had seen anything he would have changed the canvas. It was not true." According to Hitchcock, when Prince Charles's valet saw the news about McQueen's alleged subversive graffiti he contacted Anderson & Sheppard to complain. Hitchcock recalled the jacket in question, slowly unpicked the stitching and opened it up to discover—nothing. "What McQueen wanted was publicity to say that he had made jackets for Prince Charles, and he achieved that, but it was our downfall," said Hitchcock. "It was not a nice thing to do."[23] Rosemarie Bolger is in agreement with her boss. "He would not have done that as Con would have had his guts for garters."[24]

But there are many, including Sarah Burton, now the creative director of Alexander McQueen, who believed Lee's versions of events.[25] "Of course he did that," said his sister Jacqui. "If you were supposed to be swimming on the water, he would be under the water. He would do anything to be a rebel. He wasn't trying to impress anyone, there was no one to impress but himself."[26] Andrew Groves, later Lee's boyfriend, also suspects that McQueen may well have taken pleasure in leaving his mark on the fabric, a transgressive insignia that served as McQueen's own coat of arms. "Whatever he was doing he could not help but subvert it," he said. "He always wanted to undermine the idea of authority and the establishment."[27]

After Lee had been working at Anderson & Sheppard for about two years, he started to be late for work or to miss whole days entirely. McQueen's erratic timekeeping began to interfere with the smooth running of the company—if he didn't finish a particular task by a certain day it meant that other members of staff could not complete their work on time. "It was no good saying his bus was late, as our response would have been to tell him to get up earlier," said Hitchcock. "Con asked me if I could have a word with him as he really thought his behaviour was not good enough. I told him that he was putting everyone else behind, but he got a bit shirty and left. We didn't sack him, he just walked out. Later we learnt that his mum had been ill, but if he had told us we would have given him a week off."[28] It was obvious that Lee's behavior left behind a rather sour atmosphere at the company: when the journalist Lynn Barber contacted Anderson & Sheppard for a quote about McQueen to include in her *Observer* profile of the designer in 1996, Norman Halsey replied, "A problem is that people bandy our name about but nobody in this building remembers him. He maybe only worked here a few weeks. There's an army expression I could use if you weren't a lady—it goes 'b******* baffles brains.' You don't know it? Well, the first syllable of the first word is 'bull.' "[29]

From Anderson & Sheppard, McQueen moved further down Savile Row to Gieves & Hawkes, where he took a job as a tailoring apprentice. He started work on 11 January 1988 and stayed there for just over a year. "I certainly remember him working with us," said Robert Gieve in 1997, "and sadly we lost his talent—no way were we going to keep him—his mind and nature were inquisitive, never short of asking questions. Why this, why that, why put a cut in a coat here rather than there, to create a chest or create suppression in a waist? All this was very evident from the way he worked and the way he talked."[30]

McQueen claimed he endured a climate of homophobia at Gieves & Hawkes, something that in the end contributed to his decision to leave the company in March 1989. "I went straight to the head of

Gieves & Hawkes and said the situation had to change," he said. "And it didn't, so I left."[31]

He started freelancing for Bermans & Nathans, the theatrical costumers, and worked on productions such as *Les Misérables* and *Miss Saigon*. "Lee worked on the costumes for *Miss Saigon* and I worked on the props," said Andrew Groves. "We didn't realize this until we met."[32] Although Lee later said he loathed the experience—"I was surrounded by complete queens, and I hate the theatre anyway"[33]— Groves believes that that short spell working on big-scale productions influenced his catwalk shows. "His thinking was like mine—if you are going to do a show it has to be a show. You want people to go away saying, 'Wow,' or horrified or repulsed or amazed, not just, 'Oh, that's a nice skirt.' "[34]

To supplement his meager income, McQueen also started working again at Reflections, the pub opposite his old school in Stratford. By this time the pub had changed hands and, according to Archie Reed, a man who would later have a long relationship with McQueen, "it was the roughest pub in the East End," and a hangout for the Inter City Firm (ICF), the hooligan wing associated with West Ham United. The Krays owned it for a time, and then it reopened as a mixed/gay pub. "When that door locked you got scared," said Archie. "There were fights, sex, everything." Archie remembers seeing Lee walking around the pub collecting glasses with his eyes lowered to the ground. "I was always fascinated by him because he never looked anybody in the eye," he said. "Later I asked him why he did this and he said he could see everything that was going on without looking. I also asked him why he worked there and he said, 'I was so fascinated by the things that went on there. One minute there would be guys kissing, the next girls kissing, then guy and girl.' There was a helluva lot of crime too and a helluva lot of fights."[35]

After Lee saw a magazine article about the Tokyo-born, London-based designer Koji Tatsuno, he turned up at Tatsuno's studio looking for a job. His interview outfit comprised a pair of tapered trousers, a leather jacket and a piece of satin tied around his neck.

"I looked a complete freak," he said later.[36] Although Tatsuno only employed McQueen as an intern for less than a year, the designer had an enormous influence on the twenty-year-old. Tatsuno, then backed by Yohji Yamamoto, was known for his experimentation, his desire to transform fabric from a state of two-dimensional lifelessness into three-dimensional sculpture. He had run away from home at the age of fourteen and had arrived in London five years later on a buying trip for an antiques dealer. In 1982 he launched his own label, Culture Shock, a name that held a certain allure for McQueen, and Tatsuno's lack of formal training enabled him to create an aesthetic that was unique. "I like to create in a very spontaneous way," he said in 1993. "The convention is that you start from a flat fabric cut out on a surface, but that, to me, has nothing to do with the body." Instead, he taught himself how to mold material on the body to create shapes, an approach that McQueen would later follow.[37] "His work was based on British tailoring with a mix of avant-garde and I thought, there's nothing like this in London," Lee said.[38] McQueen worked for Koji at his studio in Mount Street, Mayfair, and it was there that he learnt the art of cutting without a pattern. "We never talked about trends or fashions," said Koji. "I was fascinated by Savile Row tailoring, as he was, and interested in not just following the tradition, but trying to do something new. My first impression of him was that he was a bit weird. I could tell he was attracted to the dark side of beauty, and it was something I could relate to as well."[39]

It was while McQueen was working for Tatsuno that he met a man who would serve as a fashion educator and gay mentor and who would introduce him into a world of wealth, privilege and culture.

BillyBoy* is the kind of hyperreal aesthete who seems like he could have stepped from the pages of a decadent novel. Born in Vienna and raised in New York, he was style-obsessed from an early age—at twelve he started to collect vintage Schiaparelli when he found a hat designed by the Italian-born couturier that looked like "a crushed clown's hat with an insect sewn to it" in a Paris flea market.[40] Billy-Boy* grew up surrounded by artists, writers and movie stars: Salvador Dalí drew him when he was a child; he first visited Warhol's Factory when he was only five or six years old; and both Diana Vreeland and Jackie Onassis regarded him as their protégé. His guardian and close friend Bettina Bergery, born Elisabeth Shaw Jones, designed Elsa Schiaparelli's windows in Paris. One look featured a dressmaker's dummy that sported a bouquet of flowers for a head, which, according to one commentator, may have been inspired by an incident in the designer's youth: "Schiaparelli's mother, widely recognized as a very beautiful woman, often criticized Schiaparelli's appearance as a child. To rectify the situation Schiaparelli planted flower seeds in her mouth, nose and ears to make what she perceived as her ugly face more beautiful and unique, with predictably disastrous results."[41] In her autobiography Schiaparelli wrote of her yearning to "have a face covered with flowers like a heavenly garden."[42] The image so appealed to McQueen, a young man who always felt self-conscious about his appearance, that later in his career he would take these words and make them real, sending models down the catwalk with faces covered in flowers or butterflies. "He was interested in Schiaparelli as the anarchist, the rebel," said BillyBoy*. "I told him all about the counter-culture things she did, like the skeleton gown and the lobster dress and he found it fascinating."[43]

The two men—who met in 1989 through mutual friends—were born at the very extremes of the social scale: Lee into a working-class family on a tough council estate in Stratford, while BillyBoy* was raised amongst New York's intellectual elite, had a private tutor and attended a Montessori school. "Lee once took me to see where he lived as a child and I was horrified, I had never seen anything like it," said BillyBoy*. "Of course, I couldn't say anything, but I could see where that anger came from. I had probably the same morbid curiosity towards his background as he had towards mine."[44] Lee did not go abroad until he was twenty, whereas BillyBoy* was sent by his parents on the first of three world tours at the age of eight. McQueen felt like his family, particularly his father, always had difficulties accepting his sexuality. But when BillyBoy* was in his early teenage years his mother sat him down and asked him whether he was gay; after telling her that he was, she embraced him and "nearly crying said, 'Oh, thank God, thank God, I was afraid you might not be; you'd have such a dull life as a straight and straights would NEVER get you at all!' "[45]

When BillyBoy* came to London he would usually stay at grand hotels like the Savoy or the Ritz, "and we would go out and pub crawl and Lee would come to the Ritz and on the one hand be very impressed and then, on the other, say snide things about the hotel," he said. "He had a kind of chip on his shoulder. He wanted to succeed, and have privilege and money and fame that other people had, but also he resented them for having it. It was a paradox in his personality I don't think he resolved. We were like night and day and normally speaking we would not have been friends. I don't think he liked the background he came from and also resented it. I got the impression that he admired my background, although mine is not a happy story. We related to the pain and anguish of our childhoods."[46]

BillyBoy* was born to two teenage parents—his mother, from a Catholic family, was only fourteen, and his father, who was Jewish, was fifteen. His birth was considered shameful by both families and as a result he was taken away and placed in an orphanage. "It was for very rich, very aristocratic illegitimate children to be secreted away," he said. At the age of four he was adopted by an aristocratic Russian family who were living in Manhattan and later learnt that his real parents committed suicide when they were eighteen and nineteen. "I was their sole heir, with the stipulated wish I carry their names, both names," he said. "My adoptive parents, in a conundrum, decided to call me BillyBoy* after a British earl's family member . . . named Boy, and Billy after Wilhelm (or actually Vylyam) and the other names: Zef Sh'muel Roberto Atlantide. Atlantide because I am a double Pisces. I added the asterisk, of course."[47]

Lee was fascinated by BillyBoy*'s story—the idea of the abandoned child, the gothic orphanage full of the illegitimate children of

the wealthy, the joint suicide of his parents, his extraordinarily luxurious lifestyle first in New York and then in Paris, where he moved
in the late 1970s. In the French capital, he mixed with "everyone
and anyone you can mention in art and fashion," including Marlene
Dietrich, Line Vautrin, Diego Giacometti, Bernard Buffet, Hubert
de Givenchy, Marc Bohan of Dior, André Courrèges, Yves Saint
Laurent and Alexandre de Paris, who cut his hair. When BillyBoy*
related incidents from his life—which he later described as "a bit like
Romeo and Juliet with a dash of Pop Art"—Lee was transfixed. Even
at a young age, McQueen was fascinated by the concept of reinven-
tion, the ability some people had to create themselves anew. Billy-
Boy* told him how education played a central part in saving his life.
"My education was the best thing that came out of my childhood. I
mean, my adoptive family could have been anyone, and they had the
intelligence to give me a very good education instead of making me
into one of them," he said. "I am indebted to my adoptive family for
this and in a strange way to my real family, my parents who, literally,
died to help me . . . I feel close to them . . . so between their souls,
minds and the money, and the fortune of my adoptive parents to give
me an unusual education, I turned into myself or rather had an easier
time turning into myself."[48]

The two men also bonded over their shared love of fashion. Billy-
Boy,* who is now an artist, remembers some of the exquisite clothes
Lee created while he was employed by Koji Tatsuno. He still wears a
couple of gorgeous items made by McQueen from that time: a coat
fashioned from woven peacock feathers and another inspired by an
eighteenth-century riding jacket, which, he said, "is a masterpiece of
design that I could wear for the rest of my life."[49]

One day, when BillyBoy* came into Tatsuno's Mayfair studio to
buy some show samples, Lee watched as he tried on a tight, "much
too low-cut silk dress."

"You should wear that, only you can wear that," Lee said to him.

"Don't you think it makes me look a bit like a slut, a tranny slut?"
asked BillyBoy*.

"No, looks like you have balls," he replied.

"You mean nerve?"

"Yeah, that too," he said, laughing.[50]

McQueen was also intrigued to see how his new friend would change his look: one day BillyBoy* would be wearing a smart, traditional suit from Anderson & Sheppard, the next a surreal avant-garde outfit that was designed to challenge and unsettle. Lee was "impressed I think at first by the fact I was a strange hybrid between highbrow and lowbrow and that I could wear traditional suits and ties and also John Galliano's first clothes or the weird stuff from BodyMap."[51]

Although Lee was not, in BillyBoy*'s opinion, a very talented draftsman—"he used to do these little midgety sketches on the corners of paper plates and napkins"—he had a seemingly innate sense of cut. "He had this talent to be able to make both pattern pieces and do draping or moulage, where you take the cloth, pin it on the mannequin and cut and create and mould around the body form. He had an ability that was flabbergasting."[52]

When Koji Tatsuno's business went bankrupt in 1989 McQueen started to look for new work. He asked a female colleague at the company if she knew of anyone who needed a pattern cutter and she put him in touch with John McKitterick, the head designer of Red or Dead, the street fashion brand created by Wayne and Gerardine Hemingway. "Lee was very unassuming and didn't look like he was interested in fashion whatsoever," said McKitterick. "He was very unworldly, a bit scruffy-looking, but when he came to work at the studio, which was then in Wembley, it was obvious that he knew what he was doing. He could sew and cut very well, which was surprising in someone so young, and he was very organized and always on time. We became very friendly, but we were not friends at this point. I didn't see him outside of the studio and he didn't frequent any of the places, bars or events that I went to. I liked him, he was a very pleasant guy, but he didn't know how to have a conversation. He was a little worker bee, and he did it very well. But I didn't realize he was interesting; that came later."

During this time Lee worked with McKitterick on a number of collections for Red or Dead, including *Charlie Spirograph* (Autumn/Winter 1989), *Spacebaby* (Spring/Summer 1990) and *We Love Animals* (Autumn/Winter 1990). The more Lee learnt about the intricacies of design the more he became intrigued and, as he worked, he began to ask John specific questions relating to the technical aspects of the fashion process. "He started to think that actually what he wanted to do was get into the fashion industry," said McKitterick. "I don't think he knew at what level. Out of this conversation came an idea, a suggestion that he should go to Italy. I had worked in Italy, and at that point, in the late eighties, it was a great place to get into the business. There were lots of new avenues there, such as sportswear and menswear, which at that time you didn't get in Paris or the States."

Lee, with a spontaneity that never left him, wanted to fly to Italy immediately, but John told him to wait—the best time to get a job was directly after the shows when the head designers would be looking to refresh their studios. John also opened his contacts book, and gave him a list of names—editors, headhunters, agencies, designers. Armed with this information, Lee went to see his sister Tracy, who then worked for a travel agency and who booked him a one-way ticket to Milan. "I thought he was a little crazy," said John McKitterick. "He stood there in his baggy jeans with a hole in the knee and a baggy shirt and dreadful hair and dreadful everything. I thought, 'What's he doing?'"[53]

McQueen, who was nearly twenty-one, arrived in Italy's fashion capital in March 1990 armed with a plan. Although he was prepared to work for any designer, at the top of his list was one name: Romeo Gigli. "There was nothing going on in London, and the biggest thing at that time was Romeo Gigli, he was everywhere," said Lee.[54] In *McDowell's Directory of Twentieth Century Fashion*, Colin McDowell wrote of Gigli, "His unstructured clothes with their emphasis on an elongated silhouette soon made him stand out from mainstream

Italian fashion . . . Gigli's shows have become cult affairs and his clothes are eagerly bought by wealthy young women world-wide. His designs are a synthesis of London post-punk street fashion and Japanese avant-garde style presented with Italian refinement and colour to produce clothes of extreme subtlety and elegance . . . Many fashion experts consider him the most important designer to have appeared in the eighties."[55] McQueen was drawn to Gigli's spirit of romanticism, the references to Byzantine mosaics and medieval reliefs, and his ability to stage shows that prompted a strong emotional reaction—at the end of his 1989 Paris debut fashion editors "nearly lost their head wraps and oversize eyeglasses as they sprang out of their seats at the show's end."[56] Bianca Jagger described Gigli's appeal in 1989—he was, she said, "the most exciting designer I have seen in a long time because he makes women wear men's clothes with a great deal of femininity."[57]

That day in Milan, McQueen—dressed in a pair of seventies-style patchwork flares and a checked shirt—made his way from the Porta Garibaldi metro stop down Corso Como to Gigli's studio. He did not have an appointment, but he hoped that his "book"—which he later said was the "worst portfolio" ever, "full of costume design"[58]— would secure him a job as a pattern cutter. The receptionist called up Lise Strathdee, a New Zealander who had trained in fashion and textile design at the Istituto Marangoni and who was then working as "Romeo's right hand," and she came down to meet him. "I don't remember what images were in his book, what interested me was his work experience . . . an unusual mix which I thought might be of interest to Romeo," she said. "That morning Romeo was in a meeting with Carla [Sozzani, his partner and sister of Franca Sozzani, editor of Italian *Vogue*] and although we worked in an open studio you would not interrupt meetings." Lise remembers that Lee "spoke quite softly and was probably quite nervous. We sat down and as I looked through his book I got Lee to talk and asked him questions . . . I got the impression that he wanted to get out of London and try his luck in Milan."

After flicking through his book, Lise took his contact details and thanked Lee for coming in. As she said goodbye she could sense his disappointment, but then as she returned to her table she saw that Romeo had finished his meeting. She went up to him and told him about the young man with Savile Row experience that she had just met. "Romeo had a few minutes before his next meeting so he said yeah, he'd see him," said Lise. "So I tore out of the building and turned right down Corso Como and legged it towards the Porta Garibaldi metro stop searching for him."[59] Catching a glimpse of Lee going down the steps into the station, Lise yelled out to him. Later, McQueen recalled the moment when Gigli's "assistant came running after me like a madwoman saying Romeo wanted to see me."[60] When Lise told Lee that her boss would see him but that he didn't have much time and that they would have to be quick, "his face was like the sun coming out, warm and happy and [he was] chatty and laughing . . . So we half-walked, half-ran back, chatting excitedly, laughing. Back inside the studio I took him to Romeo's desk and introduced them. I can't remember if I stayed there with them during the meeting or not, but anyway he got hired on the spot."[61] The salary was small—around 1.2 million lire a month (the equivalent price of a simple shirt at the store)—but Lee was thrilled. He called John McKitterick to tell him the news, who was "astonished, a little shocked, but pleased" for him.[62]

McQueen split his time between Zamasport, the factory in Novara situated thirty miles outside Milan, and the studio, an "airy, white-washed space" situated in a loft above "an auto-body shop" on Corso Como, a street described at the time as "decidedly dowdy."[63] Lee started working on clothes for Callaghan, another label that Gigli designed for, and one of his first tasks was to try to replicate a pleat in a shirt that Romeo had spotted in a photograph. The image, taken by Magnum photographer Josef Koudelka, showed a young gypsy whose shirt was being pulled by another boy. "Lee worked for a week on that shirt, but he never accomplished the pattern," said Carmen Artigas, one of Gigli's design assistants at the time. "Romeo came in and said, 'No, it's not like that,' and it was embarrassing, disappointing. I remember Lee sweating and being very nervous as Romeo spoke to him that day." Six years later, when Carmen visited McQueen in London, Lee brought out a plastic folder which contained a copy of the same photograph of the gypsy boy. "Remember this?" he said to her. "I thought I was going to get fired that day."

The two became friends after Carmen, who was born in Mexico City, noticed that Lee seemed to be in pain; he held his cheek as if the skin was tender to touch and so she offered him an aspirin. Later that week, the two design assistants had lunch and Lee told her about his life growing up in Stratford. "When he looked at you he had piercing blue eyes," she said. "He was shy and had a kind heart. He was a good person. I got the impression he was not out of the closet. He wore loose jeans and loose shirts, a pocket chain, he looked like a street guy. And his teeth were in bad shape, he was self-conscious about that." Lee also suffered from gingivitis—Carmen noticed that his gums were swollen and bright pink. "And he had a tooth missing—you wouldn't notice if he spoke, but if he threw his head back and laughed you could see it."

One of Lee and Carmen's tasks was to draw small sketches of the forthcoming collection on swathes of vellum paper which then would be used to wrap Gigli's designs. In order to entertain—and perhaps shock—his new friend, McQueen started to pass a series of drawings across the table, sketches that would foreshadow the imagery of his later collections. One was of a hybrid figure, half woman, half mermaid; her head, or what remained of it, was veiled, while her breasts were adorned with metallic cones and piercing her stomach was an arrow. Another showed an aggressive-looking dog next to an exotic, mythical bird. McQueen would sign his sketches, "Carmen with love, Lee," but at times she found it puzzling. "The collections at the time were very Pre-Raphaelite, all about beautiful women, and here was this guy sketching monsters," she said. "I thought, 'What is going on with this guy?' "[64]

Lee moved into a room in Lise's four-bedroom flat at Via Ariberto 1, near the Sant'Agostino metro. The apartment was in a *palazzo signorile*, a "big place with tiled floors and wooden parquet [and] high ceilings" in "an anonymous, quite grand part of town." When he left or entered the building Lee would often see an old couple sitting inside the concierge cubicle; the man had respiratory problems and would attach himself to a breathing apparatus, an image that Lise believes may have partly inspired the disturbing tableau of the over-weight naked woman wearing a mask and breathing through a tube that played a central part in *Voss*, McQueen's Spring/Summer 2001 show. "You might come home one day and walk past the glass box, all framed in dark wood, on your way to get to the elevator or go up the stairs to the flat and you'd see these two ancient people sitting side by side with a small table between them," said Lise. "He [would be] wearing a white singlet, hairy on his arms, and his face half-hidden by being hooked up to the apparatus and they would both just stare out ahead out of the glass and through you. A pungent sulphur smell ema-nating from the glass and their blank expressions in a semi-darkness. [It was] just eerie."

As well as Lise, his flatmates included Gigli colleagues Karen Brennan and Frans Ankoné. "Lee introduced me to De La Soul, blar-ing from a ghetto blaster in his room," said Lise. "He had a very 'Lon-don' energy and when he was in the house I was sort of in London. But he wasn't at home much or maybe I wasn't. We were working ten- to twelve-hour days, maybe going out to dinner, maybe dancing and then the next morning it's one bathroom to four bedrooms so we're all in and out the door. [I remember] the occasional banging on the bathroom door, 'Come on—I need the bathroom!' type stuff." She also recalls being horrified by some of the food that McQueen attempted to cook. "He didn't seem to know the first thing about cooking," she said. "So I made him at least one or maybe a few meals after that and insisted he eat them, probably just pasta, but I would have hassled him about eating well." Years later, when the two met up again in London, Lee called her his "Italian mamma," "which he must have intended as a compliment."

One night in the flat at Via Ariberto, Lise, Karen, Frans and

Lee were having dinner when Lee made some "odd" remark about homosexuality, a quip that Lise initially regarded as homophobic. "I thought he was being insensitive and/or ignorant," she said. Nobody commented on the remark and the conversation moved on as Frans started to talk about new clubs in Milan, "and Lee rattled out all these names of gay clubs," details of which "you could only know about if you frequented them or had lived in Milan for some time . . . [it was a] connoisseur's list of gay clubs in Milan." Lise remembers there being a slightly awkward, embarrassing moment before the conversation shifted gear again, but she was left thinking to herself, "Hello? You must know a thing or two then," but Lee carried on sitting there at the kitchen table, his head bowed slightly, "not looking at anyone." She realized then that "there was way more to Lee than he let on."[65] Later, Lee would regale his Saint Martins friend Simon Ungless with stories about his sex life in Italy, stories Ungless assumed were fabrications. "He talked about doing things that were absolutely physically impossible," said Simon. "Really ridiculous things about being in some kind of hoist and being lowered onto way too many men at once."[66]

There were others who were also surprised by McQueen's behavior. One weekend Lee invited Carmen and her sister, who was visiting Milan, to a party. They arranged to meet at a street corner outside a restaurant and, as it was raining, Lee turned up holding a beautiful vintage Japanese parasol made from bamboo and waxed paper. "He destroyed the parasol, which belonged to a Japanese friend of his, because it was, of course, not meant to be used in the rain," said Carmen. When she mentioned this to him, Lee just laughed and they continued to the party. There, her preconceptions of Lee were challenged once more. "The host was a handsome man who was working for Versace and the party was full of good-looking people," she said. "I wondered where did he meet all these guys?"[67]

Determined to observe and learn as much as possible from those around him, McQueen kept a close eye on the charismatic Romeo Gigli, described by Carmen as being "like a hologram . . . he was not a good-looking man, but he had something, a special, mysterious, romantic quality."[68] Lee was intrigued by Gigli's story: born into a wealthy family, Romeo lost both his parents when he was a teenager and, with his inheritance, traveled the world. "I lived like a prince for at least ten years," Gigli said. His mother had always worn haute couture (Dior and Balenciaga) and Gigli became fascinated by the structure of these exquisite items of clothing, some of which appeared to be moving pieces of sculpture. "I paid attention to how things were made," he said. "Whatever I do, I must know how it works." Eclecticism lay at the heart of his creative process, drawing inspiration from books, paintings, foreign cultures, travel. "My collection is inspired by the library of my father," he said, "never one trend but a big melange—a miscellany of my knowledge."[69]

McQueen also learnt from Gigli how to construct and maintain a public image. "Gigli had all this attention and I wanted to know why," Lee said later. "It had very little to do with the clothes and more to do with him as a person. And that's fundamentally true of anybody. Any interest in the clothes is secondary to the interest in the designer. You need to know that you're a good designer as well, though. You can't give that sort of bullshit without having a back-up. If you can't design, what's the point of generating all that hype in the first place?"[70]

Towards the end of his time in Milan, Lee had a falling-out with some of his flatmates at Via Ariberto. Lise returned one night to find the apartment dark and in silence. She opened the door to her room to find Lee lying on her bed, with his feet on her pillow. Lee was "pretty upset" as he related to her what had happened "amidst teary sobs." She recalls, "It was late. I was tired. I consoled him as best I could, got him off my bed and down the corridor into his own bed. Soon after he packed up and left." Lise was left with the image of the "front door left banging wide open into the dark palazzo stairwell."[71]

McQueen's time at the company—which would soon implode due to a breakdown in the relationship between Gigli and Carla Sozzani—was short-lived and he left in the summer of 1990. Lee told Carmen that he did not know what he would do next, but said that he would return to London, where he hoped to get work, and gave her his mother's contact details in case she wanted to get in touch. She was left with the strange and beautiful drawings Lee had given her and a couple of photographs. One of the Polaroids which remains in her possession is a close-up of Lee in which he looks disfigured, as if he had taken a scalpel to the surface of the image in order to scratch out his features.

On the surface it looked as though McQueen's life was going nowhere. He returned to London, moved back into his parents' house on Biggerstaff Road and started to work for John McKitterick again. McKitterick had left Red or Dead and had launched a label under his own name. McKitterick's vision at this time was inspired by fetish wear and McQueen worked on a number of designs made from leather and PVC, with lots of zips and detailing featuring rivets. "At this point he really started to pick my brains again about the design process," remembers McKitterick. "He had had experience on Savile Row, but as an apprentice tailor, and then as a part-time pattern cutter, a 'seamstress,' which is not a great CV to give him much confidence. He was saying now that he definitely wanted to be a designer and I told him that he had to learn the process. I said he could learn it by working with someone else, but the best way was to go to school." McKitterick told Lee about Central Saint Martins, the London art and fashion school that was then situated on Charing Cross Road on the edge of Soho, and talked to him about how he had studied for both his BA and his MA there. "I told him it wasn't too late for him to do this and that his experience in industry would be counted as the equivalent of a BA," he said. McKitterick, who was at this point teaching on the MA course, gave Lee the name and telephone number of Bobby Hillson, who was the founder and director of the MA course.

Lee knew that, if he secured a place at Saint Martins, his life would change. "I wanted to learn everything, everything, give me everything," he said.[72]

CHAPTER THREE

If you were a misfit and you hadn't fitted in anywhere, then art school was the place where you could feel at home.

—*Professor Louise Wilson*

Carrying an armful of clothes, Lee made his way down the long, rather shabby corridor towards the office of Bobby Hillson. He knocked on the door and waited. Bobby, described by one fashion writer as "patrician" and "old-school," opened the door to see a young man she thought must be a messenger.[1]

"Can I help you?" she asked. "Who are you here to see?"

"You," Lee replied.

"But I don't have an appointment with anyone."

Lee told Hillson about John McKitterick's suggestion that he call in to see her. Bobby, who was in a hurry, said that he could come into her office but that she had only five minutes to spare. Lee dumped the jackets down on a sofa and told Hillson, "I cut these clothes, I was working as a cutter for Romeo Gigli, so I thought I could come here and be a cutter for you." Bobby dismissed that idea in her head—he was, she reasoned, much too young to be a pattern cutter and her students would not take him seriously—but she was intrigued by his experience not only at Gigli, but on Savile Row.

"Have you ever designed or drawn anything?" she asked.

"I've drawn all my life," Lee said.[2]

Bobby made an appointment for McQueen to come back in

a few days' time with his portfolio of drawings. When she saw his sketches—which she later described as "sublime"[3]—Hillson immediately offered him a place on the MA course, despite the fact that he did not have the requisite qualification of a first or upper-second BA degree in fashion design, knitwear or printed textiles. "He was stunned, absolutely stunned," said Bobby. She told him that she couldn't offer him a bursary—all the grants had been assigned—but if he could find the fees then she would love to give him a place. "There is no doubt I thought there was talent," she said. "He was relatively charmless, had nothing really going for him, but I thought if he cares this much he's got to be given a chance." Hillson sent him to see Jane Rapley, then dean of fashion and textiles, and told her, "Jane, I've taken somebody; he's got none of the right qualifications, he'll probably leave in the middle, but I'm taking him."[4]

Later, McQueen described Bobby Hillson as being "like a mother" to him, "nagging, but much needed," and one fashion writer said the couple "made as unlikely a pair as a grand duchess and a football hooligan." After training at Saint Martins, where she studied under the legendary Muriel Pemberton, Hillson had worked as a fashion illustrator for *Vogue*. Steeped in fashion history, she remembers attending Chanel's comeback show in the 1950s. "That'll date me . . . Everybody went to those shows, from Marlene Dietrich to Barbra Streisand," she said.[5] During her time at the college she mentored the best and the brightest of British talent—Stephen Jones, John Galliano, Rifat Özbek, John Flett and Sonja Nuttall. "The MA course is completely different to any other course," said Bobby. "The concept behind it was to make the students work together as a team, like in the industry. So it is part fashion design, part print design. I wasn't interested in it being a purely academic exercise, the whole point of the course was to make the students more professional."[6]

Lee returned home excited at the prospect of studying at Saint Martins, but also certain that his family would never be able to amass enough money for the fees, which then stood at £1,985 a year. The solution came from his aunt, Renee Holland, who had come into a small inheritance after the death of her father, Samuel McQueen, in 1986. "Renee used to work in the rag trade, as a seamstress in the East End," said Janet, Lee's sister. "She was very aware of Lee's ability in the early days. She spotted it early and I think Lee made Renee a couple of dresses and she was over the moon with these. She knew that he could cut, she was pleased with how the material hung, how it fitted the body. So with Renee's help Lee was able to enrol on the course."[7]

When Lee started at Saint Martins in October 1990 he felt, perhaps for the first time, a sense of belonging. "What I really liked was the freedom of expression and being surrounded by like-minded people," he later said. "It was an exciting period for me because it showed me there were other people out there like me."[8] Louise Wilson, who would take over from Bobby Hillson as director of the MA fashion course, said, "That was the beautiful thing about art school. If you were a misfit and you hadn't fitted in anywhere, then art school was the place where you could feel at home." Wilson remembered the Saint Martins building at 107 Charing Cross Road with a certain fondness. "If you were trying to describe it you would say it would be like arriving at a disused hospital in Russia," she said. "It was like walking into the best broken-down warehouse that had not been revamped. There were windows that didn't work, the floor was cracked red lino, and the studio had four pattern tables that were really just slabs of wood on top of old chests of drawers, tables that were too low and gave you a horrible back. And yet it was fabulous."[9]

Central Saint Martins—which was formed in 1989 after the merger of the Central School of Art and Design, founded in 1896, and St. Martins School of Art, founded in 1854—had developed a reputation for fostering a spirit of cultural radicalism. Former graduates included Lucian Freud, John Hurt, Sir Peter Blake, Gerald Scarfe, Antony Gormley, Mike Leigh, Jarvis Cocker, P. J. Harvey and members of the Clash. Famously, in November 1975, the Sex Pistols played their first gig in the bar (onetime bassist Glen Matlock studied art at the college). Experimentation was not only encouraged, but expected. "If you can draw it you can make it," said Muriel Pemberton. "Nothing is impossible, you just have to find the way to do it."[10] John Galliano, who had graduated from Saint Martins in 1984, later told fashion journalist Hamish Bowles, "You could move among the sculptors, the fine artists, the graphic designers and the film-makers."[11] Students congregated at Dave's coffee bar, a dingy room on the ground floor filled with grubby Formica tables and battered sofas. On the sixth floor—the home of the fine art department—there was a shower block that became notorious as a gay cruising ground. "There were boys on my course who ran a rent-boy business from Soho," said Louise Wilson, "and they would bring back their clients to the showers."[12]

On Lee's first day at the college he bonded with fellow student Simon Ungless. The young men, together with the other MA students, were in the studio on the second floor taking part in a group critique. Each student had to display work they had previously made and, in front of the other tutors on the course, had to explain why they had designed their pieces and who their ideal customer was. Simon, who had created a series of prints featuring tartan, outlined his vision and Lee, obviously drawn by the patterns of the various clans, asked him how he had achieved the look.

"I thought this kid was really young, like fourteen or fifteen, and that he was the child of one of the tutors," said Simon. "He was wearing huge, disgustingly grubby denim flares and a dirty-looking vintage baseball T-shirt with a native American head on the chest. He didn't look like all the others who were trying hard to look like fashion students at Saint Martins. I must admit I was a bit dismissive of this kid asking me how I'd done my work. Anyway, we went through the critique and this one guy had done his fashion design project with these Barbie-like illustrations which were very cheesy. Bobby asked him who the customer was and he said, 'Kylie Minogue.' This was before Kylie became cool and me and Lee both started laughing. Then Lee presented his work and it was then that I said to myself, 'Oh God, he is a student.' He presented his drawings, which looked like they had been drawn with chicken's feet dipped in ink, drawings of girls with no hair, pointy noses, really high turtle-necks covering their faces and I thought, 'Wow, this is really kind of interesting.' From that day there was an instant rapport between us."[13]

The more they talked, the more Lee and Simon realized they had a great deal in common. Like Lee, Simon was working-class and gay and had taken the trouble to gain experience within the fashion industry. There was, according to Ungless, a level of unsophistication on the course that surprised him. Whereas he and McQueen were able to bandy names such as Martin Margiela and Helmut Lang across the studio like a game of stylistic Ping-Pong, some of the other students seemed ignorant of the basics of fashion. Lee and Simon laughed at one of their contemporaries who insisted on pronouncing Versace's name as "Versayz."

"From day one people either loved Lee or hated him," said Rebecca Barton, another student on the MA course. She remembers a day early on in the course when the students had to present a collection to the group. Lee had stood up and talked about how he had drawn inspiration from Eskimos—the clothes featured large coats with big hoods in white leather. "Then Lee hammered into everybody else, saying, 'This is crap, you haven't done this or that.' Some people were really upset by his behaviour and I think a lot of people found him quite difficult. But I thought he was lovely. We got on because we were both quite sarky, I think."[14]

Rebecca recalls how Lee would imitate one of their fellow students who would use the long corridor outside the MA studios as a catwalk. Apparently the boy would prance up and down the corridor in an affected way, and Lee "would walk up and down imitating him with his saggy trousers, bum hanging out, laughing."[15] One of Barton's strongest memories of McQueen is the sound of his laugh—"he laughed a lot, and loudly, almost like a squeal," she said.[16] Although Lee alienated some students with what they saw as his aggressive attitude, he was acutely sensitive to criticism himself. Fellow student Adele Clough remembers one occasion when, without thinking, she attacked him for a poster that he had made to advertise some college event. "It was really badly drawn, embarrassing and misspelt," she said. "I said to him, 'If you don't have pride in your work you will never get anywhere.' I realized I had gone too far because he said absolutely nothing. You know when someone looks at you and they've been told that too many times in their life."[17] Tony McQueen remembers the seriousness with which his brother took the course. He recalls one time when Lee had to finish a project which involved some beading work. McQueen enlisted his brothers and sisters to help thread the different-colored beads in a particular order, but Tony made a mistake and Lee told him he had to start again. "Is this going to go anywhere, Lee?" asked Tony. "Just shut up and do it," Lee replied.[18]

Lee also became friends with Réva Mivasagar, a young gay man who is half-Indian, half-Chinese. Réva arrived at Saint Martins two weeks later than the other students and at first he found McQueen's behavior quite boorish and abrasive. Lee was sitting down in the studio and sketching using a light box when Réva approached him. Lee asked him where he was from and when Réva told him that he had been raised in Sydney, he started to ask a series of "really inane questions about being Australian, clichéd things about barbecues. And then it was like, 'Don't disturb me because I'm sketching.'" The initial bond came through a love of fashion. "He disliked most designers, but he loved Helmut Lang, Rei Kawakubo and Martin Margiela." Réva recalls how Lee would buy cheap clothes from army surplus stores and then add a piece of gauze on the back and the trademark four white pick stitches in order to fool people into thinking he was wearing genuine Margiela.[19] Réva liked Lee's "creative energy, drive and the way he envisioned beauty." Lee used to tell him that both of them were "misfits"—"in truth I think it was more about the fact that we had so little in common with the other students in our year that we hung out together more through natural selection . . . Both Lee and I had a need to explore London, whether it be through gallery exhibitions, movies, theatre, museums and libraries or late-night venues and any form of alternative lifestyle. As design students what we had in common was that we were always looking for new forms of visual stimulation or eye candy to achieve that creative high."[20]

Louise Wilson, who moved from being a visiting tutor to director of the MA course during the eighteen months that Lee was at Saint Martins, remembered McQueen's insatiable curiosity. One day, Geraldine Larkin, a former Saint Martins student, came into the college with some embroidered scarves and "Lee wandered over to look at all the embroideries, and asked her all about beading," said Louise. "That's exactly what he was like—he would hoover up information." Louise, who developed a reputation for straight-talking toughness, recognized that Lee had a certain talent for cutting. There was nothing else particularly remarkable about him, she maintained. "But I remember that he was always in college, that he was somebody who made use of the pattern-cutting facilities. Lee was always around doing his thing."[21]

Sometimes, in the middle of talks by visiting designers or lecturers, Lee would interrupt and start to argue a point. Some students found this so uncomfortable that they went to Bobby Hillson to complain. "A little group, three or so students, found it embarrassing and they said to me, 'Bobby, why did you take him?' And I said because I think he's enormously talented and told them that I thought he would settle down. He was a really intelligent boy, just badly educated. He didn't know how to behave, but that was what was interesting."[22] There were times, however, when McQueen's street-savvy attitude paid off. Rebecca Barton remembers one occasion when a designer visited the college and asked the students to work on a particular project. "Lee refused to do it because he said this designer was just going to nick our ideas," she said. "He was really cynical, but you know what? I did this T-shirt with a red cross on it and it got nicked by that designer and sold everywhere. Lee said, 'I told you that was going to happen, you are such a loser.'"

As the course progressed, Rebecca and Lee spent more and more time together, mostly at her small flat in Westminster and then later at another flat in north London. The friends worked out a mutually beneficial scheme: Lee would cook for her (he made a delicious pasta bake, something he'd picked up from his time in Italy) and in return, after she had gone to bed, she would make her video recorder available for him to watch gay porn. McQueen was still suffering from terrible gum disease and when Rebecca woke up she would find that Lee, who shared the bed, had bled all over her pillows. "When he talked he would spit blood," she said. "He wasn't very attractive at that time; he was fat and spotty, he was having a lot of sex but none of it more than once with the same person. Sometimes he would go out cottaging all night and he would come back and tell me all the horrible details. He would go to Camden Lock and see someone and they would go down an alley and have sex. Everything he did was to excess." Once, the two went out clubbing, but Lee told Rebecca that she was a poor mover and that he couldn't be seen on the same dance floor as her. "Lee had a good rhythm, but he was very frantic," she said.[23]

Simon recalls his first night out with Lee. He had just spent a few weeks island hopping with his boyfriend in Greece when he returned to London and realized how much he had missed McQueen. Simon called him up and the two young men went to Fruit Machine, the Wednesday night at the gay club Heaven, situated under Charing Cross station. "That was the first time we ever went out and we just had the best time," he said. "We both loved to dance and go out and be naughty and pick up boys and basically have a lot of fun." That night Simon remembers a handsome guy cruising around Lee—he watched as the man came over and spoke to his friend, before quickly disappearing. Simon asked Lee what had happened and he replied, " 'I asked him if he'd got a big cock.' I said, 'Lee, your first chat-up line can't be, "Have you got a big cock?"'" But he was laughing hysterically."[24]

With Réva, Lee would go to the London Apprentice, a rough pub-like club near Old Street, or various "leather clubs in the East End."[25] According to Réva there was "way, way, way too much clubbing . . . there was never a dive too desperate or sleazy for us to discover . . . He wanted to go anywhere that had an edge. There were so many different clubs that I can barely remember now. There was never anything like just a nice, normal disco."[26]

Lee and Réva would also frequent the shop Ad-Hoc—a kind of dressing-up box for the perverse—on the corner of Moor Street and Old Compton Street. Here one could find a costume fit for all fantasies—Ad-Hoc sold bondage trousers, PVC vests, women's shoes in men's sizes, and its customers were a curious mix of club kids, prostitutes, gay muscle men, drag queens, stylists and designers. "One day I was working there and Anna Sui, Marc Jacobs, Steven Meisel and Anita Pallenberg came into the shop and bought a whole load of stuff," said Frank Franca, now a New York–based photographer. "Another day an elderly man wanted to buy some women's shoes. He came in and crawled around on all fours." Club promoters would drop off fliers for their nights at the shop and as a result Ad-Hoc became a hot spot for information about London's thriving nightlife. "A punk revival was happening at the time and this place was the ground zero for that," said Frank, who would become an acquaintance of Lee's.[27] The manager of the shop, Eric Rose, who had been brought up in Vancouver but who had been living in London since the late eighties, remembers McQueen from those days when he would drop into Ad-Hoc and look through the packed rails of clothes. Lee liked the Canadian's quick wit, camp humor and his varied social circle, while Eric was drawn to McQueen's sense of anarchy. Eric recalls one day when he went with Lee and David Kappo, who used to work in the wig shop in the basement of Ad-Hoc, to a house party in Mayfair in honor of Kylie Minogue. "We drank all the booze and then decided to go," he said. "Lee was like, 'It's shit, we gotta go,' and as we ran down the stairs McQueen pulled the fire alarm. I said, 'What are you doing?' and he said, 'That party was shit—if *we're* not going to have fun no one is.' I thought that was a little bit naughty. He had a fun, who-cares attitude."[28]

Often on Friday nights, Lee would meet up with Rebecca Barton at a pizza restaurant near the college in Soho. The friends would take advantage of an *Evening Standard* offer of two-for-one pizzas—"I would be the one who paid full price and he would be the one who paid a penny," said Rebecca. It was here one night that Lee told her about the sexual abuse he had suffered as a child. "He didn't tell me in any detail about what went on but I know it wasn't just a one-off," she said. Rebecca remembers that while they were at Saint Martins, Lee organized a surprise birthday party for her at a Soho pub and once he gave her a present of a necklace that he had made and a strange black-and-white photograph of himself, naked from the waist up, wrapped in what looked like cling film. On the back of the photo he scribbled, "To my dearest Becca. Lot of love Lee x." "He was a complete poppet," she said. "He was lovely and funny and naughty."[29]

He also spent a large amount of time with his friend Tania Wade, whom he had met one night in the club SubStation. At the time, Tania lived in a nearby flat on Shaftesbury Avenue and at the end of the night she would often invite a legion of young gay men back to her place to sleep the night. "There would be all these different boys in rows—one with a pillow case over him, another with a flannel or a tea towel—and Lee was one of them," she said. "I adored him straight away, he was such good fun." Tania introduced him to Maison Bertaux, the patisserie on Greek Street run by her sister Michelle; he would order a fruit cheesecake or an apple Danish and an Earl Grey tea and take his place upstairs at the long banquette. "He always wanted to make me clothes and I will never forget the sight of him sitting by his sewing machine," said Tania. "He was so absorbed, like someone with a mania, like a lunatic. I told him that some of the outfits he had made for me would take five people to help me get into them, and that some of the clothes were unwearable. 'You cheeky bloody cow,' he replied." Once, when the friends were together, he told her to pass him the material for the dress he wanted to make for her; she could see nothing that was suitable. "It turned out that he wanted to use his bedcover made from candlewick," she said.[30]

In October 1991, the fashion students, including Lee, Adele and Rebecca, traveled en masse to Paris to try and blag their way into the shows. "For London fashion students, sneaking into the shows is a rite of passage," said fashion writer Marion Hume. "Students from Central St Martins . . . are masters of it."[31] They traveled by train and ferry and stayed in a cheap hotel with the plaster falling off the walls. Rebecca had already secured tickets for the Givenchy show, which she remembers as being full of "horrible dresses with floral designs." Lee was not impressed either. "I can't believe you've made me go to this show," he told her. "It's really crap. I would never design for a place like this." Five years later, when Rebecca heard the news of McQueen's appointment at Givenchy, the memory made her smile.[32]

In Paris, Lee dared fellow student Adele Clough to try and talk her way into the Helmut Lang show by pretending to be a model. The trick worked—some of the booked models had been taken ill and Lang's team had had to call in some more girls. Suddenly, Adele, who was wearing a Gigli suit, felt terrified at the prospect of continuing the charade and the thought of walking down a catwalk and so she hid in the toilets while she considered her options. "Then I came out and found that on the chairs were all these spare tickets so I took them, went outside and gave them to Lee and the rest of the group," she said. Buoyed on by her success, Lee persuaded Adele to try the same trick again, at a show managed by PR consultant Lynne Franks. But on this occasion the security was tighter and the organizers had photographs of each of the models they had booked. Lee did not give in, however, and he came up with another plan: he told Adele that she had to pretend she was working with stylist Edward Enninful. "Lee briefed me about Enninful, what he thought he knew about him, and I duly repeated all this to Lynne Franks, who asked me to describe what he looked like," said Adele. "But then Lynne turned around and said, 'Did you not think to mention that he is black?' I realized Lee had made it all up."[33]

When the students arrived back in London, Bobby Hillson asked them about what museums they had seen in Paris. "We didn't go to a single exhibition or do a single drawing, we just had a really good time," said Rebecca. The news did not please Bobby and she told her students what she thought of them. This ticking off was nothing compared to the force with which Louise Wilson expressed her opinions. Her speech was frequently peppered with "fucks" and she would, in the words of one commentator, "drop-kick a mannequin at any student dropping their stitches."[34]

From the beginning of the course McQueen and Louise Wilson had a difficult relationship. Lee accepted criticism when he believed it was warranted, such as the occasion when Wilson pointed out that "he put these beads between organza and I remember at the time saying that he had knocked them off, that he had got that idea from Callaghan."[35] But then, as the course progressed and Louise took over the job as director, the relationship worsened. "He had many clashes with Louise, because they were actually quite similar; they were both control freaks," said Réva.[36]

One project involved designing an outfit for Dame Shirley Porter, the Lord Mayor of Westminster, but Lee refused to take part because "he said he wasn't going to make clothes for anyone who was privileged and who wasn't prepared to pay for them." Although Louise subsequently admitted that she could be brutally honest, McQueen felt that at times he was being bullied by her. "If she could have got rid of Lee she would have got rid of him," said Adele. "He could do his work in two minutes. He could sketch a pattern by eye. And the pattern tutor would tell him it was not good enough, but then he would make the toile and it would fit perfectly the person it was made for. But still they would say you've done it the wrong way. I think they were jealous of his talent. But Lee always knew he would be a success—there was never an unwavering doubt in his mind."

At one point, Lee lashed out at Louise Wilson and, in front of a group of students, said, "How can you possibly know what women want to wear when you are so fat?" From that moment onwards the attacks became more personal. "Lee was always hatching plans for the downfall of Louise," said Adele. At one point he brought in a whoopee cushion and put it on her chair.[37] Lee still felt incredibly loyal towards Bobby, the woman who had taken him onto the course because she had recognized his raw talent, and he felt protective towards her. "Lee did have a tough time under Louise Wilson," said Bobby, "but I didn't know it at the time. It only came out later when I heard that Lee had said, 'Louise did nothing for me, it was all Bobby.' "[38]

During the course, Lee had become increasingly interested in drawing inspiration from the dark side. According to Rebecca Barton, he became obsessed with Burke and Hare, the Irish immigrants who carried out a series of murders in Edinburgh at the beginning of the nineteenth century and who sold sixteen corpses to a doctor to be dissected. At the same time he also read *Perfume*, Patrick Süskind's bestselling novel about a perfume apprentice in eighteenth-century France who goes on to murder virgins in his quest to find the "perfect scent." "The character in that book is him," said Rebecca, "all visceral with all his senses heightened. He liked nasty rawness, but of course he balanced that with complete beauty."[39]

Lee told friends that his family was related to Jack the Ripper. His interest in the Victorian serial killer intensified after seeing the 1991 film *The Silence of the Lambs*, starring Jodie Foster and Anthony Hopkins. McQueen became fixated on the character of Buffalo Bill, a psychopathic tailor who kills women in order to fashion a suit made from their skin. "The idea of these women being sewn into an outfit was a huge inspiration for him," said Réva, who saw the film with him. "And also the image of butterflies or moths being encased inside the fabric, you could see that later in one of his collections."

Réva worked beside McQueen as they started to plan their final collections. Lee started the process by sketching, but the design would quickly change and evolve as he made the dress. "He would start with the collar line with a very tailored, very tight-fitting collar," Réva said. "And then very tight sleeves. If you look at those catalogues of old Victorian costume you see these very corseted tailored women's coats. He had this book on his desk about Victorian costume, a huge reference book. And he would go through it and show me the capes, he always liked the capes."[40]

Lee turned to Simon Ungless to help him with preparations for his final show. For the whole of his second year, McQueen had been spending increasing amounts of time with Simon in the print room, learning about techniques such as dip-dyeing and tie-dyeing. For one of his designs, a frock coat, Lee used a barbed thorn pattern that Simon had printed onto pink silk. "I worked with Lee on some of those pieces," recalls Simon. "I remember the day, it was just me and Lee in the studio and he was working on the toile for the jacket with the peplum that stuck out at a 90-degree angle, and I was concentrating on some rubber pieces, trying to work out a way of sewing them together. Neither of us knew how these things were going to work and Ike Rust, who was then a visiting lecturer, came into the studio and asked, 'How are these things going to work?' Lee and I looked at him and said, 'Well, we don't know,' and he said, 'You two are completely mental,' and walked off."[41]

In the run-up to the show Lee wrote a letter to Simon Costin, whose jewelry and body sculpture he had seen featured in the pages of magazines like *The Face* and *i-D*, asking if he could use some of his pieces in his collection. The two men met and Costin, who would go on to work with Lee as a set designer and art director on a number of shows, lent him seven pieces, including two large necklaces made from bird skulls. "He was always interested in the iconography of death," said Costin. "And we shared a similar sensibility, as both of us were fascinated by the macabre. Yet the first time I met him I kept thinking of Billy Bunter. Lee was so playful and funny and raucous and foul-mouthed, and he had this passion for what he was doing."[42]

When McQueen had finished the clothes, described as "day into evening wear inspired by nineteenth-century street walkers,"[43] John McKitterick came into the college to view them on a rack. He was amazed by what he saw. "What I distinctly remember is that if you looked at the collection from the side rather than from the front you saw this extraordinary silhouette, a bird-like silhouette," he said. "McQueen always said he loved birds, but there was something else to it, too. The idea of dropping the waist and making the legs shorter was quite homoerotic in a way." McKitterick was reminded of the sexualized images of Touko Laaksonen, the illustrator known as Tom of Finland, who drew men "with little stumpy legs, narrow waists and longer torsos." McQueen "used these masculine elements and made this sexy for a girl." McKitterick also remembers thinking how Saint Martins had given Lee a new confidence. "That institution really changed him," he said. "He became more knowledgeable and had a confidence about what he was talking about. He realized he was far more talented than the majority of people there. He began to be able to talk about the world, fashion and current events. He was a different person. St. Martins gave him the thing he was looking for."[44]

On the day of the final show, in March 1992, Lee and Simon Ungless left Simon's house in Tooting and made their way to Chelsea, where the event was to be held in the barracks on the King's Road. The atmosphere was tense and chaotic as there was a great deal left to do. After finishing backstage, the friends went to find Louise Wilson, as Lee wanted to check a last-minute detail with her. "And she just took out her perfume from her bag and sprayed it in his face, and yelled, 'You fucking stink,'" recalls Simon. "Lee fell on the floor and said, 'God, you're a fucking cunt.'"[45]

As the audience began to take their seats they had little idea of the toxic interchange that had just taken place. The lights dimmed and the show started. Lee's mother, Joyce, and her sister-in-law Renee, who were sitting in the audience, enjoyed the spectacle, the parade of models and designs, but it wasn't until the words "Lee A-McQueen" were projected onto the back wall that they began to feel totally engaged. After all, both women knew how far Lee had come to get to this point. "To me at that time that was the pinnacle, seeing him at his MA show," said Joyce in 1997.[46] A heavy beat began to pump out from the speakers as the models sashayed down the runway. Lee presented ten looks in total, including a black silk peplum jacket paired with a tight red skirt; a pink silk thorn-print jacket with black trousers and a black bustier top; and a calico skirt covered in papier-mâché magazine articles and burn marks which was twinned with a black jacket with fantastically long, pointed lapels.

Sewn into the designs and also encased in small pockets of Perspex attached to the fabric were locks of McQueen's own hair, sometimes strands of his pubic hair. The front page of his market report—a document that was supposed to be an in-depth analysis outlining the background to the collection—was in Lee's case "all about his mother as a genealogist and Jack the Ripper . . . and it had his pubic hair scattered on the cover."[47] Later, McQueen tried to explain the decision to incorporate hair into the clothes. "The inspiration behind the hair came from Victorian times when prostitutes would sell theirs for kits of hair locks, which were bought by people to give to their lovers," he said. "I used it as my signature label with locks of hair in Perspex. In the early collections it was my own hair; it was about me giving myself to the collection."[48]

McQueen had named his collection *Jack the Ripper Stalks His Victims*. On one level he cast himself as a kind of stylistic serial killer figure slashing and cutting up cloth to refashion the female silhouette into a form that was more aesthetically pleasing. But the incorporation of his own hair into the clothes also symbolized his emotional identification with the victims. There was something sweetly romantic about the gesture, too. As McQueen stated, in Victorian times prostitutes would sell their locks out of economic necessity to people who then gave the hair as tokens of affection. McQueen had a hope that the same narrative of romance would infuse his own life and that he could move away from the ugly realities of exploitation and abuse to something sweeter and gentler, more equal. To him, this talisman of a lock of hair sewn into those clothes meant that he believed in the possibility that one day he would be transformed by the power of love.

McQueen had invested so much energy, both physical and emotional, into that collection that he hoped that he would be awarded the finale—the honor of showing his clothes last—but instead this went to a student named Kei Kagami. At that time Louise Wilson favored Japanese-influenced design; later she told Réva that she had also given the Tokyo-born designer the prestigious slot because "he was much better organized than the rest of us, everything was finished and perfect," said Réva. "But Lee was actually very upset he didn't get the finale because he thought he deserved it."[49] There were others there that day who also believed Lee should have been given the top award. "He was a stand-out student, you could tell right from the beginning that he was marvellous," said Lesley Goring, who produced the show.[50] Bobby Hillson recalls being slightly disappointed by his degree show, "but looking back I think I was wrong."[51] Lee left Saint Martins not with a distinction, but with a pass "like everyone else."[52]

The next day, Lee and Rebecca were in college sitting in the corridor down from Bobby Hillson's room when a call came into the office from Isabella Blow. The influential stylist, who then worked at British *Vogue*, had been in the audience and had been mesmerized by McQueen's collection to such an extent that she wanted to come into the college to take a closer look. "I was sitting on the floor, I couldn't even get a seat at the Saint Martins show, and the pieces went past me and they moved in a way I had never seen and I wanted them," she said later. "The colours were very extreme. He would do a black coat, but then he'd line it with human hair and it was blood red inside so it was like a body—like the flesh, with blood. And I just thought, this is the most beautiful thing I've ever seen. I just knew he had something really special, very modern, it was about sabotage and tradition."[53] When Rebecca heard the news of Blow's interest she turned to her friend and said, "You're going to be really famous," a comment Lee laughed off. "You could see in his face that he was really excited," said Rebecca. "And everything changed overnight."[54]

CHAPTER FOUR

We'd embarked on this adventure, like travelling on this chariot, Boudica-like.

—Detmar Blow

Isabella Blow, wearing a pair of black-fringed Gaultier trousers, came strutting and squawking into the ramshackle Saint Martins building looking for the student who she later said had "a great technical ability to . . . make clothes fly."[1] She hurried up to the second floor and introduced herself to a rather startled-looking Lee. His reaction was not unusual: after all, one commentator described Isabella as looking like "a piece of public art,"[2] while another compared her to "Rod Hull's emu as styled by Salvador Dalí."[3] "He didn't know who she was and at this stage didn't really trust her," said Réva Mivasagar, who witnessed that first meeting. "She kept saying she wanted to buy his collection, but he was very sceptical about it all, whether she would really buy it. She was very flamboyant about who she knew, all her connections, and Lee thought she was pretty crazy."[4]

Blow persisted, however, and continued to pester both him and his mother, whose number Lee had given her and who she repeatedly telephoned. "Who is this loony lady calling?" Joyce asked her son, who was still living at home.[5] Finally, after a great deal of persuasion, Lee named a price of a couple of hundred pounds per outfit, and although Isabella said she could not afford to give him the whole sum all at once—"money simply passed through her fingers

81

like sand"[6]—she said she would pay him in installments. Over the course of the next few months, Lee would accompany her to various cash points around London as she withdrew money from the bank and he would hand over the clothes stashed in black bin liners in exchange. Although Lee was wary of her at first, the more he learnt about her, the more he realized how potentially useful she could be to him. She told him about her experience at American *Vogue* with Anna Wintour, at *Tatler* with style supremo Michael Roberts and at British *Vogue* with Liz Tilberis. She had been friends with Andy Warhol—she had worn a Bill Blass black suit for the artist's memorial service and had done a striptease at the party afterwards—had lived with *Dynasty* actress Catherine Oxenberg in New York, and had known Rupert Everett for years. But the bond between McQueen and Blow went much deeper than a simple patron–artist relationship. As Lee learnt more about her past—something she talked about with the same nonchalance with which she would flash her breasts—he discovered that, for all her upper-class privileges, she was just as damaged as him.

Isabella's widower, Detmar Blow, has described her early life as a "black fairy story."[7] In 1964, when Issie was five years old, she was playing in the gardens of the family's home, Doddington Park, Cheshire, with her brother Johnny, who was two and a half. Her mother, Helen, told her daughter to look after her brother while she went into the house, but something distracted the little girl and in those few seconds it seems that Johnny, who was the heir to a baronetcy dating back to 1660, choked on a piece of dry biscuit and fell into a small pond and died. Later, Isabella would claim that her mother had gone inside to put on her lipstick. "That explains my obsession with lipstick," she would say.[8] McQueen was also fascinated to hear about Isabella's grandfather, Sir Jock Delves Broughton, who had been tried but acquitted of the murder of his second wife's lover, Josslyn Hay, the Twenty-second Earl of Erroll, in Kenya's Happy Valley, a scandal that was detailed in James Fox's book *White Mischief*. In 1942, Jock committed suicide by injecting himself with morphine at a hotel in Liverpool.

Lee, whose gothic sensibilities ran through his veins like black blood, found Issie's outlandish digressions darkly compelling. Some anecdotes—such as the one about her grandmother, Vera, who unwittingly ate human flesh on a trip to Papua New Guinea—were undoubtedly amusing. There were other stories, however, that had the potency to haunt the living: Detmar's father, Jonathan Blow, had committed suicide in 1977 by drinking a bottle of the weed killer paraquat. Jonathan's twelve-year-old son, Amaury, witnessed the death. "He said Dadda never cried out, but that his fists were clenched in pain," said Detmar.[9] Isabella would choose the same method to end her life when she killed herself in May 2007.

Isabella also told her new friend of her love of beauty, a compulsion to disguise and arm herself by means of the transformative power of fashion. Like McQueen, she hated how she looked—she described her face as "ugly"—and felt self-conscious about her "bucked front teeth," which she called "her combine harvesters."[10] Although she went to see a celebrity dentist in New York in the eighties to see if he could do anything about them she was told that she had left it too late. "Her habit of smearing her lips and teeth with lipstick was in part to deal with this perceived disfigurement," said Detmar. "Her hatred of her face was another demon Issie carried with her for life."[11]

Detmar remembers the first time his wife spoke about McQueen. She came rushing home after the Saint Martins show and told her husband about the boy "who could cut like a god."[12] Despite the occasional couple of hundred pounds from Issie and the cash he received from the Department of Social Security (DSS), McQueen did not have enough money to rent his own flat. He was desperate to leave home and so Isabella offered him the use of 33 Alderney Street, Pimlico, a tall Victorian terraced house owned by Detmar's mother, Helga. Soon after graduation, Lee moved there with Réva Mivasagar. "Isabella wanted him to have the house so that he could work on her look, on her clothes," said Réva. "She absolutely adored his work, he couldn't do anything wrong. He was very excited about starting out on his own and he was experiencing a creative high."[13] From the beginning, Isabella called McQueen by his middle name as she thought it sounded grander and more appropriate for a young fashion designer who wanted to make his mark. Later, Lee would insist that he had not changed his name simply because Blow believed that "Alexander" sounded more upmarket. "I dropped my first name when I started working for myself because I was signing on at the time," he said.[14]

McQueen also began to assist Isabella on shoots. One day that summer he came to John McKitterick's studio and asked to borrow some clothes, a couple of leather pieces with zips and rivets. "He borrowed these on a Tuesday and on the Friday night I was in a gay bar in south London with a friend and who should walk in all dressed in my clothes but Lee," said John. "His hair looked all slick and he had made a little leather bow tie. To see Lee dressed like that was hysterical—he had never had access to clothes like this before—and my friend and I looked at each other. Lee saw me and his face went red, he was embarrassed, but we ended up laughing about it together."[15]

With Réva, Lee continued to explore London's nightlife. One of his favorite clubs at this time was Kinky Gerlinky, created by Gerlinde and Michael Kostiff, which was then held at the Empire in Leicester Square.

The club, which began in the mid-eighties after the closure of the legendary Taboo, developed a reputation for "polymorphous perversity," a term that was coined by Freud to mean the ability to derive erotic pleasure from any part of the body but which, by the early nineties, encapsulated the trend of free-form sexuality. Kinky Gerlinky was a space where misfits of all sorts could go to express their difference. "It's a gay club, and it's a massive gay club, it's got about 3,000 people in it," said MC Kinky. "But they don't just cater for gay people, they cater for everything and there aren't really any restrictions . . . you can do what you want, say what you want, get up to what you want."[16]

Dressing up was a requirement, the more bizarre the better. Porn star Aiden Shaw, who went on to enjoy a close relationship with

McQueen, once went dressed as Minnie Mouse. Fashion journalist Hamish Bowles, now at American *Vogue*, transformed himself into a 1940s-style Hollywood goddess. "I always think it's always very good to really go for an icon, do it slavishly," he said.[17] "Kinky Gerlinky was a big deal for Lee," said Réva. "Once I remember him wearing a hat from [milliner] Philip Treacy, which looked like a pair of ram horns but had been made from organza, and he borrowed a silver lamé frock coat that I think was John Galliano. He made his own pants using the fabric left over from the student collection and wore them with some shoes from Isabella. The look was pseudo-drag."[18]

Later, McQueen and Treacy would become both friends and creative collaborators, but at their first meeting in 1992 the atmosphere between them was decidedly chilly. Both Alexander and Philip had assumed that they enjoyed a unique status as Isabella's new protégé— she repeatedly told both of them that they were fabulous—but now they learnt that they would have to compete for her attention.

In July 1992, Lee was invited to Hilles, the Blows' country house in Gloucestershire. British *Vogue* had commissioned Oberto Gili to shoot a story about the couple and their Arts and Crafts house and Isabella had asked McQueen to design all the clothes. When Lee arrived at Hilles, designed in 1913 by Detmar Blow's architect grandfather, also called Detmar, he was enchanted by the view. In 1940, *Country Life* magazine described it in the following terms: "Its position, one to dream of but such as few would dare to tackle, is an unsuspected ledge just below the crest of the Cotswolds west of Painswick, commanding the whole valley of the Severn from the Malverns to Chepstow, with the better part of the Welsh Marches stretching range upon range westwards."[19] On the first night of his stay McQueen was placed in the best guest room in the house, complete with four-poster bed. Wherever Lee turned he saw something to marvel at: the long drawing room with its floor of raw elm; the paneling in the bedrooms remade by using coffin boards after a fire destroyed the house in 1951; the Queen Anne needlework carpet hanging as a tapestry in the "Big Hall," a room that before the fire had comprised a hall and dining room; the coat of arms of James I featuring a lion and a unicorn and the words "Beati Pacifici" ("Blessed are the peacemakers"); and the portrait of Hilles's architect Detmar Blow sketched by Augustus John. "There is little in the way of soft furniture," wrote one observer, "and the whole place has a rather dark, medieval, and slightly cold air. It is a life-size theatrical set."[20]

Although the house looked like something handed down through generations it was essentially modern, a monument to the benefits of hard work and upward mobility. "I remember Issie telling Alexander about my grandfather, that he was creative, but that the family was not posh, that we were from Croydon," said Detmar. "He knew that the house belonged to my mother and that we had no money. I had a very modest barrister's income and Issie had hers [from magazines] which wasn't much." The underlying ethos of the house was, in Detmar's words, "utopian, egalitarian," a spirit that made Lee, and many other guests, feel at home.[21] During the course of the next two decades the "magnetism" of Isabella and Detmar "attracted some of the most dazzling figures from fashion and the arts" to Hilles.[22] Detmar Blow remembers the thrill of meeting McQueen for the first time. "He was so excited, full of happiness and joy," he said. "He was lots of fun, smart and ambitious. We'd embarked on this adventure, like travelling on this chariot, Boudica-like."[23]

Isabella was ecstatic about the clothes that McQueen had made for the *Vogue* shoot: a black wool hunting jacket; a delicate white dress fashioned from layers of sheer organza with red flower petals stitched between the fabric that, from a distance, looked like blotches of blood, and the beautiful pink silk frock coat with the barbed thorn pattern that Blow had bought from his graduate collection. Detmar wore a light pink Regency waistcoat decorated with "flower petals in a see-through material" and one of his collarless barrister's shirts with a white ruff, "with yet more rose petals in the see-through gauze material." For one shot, Isabella and Detmar were pictured standing in an archway; above their heads was a bunch of flowers being held by "an upside-down Alexander."[24]

Issie now regarded Lee as "Alexander the Great": she lauded him with compliments and repeatedly told him that he was a genius. "Issie had known Basquiat and Warhol and both of them had rated her," said Detmar. "So for him to have that endorsement when he was twenty-three was extraordinary."[25] McQueen's clothes were featured across six pages in the November 1992 edition of *Vogue* in an article titled "Over the Hilles and Far Away"; as one commentator said, the equivalent price in advertising "would have run into the tens of thousands of pounds, but in that issue, young Alexander McQueen got the publicity for free."[26]

The bond between Lee and Isabella, whom he liked to describe as a cross between a Billingsgate fishwife and Lucrezia Borgia, was intense. They would talk on the telephone at least four times a day and when they were together their laughter—a dirty, filthy cackling—never seemed to end. Isabella would invite him over to dinner with the likes of Hussein Chalayan, Rifat Özbek, Philip Treacy and Manolo Blahnik. She would frequently travel over to Stratford to take tea with Joyce McQueen, with whom she also formed a close friendship. "She has a wicked sense of humour, and she's got those McQueen blue eyes," said Isabella about Joyce. "Very comely, and the minute you enter she's always got a joke. I think Alexander is very like his mother." In the same interview, conducted in 2005, Isabella went on to describe her friend's personality. "He was exactly the same back in those days as he is today: really funny, very witty, as raw as he is soft—he's still got that great mixture of fragility and strength."[27]

Around this time Isabella wanted to buy some of Réva Mivasagar's petticoats, but when McQueen discovered this he became moody, jealous and possessive. Over the course of the summer of 1992 the relationship between the two young men living in Alderney Street began to toxify. Réva discovered that not only did Lee regularly read through his Filofax, but his friend started to wear and then steal his underwear, something that understandably "freaked" him out.[28] "He used to get really angry about things and we'd have really volatile fights," said Réva. "He wouldn't clean the kitchen and one day

I said something about him not doing his part, about how his mum obviously babied him and he said, 'Don't you fucking talk about my mother!' and I said, 'Well, you don't seem to want to clean up,' and he got hold of a pair of dressmaker's scissors and started to stab me with them. I went upstairs really fast and he followed me and I had to lock my bedroom. He would try and stab me with the scissors all the time. That's when I knew I had to get out of the house."[29]

In a bid to try and make sense of the situation, Réva wrote to a friend in Paris and told him about the poisonous atmosphere in the house. His friend in France wrote back offering some advice, and after Réva had read the letter he was careful to rip it into pieces and drop it into the wastepaper basket in his room. One day, when Réva was out, Lee walked into the bedroom, took the pieces out of the bin and pieced the fragments back together. McQueen read that "he was very hard to live with" and that Réva "wanted to get out."[30] Silence descended on the house like a noxious gas and when the boys passed each other in the hallway or on the staircase they would not meet the other's gaze. "Finally he called Isabella to tell her to get rid of me," said Réva.[31]

A few months later, when Réva went back to Saint Martins, he spotted Lee with a friend and said hi. "But Lee just snubbed me and walked away," he said. "And we never talked to each other again. I think Lee was very aware of the future he wanted for himself, very aware of his path, and knew exactly where he was going."[32]

From Pimlico, McQueen moved south to Tooting and into a two-story house at 169 Lessingham Avenue already rented by Simon Ungless. Simon lived upstairs while Lee occupied the ground floor. Here he had a bedroom at the front and at the back of the house a studio, which contained his sewing machine and where he could often be seen working amidst swathes of fabric. Isabella would sometimes telephone the house and if Simon answered would say just one word, "Alexander." Simon would say, "No, it's Simon here," but Isabella would just repeat herself, breaking up McQueen's middle name into four syllables. "I said, 'God, you're so fucking rude,' and Lee would be there laughing his head off," said Simon.[33]

That summer, Simon and Lee, who were always just good friends, had spent a great deal of time together, taking poppers at Tooting Bec Lido and pretending to do synchronized swimming underwater. The boys also shared a passion for nature and Lee loved it when Simon would return from his parents' home on the Wiltshire/Berkshire border with a brace of pheasants or French partridge, which they would pluck, eat and then reuse the feathers in clothes, while crows' or pheasants' feet would be metamorphosed into earrings. Simon introduced Lee to his friend Shaun Leane, who had started his career as a fifteen-year-old apprentice in Hatton Garden, learning the craft of traditional English jewelry. Their first meeting had been at the Three Greyhounds pub on Greek Street, a hangout in those days for the Saint Martins crowd. Shaun noticed that Lee was quite shy and made an effort to try and place him at ease. It wasn't long, however, before Lee felt he could relax in Shaun's company. The three friends would go out and have fun at the Vauxhall Tavern, a gay pub in South London, where Lee used to enjoy a bottle or two of Woodpecker cider, or to the White Swan in the Mile End Road, or clubs such as Heaven or the Fridge in Brixton. Shaun remembers how, in Tooting, Lee would work in the back garden until it resembled a disaster zone, the ground covered in silicone and plaster of Paris, the plants stained by red dye.

It was in the house in Tooting that Lee first read Simon Ungless's copy of the Marquis de Sade's *The One Hundred and Twenty Days of Sodom*. "He was amazed at how the book progressed and became more extreme," said Simon.[34] McQueen was intrigued by the unremitting account of sexual abuse and torture that de Sade had written over the course of thirty-seven days while imprisoned in the Bastille in 1785. As Lee read the work, described by its author as "the most impure tale that has ever been told since the world began,"[35] he was gripped by the descriptions of the "simple passions" (non-penetrative acts such as masturbation in the faces of seven-year-old girls, the drinking of urine, the eating of feces); the "complex passions" (the rape of children, incest, flagellation); the "criminal passions" (mutilation, sodomy of three-year-old girls); and "murderous passions" (skinning children alive, the disembowelment of pregnant women, masturbation while watching teenagers being tortured). "I gather some influence from the Marquis de Sade because I actually think of him as a great philosopher and a man of his time, when people found him just a pervert," McQueen told David Bowie. "I find him sort of influential in the way he provokes people's thoughts. It kind of scares me. That's the way I think . . ."[36]

Lee's friend Chris Bird, who met him in 1993 through the illustrator Richard Gray, often thought of the parallels between McQueen's work and that of de Sade, particularly his novels *Justine, or The Misfortunes of Virtue* and *Juliette, or Vice Amply Rewarded*. "That whole aspect of chronicling man's inhumanity to other men—not condoning it but showing it," he said. "This is someone—Lee—who embroidered 'Life Is Pain' on an item of clothing for one of his collections. There was an element of romanticism in his work, but also cruelty. There was an aspect of bondage, but he wanted to liberate women and enable them to be fierce on a catwalk."[37]

Caroline Evans, professor of fashion history and theory at Central Saint Martins, has written on the links between de Sade and McQueen in her book *Fashion at the Edge: Spectacle, Modernity and Deathliness*. "Both in the cruelty of McQueen's cut and in the choice and styling of his catwalk shows, he recalled the great female libertines of the Marquis de Sade, with their repertoires of savage dominance and mastery," she wrote. "Sade's dangerous females were superwomen so exceptional that they were almost beyond gender . . . McQueen, like Sade, was fascinated by a dialectical relationship between victim and aggressor, and the parade of women he created on the catwalk resembled Sade's aggressors rather than their victims . . . In his visual imagination there operated an economy very like that of double-entry book-keeping: every instance of goodness was balanced by one of cruelty, every gesture of dominance also sketched a gesture of sub-servience. As his shows progressed the victimized model gave way to a more powerful image, as prey became predator."[38]

De Sade also outlined how morality is an artificial construct, a matrix of rules and restrictions designed to contain and control the "natural" urges of man. As McQueen read his way through *The One Hundred and Twenty Days of Sodom* the young designer felt as though he was finally being given permission to express his sexuality—which some might have seen as excessive, messy, dirty or sordid—in a way that pleased him. In his eyes, nothing was out of bounds or too shock-ing. "Lee had a voracious sexual appetite, he loved getting fucked," said his friend Chris Bird.

One morning, after Chris Bird had stayed over at the house in Tooting, he came out of the shower and was drying himself in the bedroom when Lee burst into the room and tried to seduce him. "He wasn't my type, it was like *Run for Your Wife* or something," said Chris, referring to the Ray Cooney farce. "Later I reminded him of the incident and he sort of freaked out, he didn't want to talk about the past and rejection."

One of Lee's favorite greetings, at least for "lucky" gay male friends such as Chris Bird, involved sticking a finger up his arse and as you walked into the pub he would suddenly thrust the smelly digit in front of his mate's face and say, "Meet Lee!", quickly followed by his cackling fishwife laugh. McQueen loved telling an anecdote about how one day he went into the V&A Museum and his bag was checked by security. "He had a dirty dildo in his sports bag and the guards found it, he thought that was hysterical," said Chris. "The rea-son why he and Isabella got on so well was because they loved talking about sex, about big cocks and getting fucked."[39]

Lee often regaled his friends and work associates with tales of his sexual exploits. Alice Smith—whom Lee met in the autumn of 1992 when she worked for the fashion recruitment agency Denza—likened him to a filthy-mouthed court jester who regaled her and her professional partner Cressida Pye with elaborate stories of cruising on

Hampstead Heath. "He was always interested in sex and wanted to tell us what he had been up to in great detail," said Alice. "I remember once he told us that he went to Clapham Common to meet men. One day he was tied to a tree by a man who then ran away and left Lee there until the morning. He had the most brilliant laugh, a real old hag's screeching. We used to say, 'Can you keep it down, Lee,' because we would be on the phone to Mulberry or someone and there he would be sitting in the office telling filthy stories."

Lee had registered with Denza soon after graduation and, dressed in a three-piece suit, "looking like a little hamster," went for an interview with Alberta Ferretti. "I thought he's never going to get the job looking like that, like a bank clerk, and he didn't," said Alice. When Smith and Pye left to form their own agency, based in St. Martin's Lane, he followed them in the hope that they would find him work. "He was excited that we had run away from this big agency and set up on our own," said Alice. "There was a sense of kinship between us because I think he felt like a bit of a freak, a bit of a loner. He liked the idea that Cressida and I were being these sort of pirates." The women recognized McQueen's talent immediately: on his Smith & Pye form, which Lee had filled in giving details such as his address, they had written the words, "This is a star." His drawings, sketched with an "H" pencil—pale, neat, controlled and precise, like something created by an architect—were beautiful and not in the least flamboyant.

Alice would invite Lee around to her flat in Primrose Hill to make trousers for her: she would buy the fabric from Berwick Street market and for £50 he would rustle up a pair of palazzos, trousers with a wide leg that flares out from the waist. "I would say what I wanted but he would answer back, 'I'm not going to do it like that,'" said Alice. "He would put the fabric on the floor of my tiny flat in Primrose Hill and would cut the trousers without drawing or making a pattern. I couldn't believe it. I remember he always used to walk around with a pair of big tailor's scissors, which I think his aunt might have bought for him. Money was very tight and we used to lend him cash from the company—when I say 'lend' it never came back. Although we never had any money ourselves we genuinely thought that he was brilliant, we had a lot of faith in him and so we went along with it. We were carried away by the excitement of it all."[40]

In order to bring in a little more cash—he was still living on unemployment benefit at this time—Lee started to make and sell waistcoats, some of which he brought into the offices of *Vogue*. Anna Harvey, then the magazine's fashion director, remembers seeing these "rather marvellous waistcoats" and although she thought of buying one for her son, who was a prefect, she did not do so, something that she now regrets. "Lee was quite unusual and agonizingly shy and felt rather out of place in the *Vogue* fashion room surrounded by shriek-ing girls," she said. "I remember him as pale-faced and startled-look-ing. But there was a quiet confidence to him and on the basis of seeing those half dozen waistcoats I thought this guy knows where he is going."[41]

Throughout the latter part of 1992 and into the spring of 1993, McQueen was busy at work on his first collection, which he called *Taxi Driver*. Smith and Pye volunteered their services as public rela-tions consultants. Alice rang her friend Katie Webb, who was then working on *Sky* magazine, and secured the first piece of press on McQueen. There was only one problem: although Lee knew he needed the publicity, he did not want to be photographed in case the Department of Social Security spotted him and cut off his benefits. McQueen, together with photographer Richard Burbridge, came up with the idea of wrapping his face in gaffer tape. "I think there was also an element of Martin Margiela to it," said Chris Bird, referring to the Belgian designer who refused to have his photograph taken. "It made him more enigmatic."[42] The look, borrowed from bondage and fetish wear, obviously appealed to Lee: around the same time, he gave Simon Costin a photograph of himself, his face bound by tape, with one of Costin's bird skull necklaces draped over his bare chest. McQueen told Webb, "Some of us are born the wrong shape, too short or too fat, and I'm working with patterns that make people look better and improve their self-esteem at affordable prices. I want to use everyday people in my show—after all, we can't all be Ivana Trump."[43]

For *Taxi Driver*, McQueen turned to the cinema for inspiration, particularly the films he had recently seen at the Scala in King's Cross. "I love Pasolini and Stanley Kubrick," he said. "This was my homage to film and photography."[44] Of course, Martin Scorsese's 1976 film, starring Robert De Niro as disturbed taxi driver Travis Bickle and the young Jodie Foster as child prostitute Iris "Easy" Steensma, played a central part in the collection: McQueen asked Simon Ungless to help him print a photograph of De Niro in the role, which he then printed on a taffeta tailored jacket. It's not hard to see why the film appealed to McQueen—he could identify with both the vigilante Bickle and the exploited and abused Iris, whom he tries to save.

McQueen worked hard on the collection and he told Lucinda Alford at the *Observer* that he was keen to experiment and try out new techniques. He dipped the edges of fabric in latex instead of hemming them and incorporated feathers encased in a "sandwich of clear vinyl." The attention to detail was astounding, "with sleeves often made of three pieces then constructed with twice that number of seams," wrote Alford. "Collars and sleeves are constructed using principles of origami; a seam at the elbow and lining fabric under the arm means that jacket sleeves can fit tight to the body and still allow for movement."[45]

At this time in the early nineties, Britain's fashion industry was in the doldrums—the country was still recovering from a recession characterized by falling house prices, high interest rates and an overvalued exchange rate. In 1993, four former British designers of the year—John Galliano, Vivienne Westwood, Katharine Hamnett and Workers for Freedom—together with the then current holder of the title, Rifat Özbek, had decided to show their collections abroad, either in Milan or Paris. Betty Jackson opted to present her work via a video while John Richmond also chose to show in Paris. "London Fashion Week does not attract enough international press and buyers," said

Richmond. "If my business is to expand, I must show in Paris." In 1990, twenty-one designers staged shows in London and 250 names took stands at the adjoining trade exhibition. In March 1993, only "thirteen designers are staging shows, with another sixty at an exhibition at the Ritz hotel," reported Roger Tredre in the *Independent on Sunday*. "There is no shortage of talent in Britain," said Tredre, who picked out McQueen as one of the rising stars, along with Bella Freud, Amanda Wakeley, Flyte Ostell, Sonnentag & Mulligan and Abe Hamilton. "Money, rather, is the core of the problem."[46]

In order to address this, the British Fashion Council set aside a small sum of money to sponsor six new talents: Alexander McQueen, Sonnentag & Mulligan, Lisa Johnson, Paul Frith, Abe Hamilton and Copperwheat Blundell. Lee Copperwheat had met Lee McQueen at Saint Martins when he had worked as a visiting lecturer on the MA course; the two men had become friends and enjoyed clubbing together. "He was quite wild, we liked the same things, he was up for anything, a bit naughty," said Copperwheat. "We started hanging out and became really close. But I didn't see his genius until the Ritz hotel show."[47]

The group show, held in a series of rooms in the hotel, was small in scale; the work was not exhibited on models but on rails and McQueen's clothes were displayed on coat hangers from Dorothy Perkins. "It all seemed so hopeless till I was drawn down the corridor by the sound of squawking laughter," recalls the fashion critic Sarah Mower. "It was Isabella Blow, with a Philip Treacy feathered explosion on her head, corralling people towards a rack of razor-sharp tailoring, behind which was a bullet-craniumed cockney boy."[48] Nilgin Yusuf, writing in the *Sunday Times*, also picked out McQueen's work. She was in raptures over a "quilted, bejewelled" collar, a "confection fit for an empress,"[49] while Lucinda Alford in the *Observer* wrote of McQueen's "indisputable skill as a pattern cutter. A mixture of made-to-order couture and ready-to-wear, it contains some of the most interesting cuts around. His style has evolved out of a mix of freer bias cuts, using and updating historical references as well as futuristic shapes and printing processes."[50] Lee's sister Janet went along to the hotel with her mother, Joyce, and aunt Renee; her perspective was rather different to that of the fashion editors. "I remember looking at these garments and thought to myself that I wouldn't wear them," said Janet. "I was quite classic, not experimental like Lee. But Isabella Blow was going mad for the clothes."[51]

Perhaps all the positive press attention went to Lee's head a little—after all, his name had even made it into the pages of *The Times*. "Their designs are unequivocally of today," wrote Iain R. Webb of the Ritz six, "their names should be world-famous tomorrow."[52] After packing up the collection into black bin bags, Lee and Simon Ungless went for a few drinks at Comptons in Soho and then on to Man Stink, at Central Station, another gay pub in King's Cross. Short of cash, as always, the two young men decided not to deposit the bags in the cloakroom, but hid them away under some rubbish bins outside. "We danced and drank for a few hours and completely forgot about the clothes when we left to go back to Tooting," said Simon. "Lee went back the next morning but of course the bags and clothes were gone."[53]

The reverence and awe with which fashion collectors and curators regard McQueen's clothes today—a single vintage piece can be worth tens of thousands of pounds—did not apply in the more carefree and chaotic early nineties. Alice Smith remembers one occasion in early March 1993, on the way back from a shoot for the *Daily Telegraph* on designers and their muses, in which she had been photographed wearing a McQueen leather bustier and an extravagant ruff made from pheasant tails. As she held it in her hands the feathers kept dropping out over the seat and onto the floor of the cab. "Do you want this?" she asked. Lee shook his head and so the design was abandoned in the taxi. "The Met tracked me down and asked me if I had it for *Savage Beauty* and I had to say no," said Alice. "There are so many things that are missing. Lee used to leave rails of clothes in our office and we said to him, 'Can you get these out of here?' as we really did not have enough space." Again, the clothes were consigned to the trash.[54]

On 17 March 1993, Lee celebrated his twenty-fourth birthday at Maison Bertaux with a small group of friends, including Tania Wade, whose birthday fell on the day before his. "I remember once he sent over a top with McQueen written on it, but for some reason it disappeared within the building," said Tania. "Lee wanted to know what had happened to it, and I told him the chefs probably thought it was a bloody J-cloth. 'You fucking cheeky cow,' he replied."[55] Lee also became friendly with Tania's sister, Michelle Wade. One day he told Michelle that he would like to stage a fashion show outside the shop. He had a vision of erecting a platform and scattering hay all down Greek Street, a project that never materialized. "That's when I thought to myself, 'Who is this?' This is someone with real imagination," said Michelle. "At first he was a little shy, withdrawn and awkward—he was someone who was obviously a conflicted person—but as time went on it became easier for him to deal with people. But he wasn't a fluid person. I think it was because he had so many ideas going around in his head." Lee made Michelle a long black military coat with a tartan lining, "and now even after about fifteen years I put that coat on and I feel good. That's what he did for a woman, he made you feel fantastic."[56]

CHAPTER FIVE

Sex is a big part of what I do.

—Lee McQueen

The lights went down, Cypress Hill's eulogy to drug taking, "I Wanna Get High," blasted out of the sound system and a thin girl wearing a pair of shockingly low-cut silver trousers and a beautifully tailored frock coat staggered out in front of the audience. It was 20 October 1993 and the venue was the Bluebird Garage on the King's Road, London. As the show, *Nihilism*, progressed, the "heroin chic" imagery became darker and more disturbing. One of the models gave a middle-fingered salute to the audience. Another girl wearing a long, sleeveless white cotton dress splattered with red dye looked as if she had been attacked. A few moments later a pale-faced young woman emerged in a minidress made from cling film that appeared as if it had been smeared with mud and blood. The effect was Carrie trapped in a couture house.

"Alexander McQueen's debut was a horror show," wrote Marion Hume in the *Independent*, which devoted a whole page to *Nihilism* under the headline "McQueen's Theatre of Cruelty." "In between bursts of hard house music, there was an eerie silence where usually motordrives whirr and shutters click. The photographers, many of them veterans of as many war-zones as fashion shows, had nearly all stopped snapping." Hume admitted that the imagery made her and many of her colleagues distinctly queasy. She was used to naked flesh, of which there was some, but this was something else. "But models who look as if they have recently experienced serious traffic accidents, in sheer and sweaty cling film knickers, with what appeared to be bloody, suppurating, post-operative breasts visible through muslin T-shirts, was rather a lot to take in the name of frocks."[1]

Understandably, none of the fashion journalists had a clue about the true origins of the imagery, which stemmed from Lee witnessing the endless beatings suffered by his sister Janet at the hands of her husband, the same man who abused McQueen when he was a young boy. As a result, some critics wrote the show off as distasteful and misogynistic. One reviewer, for the trade journal *Drapers Record*, even found the collection boring: "Apart from the occasional 1970s suit in a two-tone diamond print and high-collared shirts in masculine check, the rest was not worth the hour wait."[2]

Hume, however, noticed that McQueen, for all his "perverse view of women," was trying to express a new spirit of modernity through his designs. The show spoke of "battered women, of violent lives, of grinding daily existences offset by wild, drug-enhanced nocturnal dives into clubs where the dress code is semi-naked. As such, his clothes probably speak with more accuracy about real life than some swoosh of an evening gown by Valentino." She recognized that, like Rei Kawakubo and Vivienne Westwood, McQueen had something new to say. When Kawakubo first showed her Comme des Garçons collection in Europe, about half of the audience walked out. Similarly, when Westwood adorned flesh-colored leggings with drawings of penises, Hume herself admitted to feeling appalled and disgusted. It was, she added, important to let young fashion designers experiment. "The shock of the new has to be just that: shocking," she concluded. "And if that sometimes leaves us fashion hacks tut-tutting like latter-day Miss Jean Brodies, or feeling distinctly off-colour, so be it."[3]

At this time, London Fashion Week was still seen as something of the poor relation to its glitzier cousins in Paris or Milan. As Edward Enninful outlined in his introduction to a feature in the October issue of *i-D* magazine on six new talents to watch—McQueen was on the list, together with Nicholas Knightly, John Rocha, Abe Hamilton, Flyte Ostell and Copperwheat Blundell—while British creativity had been admired all over the world, the country's designers let themselves down because of poor business practice and less than perfect workmanship. "We showcase the development of innovative graduate design talent like nowhere else in the world, only to see it lured away to the fashion houses and factories of Europe," he wrote. However, a generation of fashion designers was showing that they could combine wearability and commercial prospects with canny business sense, a trio of skills that would "herald a rebirth for the much-maligned British fashion industry."[4] Lee told Avril Mair, who wrote the small profile on him that accompanied Enninful's feature, that while he was "totally unponcey" he wanted the new collection to incorporate "couture's traditional handcrafted techniques into a range of simple pieces." At the heart of his work was a certain eroticism—"Sex is a big part of what I do," McQueen said. Mair described the designer as looking "more like a football hooligan than the creator of sensitive and immaculate tailoring beautifully manipulated to flatter the female form."[5]

Lee had turned to Fleet Bigwood, a print tutor on the Saint Martins MA course, for help with his fabrics. Fleet recalls the time two days after McQueen's graduate show when Lee had turned up at the college wearing a sheepskin waistcoat, a plaid shirt and a pair of jeans and, in a state of fury, told him that he wanted to do his own collection. "I'm fucked off with it all," he had said. "Nobody's interested in me apart from this mad fucking rich woman [Isabella Blow]." "I liked his anger," said Fleet. "He was motivated to tell everyone to fuck off, the industry, the journalists and the buyers. He felt frustrated, he felt nobody gave him any recognition or understood what he had to offer." Bigwood lived in Streatham at the time, only half a mile or so from Tooting, and he would often travel over to Lee's house, where he watched McQueen "burn or scorch or do disturbing things" to the fabric. "It was so raw," said Fleet. "He was designing and cutting and developing his own fabrics. He wasn't disciplined in that because he was a cutter, but that didn't stop him from wanting to engage with every single element of the process." When Fleet saw the show *Nihilism* he recalls feeling a little underwhelmed. "I was born in 1962 and so I had been through punk, but Lee had been too young. I was a bit jaded by it—I thought he was trying to be shocking, and felt we've already been through this. Looking back now his influence on style was as big as punk and has had as much longevity."[6]

Watching *Nihilism* with excitement was Marin Hopper, fashion director of American *Elle* and the daughter of the actor Dennis Hopper. When Lee and Marin had met earlier that spring, he had told her about his time on Savile Row when he would write secret messages in the linings of suits. "I thought it was so punk of him," said Marin, who subsequently featured his work in the pages of her magazine. Later, McQueen would tell Isabella and Detmar Blow that he had slept with Marin at the Hôtel Costes in Paris. "I would be the first person to admit it if it was true," she said. "There was something very flirty about him, but we never did that. We talked about sexuality, and the crushes he had on guys, but he was absolutely 100 per cent homosexual. Maybe he thought that the idea that we had slept together would shock people—the shock of the new, or rather the shock of the old."[7]

Bobby Hillson was also in the audience that day. As she watched the girls walk through the Bluebird's faded art deco space—this was in the days before the garage was converted into a swish restaurant—McQueen's former tutor felt a deep sense of satisfaction that her gamble had at last paid off. "It sent chills through me," she said of the show, comparing her reaction to the heightened physical and emotional response one feels while watching first-rate theater.[8]

Nihilism saw the first catwalk appearance of McQueen's "bumsters," low-cut trousers that, according to one fashion writer, created "a cleavage closer to the building-site than the boudoir."[9] Fashion historian Judith Watt believed that the origins of the bumsters—which eventually resulted in a whole generation of men and women wearing low-rise jeans or trousers below the waist—could be traced back to something McQueen had seen in his copy of Juan de Alcega's 1589 *Tailor's Pattern Book* (the volume, originally in Spanish, was published in English in 1978). In the sixteenth century, men wore their breeches low, so that they sat on or below the hipline. "By blending this line with modern tailoring techniques to create a fresh area of erotic interest, he achieved something new," she said.[10]

The base of the spine was, for McQueen, an erotic cynosure. By inventing the bumster McQueen introduced both sexes to the delights of the ogee, Hogarth's S-shape "Line of Beauty." This would form the central image of Alan Hollinghurst's 2004 novel of the same name, a book which is full of yearning for the visual pleasures offered by the double curve of the lower back. "I wanted to elongate the body, not just show the bum," McQueen said in 1996. "To me, that part of the body—not so much the buttocks, but the bottom of the spine—that's the most erotic part of anyone's body, man or woman."[11]

For Seta Niland, a new friend he had met who was working as a stylist for magazines like *The Face*, the bumsters were a natural evolution of Yves Saint Laurent's "Le Smoking," the French couturier's revolutionary tuxedo suit that introduced an element of masculinity into women's fashion. "Lee called the bumsters the builders' pants or builders' trousers," said Seta, who helped McQueen organize and style *Nihilism*. "He would have seen builders with their arses hanging out and that might have looked nice to him. But to then translate that to a woman? It was scary and I had to talk the models into wearing them for the show. I didn't get it until a girl put them on. It was gorgeous, but a huge risk."

Lee had been drawn to Seta because of her own dark history: she told him that her sister had been murdered. In turn, she was attracted to his personality because of his "outsider" status. "I saw myself as a bit of an outsider too, not the right colour, although I probably had the right accent by then," she said. The two met after Lee had left Saint Martins and they used to hole up together in Maison Bertaux, making a coffee or tea and a cake last for hours on end, a treat that Seta, who like Lee was then "piss poor," would usually pay for.

"He kept banging on about producing a collection and I asked him, 'How are we going to afford this?' I had seen catwalk shows and I knew how much they cost," she said. "But he said, 'Let's just give it a go.' To begin with it was my role to coerce people into giving us stuff for free. I went to the Bluebird Garage and told them that we were staging a show off schedule, which was a lie. I got some guys I knew who did the lighting at Glastonbury to do the lighting for the show. We cobbled some chairs together from people in the rest of the building and begged and borrowed people to help with the press and the invites. I used all my contacts to get the models for free and we got some good girls for nothing."

Throughout the process of putting the show together it was in danger of falling apart because of a lack of resources: Lee was still on benefits and Seta, who was living in a council flat in Kennington, did not earn much from her work for style magazines. On the day of the show itself Lee and Seta realized they had no money to buy underwear for the models. Seeing a roll of cling film, Seta had an idea and she started to pull out swathes of it and wrap it around the models. "Necessity breeds genius and creativity," she said, laughing.[12] There were consequences, however. "Nobody got paid at all and at the end of the show the models were just throwing the clothes into bags," said Chris Bird.[13]

Seta also had to organize the music for the show. One of the tracks she chose was Radiohead's 1992 single "Creep," which depicts the "self-lacerating rage of an unsuccessful crush."[14] Backstage, when the show was over, Lee turned to Seta and told her he hated her for that choice of song. "He was absolutely pissed off, but he didn't understand why I had chosen it," said Seta. "I wanted people to say, 'Yes he may look like a creep but look at what he can do.' The fashion industry did see him as odd, as a lout, until his designs started to speak for themselves and then they all had to bow down. It was an ironic ending to the show because he was not a creep. Looking back it might all have been a bit rough and ready, with not much polish, but that was the beauty of Lee. The tailoring was amazing, the textiles were so innovative. But there was a brutal elegance to it, a phrase that I think really sums Lee up."[15]

Nihilism also saw the first outing of another important McQueen signifier: the designer's distinctive logo formed by a lowercase "c" encased within an uppercase "Q." Alice Smith had the initial idea, while her boyfriend at the time, a graphic designer, sketched the logo. "Lee didn't pay for it, of course," said Alice. "Nothing was paid for, which I forgive him for. Those early shows were unlike anything you had ever seen before. They had immense shock value but also everything was beautifully made and conceived. Cressida and I would be practically in tears because we were so excited for him. You were never quite sure whether he would pull it off, and so it was with unravelling amazement that he would produce show after show and each show was bigger and better. But we always felt it could all collapse at any minute."[16]

Towards the end of 1993, McQueen's housemate Simon Ungless told Lee that he was moving in with his boyfriend. This meant that McQueen had to find somewhere else to live, but he still did not have enough money to rent his own place. Lee's sister Jacqui, who had gone to live in Budapest for work, offered Lee the use of her flat in Chadwell Heath, and his brothers Tony and Michael said that they would help him move. One Saturday morning, Michael drove a van across London to Tooting and turned up only to find his brother still in bed. "Nothing packed, nothing done," recalls Michael. "I said, 'Fucking get out, we've come all the way down here, get up.' That was the way he was."[17]

Lee was grateful to be able to use his sister's vacant flat in Spring Close, Chadwell Heath, but life in suburban Essex seemed dull after the grit of south London. Seta Niland remembers getting the train to Essex with McQueen from Liverpool Street—they used to jump over the barriers in order to avoid paying the fare—and being amazed by the sparseness of the flat. It was like a blank canvas, she said, but perhaps he found that creatively stimulating. "From the beginning, he kept coming out with these references to art, and he taught me so much," she said. "He wasn't the 'normal' fashion type, he did not progress from O levels to A levels to degree, but not having that made him much more driven. I met him with Isabella Blow once and I don't think he was offended by the class difference between them, I think he was intrigued."[18]

Throughout 1993, Isabella had been trying to persuade Steven Meisel to photograph a story for British *Vogue*. Meisel, who had been working for Italian *Vogue* and its editor Franca Sozzani since 1988, was reluctant. "There's absolutely a queer sensibility to my work," he said, "but there's also a sense of humour . . . a sarcasm and a 'fuck-you' attitude as well as a serious beauty."[19] His profile was so high—he had just worked with Madonna on her 1992 *Sex* book—that the New Yorker was said to be the world's highest-paid fashion photographer. "He's widely regarded as one of the superstars of fashion photography," said Anna Wintour at the time.[20] After Meisel finally agreed to take the job—the black-and-white photographs appeared in the December 1993 issue of British *Vogue* under the title of "Anglo-Saxon Attitudes"—the bill came to a rumored £80,000, the most expensive shoot in the history of the magazine.

The brief for the story, which came to be known as the "London Babes" shoot, was to find the most beautiful, blue-blooded British girls imaginable, said Plum Sykes. Sykes was then working as Isabella's assistant and ended up modeling for Meisel, along with Stella Tennant, Bella Freud, Lady Louise Campbell and Honor Fraser. Blow had invited McQueen into the offices of *Vogue* to discuss which of his designs could be featured in the shoot. "But some of the editors at the magazine did not rate him at all," said Plum. "At that time people were still very interested in Paris and Christian Lacroix and Chanel and so London was dismissed. Some editors at *Vogue* thought that Alexander, as I called him, was some scruffy common boy. I remember he came into the office with a ripped-up lace punky dress—I think it ended up on Stella Tennant—and he did cut quite an odd figure. The office was very upper-middle class and he seemed so rough. He was wearing an old lumberjack shirt, jeans falling down with his bottom crack showing and a keychain. He was always a bit smelly and sweaty and grubby. I remember just being quite frightened of him. I was quite a prim Oxford girl and I didn't understand his clothes. At the time, Issie said, 'This boy is so talented, he is a superstar, look at his tailoring.' But I had only worked at *Vogue* for a year and didn't understand great tailoring. Now I totally understand that he created this silhouette that was completely different from everyone else."

At the end of 1993, Plum Sykes asked McQueen to make her a punk-inspired dress in black lace and chiffon for *Vogue*'s Christmas party. She gave him £20 to buy the fabric and an extra £50 for his time. "He made the dress, brought it to *Vogue* and came into the ladies loo and just chopped it and slashed it on the bottom and said, 'There, it's finished.' He was very hand to mouth, still officially unemployed and didn't have a bank account. I quickly realized that he was very quick, clever and sharp—Artful Dodger sharp. I remember thinking, 'This guy is so much cleverer than me and my [Oxford] friends.'"[21]

Lee and Isabella—who had herself agreed to model—persuaded Plum to walk down the catwalk of his next show *Bheansidhe (Banshee)*, held at the Café de Paris in London on 26 February 1994. Two days before, McQueen gave an interview to Kathryn Samuel, the fashion editor of the *Daily Telegraph*, in which he came out publicly as gay for the first time, something that made his mother furious. "Why do you have to publicize your private life?" she asked him. "But it's not my private life," he responded, "it's just the way I am."[22] He also told Samuel that while the intention of his last show was to "give London a kick and shout" he wanted his new collection to be more saleable. "My aim is to marry Savile Row with ready-to-wear," he said.[23] The invitation for the show consisted of a black-and-white photograph taken by Rankin of an old, naked woman holding her arms behind her head, while the inspiration for the collection "came from Irish folklore about banshees heard wailing when a boat sank," said McQueen. "It's about women being at the helm, being strong."[24]

When Rebecca Lowthorpe, now assistant editor of UK *Elle*, turned up backstage that day to model she had no idea what McQueen wanted her to wear on the catwalk: a body mold made from chicken wire and plaster of Paris. She remembers that it was so uncomfortable that she could not bend at the waist; when she wanted to rest she had to lie on the floor and other models fed her Coca-Cola through a straw. The atmosphere backstage was "electric," she said, and the show itself was memorable for its spirit of irreverence. It was "an almighty fuck-you to the industry at large," said Rebecca, who had modeled for McQueen and other students at Saint Martins. "He had the temerity to put these things called bumsters on the catwalk and have models striding down with their arses hanging out. It felt like a mini revolution. It was a punk moment in the purest sense."[25] Filmmaker John Maybury, who had been born in 1958, had lived through punk and he recognized that Lee embodied the spirit of the anarchic movement. "Lee was a natural punk, it was inherent in his attitude," he said. "Punk wasn't about that later wave of gobbing and spitting plebs, it was really driven by a bunch of art students and old Bowie fans. The aggression was more about visual violence, contesting the status quo, and that's what Lee was all about."[26]

Isabella Blow had ensured that Michael Roberts, Joseph Ettedgui, Manolo Blahnik and Suzy Menkes all attended the show, but McQueen was far from intimidated. If anything, he was deliberately provocative. In an interview with Mark C. O'Flaherty in the *Pink Paper* he called the eminent fashion journalist and historian Colin McDowell, author of the then recent book *The Designer Scam*, "a right fucking queen" and went on to attack the power of the fashion pack. "I always try to slam ideas in people's faces," Lee said. "If I get someone like Suzy Menkes in the front row, wearing her fucking Christian Lacroix, I make sure that lady gets pissed on by one of the girls, you know what I mean? These people can make you or break you, and they love you for just a moment. I may be the name on everyone's lips at the moment, but they can kill you."[27] Adrian Clark, then a journalist at *Fashion Weekly*, awarded the collection 9/10 for creativity and only 7/10 for commerciality. "One of the hottest collections in town, helping London back to its feet as the creative capital of Europe," he said.[28] Ettedgui, a respected designer and owner of several shops in London, believed that McQueen represented "a new energy in British design" and labeled him the next John Galliano or Vivienne Westwood, while Blahnik raved about the designer's finishing. "It's modern couture: you just don't find work like this in ready-to-wear," he said. "If he has any problem, it's too many ideas."[29]

McQueen told journalists that he was responding to imagery from Luis Buñuel's 1967 film *Belle de Jour*, starring Catherine Deneuve as a housewife who spends her days as a prostitute while her doctor husband is at work. As he said to O'Flaherty, "I took the themes of the Buñuel film and made something ethereal, with long gowns; people who are cloistered and restricted but then all of a sudden they find a part of their life that's been closed. There's a lot of sexuality in there."[30]

Plum Sykes thought that McQueen had also gained inspiration from the work of Edvard Munch, the Norwegian artist whose paintings he had seen in the November 1992 issue of *Vogue*. (It is also likely that Lee went to see the Munch exhibition *The Frieze of Life* that ran at the National Gallery between November 1992 and February 1993.) "Alexander made the make-up artist paint all our cheeks brown so it looked as though we hadn't had any food for about three and a half years," said Plum. "I couldn't understand what he was doing—why did he want to make us look so ugly, why did I have to have my face painted like a skeleton or *The Scream*?" The women— including one model who was heavily pregnant—had the word "McQueen" stenciled in silver on their heads. "He did everything. He wasn't sitting in state. He put the clothes on the girls, designed the make-up, designed the hair. I remember him backstage, screaming with squawking cockney laughter."[31]

• • •

Lee's twisted sense of humor was one of the things that first attracted fashion designer Andrew Groves to him when they met in the summer of 1994 in Comptons, the gay bar on Old Compton Street. "I seem to remember he was laughing at one of his own jokes hysterically," said Andrew, who was a year younger than Lee. They were introduced by mutual friend David Kappo, the fashion student who had been persuaded by Louise Wilson to leave behind the delights of the Soho wig shop to return to Saint Martins. Towards the end of the night, when everyone had had a lot to drink, the men in the group were passing around a joint, at which point they were spotted by a barman and threatened with being thrown out of the pub. Lee asked Andrew whether he would like to come back to his flat in Chadwell Heath. "I remember it was miles out, a train ride, and when you are that age everything seems like a bit of an adventure," said Andrew. "You've got no work so it's not like you need to get up the next day. I just thought, 'I'll go and see what happens.'" A relationship began and lasted, in fashion terms, "four seasons," until the couple split in 1996. "He was exciting," said Andrew. "Lee was sort of my first proper relationship and I didn't have a guide to what was normal or not normal. It was a bit like Elizabeth Taylor and Richard Burton—I just thought all that high drama and energy and fighting were part of being in a full-on relationship."

There were many funny and tender moments, too. The pair enjoyed a holiday to south Wales, where they donned wet suits and went surfing. Andrew and Lee would often go and visit Joyce McQueen in Biggerstaff Road. One day Andrew was there and, in a rather thoughtless way, said something was "shit." Lee turned around and said, "Don't you fucking swear in front of my fucking mother." Although Andrew tried to explain the irony of the situation, Lee did not find his comments funny.

Andrew, who designed under the name Jimmy Jumble, was keen for Lee to teach him everything he knew. McQueen, who at this point was selling a few chiffon dresses in Pellicano on South Molton Street—"the clients were women who dressed in Miyake and liked their arms covered," said Andrew—showed him how to pin-hem chiffon. "Underneath all that theatricality he was able to create really desirable and wearable clothing," said Groves. "It wasn't just about doing the shock-value stuff that you saw on the runway."

One day, soon after he first met Lee, Andrew returned to the flat he was renting with five others in Clapton Pond to discover that the building had been burgled. He also realized that the man upstairs was a drug dealer and had a stash of 200 Ecstasy pills. Perhaps it would be best to find somewhere else to live, he thought. At the same time, Isabella invited McQueen to move into the basement of 67 Elizabeth Street, which was owned by Detmar's mother. The offer of a free place in a house in Belgravia might have sounded extraordinarily generous, but there was a reason why the building was empty. Numbers 69 and 71, both part of the Grosvenor Estate, had started to collapse and needed extensive refurbishment; the party wall to number 67 was cracked and the Blows had been instructed that it was unsafe to carry on living there. Despite the poor conditions—there was no hot water, the bare floorboards were covered in dust and dirt and they had only a dirty mattress to sleep on—Lee and Andrew were overjoyed that they could live together in central London. "In the front room there were boxes and boxes of Philip Treacy's hats for Versace which we tried on," Andrew said. "We thought how hilarious that these hats that had gone down the runway in Milan were actually shoved in a cardboard box in one of the dirtiest places I had ever been to."[32]

Soon after meeting Andrew, Lee shaved his head and began to change his look. Simon Ungless, who was used to seeing him most days, recalls how at this time Lee seemed to disappear from his life for about three weeks. The next occasion he saw him he was going down the escalator at Tottenham Court Road tube station when a couple of skinheads pushed past him; it took him a few seconds to realize that one of them was his friend Lee with his new boyfriend, Jimmy Jumble.

The couple's social life was a wild one. Ad-Hoc manager Eric Rose remembers going to a party with them in the upstairs room of a pub in Islington Green. The men knocked back a series of free drinks and then Lee and Andrew "started throwing each other about." Rose looked around the room at the horrified faces of the fellow guests and realized that they had crashed somebody's party. "I was laughing so fucking hard I nearly pissed myself," said Eric. "It was like, 'Who are these hyenas that have arrived?'"[33]

One day in Comptons, Eric introduced Lee to Dai Rees, who had studied ceramics at Saint Martins and the Royal College of Art. Rees, an artist and a course director at the London College of Fashion, remembers how he and a little group would congregate at the back of Comptons in an area they styled the "Saint Martins step"; no one who was not a part of their clique dared to venture near. "We were an odd, quite fierce group," he said. "My first impression was that Lee had a very strong link with his class, his background. We had a connection because we were both makers, a working-class trade, not screaming and shouting fashion, it was just something we did." When Dai was at the Royal College he would invite his friend over to the Art Bar on a Thursday night. "When we didn't have any money we would go around stealing drinks," he said. "One trick we had was to wait until it was very busy and then at about ten thirty set the fire alarm off. Everyone would leave the building and we would fill up our glasses and stash them in the back of the toilet until we went back inside."[34]

Eric also introduced Lee to Nicholas Townsend, also known by his drag name "Trixie," who was then working at Ad-Hoc. To begin with, Trixie thought Lee was quite shy and innocent. Although there was only two years' difference in their ages—Townsend was born in 1967—Trixie assumed that Lee was much younger. "He had a very child-like quality to him," he said. "He had a young spirit. He wasn't jaded or bitter." Trixie remembers one occasion when he and Lee were at Andrew Groves's studio and they knew that Isabella was about to drop by. "For some reason we had this muslin body bag and, for a joke, we cut two holes in the arms. She came in and said, 'I love this darling, I love it,' and when she walked out we laughed so much. Lee and her were like brother and sister, they were as crazy as each other."

Lee would drop by Trixie's flat in Covent Garden and, while Michael Nyman's soundtrack to *The Piano* was playing in the background, he would listen to his new friend's stories of going to Taboo and the Asylum Club in the eighties. "I used to call the eighties the 'Haties,' which he thought was really funny," said Trixie. "I remember telling him I had met Ossie Clark, who had said, 'You remind me of Bianca Jagger in Monte Carlo in 1976,' which Lee thought was hysterical." Lee regarded Trixie as something of a gay "mother" or "older sister," someone he could turn to for advice. "He was interested in the history of the AIDS epidemic, which I had lived through," he said. "He asked lots of questions about safe sex and situations you might end up in such as, when do you bring up the point about the condom?" Although Lee didn't talk about his own childhood he was interested to hear how Trixie had grown up in a children's home and how, on arriving in London, he had worked as a male prostitute. Lee was also fascinated by Trixie's style, the way he would mix items of male and female clothing. Some items in his wardrobe would come under particular close scrutiny, such as a copy of a Thierry Mugler suit. "He liked the tailoring of Mugler, but never Vivienne Westwood, who he thought was really tacky," he said.[35] Trixie loved to dress in McQueen—"he was like McQueen's muse," said Eric Rose[36]—and for his birthday Lee made him a pair of bumsters. On the day of the fitting Trixie had to strip down to a G-string and stand on a chair. When he wore them out he would always attract attention. "Even gay people found them shocking," said Trixie. "Some people giggled while others were angry. 'Can't you afford to finish those off?' gay men would shout at me. I don't know what it was about those trousers because it wasn't as though your whole arse was showing. I suppose it was the fact someone had the nerve to wear them. His clothes made me feel quite masculine. With the bumsters you had to stand quite tall, you had to hold yourself very upright."[37]

Through Eric Rose and Trixie, McQueen met actress and filmmaker Paulita Sedgwick, descended from the "bluest of American bloodlines" and the cousin of the actress and Warhol superstar Edie. Paulita, dressed in black Vivienne Westwood jeans, would invite a diverse range of people—her friends included "transvestites, tattooists and a sprinkling of ex-rent boys"—to her flat in Whitehall Court, on London's Embankment.[38] As soon as she met Lee she became fascinated by his tough look and "authentic" life experiences and she quickly cast him in two short films, *On the Loose* and *Fit to Be*. "She was looking for someone who was an East End thug, a gangster, and that's precisely what she got from him," said Paulita's friend Frank Franca.[39] "One was filmed in Whitehall and the other in a studio warehouse at the back of Tottenham Court Road," said Trixie, who starred in them too. "Lee played a rapist, and raped one of my friends, who was cast as a model."[40] Later, Paulita would tell friends that she was disappointed in McQueen when he slimmed down and had his teeth fixed. Frank noted, "She thought that he was far more interesting before."[41]

Trixie would often go clubbing with Lee and Andrew Groves. On one occasion, in preparation for a night out at a club in Leicester Square, the friends decided that the boys should wear nothing but Gaffa tape. Lee and Andrew stripped naked and they fashioned a boob tube for Lee and a dress for Andrew. "I seem to recall Lee ripped the tape off Jimmy [Andrew Groves] on the way back and so he was naked outside Stringfellows in the street," said Trixie. "When we got back Lee had to rip the tape off his chest and it was really painful, but it was even worse for Jimmy because he had more hair."[42]

One of the couple's favorite clubs was the Beautiful Bend, a night held at Central Station, King's Cross. It was a surreal vision dreamt up by the artist Donald Urquhart, drag queen Sheila Tequila and DJ Harvey. "We were bored of everywhere and wanted to get away from the whole branding thing that was making clubbing stagnate," said Urquhart. "We had an idea of a club that totally changed every time you went there. We put together different themes for each party and really went to town on the décor."

113

Donald had first seen Lee's work at his Café de Paris show, which he had attended with his friend Fiona Cartledge, who ran the shop Sign of the Times, and Sheila Tequila. "This was unlike anything I had seen on a catwalk," he recalls. "It was vaguely grim and not conventionally sexy, I thought some of the numbers were positively frumpy, but I was thrilled by the icy models—the cinematic drama was really something else. We went backstage after the show and there was Lee, wrecked, his little eyes vanishing into his head, with Isabella Blow taking all the photo calls like a prize fighter."

Donald, born in Dumfries, Scotland, in 1963, had moved to London in 1984 and became a friend and collaborator of the performance artist Leigh Bowery. "I was everywhere in drag, day and night through the early nineties—at Tasty Tim's Beyond, Powder Room at Heaven, Ron Storme's Tudor Lodge, Kinky Gerlinky, Pushca. Of course when I say 'drag' I don't mean traditional sequins and feathers drag; I had something rather more sick yet sophisticated going on." Donald remembers how Lee and Andrew Groves would love to perform at the club in a pantomime cow suit. One night in 1994 Urquhart organized a night called "ArtBend: Paint Along with a Nancy," which centered on several "jokey art installations" and an Yves Klein–inspired "performance" which featured Donald and Sheila in bathing costumes and covering each other in paint. At the same time, Lee and Andrew—inside the cow costume—staged a silent protest against Damien Hirst. "Of course, we all started falling over on the slippery paint for some cheap slapstick laughs, but I wasn't laughing when the cow fell on top of us and I couldn't get back up," said Donald. "I was under their dead-drunk bodies, pushing and wriggling, trying to get out from under them but they couldn't move. It even crossed my mind that they were deliberately trying to suffocate me."

Perhaps Donald was motivated to get his own back on his two friends when he invited them to a live broadcast at the Freedom Bar, the venue on Wardour Street opened by Roland Mouret, who is now a famous fashion designer. Urquhart regularly contributed short plays and sketches—"inspired by *Round the Horne* but rather more edgy and provocative"—to the gay radio channel Freedom FM. One of the most popular skits was *Pamela's Party Planners*, "in which someone calls an agency looking for outrageous drag queens and over-dressed nonentities to add some glamour to their party." The character of Pamela had a sharp tongue and she regularly turned her cruel wit on the stars of London's underground scene—her victims had included Leigh Bowery, Nicola Bateman, Princess Julia, Transformer and Matthew Glamorre. That night, in September 1994, as she spotted Lee and Jimmy lurking in the audience, Pamela decided to single them out for ridicule:

> *PAMELA: Who else do we have? Ah . . . you might want these two. They're always really really drunk, teeth like tombstones, spitting bad breath and plaque at you and they misguidedly think they dress like East End barrow boys but really look like a couple of dirty Marys who just came off Hampstead Heath. If you're lucky your guests might catch something off them.*[43]

The performance captured the spirit of campness and bitchiness that seemed to have infected a certain section of the gay scene in London. "That was the mood of the time," said the artist BillyBoy*. "Lee could be really witty and sometimes cruel. When he was on the way up the ladder of drunkenness he was amazing. He would talk about feelings and art, that was a part of him that I loved, but unfortunately he had to climb the ladder of insobriety to be that person." According to BillyBoy* there were at least three different personalities trapped inside McQueen. "There was the sober him, an insecure, unhappy person," he said. "Then there was this intermediate one, this brilliant genius who was escaping with the aid of alcohol and drugs; and then this drunken jerk that went into a state of psychotic weirdness that I did not understand. Then he would be violent or morbid or sexed up and horny, and it was very unpleasant. He always used to talk about suicide. He would say horrifically scary things and at times I was worried about him. Suicide is a very touchy subject for me because of what happened in my family, but when he was drunk he would talk about it and he knew how much it disturbed me."[44]

The fashion designer Miguel Adrover witnessed his friend's quixotic personality at close quarters. He remembers Lee as both shy and insecure and "the most fun person I ever met on this fucking planet." McQueen was "a joker, a super joker" and someone "really dark," a man who in the end no longer gained "pleasure from that darkness." The two had first met in London in 1993 through Lee Copperwheat. Miguel, who had been born in Majorca but who was living in New York, immediately recognized a kindred spirit in Lee. Like McQueen, he grew up in a poor family—he didn't have a television until he was fourteen years old—"and we had a connection somehow, we both came from the same place and both of us really needed to fight the world."[45]

Adrover had told McQueen all about New York and in the spring of 1994 Lee got the chance to visit Manhattan for the first time. After the success of *Nihilism* and *Banshee*, Lee had been contacted by Derek Anderson, then the agent for Martin Margiela, and invited out to America. He put a show together in a downtown loft which was, according to journalist Ingrid Sischy writing in the *New Yorker*, "a frenzy of bodies, male and female, rushing in and out of remarkably intricate constructions that showed a remarkable amount of flesh."[46] In her feature Sischy examined the way that AIDS had influenced culture—"the fact that there's been so much mourning, so much terror of sex, that people feel they have to break out. Some of the designers apparently felt the same thing." She fantasized about a time when "the wide range of desires that live in human beings might finally come out in public" but doubted whether fashion had the capacity or power to express such feelings.[47] The visions that sprang from McQueen's mind over the course of the next fifteen or so years would do just that.

In New York, McQueen enjoyed some positive responses and initial good sales, but he was less than taken with the city itself. He could never imagine living there, he told Samantha Murray Greenway from *Dazed & Confused* magazine, which ran an interview with him in the September 1994 issue. "It's such an air-brained city," he said. "The money system, their class system, it's so blatant: power by wealth. There's the homeless and there's the rich, there's no in between. Money buys everything. Money buys you stature."

He dreamt of taking time out to travel to Spain—"to some desolate place where there are no clocks"—as he felt as though he was beginning to lose control of his life. He could think of nothing but the preparations for his new show, *The Birds*, scheduled for 9 October 1994. "It's doing my head in," he said. "It's getting to the point where I'm not doing it because I enjoy it but because it's what's expected. I've got a feeling I could lose grip altogether, but that's why I work on my relationship with Jim [Andrew Groves] because hopefully he's there to bring me out of that."[48]

McQueen enlisted Andrew to help work on the new collection—"only because he found out that I could sew," said Groves. It was always fascinating for him to watch Lee making clothes. Once, Andrew related a story to Lee: how, a few years earlier, he had met an American man through the personal ads of a gay magazine. The two met up and the American guy wrapped him in cling film. A few days after telling him this story Andrew and Lee were walking down Elizabeth Street when McQueen spotted a roll of clear plastic wrap. "Let's make a dress out of this!" Lee said.[49] At the same time, McQueen realized that if he wanted to continue to improve his image and bankability—he had just signed a distribution deal with Eo Bocci, one of the original backers of Ann Demeulemeester and Jean Paul Gaultier—he would need to draft other style professionals.

One day that year Lee walked into a bead shop in Soho, London, and spotted the stylist Katy England. He had first seen her in 1991 when he had traveled with his Saint Martins friends to Paris to see the shows. "She was standing there in this second-hand nurse's coat, very severe, perfect for that time," he said. "I thought she looked fantastic. I didn't have the guts to go up to her, though. I thought she'd be too elitist." Within a few moments of talking to her this time he discovered that she was one of the least affected people he had ever met.

"Are you Katy England?" he asked.

"Yes," she replied.

"Will you style my next show?"

"Yes," she said, slightly taken aback, and perhaps even more amazed with herself for agreeing to work for him for nothing.[50] "At first, my parents thought I was mad working for no money," she said later.[51]

Katy England—who would later be known as McQueen's "second opinion"[52] and "the hippest woman in Britain"[53]—initially considered herself to be something of an outsider in the insular world of fashion. Born in Warrington, Cheshire, in 1966, the daughter of a bank manager and a mother who worked in a GP surgery, she started to be fascinated by clothes at the age of ten. She loved dressing up in her sisters' clothes and remembers as a girl ripping out the pages of *Vogue*. She was "interested in the power and confidence [clothes] can give you," she said. "I found the way I felt completely different depending on what I was wearing really fascinating."[54] After graduating with an MA in fashion design from Manchester Polytechnic in 1988, she came to London and started work at *Elle* magazine, where she had secured an unpaid placement. "I came down to London and got interested in magazines and didn't understand the fashion world," she said. "I didn't even know about the people at Saint Martins and how difficult it was to get into things."[55] From *Elle*, England moved to *You* magazine, the *Mail on Sunday*'s women's magazine, where she worked as a fashion assistant for four years. In fashion terms, England was positioned at the heart of the British mainstream; *You* magazine was extremely popular but it was far from cutting-edge. England, however, believed this had its advantages. "It was very good for me because I was put through the ropes in quite a formal way," she said. "I think that's really useful. Also, because it's a weekly, I was thrown right in at the deep end."[56] From *You*, England started working for the *Evening Standard*, where she believed she started to forge her own, more experimental, style. Journalist Nick Foulkes, who at the time edited a section of the London newspaper, remembers that "the pictures she used to turn out were vaguely fetishistic and, I thought, slightly sinister. England, herself, though, never showed any of the self-regarding 'attitude' so common among the priestesses of fashion."[57]

Using his finely tuned instinct, McQueen started to pick the team for the *Birds* collection, some of whom he would continue to work with over the course of his career. Fleet Bigwood, Simon Ungless and Andrew/Jimmy helped with the fabrics; Simon Costin was drafted in to design the set and supply some of the "jewelry" (including neck braces fashioned from jet and enamel and cockerel feathers); Val Garland, who had just arrived from Australia, was in charge of the makeup; Alister Mackie, a recent graduate from Saint Martins, helped Katy England with the styling; and Sam Gainsbury, who had studied fashion and textiles at Birmingham Polytechnic, was brought in as a freelance casting assistant.

"In the run-up to the show, in the weeks before, it would be fun, fun, fun, but then two weeks before [the day] it was, 'This is serious, I need to get on, I can't speak,'" remembers Trixie. "At the time a lot of the designers were taking diarrhoea pills, emetics. I am sure that is what Lee would do, as he seemed to lose a stone really quickly. And he was probably doing speed as well. Andrew would be up too, twenty-four hours a day, for a week before the show. If I saw them at this stage I would say, 'Honey, you look fabulous, you've lost so much weight,' but they would be ratty because they had only had one hour's sleep."[58]

The news, on 6 October 1994, that he had not won the coveted Young Designer of the Year award at the Lloyds Bank British Fashion Awards, did nothing to help lighten Lee's mood. McQueen had already gone into print with an attack on the body that granted the awards, and so the failure to win could hardly have come as a surprise. "London gives me fuck all," he had said. "If they offered me Young Designer of the Year I'd throw a right tantrum—they haven't given me shit."[59]

Inspired by the work of the Dutch graphic artist M. C. Escher, particularly his illustrations showing birds that transform into geometrical patterns, Lee shared his vision with Simon Ungless, who was enlisted to print the fabric for the new collection. Ungless, then working as a print technician at Saint Martins, helped himself to the material in the college's fabric store. Yet, in the run-up to the show, McQueen kept many preparations secret. For instance, Andrew Groves knew nothing of Lee's intention to use Mr. Pearl, the corsetiere with an eighteen-inch corseted waist, as one of the models. "He liked the idea of surprising people," said Andrew. "It wasn't just shock, it was about subverting expectations. Lee had this thing—it's not about the clothes, he would say, it's about the set and the theatre and the emotional spectacle."[60] Mr. Pearl had first met McQueen at the club the Beautiful Bend in King's Cross and had found him "amusing." "He convinced me to model in his next show for £100, which in the end I never received," he said. "The show was chaotic and very late, everyone was freezing and I found the whole thing boring. In retrospect, I was pleased to have met him—he inspired many people, and this contribution to beauty is part of his legend, but he paid for it with his life. I think he was not a happy man."[61]

McQueen was becoming an expert at creating heightened levels of expectation around a show through a not-so-subtle manipulation of the media. Sometimes he would get a thrill from telling journalists elaborate stories that he had invented. Once, remembers Andrew Groves, he told a reporter how he had joined a traveling circus, but had got into trouble for shaving the bearded lady; her fresh-faced look meant that she could not work for three months. "He was very good at his own PR," said Alice Smith. "He said that Michael Jackson and Karl Lagerfeld were coming to his show. At the time, we believed him, but a lot of that was complete fantasy."[62] As a result, the excitement surrounding *The Birds* had reached such a level of frenzy that when friends turned up at Bagley's, a disused warehouse in King's Cross, there were huge queues around the block. Luckily, Donald Urquhart only lived around the block and so he, together with Sheila Tequila, went back to his flat, enjoyed a few drinks and returned to Bagley's wearing the pantomime cow costume. "We still had to wait for ages for the show to start, but at least we were warm in our fun fur," he said.[63] Joyce McQueen sat proudly at the front; Lee's dad, Ron, watched from the shadows at the back after arriving late.

McQueen said he drew inspiration from Hitchcock's 1963 film *The Birds*—in which the heroine played by Tippi Hedren gets attacked by a series of different birds—but in his catwalk show the women are more than mere passive victims. The models who strutted down the runway, a dirty warehouse floor painted with white road markings, were powerful Amazonian creatures. Some women had been fitted with white contact lenses, making them appear otherworldly, while others wore skirts so tight that they found it difficult to walk. The fabrics were printed with images of birds and tire prints, symbols of freedom and roadkill. The tire-print effect was achieved by the low-tech method of running a car tire dipped in black paint over the bodies of the models backstage. "He had all our hair crimped, he called it 'angel hair,'" recalls Plum Sykes, who modeled in the show. "At the time I thought it was so bizarre, not pretty. But he was trying to get into a new genre, a new look."[64]

Hamish Bowles—who in 1993 had arranged to feature McQueen in the pages of American *Vogue* only for the designer to tell him that he didn't "give a flying fuck" about the magazine[65]—called the show a "revelation."[66] Later Bowles wrote, "It was, quite simply, astonishing and one of those electrifying moments when you realized that a designer had arrived possessed of the single-minded vision and passion and talent to challenge the paradigm. It seemed even then that fashion would never be the same again, and McQueen's low-slung silhouette and savage imagination would come to define the decade."[67]

Amy Spindler of the *New York Times* said that "the jackets in the collection were nothing short of perfect" but the influential fashion critic did have one reservation: while McQueen might have been the "most talked-about designer to be showing" in London that year, she believed his restrictive skirts and his bumster trousers were essentially unwearable.[68] McQueen was determined not to be sidetracked by the opinions or demands of fashion journalists. "I don't want the press or anyone making me into something I'm not," he said. "Someone said John Galliano only does clothes for press, but that's what the press made him and now they're knocking him for it. I can see myself going that way as well if I don't take control because my shows have been getting so much press, because they're so different from what's going on. But I want to see people wearing my clothes, not just a handful of fashion editors." In an ideal world, McQueen said, he would like to make just one beautiful jacket a week, but the demands of the market meant that he had to finish five. "I've got a feeling I might become a recluse one day," he said.[69]

Stylist Seta Niland wondered to herself about the effect of her friend's increasing success. As McQueen became more high profile— it was rumored that the jacket worn by Mr. Pearl in *The Birds* had been bought by Madonna—she felt as though she was being marginalized by some new arrivals in his team. "It was a battle for me to stay with him and I didn't give it the fight I should have, perhaps," she said. "But Lee needed to be on that bandwagon. It was all rolling too fast and as more and more people jumped on to the bandwagon I had to ask myself, 'Where was Lee?'"[70]

CHAPTER SIX

I want heart attacks. I want ambulances.

—Lee McQueen

On 24 November 1994, a Thursday evening, Lee took his seat next to Simon Ungless downstairs at the Freedom Bar and waited for the act to start. To say that there was an air of expectation in the smoke-filled room would be an understatement. Lucian Freud, Marc Almond, Anthony Price, Björk, Jane and Louise Wilson, Cerith Wyn Evans and some of the members of Blur and Suede were all in the audience, and countless numbers of record company scouts, journalists and fans had been turned away. Lee watched as the venetian blinds that shielded the stage began to open, casting slivers of light into the darkness. McQueen was here to see Leigh Bowery, a man who made Lee's own shows look tame and tasteful by comparison. "In this jaded age, when nobody gets shocked by anything any more, Leigh [Bowery] still managed to shock people in an intelligent way—in an original way," said John Richardson, the art historian and biographer of Picasso.[1]

That night, Leigh Bowery, who was appearing with his band Minty, did not disappoint. After performing a song about Comme des Garçons, Bowery, dressed in an enormous yellow and black striped dress, began to feed his "baby"—his real-life wife Nicola Bateman—who was attached to him by a harness. "I was released from my harness and Leigh continued to undress until he was naked," remembers

Nicola. "I had to say, 'Feed me,' and then Leigh vomited into my mouth. I had to say, 'Feed me,' again and then Leigh did a pee in a cup which I drank."[2] Watching from the side of the stage, and taking photographs of both the event and the audience, was photographer A. M. Hanson, who had first met Lee in 1993 in Comptons. "I didn't know Lee was there that night—it was so dark—and it wasn't until the next day when I got the photos back that I saw him sitting there in the front row, his eyes agog at what he had just seen," said Hanson. "Later he told me that he loved Bowery's shows for their unpredictability."[3]

"Leigh Bowery was a huge influence on him," said Réva, Lee's friend from Saint Martins. According to Stephen Brogan—who, as Stella Stein, was one of the members, with Leigh, of the band Raw Sewage—McQueen "worshipped" Bowery. Leigh and Lee shared a mutual friend, Wayne, and according to Stephen, "McQueen pumped him for stories of Bowery and he was obsessed over his designs."[4] McQueen borrowed many elements of Bowery's style and incorporated them into his work: the bumsters, the makeup from the *Horn of Plenty* show (Autumn/Winter 2009) and the ten-inch-high "armadillo" shoes made famous by Lady Gaga. Leigh had worked with a number of McQueen's friends and associates, including Donald Urquhart and Mr. Pearl, who would transform himself into a "human bustle, doubled over beneath the fabric at Bowery's back end."[5] Bowery and Pearl—both of whom, like Lee, were interested in transforming the shape of the human body through costume—adored getting their hands on a piece of couture and ripping the lining out of the jacket to see how it had been engineered, a process that McQueen would have savored too. Although Lee and Leigh both used fashion as a form of catharsis—the extremities they expressed on the catwalk or in the nightclub reflected their own fears and desires—the ways they chose to do this were very different. McQueen projected his feelings and fantasies onto the girls who walked down the runway, while Bowery used his own body as the canvas.

Leigh Bowery, who had been born in 1961 in Sunshine, Australia, arrived in London in 1980 and had set about a process which one observer called the "total theatricalization of the self, using the night club as his stage."[6] Although he occasionally made clothes for friends—BillyBoy* bought a number of his designs, as did Boy George, Holly Johnson of Frankie Goes to Hollywood and Al Pillay (as the transsexual diva Lanah Pellay)—he knew that he could never marry his taste with that of the masses. "Fashion is a business, first of all. You have to appeal to too many people," he said.[7] As he explained in his diary in 1981, "I believe that fashion . . . STINKS. I think that firstly individuality is important, and that there should be no main rules for behaviour and appearance. Therefore I want to look as best as I can, through my means of individuality and expressiveness. I think that the clothes I am interested in are strictly the opposite to what's in mass taste, and that there is a minority that like the same style as me."[8] One of Bowery's most infamous "looks" was the one he described as the "Paki from Outer Space," which made its first appearance in 1983. This involved covering his face with red, green or blue makeup decorated with gold writing and accessorized using items of cheap Asian jewelry that he had picked up in Brick Lane. "His next make-up look was to complement his new frilly designs, when he made stockings with frills at the top, pinnies and very detailed blouses covered in pockets, intricate collars and full sleeves," said his friend Sue Tilley. "The cutting was very unusual and lots of the garments had uneven sleeves and clever capes and flounces . . . If Leigh was feeling particularly daring he would wear this look without the frilly knickers so that his bottom was bare."[9] The bare-bottomed look made numerous appearances—on the catwalks of Japan when event producer Susanne Bartsch flew Bowery out there to show his designs; on the television show *The Tube* in 1984; and when the choreographer Michael Clark commissioned him to design a set of costumes, exquisitely tailored clothes described as "haute-couture surrealism." "Dancers wore caps with little wiglets attached at the back, silver platform shoes, ruffled see-through aprons, loud briefs, knee socks, and stretchy knit tights with the ass missing," wrote Hilton Als in the

New Yorker. "This was at least eight years before the English designer Alexander McQueen would come out with his 'bumsters.'"[10]

That night, in November 1994, Bowery's show proved too much for some spectators—Lucian Freud, who used Leigh as a model for some of his most revered paintings, found the noise levels too intense and had to leave early. The next day the Freedom Bar received notice that if they carried on with the show they would have their license revoked by Westminster Council. The show proved to be Bowery's last performance—he died on 31 December 1994 from an AIDS-related illness, a condition that he had kept from most of his friends. "A very definite line was drawn when Leigh Bowery died," said Donald Urquhart. "It was time to drop the acid-tongued severity and disposable decadence and respond to life with a new seriousness."[11]

McQueen, however, was not quite ready to grow up. "My shows are about sex, drugs, and rock and roll," he said. "It's for the excitement and the goose bumps . . . I want heart attacks. I want ambulances."[12] Lee still loved hanging out with Nicholas Townsend and listening to Trixie's camp repartee. "Why do you always wear red lipstick?" asked Lee. "Because it looks better on a cock," Trixie replied. Another of Trixie's lines that used to make McQueen laugh was: "Heels always look better on shoulders than they do on the street." Lee liked to visit Trixie when he was working in a club called Burger, where he would dress up as a 1950s-style diner girl. "We liked to go out to Popstars, the Scala and Sean McLusky's Fantasy Ashtray," said Trixie. "Jimmy and Lee loved dancing and at that time we did alcohol—snakebite—and speed. One of my favourite memories is dancing with Lee and Jimmy to Pulp's 'Common People' at Popstars. We were drinking pints of cider and just laughing. That was one of the best times we ever had. That's how I prefer to remember him, as he still had that innocence then. We were like a little family, and we looked after one another. We might only have had ten quid each on us, but we made sure we got home and we were OK. The next day we all chipped in together to have breakfast."[13]

Lee and Andrew often dropped in to see mutual friend Fiona

Cartledge at her shop Sign of the Times in Covent Garden. The influential outlet began life in Kensington Market in 1989 when it sold rave gear. From there it expanded to a stand in Hyper Hyper and, because of the falling rents triggered by the recession, by December 1994 Fiona could afford to open a shop just off Neal Street. Fiona stocked a wide range of clothes by young designers, including Jimmy Jumble (Andrew Groves), and her shop became something of a mecca for stylists and fashion junkies such as BillyBoy*, who became a close friend. When Isabella Blow was preparing to shoot "Anglo-Saxon Attitudes" for *Vogue* she sourced many of the clothes from Sign of the Times. "And it was Isabella who took me to Lee's show at the Bluebird Garage," recalls Fiona. "I didn't meet him properly until after we had opened in Covent Garden when I noticed he seemed much more sophisticated than other designers, probably because he had worked in Italy. He was sure of where he was going." Fiona also organized club nights, using the profits to channel back into the shop, but by November 1996 lack of funds forced her to close. "When the shop shut I was dropped by lots of people, but McQueen never forgot me and continued to invite me to every show in London and he made sure I had a good seat. I never forgot that."[14]

On New Year's Eve 1994, Lee and Andrew went to a Sign of the Times party at the Hanover Grand in central London. The theme of the night was *West Side Story* and guests such as Liam Gallagher and Tricky enjoyed a range of acts such as Mark Moore, Harvey and Jon Pleased Wimmin. That night the artist Jeremy Deller took a photograph of the pair dancing, with Lee holding Andrew from behind. A couple of months later another photograph told a very different story. On Valentine's Day 1995, Lee and Andrew went to Link Leisure's Red Party in a warehouse in Bethnal Green, where they saw a performance by David Cabaret, a self-taught tailor whose act involved transforming himself into iconic art works such as Warhol's *Marilyn* and Vladimir Tretchikoff's *Green Lady*. A photograph taken that night by another artist, A. M. Hanson, showed the couple leering into the camera, their eyes heavy with drink, their faces scratched, with Lee sticking a finger up to the world. "Lee told me that they had just had a fight," said Hanson. "I remember taking pictures of people dressed up in various pink outfits and rouged-up characters, then came across Lee and Jimmy in the corridor. I think Lee was being reactionary because of the fight they had had and Jimmy's affection shows they had made it up, I guess."[15]

Trixie remembers, in the spring of 1995, going to the newly opened Belgo Centraal restaurant in Covent Garden with Lee and a couple of other friends. "As soon as we went in we knew it wasn't right for us," he said. "Lee wanted a burger and it was clear he didn't like the idea of mussels. We ordered chips and we ended up having a food fight and we were asked to leave. Lee jokingly said, 'Don't you know who I am?' and they were like, 'No, we don't.'"[16]

This may have been surprising to McQueen given the controversy surrounding his March 1995 show *Highland Rape*, in which he sent women down the catwalk wearing tartan and lace dresses ripped at the chest to show their breasts. The newspapers accused him of misogyny, of using rape and violence as a form of entertainment and of featuring models with tampon strings attached to their skirts (the "tampon strings" were, in fact, beautifully fashioned Albert fob chains made by Shaun Leane). "I remember the critics putting down their pads and paper during that show," said Detmar Blow.[17] "I thought that he had gone a bit far and I think a lot of people thought that," said *Vogue*'s Anna Harvey.[18]

The *Independent* was fierce in its criticism: "The Emperor's new clothes: rape victims staggering in dresses clawed at the breast were a sick joke, as were knitted dresses that M&S would make better for a fraction of the price. McQueen likes to shock. To admit to not liking his collection is to admit to being prudish. So, we admit it. He is a skilful tailor and a great showman, but why should models play abused victims? The show was an insult to women and to his talent."[19]

The response infuriated McQueen, who appeared at the end of the show wearing black contact lenses. How could the critics not see what he was trying to achieve? The rape in the title of the show referred not to the rape of actual women, he said, but the rape of Scotland by the English. He was referencing both the Jacobite Rebellion and the Highland Clearances, and also the way in which Scotland had been portrayed by contemporary fashion designers. "It was actually anti the fake history of Vivienne Westwood," he told Colin McDowell. "She makes tartan lovely and romantic and tries to pretend that's how it was. Well, eighteenth-century Scotland was not about beautiful women drifting across the moors in swathes of unmanageable chiffon. My show was anti that sort of romanticism. You needed only a little intelligence to take the clothes out of context and look and see how they were cut. I can't compensate for lack of intelligence, but I wish people would try a bit harder."[20] Later, Westwood would issue her own barbed attack on McQueen—"His only usefulness is as a measure of zero talent," she said.[21]

Perhaps Westwood was thoughtful of the frenzied attention McQueen was beginning to attract. Before *Highland Rape*, which was held on 13 March 1995 in the British Fashion Council tent on the east lawn at the Natural History Museum, the show was already being talked about in terms reserved for sold-out rock concerts or over-subscribed theatrical events. Such was the hysteria surrounding the show that on the night it was staged some students tried to crawl under the tent to gain entry. Others, thought to be from Saint Martins, managed to get past security by flashing the photocopied invites of a close-up of some sutures stretched across a piece of skin.

Backstage, before the show, Joyce McQueen—who liked to make sandwiches for the models and crew—watched as her son attacked the dresses with a pair of shears. "There were all these beautiful blue lace dresses and he was hacking at them with his shears and I was crying, 'No, don't spoil them,'" she said.[22] John Boddy, a twenty-year-old student who had come to McQueen on a four-month-long work placement from Saint Martins, recalls being told by the designer to take a Stanley knife and a can of spray paint to a range of beautifully finished dresses. "He had a certain kind of Jackson Pollock–like energy about him," said John, who had also worked as one of the dressers on the *Birds* show. "There was a sense of anarchy and chaos within that creation. I liked his oddness, there was something very magical about him. He was almost like a boy at times, but then he also had a wicked sense of humour and would say the most disgusting things. His laugh was like a cackle—at times you would think that there was a coven of witches in the room."[23]

The tartan for *Highland Rape* had been paid for by Detmar Blow, who lent Lee £300 to buy it and never got the money back. The rest of the material came from Berwick Street market in Soho. "All the lace came from Barry's stall there, mainly because both of us fancied Barry, he was an ex-boxer, and also because it was a pound a metre," said Andrew Groves. "So Lee ended up making a dress for a quid. The funny thing was the same dress was shot by Richard Avedon and was flown over [to New York] on Concorde. There was a seat for someone to take it and a seat for the dress. And it cost a quid. He loved the humour of that, that he could take a bit of crap and make it into something."[24]

McQueen had worked on *Highland Rape* at his new studio in Clerkenwell Workshops, a space he began to rent after Detmar's mother asked Lee and Andrew to leave her house in Elizabeth Street so that it could be renovated. The relationship between the two designers had started to become increasingly difficult and although Lee and Andrew put a deposit down on a rented flat in Hackney they never moved in because they had "a bust-up." Soon afterwards, Lee moved into Andrew's flat in Green Lanes, where he stayed for a few months. "It was horrible, it needed an electricity key for electricity, the bath was practically in a freezing cold outside lean-to, we had absolutely no money, and it was really depressing," said Andrew. "There were no chairs or furniture, only a mattress on the floor. And as we couldn't afford heating we stayed in one room. Looking back, I can't think of a worse place for either of us to be living. It certainly would have made anyone's depression worse."[25] At times, Lee seemed uncommunicative and self-contained. "He kept lots of things secret," said Andrew. "There was lots of stuff going on in his life that he never really shared. For instance, I never knew where the money came from to do the shows. And then one day, around four o'clock in the afternoon, he said, 'I've got to go to the fucking Palace now to see Princess Diana.' I said, 'What?' And he just said, 'Yeah.' He put on a dirty shirt inside out to see her."[26]

Although Andrew Groves said he never saw Lee take drugs, it soon became obvious to him that McQueen had started to experiment with them. The couple's fights got nastier and more physical. "Once Lee came around and he had had a fight and had lost one of his teeth," said Trixie. "When he was going out with Andrew they used to fight a lot. He would come around and there would be scratches on his face."[27] Chris Bird said, "Andrew and Lee had a very violent relationship. There were punches, doors being ripped off."[28] Lee also started to frequent gay clubs in London with a harder, cruisier feel such as Trade and FF. "It was an experience, but one I don't really want to repeat," he said in 1996. "The whole sex club scene turned out to be a really horrible time in my life. A time of total nervous destruction."[29]

McQueen would stay out all night and return to the flat in Green Lanes at dawn. Once, he returned home and spotted a piece of paper with the numbers "362436" scribbled on it, a sign—in his eyes at least—that Andrew had been unfaithful. Groves recalls, "He was going mad, saying, 'Whose is this fucking phone number?' And I said, 'That's the measurements of the dummy—36-24-36.' He was insanely jealous. He was always waiting for someone to betray him and to be proved right, that in the end all men were bastards and everyone was going to let you down or fuck you up."[30]

In July 1995, just after John Galliano had been appointed the head of the Paris-based couture house Givenchy, McQueen met up for a drink with John McKitterick in a bar in the East End. Lee could not believe that Galliano—who after his graduation from Saint Martins had established his own label, based in Paris—would want to work for the corporate giant LVMH.

"Why has he gone to work at this really boring place?" said McQueen.

"He needs the money to support his own business," replied John.

"But why would he want to leave London, which is so great? Why does he want to design for someone else?"

John tried to explain the economics of the decision, but Lee did not understand Galliano's motivation. "At that point, Galliano was the only other designer he really spoke about," said McKitterick. "He felt that John was not the one to beat but the one to measure himself by. At this point, fashion was changing; it was the beginning of the trend of big fashion houses coming back into style and Galliano started that."[31]

Ever since he had been a student at Saint Martins, McQueen had set himself up as a rival to Galliano. Fellow student Adele Clough remembers going to a Galliano sample sale with him where Lee declared everything to be "a load of rubbish."[32] "I never heard him say Galliano was brilliant," said Alice Smith. "But he never said Dior was brilliant. He had his own ways of thinking about fashion and that was all he knew."[33]

In 1995, McQueen expressed some of these ideas in a debate held at the Institute of Contemporary Arts in London when he appeared on a panel with designers Paul Smith and Helen Storey, the stylist Judy Blame and the design director of Marks & Spencer, Brian Godbold. It was clear that McQueen, dressed in jeans and a simple blue shirt, felt angry about the state of the fashion industry in Britain. He told Sally Brampton, who was chairing the debate—titled "Balancing Acts: Commerce Versus Creativity"—that he sold only to one shop in the UK compared to fifteen shops in Japan. When it came to getting his clothes made he also had to look outside his home country. "It's just ludicrous to think about trying to get a manufacturer to produce a sample from any of my collections," he said. "They don't want to know." He also blamed fashion students for their lack of technical abilities. "It's all very well being a fantastic designer on paper, but give it to a student to put together or construct or put the run through from paper to manufacturing—I would say three quarters of them don't know what they are doing."[34]

In the early summer of 1995, McQueen moved out of Andrew Groves's flat in Green Lanes and into a basement loft in Geller House, 51 Hoxton Square. The area had not yet been touched by gentrification—there were no cool bars or restaurants and the only place to buy food, as Gregor Muir notes in his book *Lucky Kunst*, was a twenty-four-hour garage "that offered a very poor selection of sweets, fizzy drinks and crisps, as well as the occasional Scotch egg."[35] McQueen described the area as "desolate and rough" but the benefit was "you got a lot of space for your money."[36]

In addition to the low rents, McQueen had been attracted to Hoxton because of its association with the new breed of artists who had started to shock Britain—the so-called YBAs (Young British Artists). In July 1993, Joshua Compston, who ran the art space Factual Nonsense at 44a Charlotte Road, Hoxton, had organized an event called "A Fete Worse Than Death" at the junction of Rivington Street and Charlotte Road. Artist Gary Hume, who lived and worked in Hoxton Square, dressed as a Mexican bandit and sold shots of tequila; Tracey Emin read palms; Gillian Wearing dressed as a schoolgirl and walked up and down the street with a figure known as The Woman with Elongated Arms; and Damien Hirst and Angus Fairhurst disguised themselves as clowns and set up a stall selling paintings for one pound made from a spin machine, works that they would sign on the back. "For an extra 50p the artists would reveal their spot-painted bollocks, an elaboration on the part of their make-up artist for the day, Leigh Bowery," said Muir.[37]

Lee turned up at his new flat in Hoxton Square with one black bin bag full of his possessions. There was nothing in the loft apart from a makeshift shower and a small mattress on the floor; he shared a toilet, down the corridor, with his neighbors. On the day of his move he was coming into the building when he met Mira Chai Hyde, a hairdresser and men's grooming artist from America, who lived on the first floor. She invited him into her loft for a cup of tea and within five minutes he had asked her whether she wanted to work on his next show. Their bond, she said, was instant. "I loved him immediately," she said. "You could tell straightaway there was something special about him. He was very, very funny; he used to make me laugh a lot and he had an incredible energy. Everyone in the fashion industry had heard about *Highland Rape*, about this brilliant young man who had done this amazing show. From day one, I felt very bonded to him and loved him like a brother." Lee started to come up to Mira's for dinner and then, after a month, he moved into the loft that she shared with her boyfriend Richard. "I have a picture from that time and you can see how poor we were because material covered crappy chairs, the bookcase was made out of wood and bricks and a curtain separated our two sleeping areas," said Mira. "For me to survive I had to cut hair, because I made no money in fashion. At the end of the day Lee would collect the hair from the floor and use it in the plastic labels in his clothes." Lee loved it when Mira cut his hair, which was incredibly fine, but he could not sit still for long. Once he asked her to cut a tramline into his hair in the form of a heart monitor that had flatlined, a symbol that he incorporated into his shows and an image that haunted him until his death.[38]

On Sunday, 3 September 1995, after a night out, Lee turned up at Andrew's flat in north London. "He came in, going 'I'm in pain,' but I just said, 'Oh, piss off, it's because you've been on drugs,'" said Andrew. "He said that he really was in pain, but I ignored him for about three hours and then called an ambulance. It turned out he had burst his appendix and he had to be rushed to hospital, to the Whittington in Archway."[39]

When he came out of hospital Lee got straight back to work. Mira remembers occasions when late at night, after enjoying one of her suppers, McQueen would go back to his loft and start work on a jacket. "The next morning I would go down and it would be finished," she said. From the beginning, Lee started to give Mira clothes he had designed, including a green wool jacket embroidered with gold military braid and a pair of bumsters with "pee" stains on the fabric, both from *Highland Rape*. "He had used bleach to get that effect," she said. "It was supposed to symbolize fear, the girls were so frightened they had peed their pants. I was called the bumster girl, because I was the one who always wore them. I wouldn't have my ass hanging out in daylight, but in the evening I might do. Lee could tailor something to make you look like you had the most amazing ass in the world. His tailoring was exquisite. When I wore his clothes I felt powerful, strong, beautiful and quite sexy."[40]

Earlier that year, Mira had played Lee an LP of the sound track from the film *The Hunger*, Tony Scott's art-house vampire film starring David Bowie, Catherine Deneuve and Susan Sarandon. McQueen loved the music, both Bauhaus's gothic rock song "Bela Lugosi's Dead" and "The Flower Duet" from Delibes's opera *Lakmé*, and, after seeing the movie, named his next collection *The Hunger*. Mira noticed how the basement—which he still used as his studio—started to fill up with people: creative director Katy England; Sam Gainsbury, whom Lee had appointed as producer of the show; Trino Verkade, who had the role of coordinator; and a number of other design assistants, including Ruti Danan and Sebastian Pons. Sebastian, from Majorca, a graduate of Saint Martins who had met McQueen through Simon Ungless and Lee Copperwheat, remembers his first day of work at the studio in Hoxton Square. "I went down to a horrible, dingy basement, nobody was there, just him and me," he said. "He had just bought a table from Ikea that was still in its box and our first job was to put this table together. In the afternoon we designed this thorn print. He told me he was crazy about thorns, 'They really represent me, they represent who I am,' he said. He said he wanted to break some rules and do something a bit shocking. He created this team of people around him to help him achieve that."[41]

To model in the show, which was held in a tent at the Natural History Museum on 23 October, McQueen drafted Tizer Bailey and her boyfriend at the time, Jimmy Pursey from Sham 69, a bare-chested Goldie (who ran a drum-and-bass night at the Blue Note, on the north side of Hoxton Square) and journalist Alix Sharkey. The clothes, many of which had been manufactured by MA Commerciale in Milan, incorporated plaster cast molds. There were men's shirts patterned with bloodied hands, slashed trousers and dresses, and a piece of transparent body armor inside of which squirmed a batch of worms. Models gave V signs and single-finger salutes while at the end of the show Lee, sporting a blond streak in the middle of his hair, dropped his green combat trousers and flashed his bum at the audience. Later he said, "I showed my bum to the press because I thought I was getting a very raw deal . . . I was on my own, I didn't have a backer and I couldn't do as much as the British Fashion Council wanted me to do, so I started doing silly things to fill in the gaps."[42]

As he rushed backstage, he realized that perhaps his shock tactics had gone too far. "I was saying to myself, 'I may as well write my obituary now,'" he said. "No one was coming backstage apart from people from a few mad shops around the world."[43] Fashion editor Suzy Menkes recalls going backstage and seeing him "sobbing his heart out." She put her arms around him and tried to reassure him that he still had a future in fashion. "He was tremendously overwrought," she said. "At that time he always cared so much, he really put his heart and soul into everything. I remember the first time I went to see him he told me he had been up all night because he had been working on a shoulder and he couldn't get it right. He was effing and blinding and talking about Yves Saint Laurent shoulders. He was so passionate about it."[44]

The press were far from kind. Iain R. Webb, writing in *The Times*, said that it was a shame that McQueen had allowed his "angry young man pose" to dominate the show as it was obvious that the designer possessed some "unique cutting skills and fresh perspectives . . . If only it didn't hurt so much to watch."[45] Colin McDowell of the *Sunday Times* outlined how there was a crisis in British fashion, believing that London lacked "a common core"; that the majority of clothes on display during Fashion Week were tame and commercial and repetitive. He criticized both Vivienne Westwood and John Galliano, who had just won his third Designer of the Year award, for churning out fashions which were "part *Gone with the Wind*, part nine-teenth-century Balmoral." And while he congratulated McQueen for spearheading a much-needed spirit of originality, overall he found his collection immature and childish. "What McQueen has he shares with Man Ray and Magritte, the wit and awareness to take the present and catapult it into the future before anyone knows what he is up to," he continued. "That is where his strength lies. Frankly, most of his clothes this season were an ill-thought-out mess. Many of his ideas will need some years' work if they are ever to become reality. And it matters not at all because he . . . understands that the new femininity is more about giving the finger than it is about mincing along in court shoes like a 1950s deb."[46]

Although Lee later said that *The Hunger* marked "the end of the old, reckless McQueen" this was, of course, far from the truth.[47] According to friends, he seemed just as irresponsible as ever. In the run-up to the show Lee had asked Simon Ungless to help him with the prints. McQueen told him that he could not afford to pay him very much, only £500, but Simon thought that it would be good for his career. "Some of them were really filthy," he said. "I think there was one about fisting that went into *The Hunger*." After the show Lee had to admit to his friend that he did not have the money to pay him, but presented him with a gift certificate for the fashion shop Browns for £1,000. "I thought I don't really want this as there is nothing in Browns that I like, but he persuaded me," he said. "I was working at Saint Martins at the time and so we walked all the way across town to Browns. I picked out some Helmut Lang stuff and then when I got to the register suddenly all the doors locked and the alarms started to go off. Lee had already gone. It turned out that the gift certificate was stolen, and Lee had filled it out and signed it. I explained everything to them and they asked me who gave it to me and I told them. 'Oh, Alexander McQueen, we don't carry him, but we love him,' said the woman behind the counter. 'Well, I fucking don't, not right now,' I said. I walked back to Saint Martins and as I was crossing Old Compton Street I saw him slink down a side street, laughing his head off.

When I told him what I had said in the shop he was so mad with me. 'How could you do that?' he said. 'I've got a name. I've got a reputation and you're going to destroy me.' I said, 'Well, I've got a job and I've got to live. Fuck you.' And then, of course, we started laughing about it."[48]

This kind of behavior was not unusual. Soon after leaving Saint Martins, Lee had tried to steal a couple of mannequins and was only stopped from doing so by a hawk-eyed Louise Wilson. Design journalist Liz Farrelly remembers the time when, in the summer of 1995, she had been trying to finish her book *Wear Me: Fashion + Graphics Interaction* at the studio of Silvia Gaspardo Moro and Angus Hyland in Wardour Street, a place that Lee used as an occasional work space. Liz had called in a number of items of clothing featuring graphics and had left them in the studio in preparation for a forthcoming photo shoot. One Monday, she walked into the studio to find all the clothes had disappeared. "We couldn't figure out what had happened, if there had been a break-in or what," she said. "We were stuffed—we were right up against the deadline, the photography was booked and there was nothing to snap. At some point Lee appeared, maybe the next day, really the worse for wear. He'd been off somewhere for the weekend. I walked into his room and saw his bag or case open on the floor and there, all screwed up and 'club soiled,' were our T-shirts, which he'd just 'borrowed.' I was livid, but Silvia stepped in, calmed us down, and I think she either suggested he wash them, or she did it. In an attempt to build bridges, he offered, or perhaps Silvia suggested, a peace token and he said I could have anything out of the cardboard box full of his designs in his room." Liz was not a great fan of the bumsters, but she considered a black lace frock coat, which she described as a "beautiful mix of crude and sophisticated," made from a "stiff sort of lace." But she found the cut across the back too narrow for her and so she declined, to her "very great annoyance later."[49]

In November 1995, McQueen, together with fellow designers Joe Casely-Hayford and John Rocha and fashion historian Judith Watt, flew out to South Africa to judge the Smirnoff International

Fashion Awards. On the first night in Sun City, Lee had his wallet stolen. After feeling angry, he resigned himself to the loss and told Joe that perhaps it had been taken by someone who needed the money more than he did. McQueen managed to scrabble together a few coins, which he then fed into a slot machine and promptly won £2,500. From there, the group moved on to Cape Town, where they judged the competition. Linda Björg Árnadóttir from Iceland recalls walking into the room with her work, a dress made out of transparent leather which was inspired by the parkas the Inuits made from the stomachs of seals. On seeing this McQueen became immediately animated. "What the hell is this made of?" he asked. "And when I told him the story he was very impressed and just kept on talking," said Linda. "He looked like a skateboarder to me and I didn't pay him a lot of attention at first. He seemed very nice and down to earth, but not very sophisticated." When Linda was named as the winner of the competition at the press conference some of journalists in the audience started to laugh. "There was some criticism about my clothes not being wearable and not being real fashion," said Linda. "I was a bit stressed out and he answered some of the questions that were meant for me and defended my work, saying that a competition like this should emphasize new ideas even though they weren't ready for the market."[50]

McQueen had always stood up for people whom he perceived to be vulnerable. Janet, his sister, recalls a family party in the late 1970s when Lee, who was still a boy, spotted her mother-in-law from her first marriage—the mother of the man who abused him—standing alone in a corner. "She was a very small woman, timid, and he made a point of going up to her to make sure she was OK," she said. "That was Lee all over. He had a very soft heart and would always be drawn to the underdog."[51] In 1995, McQueen paid a visit to Battersea Dogs Home and returned home with a light-brown-colored mongrel that he named Minter, after the boxer Alan Minter. In addition to meaning something secondhand that was in mint condition—appropriate then for a pet from Battersea Dogs Home—the name also signified

139

somebody who had acquired special skills. The root of the word had its origins in the Old English word "mynet," which meant "coin" or "money." This was ironic in Lee's case. At the beginning of 1996, when he was still broke, Edward Enninful, then working for *i-D* magazine, asked him in an interview about the secret of his success. "You just wanna see my bank balance!" he said. "If success is counted by pounds, I'm fucking unsuccessful. I'm a really bad businessman."

Enninful, who would become a friend of McQueen's, went on to ask him a series of personal questions. What would he take to a desert island? "Well, it wouldn't be a sewing machine," he said. "A bottle of poppers, a vibrator and a ready supply of Coca-Cola." What did other designers think of him? "A slice and a dice of twisted lemon," he said. What did he think distinguished him from other designers? "I think when they sent that probe to Jupiter, they found me there," he replied. What was his idea of a good night out? "With a man called Charlie." What was his most embarrassing moment? "Being born," he said. And, lastly, was he a fashion victim? "No, a victim of the fashion industry," he said.[52]

Just after he gave this interview his luck changed when he got a backer. He signed a deal with Gibo, the Italian subsidiary of Onward Kashiyama of Japan, who also supported Paul Smith and Helmut Lang. Instead of having to put together a show on a shoestring, McQueen now had a budget of £30,000. The increased investment in the label was immediately obvious. For his new collection *Dante*, McQueen sent out a glossy, expensively produced invitation, a full-color gatefold with a pair of angels on the front and a black-and-white photograph of a close-up of a dog's mouth inside. The fabrics too were more luxurious than anything he had used before. "We have developed a pure white fine cashmere and printed a black paisley pattern on it for a simple dress," he told Paula Reed of the *Sunday Times*. "A black lace dress has a flesh-coloured chiffon base, so it looks almost weightless, but sumptuous, too. A lavender silk jacket is fitted close to the body with sleeves cut in a spiral and slashed at the elbow. Much of the work is done by hand, which makes some of the pieces expensive, but also original. I think people want that now, they don't want to look as though they bought their clothes in a thrift shop."[53]

Instead of showing inside a functional but rather bland London Fashion Week tent as he had done for his last two shows, McQueen had managed to secure Nicholas Hawksmoor's Christ Church in Spitalfields as a venue. The idea for the collection grew out of a conversation Lee had had with Chris Bird, whom he often teased for being a bookworm—" 'You're always fucking reading these fancy poncey books, aren't you?' he would say. I said, 'You should call your collection *Dante*,' who he had never read," Chris said. Later, when Chris jokily challenged him that he had taken up his suggestion, McQueen looked a little "sheepish."[54] Simon Costin had recently given Lee an art catalogue of the work of Joel-Peter Witkin, the American photographer famous for his studies of hermaphrodites, corpses, dwarves, transsexuals and people with physical deformities. McQueen was entranced by the beauty with which Witkin—who when he was a child saw a girl get decapitated in a car accident outside his family home—shot these unsettling images and he was determined to reference the photographer in the show. He wanted to copy a Witkin self-portrait from 1984, in which he shot himself wearing a black eye mask that had a small crucifix that ran from between his eyebrows to just above his mouth. McQueen sent a fax to Witkin's office outlining how he intended to use the same mask design in his show, but, according to Chris Bird, the fax he received back informed him that the artist refused to grant permission. "I think Lee sent a really shitty fax back saying, and I'm not even paraphrasing, 'Fuck you,' and he proceeded to use it."[55]

In an interview with *Women's Wear Daily* McQueen stated that he had wanted to use Christ Church on Commercial Street because most of his relatives had been baptized and buried in the grounds in the nineteenth century; in fact most of his ancestors, on his father's side at least, were interred in the less alluring setting of St. Patrick's Cemetery in Leytonstone. The truth of the matter was that he was drawn to Hawksmoor's church because of its proximity to the Ten

Bells Pub, associated with two of the victims of Jack the Ripper, and its rumored associations with the occult. McQueen had told Mira Chai Hyde that he believed that Hawksmoor was a member of a secret society and "if you looked at London from the air it formed one point of a pentagram with the other churches he had built." Before the show started the atmosphere was tense. "We were all very spooked out and weird things were happening, like a crucifix fell onto the ground," said Mira, who was in charge of men's hair and grooming.[56]

On 1 March 1996, as the fashion crowd pushed their way into the church, a religious fanatic handed out pamphlets titled "Homily Against excess of Apparell [sic]."[57] The audience took their seats amidst apocryphal whispers of how victims of the Black Death had been buried beneath the floor of the church and how their ghosts still haunted the catacombs. Atonal music started to echo around the building and the stained-glass window of Jesus Christ at the back of the church seemed to blaze brighter for a moment before everything was pitched into darkness. The lights came on briefly before the audience was shrouded in blackness once more, an effect that produced gasps of astonishment. Then, from an archway of roses, a model wearing a Witkin-style black mask emerged wearing a beautifully tailored black dress with two reverse V-shaped slashes that revealed her breasts. Male models were styled as members of an American gang, men who seemed both attracted to and fearful of the powerful women who strutted down the cross-shaped catwalk. In fact, some of the women on display here looked as though they had transformed themselves into members of an unclassifiable third sex or a mutant hybrid of animal and human. Some wore antlers or unicorn horns on their heads, others sported masks that looked like something from *Alien*. One model had what appeared to be a crown of thorns circling her head; another, with spikes protruding from her pale face, seemed as though she had stepped from the set of the film *Hellraiser*. One outfit that drew the loudest applause from the audience was a black lace dress with an exaggerated mantilla headdress, supported by antlers, which increased the height of the woman wearing it to around eight feet. The message was clear: these were women you wouldn't want to mess with. "I like men to keep their distance from women," McQueen said. "I like men to be stunned by an entrance."[58]

Counterpointing the organ and choral music was the sound of helicopters and the splatter of gunfire. T-shirts were printed with the faces of the victims of violent conflict. "The show's theme was religion being the cause of war," said McQueen. "Fashion's so irrelevant to life, but you can't forget the world."[59] To hammer home his point some garments were emblazoned with images taken by Don McCullin, the war photographer. "When McCullin's agent saw the images they not only wanted everything destroyed but they wanted to sue," said Simon Ungless, who helped McQueen with the prints. "Lee passed everything on to me as if it was 100 per cent my fault. We got around it—we destroyed everything apart from one T-shirt I have."[60]

Yet, looking beyond the unconventional styling, the fashion critics could discern a set of exquisite clothes fashioned from gray wool, gold brocade, lavender silk taffeta and nude chiffon that women could wear, a sign that, at last, McQueen had matured. "In the past, the lewdness of Mr. McQueen's fantasies has limited the appeal of his inventive designs," wrote Amy Spindler in the *New York Times*. "This collection could be enjoyed by all."[61] Suzy Menkes, writing in the *International Herald Tribune*, said that McQueen had "hit a fashion moment." Her review was called "The Macabre and the Poetic," a phrase that summed up McQueen's gothic sensibility and the beauty with which he had expressed it; the designer had even placed a skeleton in the front row. Menkes wrote how McQueen's fascination with death mirrored that of contemporaries such as Damien Hirst—whose 1990 work *A Thousand Years* consisted of a series of glass cases containing maggots, flies and a rotting cow's head—and the narrator of the film *Trainspotting* who says, "Choose life—but why would I want to do a thing like that?" When Menkes questioned McQueen about the theme he replied, "It's not so much about death, but the awareness that it is there." She concluded her review with the words,

"[McQueen] proved that he is not just a fine tailor with a soaring imagination, but one of those rare designers who capture the spirit of the times."⁶²

At the end of the *Dante* show, a shy-looking McQueen, dressed in a baggy plaid shirt and his head shaven with a series of geometric tramlines, stumbled down the catwalk to take his bow. Applause echoed through the church as he kissed the two most important women in his life: first his mother, Joyce, who had been sitting in the front row, and then an ecstatic, black-befeathered Isabella Blow, to whom he dedicated the show. As Lee rushed backstage, models, friends, stylists and photographers all told him that the show had been an enormous success.

What nobody but a small group of trusted friends knew, however, was that his relationship with Andrew Groves had reached a crisis point. On the day of the show, Andrew had been bleaching some jeans in the bath and had not had time to wash them. "So the model's legs got bleached," he said. Lee was already in a foul mood just before the show. "And he thought I had laced up a corset the wrong way, like sabotage," he said. "He went to the pub afterwards and I didn't get invited. And that was the end of it."⁶³

Seven days after the show, McQueen found himself invited to Downing Street to meet the prime minister, John Major, at a reception held to celebrate London Fashion Week. Lee was far from impressed. In a photograph taken at the event McQueen, dressed in an overcoat from the collection *Dante*, and sporting a goatee beard, shaved head and what appears to be a large gold earring, looks distinctly uncomfortable as he stands with John and Norma Major and fellow designer John Rocha. "I haven't a clue about your world," said the prime minister to him. McQueen, in typically combative mood, responded, "We're only the third-biggest industry in this country." How was business? Major asked. McQueen said that he didn't have to worry, as his backers were Italian and so he did not have any dealings with London, after which Major turned away from him.⁶⁴ Later, he said of Major, "He's such an idiot. A real plank. I mean, you want someone with bollocks to rule the country. My mum could do better. She'd get the country shipshape."[65]

McQueen related his experiences at Downing Street to Colin McDowell, who interviewed him for the *Sunday Times*. Although the fashion journalist and historian had had his doubts about McQueen, now he believed him to be "the most stimulating designer of the moment." He outlined how he thought McQueen could be the savior of British fashion—"his desire to sweep away the barriers of taste might be the kick-start that fashion needs as we approach the millennium," he said. "Then again, bearing in mind that fashion is a conservative world, he could well end up going nowhere, yet another short, brilliantly iconoclastic career beaten by the system." McQueen was honest about his frustrations. What was the point in just reproducing classic, tasteful designs? "If people want a boring coat, they can go to DKNY," he said. He thought that it was his mission to try and change the way people thought about clothes. "I'm not an aggressive person," he said, "but I do want to change attitudes. If that means I shock people, that's their problem." (After the show McQueen said that he had received a fax from Christ Church complaining that the show was unnecessarily perverse.) He was ambitious—he confided to McDowell that one day he would like to follow John Galliano to Paris and take over the house of Yves Saint Laurent—but stated that he would rather give up everything than compromise. "I don't know whether I can survive in fashion without murdering somebody," he said.[66]

From London Lee flew to New York, where he was due to restage a more "aggressive" *Dante* at a synagogue on Norfolk Street, on the Lower East Side. New York Fashion Week was in a state of stagnation—one observer commented that it possessed all the excitement of a "Labor Day telethon"[67]—and so McQueen's spectacle injected a much-needed shot of adrenaline into the season. ("At this point it's a matter of what sucked the least," sneered one fashion writer.[68]) McQueen's reasoning was that his label had already amassed a good amount of sales in Milan and Paris and so he could afford to put on a show that was more about creativity than commercialism. "This show is really more to promote the label and maybe scare a few people—though hopefully they won't cancel their orders," he said. "New York has this very brash image, but then the clothing is so conservative. I think it's good to bring a little excitement to New York."[69] Since arriving in Manhattan, McQueen had experienced his own fair share of excitement. Two male models—who were straight—offered to sleep with him if he could help advance their careers. Despite his reputation, he told them to "fuck off" as he found the idea "disgusting."[70]

Such was the buzz surrounding the show that, despite a snowstorm, it attracted New York's fashion elite, including *Vogue*'s Anna Wintour and André Leon Talley. Kate Moss modeled a pair of bumsters and Helena Christensen wore a black lace dress and military jacket. David Bowie had just got in touch to ask if Lee could work on some designs for his forthcoming tour—the rock star sported a McQueen Union Jack waistcoat at his appearance at the Phoenix Festival in July and the following year the designer created a Union Jack coat for the *Earthling* album cover. Upmarket American outlets such as Neiman Marcus and Bergdorf Goodman placed thousands of dollars' worth of orders, while in the UK the influential Joan Burstein of Browns declared that she had bought McQueen's collection for the first time.

In April 1996, McQueen flew to Florence for a shoot for American *Elle*. Lee's friend Marin Hopper, the magazine's fashion director, had persuaded her father, the actor Dennis Hopper, to photograph McQueen's latest collection. There was only one problem: the actor had just married his fifth wife, Victoria, and the couple were on their honeymoon. According to Lee, Victoria "was getting pissed off. We were all in the same hotel as them, and these people wanted time alone." Lee served as the art director on the shoot and almost as soon as the actor started to take photographs the two men began to argue. "We have a bit of a blow-up . . . me and Dennis, because I give people one chance and if it doesn't work, then I'm not gonna be bothered again," recalled Lee. "I said something and he said, 'Who's doing the fucking shooting here?' and I went, 'Easy tiger, carry on . . .' and I never spoke to him after that." But then, on the last night of his stay in Florence, Lee was asked out to dinner by Hopper, who then invited him out to Los Angeles. "I was sure I would be the last person they'd want to see after their honeymoon," he said.[71] Yet according to Marin, Dennis Hopper had nothing but respect for McQueen. "My father thought he was a beyond-talented genius," she said.[72]

From Italy, McQueen flew to Japan, where his clothes were in high demand. Surely, asked one New York journalist, it was only a matter of time before the super-successful designer had his own perfume? "Yeah," replied the quick-witted McQueen. "It's called Eau de Scat."[73]

CHAPTER SEVEN

Where the dreams of your life in fashion become reality.
—*Lee McQueen on couture*

On 13 July 1996, a balmy Saturday evening, Lee was at a party given by Lee Copperwheat at his flat in Cheshire Street, just off Brick Lane, London. He was in a good mood and, after a few drinks, felt himself beginning to relax. As the party progressed he noticed a tall, dark, handsome young man wearing a blue Copperwheat Blundell bomber jacket, a pair of tight blue and black striped Copperwheat Blundell cigarette pants and Fila trainers, who seemed to catch his eye whenever he looked in his direction. McQueen, who was wearing a pair of green army pants and a Burberry shirt, watched as the man knocked back drink after drink and staggered into the bathroom, where he was sick. Lee, who was concerned about his well-being, followed him out to the garden, where he helped him vomit once more, holding his head and stroking his back as he did so. "It's better out than in," he told him.

The man was Murray Arthur, and when he began to feel better he thanked Lee for his kindness. The two men started to talk and it was immediately obvious that they were attracted to each other. "I thought he was the nicest person ever," said Murray, who was then twenty-six and working in the Donna Karan shop in Bond Street. The couple left the party and returned to Lee's loft in Hoxton Square. The next day McQueen took one look at Murray's cheap plastic watch and pulled off his own, one from Paul Smith. "You've got a shit watch," he said, passing his over to Murray, "so I better see you again because I want that watch back." They arranged to have another date later that week, on Thursday, 18 July. They met at the Freedom Bar in Soho and had a drink with Roland Mouret, but Murray felt so nervous and tongue-tied he hardly said a word. From there they went to Lee's favorite Chinese restaurant on Shaftesbury Avenue.

"Lee knew that I had just arrived in London—I grew up in a village outside Aberdeen—and said that he would understand if I didn't want to take it any further, if I just wanted to have fun," said Murray. "I told him that I would like to take it further as I really liked him. I had the next day off work and I remember going back to the hideous, tiny flat I shared in Camberwell and phoning a friend and saying that I thought I was in love, that I had met the person I wanted to spend the rest of my life with. I liked his personality, his incredibly infectious laugh. I liked being around him; he made me laugh more than anything else. He had the most amazing colour eyes, so beautiful, and they would change colour—often you get that with people with blue eyes—sometimes they would be pale, sometimes they would be dark."

Lee went on a quick trip to the factory in Italy where his clothes were made—he usually traveled there twice a month—and when he returned to London he met up again with Murray for a walk on Hampstead Heath. There, the two men carved their names into the bark of a tree. Three weeks after that first meeting Lee asked his new boyfriend to move into his loft with him. Murray would go to work each morning and he would often come back to find Lee still hard at work in the studio. "I remember once in the middle of the night he told me he had just made a sleeve out of one piece of fabric for the first time and I was like, 'Big deal,'" he said.

Lee was enamored of Murray and within a few days of meeting him he had given him the silver pendant that he always wore around his neck with "McQueen" engraved on it. Murray adored Lee's dog, Minter, and taught him how to sit, lie down, pat and roll over. "We had loads of fun and I have really happy memories of those times," he said.[1] When Murray got a promotion at Donna Karan from sales assistant to supervisor, Lee wrote him a postcard telling him that he loved him and that he was happy for him. After Murray returned home to Aberdeen for a few days, Lee wrote another card that said, "I think of you often, especially when I go to bed and when I wake up and you're not there."[2]

Soon after they first met Murray told Lee about his epilepsy, a condition from which he had suffered since the age of twenty. If Murray had a seizure—and sometimes he would have two or three a day—Lee would hold him still, stroke his head and make sure his boyfriend did not swallow his tongue. "I'm there to bring him back out of it," he said. "No other queen in the world would, I don't think."[3] McQueen, through Isabella, introduced Murray to Dr. Charles Levinson, the husband of Detmar's sister Selina Blow, who arranged for him to see the best brain specialist in Britain. "Lee used to worry himself sick," said Murray. "He did everything he could and was very compassionate about my condition."[4]

One Saturday, after a heavy night out, Lee told Murray that he had booked himself into a tattoo parlor on St. John Street, Clerkenwell. McQueen loved tattoos—he had his first one, an intricate image of a koi, etched into his chest soon after moving into the loft in Hoxton Square. Mira Chai Hyde remembers going with him to the tattoo parlor to hold his hand. "He was squeezing my hand so hard I came out with fingernail marks," she said. "My hand was so bloody afterwards."[5] That day in 1996, McQueen planned to get a tattoo of a peony together with Murray's name beside it. Lee asked his boyfriend if he would let the tattoo artist inscribe his name on to his arm. ("His and hers" tattoos—or in this case "his and his"—were very much in vogue at the time, and the celebrity couple of the moment, Patsy Kensit and Liam Gallagher, had proclaimed their love by having each other's names etched onto their skin.) Murray agreed and had "McQueen" tattooed on the upper part of his right arm in black ink. But when Lee sat down in the tattooist's chair he suddenly changed his mind, telling his boyfriend that the process was too painful and he was too hungover to go through with it. Later that night Murray went to a party where he met some friends from Scotland; when they saw the tattoo they told him that one day he would regret it.[6]

Often, Murray and Lee would spend the weekend at Hilles, Isabella and Detmar's house in the country. "He comes up maybe four times a year, maybe half a dozen, and completely takes it over," said Isabella. "As soon as he arrives it becomes his office and it becomes his play den and he relaxes and he feels very at home."[7] Isabella had arranged for herself and Lee to have lessons in falconry. "I think he goes into another world when he's up there, especially when he's with his birds," said his mother.[8] Isabella said this was one of "the most exciting" things the friends had ever done together. She employed two local mechanics who were "obsessed about training wild birds," particularly Harris's hawks.[9] "McQueen was a natural and soon had them flying and landing on his arm," said Detmar. "He liked the big leather glove he had to wear to protect himself from their claws."[10] Murray was less keen—even pigeons scared him, he said—but he would love to stand back and watch as Lee handled the birds.

Visiting Hilles was, said Murray, always "quite heavenly." The couple would stay in the room with the four-poster and pull the curtains around the bed so that they felt secure in a self-created, womb-like space. They would sleep in for as long as they wanted, and in the mornings, wander down to the kitchen to make themselves a cup of tea. They liked going for walks with Minter in the lush countryside and sitting around a hot fire. One weekend Princess Michael of Kent, who lived in nearby Nether Lypiatt Manor, arrived for Sunday lunch. "She was really nice, and being really funny and cracking loads of dirty jokes and suddenly there was the most god-awful smell," said Murray. "I lifted up the tablecloth and there was the biggest dog shit you can ever imagine—Minter had just done it under the table. I turned to Isabella and told her what had happened and she told me to go and get the housekeeper. I put my napkin over the top of it and excused myself from the table. By the time I came back Princess Michael of

Kent was laughing her head off, saying, 'Don't worry, my husband [Prince Michael of Kent] is president of Battersea Dogs Home. We've got dog shit all over our house, you wouldn't believe the mess.' "[11]

Towards the end of the summer of 1996, McQueen was busy preparing his next collection and show, which he had decided to call *Bellmer La Poupée*. The inspiration had come from the work of Hans Bellmer, a German artist who in McQueen's words "dissected dummies and reconstructed them."[12] In 1933, Bellmer had originally been motivated to make his strange-looking dolls in response to the cult of the body beautiful promulgated by the Nazi Party. Some of the unsettling images he produced, such as the 1936 photograph *The Doll*, a surreal shot of a disembodied female torso missing arms and legs, resembled the work of Joel-Peter Witkin. Both artists appealed to Lee's fascination with the macabre and his unconventional view of what was aesthetically pleasing. As he would write just days before his death, "Beauty can come from the . . . strangest of places, even the most disgusting places."[13] In order to transfer these ideas to the catwalk, Lee turned to his friend Shaun Leane for help. McQueen wanted him to design a shackle that would fit onto a model's wrists and legs, which would force her to walk like one of Bellmer's dolls. The friends would meet up for a drink and Lee would sometimes draw a sketch of what he wanted on the back of a beer mat.

McQueen asked his friend Dai Rees to create face- and headpieces for the show. Rees remembers taking them round to the Hoxton Square studio, where he met Isabella for the first time. Lee knew that Dai had studied ceramics and so when his friend turned up at the loft and said he had something to show him McQueen assumed he meant pieces made from pottery. He was surprised when he saw Dai take out three head cages made from quill feathers. "There was this huge mirror at the bottom of the stairs and Lee and Issie were both having a laugh trying them on," he said. "I remember Lee saying, 'This will really fuck Philip [Treacy] off,' as he knew that Philip and I didn't get on. At that point, Lee asked me to produce another five of these in specific colours." On his second visit to the studio Lee asked Dai if he could make a number of leather pieces for the neck and face. Rees told him that he had never worked with leather, but Lee convinced him that he would be able to do so. Two weeks later Dai returned with ten hand-molded leather neck and face braces with quill feathers and Lee "was blown away by them."[14]

Lee had recently seen Richard Wilson's installation *20:50* at the Saatchi Gallery, a specially constructed room that had been filled with highly reflective sump oil, and wanted to somehow create the same effect on the catwalk. "How can we do it?" he repeatedly asked Simon Costin. Once the venue had been organized—the Horticultural Halls in Victoria—Simon went along to inspect the site. "I went with a plastic sheet and some pieces of two-by-two which I screwed together and filled with water," said Simon. "We jumped up and down next to it to see how solid the floor was, and to see if it would ripple." He then made a frame two feet high and 150 feet long with a black lining, "as large as I could make it within the space and still get the audience in—the aim was to make it look like a black mirror." It seemed as though it would work perfectly, but then the sponsors of the show, Tanqueray gin, demanded that their logo should be on view. "I thought why not do a black logo for them and so that's what we did," said Simon. "It was so black you couldn't see it."[15]

Helping McQueen to finish the pieces ready for the show was Sarah Heard (now Sarah Burton), a student at Saint Martins who had been introduced to Lee through one of her tutors, Simon Ungless. Born in 1974 in Prestbury, outside Manchester, Sarah started drawing clothes when she was a girl. "I remember buying *Vogue* from a very early age," she said. "I would tear out the pages and put them on my bedroom wall. The early Calvin Klein pictures, Avedon pictures . . . My art teacher said, 'You have to go to Saint Martins.'" In her third year at the college, Ungless arranged for her to have a year's internship with McQueen, an experience she described as "beyond inspiring." "I realized almost immediately: pattern-cutting, that was what it was all about," she said. "It was like a baptism of fire. Saint Martins taught me a lot but a year at McQueen you discovered the whole process."[16] Lee would cut the patterns and Sarah would help make the clothes. She recalls how McQueen showed her how to cut an S-bend and how to put in a zip. "I remember him being able to have a piece of flannel on the floor and being able to draw a pair of trousers with a piece of chalk, cut it out, sit at a sewing machine and 'Rrrrr,' sew up a perfect pair of trousers just by eye," she said. "It gave you goosebumps."[17]

The autumn of 1996 was an intense, highly stimulating time for McQueen. On 12 September, *Jam: Style + Music + Media*, an interactive exhibition that aimed to re-create a snapshot of nineties urban culture, opened at the Barbican. A whole room was devoted to McQueen, beginning the process by which the designer's work was appropriated and legitimized by the lofty world of museums. Lee was asked by the curators how he would describe his work. "Eclectic verging on the criminal," he said. And his attitude towards life? "Criminal verging on the eclectic."

Liz Farrelly, one of the organizers of the exhibition, explained how fashion could be viewed as art. "Forget the accusations of elitism and irrelevance which are levelled at cutting-edge British fashion," she wrote in *Design Week*. "When it comes to the crunch, here are designers and image-makers whose personal vision inspires and produces commercial successes and where self-motivation equals creativity." Citing the work of McQueen, Hussein Chalayan, David Sims and Juergen Teller, she believed that the "frocks look just as believable hanging on a wall as they do on a model, and the photographs look doubly so, freed from the confines of magazine spreads. In fashion, novelty has been superseded by innovation and self-expression, and that's what I call art."[18] When critics asked McQueen the question "Is fashion art?", he would dismiss it with a sneer; all he was doing was making clothes for people to wear, he said. But over the course of the next two decades various museums—the Moderna Museet, in Stockholm (*Fashination*, 2004–2005); the Metropolitan Museum in New York (*Savage Beauty*, 2011) and the V&A (*Savage Beauty*, 2015)—would display his designs in a way that presented them not so much as utilitarian items of clothing but as exquisitely crafted, deeply engaging pieces of art.

At the same time as the Barbican exhibition, McQueen had been asked to contribute a piece of work to the Florence Biennale's city-wide exhibition, *Il Tempo e la Moda* (*Time and Fashion/Looking at Fashion*). Curated by Germano Celant, Ingrid Sischy and Pandora Tabatabai Asbaghi, the exhibition analyzed the relationship between art and fashion. A number of contemporary fashion designers were asked to work with artists to produce specially commissioned pieces for the Biennale: Karl Lagerfeld and Tony Cragg; Gianni Versace and Roy Lichtenstein; Azzedine Alaïa and Julian Schnabel; Helmut Lang and Jenny Holzer; Miuccia Prada and Damien Hirst; Jil Sander and Mario Merz and Rei Kawakubo and Oliver Herring. When the curators approached McQueen he made it clear that he wanted to work with the photographer Nick Knight, whose startling images he had seen in magazines like *i-D* and *The Face*.

The two men had first met at a *Vogue* Christmas party, a meeting that Nick described as "quite romantic in a way." Both of them were shy and it was clear each of them respected, even worshipped, the other's work; later that same Christmas, McQueen sent Knight a fax saying, "Happy Christmas, Alexander McQueen." Lee made contact again in the summer of 1996 and they met up to talk about ideas. Nick wanted to produce a piece of work based on the sex ads at the back of porn magazines, an idea that intrigued McQueen. One of the recurring themes of McQueen's work, he said, was the idea of hidden beauty. "He seems very preoccupied with the notion of what's inside, the hidden beauty that comes out after destroying the surface beauty," said Knight, in an interview with Charlotte Cotton for the British Library's Oral History of Photography project. "He comes from a working-class background, but he is producing for the elite. From the difficult comes the beautiful, like the lotus flower blossoming in stagnant water."[19] One of the images they settled on for the Biennale, which opened on 20 September, was a portrait of McQueen's head exploding, an image inspired by the David Cronenberg film *Scanners* and one that was reproduced in the November 1996 issue of *The Face*; next to the photograph the captions reads, "Alexander McQueen, Victim of the Fashion Industry, 1996."[20] When, in the same issue of *The Face*, writer Ashley Heath asked McQueen about his best wind-up, the designer replied, "Getting my head blown up by Nick Knight in these new pictures, that's my best wind-up yet. I mean, that's not what I'm like." Really? "Well, when I've done too much charlie [cocaine] I feel like getting my head blown up but, no, that's not what I'm like. Not really."[21] McQueen and Knight would continue to work together over the course of the designer's career. "It has been quite a strange relationship," Knight told Charlotte Cotton in the late nineties, "and I am not sure how it will end."[22]

On 27 September 1996, at the Horticultural Halls, the fashion world experienced a catwalk show that looked like an artwork in itself. The audience watched as the first model walked down a flight of stairs and onto the mirrored black surface; the realization that the girl was walking through water drew a collective gasp of surprise and delight from the crowd. The models, including Kate Moss, Jodie Kidd and Stella Tennant, wore Perspex wedge-heeled shoes and "they appeared, quite literally, to walk on water."[23] The reference to water also held a more personal meaning for McQueen and his team. *La Poupée* was dedicated to David Mason, a close friend of Katy England's, who had committed suicide by filling his backpack full of bricks and throwing himself into the Thames. The theme of the transiency of life was expressed at the end of the show when a model staggered down the watery catwalk with a transparent geometrical structure enclosing her head and half her body; inside fluttered dozens of moths. (The imagery would be explored further in McQueen's show *Voss* in September 2000.)

The most controversial aspect of the show, however, was McQueen's decision to send a black model, Debra Shaw, down the catwalk wearing the shackle-like piece of body jewelry made by Shaun

Leane. The audience went wild, but later the designer was accused of using the imagery of slavery to sell clothes, something he vehemently denied. "When Debra Shaw, the black model, walked contorted in a frame that image had nothing to do with slavery," he said. "It was the idea of the body reconstructed like a doll-like puppet."[24] The use of a photograph of a skeletally thin African child on the back of a jacket also drew some criticism from Christian Aid. The head of campaigns, John Jackson, said, "It is basically simply crass. If this jacket is designed to shock then it's worked on me. I think it is tasteless to turn famine into a fashion statement."[25]

However, the majority of the reviews were ecstatic. McQueen's show was the highlight of London Fashion Week, wrote Iain R. Webb in *The Times*. "Exquisitely beaded Jazz Age fringed dresses looked remarkably sophisticated, as did clingy transparent dresses embroidered with cherry blossom and swirling Chinese dragons," he said. "Likewise his viciously tailored trouser suits in rose-pink brocade and icy-white matt sequins. However, McQueen could not resist a little anarchic fun, so he sliced them up with zip fasteners, or spray-canned them with slashes of brightly coloured paint."[26] Tamsin Blanchard of the *Independent* said that *La Poupée* was McQueen's "most accomplished collection to date." The whole London fashion scene seemed reinvigorated due to the creative genius of Hussein Chalayan, Antonio Berardi, Clements Ribeiro, "and above all, Alexander McQueen," whose clothes were both wearable and desirable. "Every pair of fine brocade trousers, each dusty pink catsuit, and every stitch of his bias-cut evening dresses, was masterful," she said. "A fine, sheer mesh dress embroidered with dragons; a razor-sharp, shiny, sea-green trouser suit; a bias-cut dress with a train trailing out into the dark ripples of water. This was a collection to leave no one in doubt that the designer could take on a couture house and breathe fresh life into it." Sitting in the audience were representatives from LVMH, the French multinational luxury goods conglomerate that owned both Dior and Givenchy, figures who "could not have failed to be impressed" by McQueen's extraordinary vision.[27]

• • •

Throughout the summer of 1996 there had been rumors about possible changes at Givenchy. In July, Gianfranco Ferré announced his departure from Dior, a move that opened up a series of tantalizing possibilities. At first it was thought that Vivienne Westwood had secured the top job at Dior, something she was forced to deny, while other names mentioned in the press included Marc Jacobs, Martin Margiela, Jean Paul Gaultier and Christian Lacroix. When McQueen was asked whether he would take the position if it were offered to him he said, "There is only one Paris fashion job for me—Yves Saint Laurent."[28] Joyce McQueen called the prospect of her son taking over a Paris atelier "a fairy-tale," while Lee himself said of couture, "It is where the dreams of your life in fashion become reality."[29] In an interview with *Le Figaro*, the head of LVMH, Bernard Arnault, outlined what he was looking for: "I want modern creativity in the spirit of Christian Dior himself," he said.[30]

At the end of the summer Arnault offered the position to John Galliano, which in turn left open a vacancy at the esteemed couture house established by Count Hubert Taffin de Givenchy in 1952. Famous for dressing Audrey Hepburn, Givenchy was known for the elegance and refined tailoring of his clothes. According to the entry in *McDowell's Directory of Twentieth Century Fashion*, words that McQueen himself would have read, Givenchy "was a designer of lasting quality who, without gimmicks or vulgarity, would create clothes in the great tradition of couture."[31] Would McQueen go to Givenchy? When the designer was contacted by Constance White of the *New York Times* at the end of September with this very question his response was, "I can't say nothing."[32] All he would tell her was that she would have to await an announcement on 14 October. McQueen had been contacted by representatives of LVMH in September, but as Sarah Burton remembers, "Lee thought he was being given a job to design a handbag for Vuitton."[33] The news that he was being offered the job of creative director of Givenchy unsettled him to such an extent that he had to go to the bathroom. "I heard that after they phoned him he put the phone down and had a shit and came back to the phone," said Andrew Groves.[34] "The first thing he did was he called me from the toilet at home," said Murray. "He said, 'I have been offered this job in Paris, if I take it will you come with me?' I said, 'Yes, of course, why not?' "[35]

McQueen felt ambivalent about taking the job and, unusually for him, sought out the advice of others. Alice Smith tried to persuade him to turn it down, believing that he would not be able to cope with the elitism of Paris. Isabella Blow, meanwhile, hoping that Lee would secure her services as a consultant, pleaded with him to take it.

In the end, Lee agreed and LVMH sent him a draft contract. At the beginning of October, Detmar Blow rang his accountant John Banks, as he knew he spoke French, and asked him whether he could cast his eye over the paperwork. Lee and John spoke over the phone and made an arrangement for the accountant to travel from his home in Gloucestershire to the studio in Hoxton Square. When John arrived in Shoreditch in the early evening of 8 October he was told that Lee was in bed. McQueen finally emerged and told John that although he was supposed to travel to Paris to sign the contract the next day he had decided not to take the job. Just then, the telephone in the studio rang—it was one of the representatives of Givenchy on the telephone. Lee didn't know what to do.

McQueen passed the telephone to John, who told the executive from Givenchy that he would call him back in half an hour. The two men then sat down and talked. The problem with the job, said McQueen, was the money—it wasn't enough. "I think they were offering something like £300,000 a year," said John. "Lee wanted more. I said, 'What, £400,000?' No, he wanted more. '£500,000?' No, that was probably too much. So we settled on something like £450,000. He also said that they wanted him to sign a three-year contract, but he only wanted to do it for two years. So I got on the phone and said, 'These are the things that Lee wants. He's not coming to Paris tomorrow unless he gets them.' The man had to go off and speak to Mr. Arnault and about half an hour later he called back and said it was a deal. But he also said that Mr. Arnault wanted to know whether Lee was committed to this. I asked Lee and he said yes, he was. I put the phone down and said it was all sorted but that was when Lee told me that he wanted me to go with him the next day."

John returned home to Gloucestershire to pick up his passport and early the next morning took a train to London. He bought a copy of *The Times* at Swindon station and opened it to see the headline "French Fashion Has Designs on Britons," and underneath a story about how McQueen had been offered the job at Givenchy. "I don't know if they realized how close they got to getting this wrong, as they had obviously got this ready to print before I had had a conversation with Lee," said John.

On 9 October, Lee met John in the Eurostar terminal at Waterloo to get a morning train to Paris. Accompanying them on the trip, in standard class, was Isabella Blow, who had turned up with six or seven hatboxes and a couple of suitcases. As Lee and John tried to go through the contract, Isabella started to wander up and down the train looking for friends who happened to be traveling to Paris; it was Fashion Week and so she hoped there might be other designers or models she could talk to on the train. Twenty or so minutes later, Isabella returned with a young model and the two women proceeded to strip down to their underwear and swap clothes. The women thought this was a hoot; McQueen was far from amused. "She's doing my fucking head in," Lee muttered to John.

The party from London was met by a car at the Gare du Nord, but as Isabella's proliferation of hatboxes and suitcases would not fit in the boot, a taxi had to be ordered to carry the excess luggage. "We went to Givenchy, and had lunch with the managing director," said John. "I remember Lee being really quiet and Isabella did most of the talking. Then she went off, as she was staying in an apartment. Lee went to see Mr. Arnault and I sat down with the lawyers. In the middle of this, Isabella called to say she had locked herself out of the flat, and Givenchy had to find a locksmith for her. We were running through the documents with Lee and the lawyers when Isabella burst into the room with a bizarre hat on, all wires and beads." Finally, in the early evening, McQueen signed the contract and John left the building to get his train, while Isabella and Lee enjoyed a celebratory dish of caviar, washed down with vodka and champagne.[36] From now on, when McQueen returned to Paris, he would no longer have to take the metro or hail a taxi, as Givenchy had provided him with a Mercedes sedan complete with a chauffeur.

McQueen stayed in Paris to enjoy the shows. That night, after signing the contract, Lee, dressed in a suit and a pair of trainers, went with Isabella to see Rifat Özbek at the Moulin Rouge and Ann Demeulemeester, whose simple jersey dresses were worn by a parade of androgynous models. On 10 October he took his place in the front row at the Christian Lacroix show, "the master of eccentric French dressing," who reportedly had turned down the Givenchy job earlier in the summer. While in Paris, McQueen gave an interview to Hilary Alexander of the *Daily Telegraph*, who described him as "tousle-haired, unshaven, wearing a strange conglomeration of what I take to be pyjamas, but turns out to be a Comme des Garçons shirt and 'Bosnian' combat pants." Lee told the newspaper's fashion editor of his admiration for the chairman of LVMH. "Arnault is a man of unusual vision," he said. "He has seen videos of all my shows and he understands what I am trying to do, better than most of the press. He is also committed to creativity 120 per cent. Otherwise, I wouldn't be here." McQueen accepted that his workload would be heavy— he would have to produce four collections a year for Givenchy (two haute couture, and two ready-to-wear), plus two shows a year under his own label—but he said that he felt far from "overwhelmed." He had reached a certain level of maturity to know what was appropriate for certain audiences and said, "Of course, I'm not going to have 'bumsters' on the [avenue] George V [the location of the Givenchy atelier]. I may be quite mad on the public circuit, but I've got my head screwed on—tight with a wrench."[37]

Before John Banks, who would continue to work as McQueen's

accountant for the next four years, had left Gloucestershire for Paris, Detmar Blow had told him to make sure that Isabella "got something" from the deal.[38] Indeed, on 1 November it was reported in *The Times* that Isabella had secured a job with her friend, in charge of preparing advertising campaigns for Givenchy.[39] "Isabella did talk about a role for her at the time of the Givenchy deal, but this would not have been with Givenchy, but between Lee and herself," said John.[40] When John Banks tentatively questioned McQueen about such a role, he supposedly replied, "Issie and I are not about money."[41]

Isabella had already imagined the kind of work she could do at Givenchy—she would serve as McQueen's muse and she also wanted to launch a salon, "as they did in the eighteenth century," she said, or a "kind of Warhol, Factory thing."[42] It was, in Detmar's words, "utterly devastating" for Isabella when she discovered that McQueen decided not to include her in his plans. It was, in Detmar's eyes, nothing short of a betrayal. "People said Issie shouldn't get so worked up about it," said Detmar. "Fuck off, well she was and nothing was going to convince her otherwise. But the problem was Issie couldn't fall out with him because she was addicted to McQueen. She didn't want to lose the clothes."[43] During one interview, when Isabella had enjoyed a few mugs of Bollinger champagne, she stated that in future she wanted to get paid for her role as muse. "If Alexander uses some of my ideas in his show, and he has, I don't get paid; he does," she said.[44] "There was a moment of bad blood on her part," said film-maker John Maybury, friends with both Lee and Isabella. Fundamentally, McQueen was "quite a pragmatic person and when someone is fragile and unreliable it's kinder not to drag them into a situation that could overwhelm them."[45]

Daphne Guinness—the socialite who was friends with both Lee and Isabella—believed that although Isabella had been terribly hurt by the failure of Givenchy to give her some kind of role, she saw the fault lying more with the couture house than with McQueen. "It wasn't his fault," she said. "She was more upset with the system. There was a place for her as a kind of Amanda Harlech to John Galliano, but they never had the imagination to employ her. I know from him that he was trying to steady his position. I think he was also trying to make Isabella be more responsible."[46] McQueen also needed people around him who did not jar his nerves, assistants who were stable, reliable and not prone to flights of fancy.

The news of McQueen's appointment as design director of Givenchy was greeted with astonishment by the British press. Not only was he so young and relatively inexperienced—at twenty-seven he had only produced eight collections—but, in contrast to the refined and genteel house of Givenchy, he was a "self-proclaimed East End yob." The *Guardian's* profile of him, headlined "Bull in a Fashion Shop," outlined how he was "more East End bruiser than haute couturier." Journalist Susannah Frankel interviewed his former tutor Louise Wilson, who called him a "creative genius" and highlighted his extraordinary tailoring skills. Yet there were other people within the fashion industry who voiced "doubts, worrying that McQueen and Galliano" were mere "pawns in a sophisticated publicity stunt."[47]

After a few days in Paris, McQueen took the train back to London. On 21 October, he went to the opening of a new Valentino shop in Sloane Street; a photograph taken by Dafydd Jones showed an ecstatically happy Lee standing next to Murray Arthur. After the opening the couple went back to Supernova Heights, Liam Gallagher's house in Steeles Road, Belsize Park. "That was quite a night," said Murray.[48] The following evening they attended the British Fashion Awards at the Royal Albert Hall, where McQueen won his first British Designer of the Year award. "I never thought it was important to have recognition from your colleagues, but when it finally happens it justifies everything," Lee said, after being presented with the award.[49]

Some designers reacted with astonishment at the news, as they believed McQueen to be vastly overrated. Sir Hardy Amies, who attended the awards ceremony—the "naffest thing I've ever seen," he sneered—said that he was dismayed by the recent appointments. "They have John Galliano for Christian Dior, and this other yobbo for Givenchy," he said. "And they have fallen into this trap that Paris sets for them to get publicity to sell scents. I don't know anybody who would wear that stuff—but then I don't dance around in nightclubs any more."[50] One anonymous student or staff member at Saint Martins aired their opinion in a piece of graffiti on a newspaper cutting kept by the college's library. "From what I remember of him—I find it hard to believe he's got this far! He seemed to be really dippy," they scribbled next to an interview with McQueen in the *Independent on Sunday*. "I think it's all a *con*!!"[51]

Lee could hardly begin to imagine how the Givenchy deal would change his life. "I thought, all this time I've been freaking out about not being able to feed myself, and it was just, like, instantaneous," he said of his newfound wealth.[52] His father had once advised him that if he wanted to sell clothes he should get a job on a market stall; after the news of the Givenchy deal he reportedly turned around to his father and said, "Now, that's the way to sell clothes."[53] With his first paycheck from Givenchy, Lee finally paid back the money his aunt Renee had lent him to attend Saint Martins six years earlier.

Back in London, McQueen started to gather his team together to take to Paris: Katy England, Trino Verkade, Simon Costin, Sam Gainsbury, Sarah Burton, Shaun Leane, lighting expert Simon Chaudoir, Sebastian Pons and design assistant Catherine Brickhill. "I chose these people because they are special and individual, the very best in their own professions," he said. "It's like a soufflé really: if none of the ingredients are right, you get sludge; but if they are right, the whole thing rises."[54] McQueen also found a position for his boyfriend, Murray. "Within a few days he had said, 'Come and work with me,'" said Murray. "And I basically went into work on Thursday and told them I was finishing on Saturday. Because I had studied business at college Lee was like, 'You can do the accounts.' I also helped with the PR and did anything that needed to be done."[55] When McQueen and his employees arrived in Paris, one French journalist called them "street urchins," which slightly upset them at the time. "But looking back on it we were," said Catherine Brickhill. "We were in bleached jeans, zip tops and there was a healthy disrespect for the house."[56]

Since leaving home Lee had lived in a series of squats, studios and rented or borrowed flats, places he had been forced to leave because the owners wanted to refurbish or sell or move back in themselves; now he wanted somewhere he could feel secure. Just as he was beginning to look for a house in north London he was contacted by the *Independent on Sunday* who asked him if he would be interviewed for the regular Ideal Homes column. The question-and-answer feature ran in the newspaper at the beginning of November 1996. His ideal house would be located somewhere secluded on a hillside in Spain, overlooking the sea. "I have an affinity with the sea, because my ruler is Neptune and I am a Piscean," he said. Local amenities would have to include at least one bar, preferably a gay one, with a disco, and a supermarket that sold Marmite, baked beans and beluga caviar. It would be modeled after Le Corbusier's chapel at Ronchamp: "My house would also have a glass roof so I could look up and see the stars when I'm in bed—it's kind of nice when you're with someone you love," he said. It would have five bedrooms and would be constructed from steel three inches thick so "even if there was a nuclear war maybe it wouldn't get blown away." The house would be equipped with three bathrooms, one of which would be made of slate with a sunken bath. "It would have a Gothic, dungeon feel about it and would double as a sauna and a sex playroom," he said. "I'd have harnesses and collar restraints and a few rats scurrying around for added atmosphere. Sound-proofing would be a big feature." In the reception room he would construct a glass table and chairs suspended from the ceiling, "hovering above the floor so your feet wouldn't touch the ground." Also he said he would love a sunken fishpond in the floor of the living room, constructed in a figure eight and with a number of little footbridges over it. The kitchen would be made from stainless steel and granite; he loved to cook, he said, but hated doing the washing up and so he would either get a dishwasher fitted or hire "a family of gypsies" to do it. Ideally, he would not have any neighbors and the garden would stretch to 200 square miles around the house, land that he would let grow wild. The motto above the door of his home would read, "Enter at your own risk."[57]

His flatmate Mira, who was upset at the prospect of him moving out of the loft in Hoxton Square, helped him search for houses. The friends looked at only two places before Lee settled on a three-story Georgian end-of-terrace house at 9 Coleman Fields, Islington. "I said, 'Lee, you've only seen two houses.' I didn't much like the one he had chosen, I thought he could do much better. But he said, 'No, I'm buying it.'"[58] McQueen completed the purchase on 17 December 1996 for £260,000, and spent thousands on renovations. Although his dream of having a sunken fishpond in the living room did not materialize, he did pay for an aquarium to be fitted into the wall of the dining room.

The end of 1996 and the beginning of 1997 were a manic period for McQueen. He had signed the Givenchy contract in mid-October and he only had eleven weeks in which to prepare for his first couture show for the fashion house in January. McQueen and his team commuted between London and a four-bedroom flat near the Place des Vosges. "The apartment to begin with was a little bit bare and it had just been repainted and refurbished," said Catherine Brickhill. "I remember he wanted to take a big pot of red paint and splash it across the whole apartment."[59] The money from Givenchy also allowed Lee to channel funds into his own label, beginning with a move into new business premises, a studio on Rivington Street, just around the corner from Hoxton Square, described by one observer as "*The Young Ones* meets a bypass-protesters' encampment . . . Instead of a curtain, a ragged bit of fabric is pinned over one window. A spray-painted dummy stands in the middle of a floor strewn with old newspapers. A board pinned with pictures of models, running the gamut from Yasmin Le Bon to some young women who manage to make Karen Elson look chocolate-box pretty, leans against the wall of a boxed-in office-within-an-office."[60] Sarah Burton, who rejected a placement with Calvin Klein to work full-time with McQueen, remembers that before Lee started at Givenchy they had one pattern-cutting table that used to belong to BodyMap and Flyte Ostell, "with chairs that didn't reach properly," she said. "When Lee got the Givenchy job, we got chairs that reached the table. And he was really excited because it meant there was money coming in, and he could do things he'd never done before."[61]

Lee had no intention of learning French, but he hoped that he would be able to communicate with *les petites mains* in the atelier using gestures and signs. "I remember being in a fitting with him and he was asking the guy to take in the shoulder, 'un petit pois,' a 'little pea,'" said Simon Ungless.[62] Lee showed him his initial designs for the couture show, but Simon thought they were so bad that he urged him to start again. "You can't expect Alexander McQueen to take over and suddenly it's the greatest thing since sliced bread," Lee said.[63] McQueen's way of working was a shock for many at Givenchy. "Our house has extraordinary know-how, but it's strictly classical," said Richard Lagarde, a senior tailor at Givenchy. "We weren't used to having things shaken up, we had to completely change the way we worked."[64]

In December, Lee and Murray took a break from the preparation of the show to travel to New York for the Metropolitan Museum Costume Institute's gala celebrating the fifty-year anniversary of the founding of the house of Dior. At the dinner that night, the two men chatted to Princess Diana, who wore a John Galliano for Dior navy silk sheath dress, "the one that looked like a nightie," said Murray. Earlier in the day, while at Heathrow Airport, Lee and Murray had decided to order some oysters. McQueen ate one and immediately declared them to be off, but Murray finished the plate, as well as a few glasses of champagne. Murray felt unwell throughout the dinner at the Met and back at the hotel, the newly opened Soho Grand, he had to confine himself to the bathroom. The following night, after Murray had received some treatment from the doctor, McQueen was invited out to dinner with David Bowie and his wife Iman; as his boyfriend was too ill to go out, Lee took along his assistant Trino Verkade. "David phoned the hotel the next day and said he wanted me to come over and meet him, so I went to his apartment, where he was wrapping Christmas presents," said Murray. "He made me two cups of black coffee and showed me this piece of art, a ball that moved around the floor."[65] Bowie told Lee that he "was so impressed by McQueen's designs that he insisted on whipping out his chequebook" to buy some clothes.[66] While in Manhattan, Murray and Lee met up with Shaun Leane and photographs taken at the time show the three men wrapped up in overcoats, standing by the skating rink at Rockefeller Plaza, smiling for the camera.

Back in Paris, McQueen continued to work on the couture collection. He had taken inspiration from both Givenchy's white and gold label and also the mythological story of Jason and the Argonauts, whose mission it was to capture the fleece of the golden ram. Two weeks before the show the French photographer Anne Deniau began to take a series of behind-the-scenes images documenting McQueen at work, a process that would continue over the course of the next thirteen years. She had been working at Givenchy, capturing the backstage of Galliano's shows—she liked, she said, "the panache, the craziness and the unbridled romanticism of Galliano" and she was afraid that she "would not understand Lee." She was wrong, she said. Before she had met him she had been handed a folder containing a few photographs from *La Poupée* and a profile of him. After reading through it she closed the folder and "said the two other words that would come up again and again: 'Strength and fragility. Both, extremes; it won't be easy.'"[67]

On first meeting Lee, Anne realized that he was, like her, a shy person. "When two shy persons meet, they hardly speak," she said. "They are looking at their shoes."[68] Deniau remembers the occasion when late at night on 18 January 1997, the night before the show, the model Eva Herzigova turned up for her final fitting. Lee took one look at her and knew something was wrong. "He walked around her like an animal in a cage, he kneeled, stood up, took two steps back, forward, back again," she said. "He remained still for a moment, then said, 'Scissors,' and started cutting. One sleeve came off, then the other."[69] After the fitting, the designer and photographer shared a cigarette and McQueen asked her what she thought of the collection. Anne told of her likes and dislikes, at which point Lee said, "Yeah, you're right, that's crap, I failed." Anne tried to reassure him—the work was not worthless, she said, and he should give himself some credit, but she did think some of it was unfinished. "It's done now," said Lee. "It's too late."[70] Lee returned to the apartment—described by Eric Lanuit, then the press officer at Givenchy, as "a typical flat of a young English rocker, beer cans everywhere, bowls of crisps, ashtrays full of cigarette butts and joints"[71]—where he and his small team enjoyed more than a few drinks. "We were partying, we had the shoes [from the show] there and we were parading around the house," said Murray. "We were so hungover the next day."[72]

On the day of his first Givenchy show, on 19 January 1997, the atmosphere backstage at the École des Beaux-Arts, where Hubert de Givenchy himself had once been a student, had reached fever pitch. Naomi Campbell had to be fitted with a pair of ram horns that had been sprayed gold, horns which had come from a ram at Hilles with particularly "curly headgear,"[73] while another model had to be patient while a large bull's ring, again sprayed gold, was attached to the insides of her nose. Model Jodie Kidd recalls, "We were all corseted to the nines and I swear to God I thought I was going to have a heart attack because I was so nervous. I can't breathe and he [Lee] is hyperventilating." Catherine Brickhill remembers how cramped the space seemed, with models and stylists and hair and makeup people running around "like crazy." She recalls McQueen "legging it over to Eva Herzigova and cutting the laces on her corset and him saying, 'You fucking bitch' and dragging her to get to her exit on time. She was in tears by the time she was out there. Nobody, I don't think, had treated her that way."[74]

The show, which started an hour late, was presided over by Marcus Schenkenberg, then the world's highest-paid male model, who had been cast as Icarus. Sprayed with gold dust by Mira, and wearing nothing but a giant pair of wings and a loincloth, Schenken-berg watched the proceedings from a stone balcony in the eaves. In the front row sat American *Vogue* editor Anna Wintour, with col-league Hamish Bowles, the designer Azzedine Alaïa, the German photographer Peter Lindbergh, Isabella Blow, sporting a black hat shaped like a satellite dish, and Joyce McQueen, wearing a checked suit from Evans. The reaction to the show was divided. Isabella Blow applauded at every outfit—Jodie Kidd dressed in a white satin coat with an enormous train over a gold bodysuit; a model who looked like Maria Callas (a reference to her role in Pasolini's *Medea*) wearing a white dress and a hairstyle one observer likened to a "black bubble"; and numerous models with bare and gilded nipples. But there were many in the audience who were less than enamored of what they saw on the catwalk. "The ladies of couture . . . were taken aback, it seemed, by the sheer excess of youthful vitality and confusion parad-ing before them in outrageous clothing," wrote Hilton Als in the *New Yorker*. "The distinctly now was clearly passing them by." One French fashion journalist was heard to whisper, "Oo-la-la. If he con-tinues with that kind of styling, he'll lose them," and another said, "Disaster. *Point*."[75]

McQueen gained positive reviews from Hilary Alexander at the *Daily Telegraph*, Susannah Frankel at the *Guardian* and Mimi Spen-cer at the *Evening Standard*, but there were others who were less than kind. "You can't come to Paris and compete with the Valentinos and the Chanels . . . and expect to win at twenty-seven," said Liz Tilberis, the editor in chief of American *Harper's Bazaar*. "It was OK and fine if you showed it in London, but it was too derivative and the tailoring wasn't quite what it should have been."[76] Colin McDowell of the *Sun-day Times* attacked the show for being both "boring" and "terminally naff"—in fact, he said, "the whole thing began to look increasingly like a casting for *Carry On Up Mount Olympus*. It only needed Ken-neth Williams to complete the camp picture of golden breastplates, rams' heads and endless white. It wasn't McQueen's best game by a long way." His advice to McQueen was simple, he said: "Get rid of your stylists and accessory makers—they are spoiling your game—and resist the temptation to hide behind your youth. Yves Saint Laurent was only twenty-one when he took over the house of Dior."[77] The French press was even more vicious. *Le Nouvel Observateur* magazine attacked him for his appearance, "his slightly soiled shirt open at the neck; the chic way he carries a can of beer; and that haircut 'très football-club de Liverpool.' Compared with him, an audience of AC/DC heavy-metal fans would win prizes for couture."[78]

McQueen knew that he could have done better. Instead of a night out partying, Lee had a cup of tea with his mum and then went back to the flat with Murray. "I had one month to make everything and embroider it," he said later. "We got slammed by quite a few people in Paris, which, in a way, I was more upset about because I didn't have control. If it were my own label, I wouldn't care. But it's like I'm working for someone and I can't take an aggressive stand and say, 'Well, I don't give a toss what you think, this is why we did it, this is what we think, it was a McQueen collection.' All of a sudden we had these wallies saying, 'This is not couture, this is a lot of bollocks.' But being about couture is trying to find new clients for couture, and it's hard to do that when you have the press saying this is not for Anne Bass," referring to the Manhattan socialite and philanthropist who regularly spent hundreds of thousands of dollars on pieces of couture. "I mean, I don't want to bloody dress Anne Bass anyway." His new ideal customers were women like Courtney Love and Madonna, he said.[79]

The morning after the show McQueen endured a string of interviews, some of which he found embarrassing. One French journalist asked him what he thought fashion would be like in the year 2000—"I mean, what a load of crap. I mean, I make clothes. I'm not a fortune teller," he said—while another wondered whether, as a designer famous for using corsets, he had ever thought of restraining the male genitalia. Lee burst out laughing at the idea. He had four appointments that day, one with a Saudi Arabian princess who wanted him to design her wedding dress. "I'm really nervous because I can only be myself, and couture's not for the average person on the street. It's about paying £20,000 for a dress." He realized that restraint was one of the secrets of success. "Structure and finesse are what couture is all about," he said. "I don't want to embroider everything in sight or play around with loads and loads of tulle. That has no relevance to today's market. You've got to take couture into the twenty-first century."[80]

The experience of his disappointing first show for Givenchy had left him hurt and more than a little damaged, but he tried to be stoical and put his job in perspective. "I don't see fashion as curing cancer or AIDS—or anything else, for that matter," he said. "At the end of the day, they are just clothes."[81]

CHAPTER EIGHT

You know, we can all be discarded quite easily.
—Lee McQueen

On 1 December 1996, Hedingham Castle in Essex was the setting for an extraordinary photo shoot. A fire was staged inside the building and as the flames appeared to lick the walls of the twelfth-century stone keep, Lee McQueen and Isabella Blow posed in the foreground for the American photographer David LaChapelle. The resulting picture still startles: Lee, dressed in a black corset, long red leather gloves and a generous ocher-colored skirt, and holding a flaming torch, opens his mouth to shout. Isabella, wearing a beautiful, funnel-necked, pale-pink cheongsam and a red, lozenge-shaped Philip Treacy hat, holds the tip of McQueen's gown as she kicks her left leg up in the air. In the background, a horse equipped for battle rears upwards as a dead or injured knight in armor lies by its side. On the far right-hand side of the grass, a human skull suggests the atrocities that have been committed in the past and also serves as an omen for the tragedies of the future.

The shoot had been commissioned by *Vanity Fair* for its twenty-five-page special report, "London Swings Again." The magazine, which featured an image of Liam Gallagher and Patsy Kensit lying on a Union Jack bed on its cover, investigated the phenomenon of what it called "Cool Britannia," a heady blend of genuine cultural excitement and overhyped media invention. "As it was in the mid-sixties, the British capital is a cultural trailblazer, teeming with new and youthful icons of art, pop music, fashion, food, and film," it said. In addition to McQueen and Blow, the magazine photographed and interviewed Damien Hirst, Jodie Kidd, Terence Conran, the Spice Girls, restaurateur Oliver Peyton, the head of Creation Records Alan McGee, Noel and Liam Gallagher of Oasis, *Loaded* editor James Brown, Damon Albarn from Blur, Nick Hornby and Tony Blair (whose New Labour Party would win the general election in May 1997). "The hope that change will bring is outweighing the fear of change," said Blair, whose choice of song during the campaign was D:Ream's "Things Can Only Get Better."[1]

The *Vanity Fair* issue was a response to an influential cover feature in *Newsweek*, published at the beginning of November 1996 and written by Stryker McGuire. The opening sentence of that article traced the birth of London as "the coolest city on the planet" to the moment "two weeks ago, when the grand Paris fashion houses Givenchy and Dior decided to install two brash young London designers as their top couturiers."[2]

Certainly, McGuire, who had first come to Britain in the early eighties, noticed a difference in London when he returned in 1996. The "drab place with great history, poor heating and worse food" had been transformed. The banking industry was booming, "sheer energy . . . crackled through the Square Mile" and money flowed between London and New York; the art scene was thriving and "some London art dealers and collectors, such as Jay Jopling and Charles Saatchi, were more famous than their artists"; architecture was experiencing something of a golden age (the week before the *Newsweek* piece ran plans were announced for the building of "a glorious Ferris wheel on the Thames," now the London Eye); Eurostar, which entered service in 1994, "brought the continent right into the heart of London"; and clubs such as Ministry of Sound "were pulling in young people from Europe and beyond."[3]

Isabella Blow had been commissioned by *Vanity Fair* to work on the issue as a freelance consultant. Although the owners of Hedingham Castle, the Lindsays, had been reluctant to let it out for film or photographic projects, Isabella and Detmar used their connections with the family to secure its use for *Vanity Fair*. "Issie told me that Lee had said, 'Who is the most expensive photographer? David LaChapelle—we will get him to shoot us,'" remembers Detmar. "Issie loved this strategy. It made her laugh. It was classic chutzpah, clever, defiant and proud. The title of the photograph was *Burning Down the House*, which was so true to them both."[4] Isabella would have noticed the resemblance between the keep at Hedingham Castle and the medieval castle that stood in the grounds of her ancestral home at Doddington Park, which she had explored as a child. "Issie loved to play in this perilous, weed-filled tower, conducting dramatic re-creations of medieval rites and myths with her sisters as willing or unwilling participants," wrote Detmar. "The tower was a formative element in Issie's medieval aesthetic."[5] The shoot functioned as an extension of the games Isabella played as a girl, and she would have been thrilled that she could cast McQueen in the role of a transgressive medieval drag queen. However, "Lee's mother, Joyce, was upset by Lee wearing a dress," said Detmar.[6]

Isabella had also managed to persuade Lee to grant an interview to *Vanity Fair* writer David Kamp. "McQueen was a hot media commodity at the time, arrogant and disinclined to give press interviews," said Kamp, "so I couldn't pass up the opportunity for a sit-down." Unfortunately, Kamp had come down with flu, and perhaps without thinking started the interview with the question, "You're obviously not from a wealthy background so I wanted to know if—", at which point McQueen interrupted, "What do you mean, obviously?! What a snobby thing to say." The designer stood up and demanded to know what kind of writer Kamp was since he obviously didn't know much about fashion. "Look, I know I'm not Amy Spindler [the *New York Times* fashion critic]," said Kamp, at which point McQueen began to soften a little. "I love Amy Spindler," he said. "Let me show you some things I showed her." McQueen confessed that he too was feeling a little under the weather, "which accounted for at least some of the irritability," said Kamp, and the interview resumed.

Kamp described McQueen as a man with "buzz-cut hair, a dome of belly visible under his sweater, and little button eyes set atop huge, Muppety cheeks, making him, despite his gruffness, adorable."[7] The designer told the *Vanity Fair* writer that he was influenced by everything around him, even sights that most people would find anathema to fashion. For instance, he had recently spotted a tramp with a string tied around his coat, an image that inspired him to copy the vagrant's silhouette and create a version of the garment with Mongolian-fur collar and cuffs and a belt instead of a piece of string. "I wasn't laughing at him," Lee said. "Who should be laughing? My coat costs £1,200, his cost nothing."[8]

At one point during the meeting, which was held inside Lee's studio, "an unmarked, graffiti-covered building," Kamp told McQueen about a speech made by John Major, on 11 November 1996, at the Lord Mayor's Banquet.[9] Towards the end of his speech the prime minister had referred to the *Newsweek* article as evidence that the country, particularly London, was experiencing something of a creative explosion, and had said, "Our country has taken over the fashion catwalks of Paris," a clear reference to Galliano's and McQueen's appointments. "Did he say that?" responded McQueen. "Ah, fucking plank! I'm not one of his own! He didn't get me there, the fucker! Fuck him! So fucking typical of government! They do nothing to help you when you're trying to do something, then take credit when you're a success! Fuck off!"[10]

Lee and Murray Arthur spent Christmas Day 1996 at the loft in Hoxton Square since the house in Coleman Fields was still being renovated. That Christmas the building was empty, but as Lee started to cook he began to hear strange noises. "Then the fridge door slammed really hard shut," said Murray. "Lee thought that I had come out of the shower and shoved it, but I was still in the shower. Later, we heard footsteps above us and he made me go and have a look. I had to go out the back door to the metal staircase, but it was pitch black and I couldn't see anything. I came down and told him that there were no lights on. He was so scared we had to go to the vicarage on Hoxton Square and knocked on the door and asked if the vicar could come and exorcise the flat."[11] Lee also telephoned Mira, who was staying with her boyfriend, and begged her to come home. "It was well known the loft was haunted," she said. "Friends didn't want to come over and I think Lee heard things. There were a few people who saw stuff, like a black figure of a man with no face, almost like a paper cut-out in the shape of a man. It would appear in the hallway by the loo. Also, we could never get the place warm whatever we did. I spent a fortune, but nothing could keep that place warm. I learnt that the building used to be a furniture finishing factory. The men who were working on the Blue Note building across the street told me that one day they had been working in my loft and went back and all the tools that they had laid out had been reversed."[12]

In February 1997, Lee and Murray moved into their new house. The couple went shopping for furniture to SCP—a contemporary design store in Hoxton—for an expensive Matthew Hilton leather chair and sofa, which Murray subsequently spilled Chinese takeaway on, and to an antique dealer from whom they bought a beautiful, French seventeenth-century carved wooden bed. "Lee had one room just for his clothes," said Mira.[13]

Five days after his first Givenchy show McQueen got the opportunity to experience what it was like to be a model when Rei Kawakubo asked him to walk down the catwalk for her menswear show at the Musée national des Arts d'Afrique et d'Océanie in Paris. The clothes—baggy tartan trousers and light cream suits filled with wadding between the layers—stretched over McQueen's bulky frame making it look, in the words of fashion journalist Stephen Todd, as though he was wearing an outfit cut from a white duvet, a look that was "not particularly slimming." Todd had been assigned to interview McQueen for the Australian gay magazine *Blue* and Lee had so little time to spare—he was heading straight back to London that day—that he had to talk to him backstage at the show. McQueen was, Todd remembers, "extremely polite, not self-consciously so, but naturally so," he said. "This may appear a facile comment, but consider the context: the kid's not long been in the spotlight, is extremely conscious of his weight, about to walk out in front of a room of his critics looking like a *boudin blanc*, and is in the presence of his uncontested idol, Rei Kawakubo, who is quietly prepping the show alongside him. He took the time to speak with me, gave lengthy, considered and coherent answers, thanked me for my time, and ten minutes later there he was on the catwalk."

Over the course of that year the two became friends—Stephen was based in Paris and so whenever Lee came over to work in the French capital the pair would meet up. "He was calm, centred, not interested in the air-kissy side of things," said Stephen. "Physically imposing, he appeared tough, but on second glance there was an evident softness to him. It's this softness I found most touching. It may have been the recognition of working-class lads, but we seemed to bond surprisingly easily, with no agenda. But this was before he'd entered the big business area of Paris fashion. In those days we used to hang out at quite louche gay bars, since I was one of the few Anglophones he knew who lived in Paris full-time. He'd been given an apartment near the Place des Vosges, and would joke about kitting it out with Ikea to upset Arnault and his cronies. I also cheered on his underdog, two-finger salute to authority; again, that may be working-class recognition. But equally, I recognized all too well that he could be his own worst enemy in such matters. I remember going to meet him, not long after he'd taken over at Givenchy, and him walking out into the courtyard, cursing the atelier up on the sixth floor, seeing them as an entrenched expression of a faded French way of doing things, but also as Arnault's army."[14]

At this time Lee also told Stephen, who wrote a feature for *Blueprint* magazine on McQueen and Galliano, about one of the real reasons he had been appointed at Givenchy: publicity. "Let's not bullshit around, the haute couture's not about selling clothes," he said. "Everyone knows it's purely about selling perfume and all that other stuff." As Todd outlined in the piece, "Arnault understood early on that as haughty as fashion may be, it's the tons of sunglasses, scarves, handbags and perfumes that get cash registers swinging. And it's the high profile of the marque which keeps the schmutter turning over." Todd also interviewed Stéphane Wargnier, professor and lecturer in communication at the Institut Français de la Mode, who said, "If we accept that much of haute couture is about squeezing out maximum media coverage—good or bad—then the more spectacular the collection and presentation, the better. And from that point of view the English are the best by far."[15]

In February 1997, Patsy Kensit asked McQueen to "knock up a short-order wedding dress"[16] for her forthcoming nuptials to boyfriend and fellow *Vanity Fair* cover star Liam Gallagher (the couple married on 7 April that year but the relationship, like the "Cool Britannia" phenomenon itself, eventually turned sour). Although Lee said he was too busy—he had two collections to finish before the second week of March—he did invite the couple to his London show for his own label at the end of the month. Called *It's a Jungle Out There*, the show grew out of images he had seen in the *National Geographic* magazine. "I think he found this pile of *National Geographics* in a Sue Ryder charity shop for fifty pence or something," said Simon Costin, McQueen's art director. Specifically, Lee was drawn to the plight of the Thomson's gazelle. "It's a poor little critter—the markings are lovely, it's got these dark eyes, the white of the belly and black with the tan markings on the side, the horns—but it is in the food chain of Africa," he said. "As soon as it's born it's dead, I mean you're lucky if it lasts a few months, and that's how I see human life, in the same way. You know, we can all be discarded quite easily. Nothing depicts it more than animals. I was also trying to say the fragility of the designer's time in the press. You're there, you're gone. It's a jungle out there."[17] He also compared himself to the Thomson's gazelle. "Someone's chasing after me all the time, and if I'm caught, they'll pull me down," he said. "Fashion is a jungle full of nasty, bitchy hyenas."[18]

But the creatures that McQueen sent out onto the catwalk on

the night of 27 February 1997 were not ones that a spectator would describe as either vulnerable or victim-like. The hybrids that stalked the runway—half women, half gazelles—had the ferocity of predators. "The idea is that this wildebeest has eaten this really lovely blonde girl and she's trying to get out," he said.[19]

The week leading up to the show was even more tense than normal. Katy England, who kept a diary of the preparations, had to find men and women to model who could communicate a certain aggressive quality. She called in some girls on Friday, 21 February, and asked them to walk for her. "The way they walk is really important," she said. "They must be able to carry off the clothes, as well as being beautiful . . . We need strong, ballsy girls. The boys are more complicated; we don't want modelly types, we want guys who are weird, brutish and extreme-looking," and so she employed someone to scour the streets for her. The men's clothes arrived from Italy on Sunday and that day she and Lee styled them. "He likes to get more involved with the way the men wear his stuff, because he styles it the way a bloke would wear it," she said. The studio had to cope with the presence of a TV crew—the BBC were making a documentary called "Cutting Up Rough" for the *Works* series—and a journalist from *Details* magazine. "Lee and I had to get out of the studio for some fresh air it was so mad," Katy said. She discussed the men's grooming with Mira Chai Hyde, and the two women decided that the men would all wear nail varnish and eyeliner to give them a bruised look. Katy also heard that two models, Esther de Jong and Carolyn Murphy, could not make it for the show as they had been booked to work in New York. "But Naomi Campbell is looking good . . . I'm not sure about Kate Moss," she said. That day half of the women's clothes arrived from the manufacturer, but they were all creased.

On Tuesday, Katy wrote in her diary that Kate Moss had decided not to model for the show as she wanted to stay in New York and she noted that the clothes that were supposed to arrive that morning were still stuck at Heathrow. "Stella Tennant is due to arrive in five minutes for a fitting and we have nothing to put her in, except the show pieces

Lee has made here," she wrote. That night, Katy did not sleep at all, because late on Tuesday Lee had "flipped and decided we couldn't wait any longer for the clothes." McQueen had shouted at Katy and made her cry, but later he bought her a diamond costing £400 as an apology. Katy hired a van and asked her boyfriend, the photographer Phil Poynter, to drive her over to Heathrow. They left at 10:30 p.m., but the clothes were not released until two in the morning, meaning that she did not get back to the studio until 4 a.m. On Wednesday it was manic, she wrote. "I styled sixty of the eighty women's outfits before midday today," she noted. The makeup artist Topolino arrived from Paris and he tested the look on Catherine Brickhill. Katy also booked two male models at the last minute, including Maxim Reality from The Prodigy: "he's the one with a row of silver teeth," she wrote. On the night before the show Katy only managed to snatch four hours' sleep. "We're running on coffee and cigarettes," she observed. "We are all feeling very stressed." By noon on the day of the show she still had not finished the running order and Lee was frantic doing the last fittings on the 100 outfits that would be featured in *It's a Jungle Out There*. That afternoon the vans would arrive to take the clothes to the venue at London's Borough Market.[20]

Lee had chosen the market, just south of London Bridge, because of its unsettling atmosphere. "It's nice to show them [the fashion crowd] the rough part of London and make them a bit scared and look over their shoulder once in a while," he said.[21] McQueen and Simon Costin wanted to try and re-create a scene from the 1978 film *Eyes of Laura Mars*, starring Faye Dunaway, in which the heroine photographs a group of models against a backdrop of two burning cars. Costin scoured salvage yards for old cars and then proceeded to smash them up. The designer and art director also took inspiration for the set from a scene in *Bonnie and Clyde*, in which a barn is riddled with bullet holes, and replicated this by positioning lights behind forty-foot-high sheets of perforated corrugated iron. McQueen had recently secured sponsorship from American Express and, according to Costin, most of the money had to be spent on security. The set, which only had a series of black curtains to shield it from public view, had to be guarded twenty-four hours a day during construction.

The show, which started nearly two hours late, was described by one observer as a "vision of urban chaos . . . both on and off the catwalk." In the scrum of people trying to gain entry, students from Central Saint Martins managed to force their way into the venue and as one of them rushed towards the audience they kicked a fire pot towards one of the cars. "The audience screamed and clapped as a fire broke out in a van," said journalist Grace Bradberry.[22] Little did the fashion crowd realize that the fire was not part of the spectacle. Simon Costin confessed that he nearly suffered an embolism as he prepared himself for the resulting inferno, but luckily a security guard spotted the fire and quickly dealt with it. "I'm always a bundle of nerves," said Lee's mother, Joyce. "I think, 'What am I going to see this time?' "[23] She was not disappointed. Horns sprouted from the shoulders of a model and the head of a crocodile grew out of the back of a man's coat. "I thought it was absolutely mad, absolutely mad— the horns in the back of the jacket sticking up!"[24] McQueen himself was thrilled by the chaotic energy of the show, something which he said was particularly special to London. "This is where I come from, this is why people come to London," he said. "They don't want to see shift dresses—they can go anywhere in the world to see that."[25]

However, there were some influential fashion commentators in the audience who were not so happy. "I came all the way from America and all I could see was the coiffeur," said André Leon Talley, then the European editor of *Vanity Fair*. "Someone—the sponsors or the British Fashion Council—should take control and do something about this."[26] Tamsin Blanchard of the *Independent* said that the show "fell flat on its face," and Katherine Betts, American *Vogue*'s fashion news director who was writing a long profile on McQueen, was "patently underwhelmed."[27]

McQueen had dedicated *It's a Jungle Out There* to his parents. Ron had recently been diagnosed with bowel cancer—"Things are a little difficult at the moment, but we keep our feet on the ground,"

Lee's paternal grandparents, Samuel and Grace McQueen.

Lee's parents, Ron and Joyce McQueen, on their wedding day, 10 October 1953.

Left: 43 Shifford Path, Wynell Road, Forest Hill, as it is today. Soon after the birth of Lee, the McQueen family moved from south London to Stratford, into a council house at 11 Biggerstaff Road (right).

Lee said that he was six years old when he first realized that he was gay. On a family holiday he won a "Prince of Pontins" competition, but he wanted the boy who came second to win "because I fancied him!"

Lee with fellow students at Rokeby comprehensive school in Stratford, east London. Lee's nickname was "Queeny" or "Queer boy Queeny."

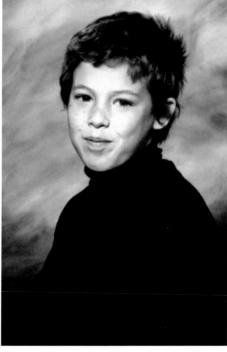

Lee's childhood was full of dark secrets that continued to haunt him throughout his life.

Lee as a student at Central Saint Martins, the London college that changed his life.

From the beginning, Isabella Blow called McQueen by his middle name as she thought it sounded more appropriate for a young fashion designer who wanted to make his mark.

Lee the apprentice tailor at Anderson & Sheppard, Savile Row, where he started work in 1986.

Lee with boyfriend Andrew Groves, or "Jimmy Jumble."
The couple met in 1994 in London.

Lee with his Spanish friend Miguel Adrover (left) in the mid-90s.
He remembers Lee as both shy and insecure and "the most fun person
I ever met on this fucking planet."

Lee with flatmate Mira Chai Hyde, a hairdresser and men's grooming
specialist, and his dog Minter in their Hoxton Square loft, where he lived
from 1995 until early 1997.

Lee with Minter in the Hoxton Square loft (above), where he lived with his Scottish boyfriend Murray Arthur (left). The couple met in July 1996 and their relationship lasted two years.

Lee's boyfriend Richard Brett, whom he met in April 1998.

McQueen backstage at a Givenchy fashion show with models Carla Bruni and Helena Christensen.

Lee had to travel between London and Paris for Givenchy, but he had little intention of learning French. "I remember being in a fitting with him and he was asking the guy [in the Givenchy studio] to take in the shoulder, 'un petit pois,' a 'little pea,'" said one friend.

said Joyce.[28] Ron's weight had dropped down to seven stone and after being admitted to hospital he had undergone surgery and chemotherapy. "He was a small man but such a fighter," said Janet. "And gradually he made a good recovery."[29]

After the London show McQueen had only twelve days to put the finishing touches to his first ready-to-wear collection for Givenchy. The show, held in La Halle aux Chevaux, the horsemeat market in Paris, with its floors that sloped to "drain the room's cobblestones of blood," had attracted a certain amount of hype even before it began.[30] Fashion editors gossiped about how, during rehearsals, the loud music had driven the rats in the sewers wild and as a result the maintenance staff had had to seal the drains to stop them swarming out. "Bullshit," responded one American journalist on hearing this.[31] "If that was true, Alexander McQueen would have opened the drains wider. He'd love rats running around."

The reviews were mostly positive—Colin McDowell, who had previously criticized McQueen, said that the collection, which showcased "the clothes of women on the rampage in the most uncompromisingly sexy kit imaginable," was presented with "astonishing conviction and assurance."[32] Yet McQueen generated most column inches not for his new collection, but for an offhand comment he made during an interview with *Newsweek* magazine when he compared his critics to Nazis. "Hitler destroyed millions because he didn't understand, that's what a lot of people have done to me because they don't understand what I do," he said. Carole Malone, writing in the *Sunday Mirror*, responded, "If he can't find a way of dealing with the pressure of his job—it's only fashion after all—he might very soon find himself being carted off the catwalk in a straitjacket (designer of course) with a one-way ticket to the funny farm."[33]

Murray realized that after all the hard work his boyfriend desperately needed a break. So Lee booked a holiday for them to Antigua. The couple flew first class to Barbados—they chatted to Paul Smith on the flight—and from there they traveled on to the Caribbean island. They hired a yacht and sailed around the blue waters and sandy beaches, but Murray became seasick. Lee read books on tropical fish and experienced the wonders of the sea on his first scuba-diving expedition. It seemed McQueen felt more at ease when free of his body. He had a deep affinity with animals and fish and could easily imagine what it was like not to be human. In one interview, he spoke of how he had once watched a television documentary fronted by Caryn Franklin in which she had sailed with a school of dolphins. "She was crying on camera," he said. "They took her on a boat in the North Sea and these dolphins started swimming beside [them] and she just burst out crying, saying, 'I wish I wasn't human, I don't want to be here right now, I want to be under the water with these dolphins.' It makes me feel quite emotional."[34]

On the last day of the holiday, Murray forgot to put sunscreen on his feet. On the flight home his feet became so swollen that once he had taken his trainers off he couldn't get them back on again. At the house in Coleman Fields, Lee tended to his boyfriend. "I had second-degree burns on my feet, and I had to roll off the bed and crawl to the bathroom," said Murray. "He was really good and looked after me. I think that was the time he bought this huge TV, which took up half the bedroom. He was so generous to me, very kind and thoughtful."[35]

In May 1997, Lee and his team traveled to Tokyo for the promotional launch of Givenchy's ready-to-wear collection. In Japan, Murray took a number of backstage photographs including one showing Lee, now sporting a blond Mohawk, with the models Helena Christensen and Carla Bruni (both wearing fantastical wigs). The photographer Anne Deniau had also been invited to Japan to follow McQueen and take a series of behind-the-scenes images. She remembers one day going up to his room at the hotel. "Can you play the piano?" Lee asked her. She said she could not, but why had he asked? "Because I have this indecent suite, with a piano, it's so stupid if you can't play."[36] At this stage in his life, McQueen loathed displays of conspicuous consumption. He said one of the reasons why he would prefer not to dress Mouna Al-Ayoub, the former wife of the Saudi billionaire Nasser Al-Rashid and one of haute couture's biggest spenders, was because of the way in which she flaunted her wealth. "Last season she sent me a huge bouquet of flowers with a note that said, 'From a future client.' I should have written back, 'I think not.'" When he witnessed people boasting about how much money they had in the bank he felt angry. "There is no style in gloating about money," he said. "These silly cows who gloat about it in the press. It makes me quite sick."[37] Murray recalls one time when Lee's friend Annabelle Neilson invited them to Caviar Kaspia, the upmarket restaurant in Mayfair. The bill for champagne and caviar for three people came to £1,200. "But we were both hungry and as soon as we came out Lee and I went to McDonald's," said Murray.[38]

There were friends, however, who were beginning to notice a change in McQueen. One night Trixie bumped into him and Shaun Leane in Comptons'. Lee asked Trixie what he was doing in a tone of voice that implied that he should by now have secured some kind of serious position. "It was almost like he was very career-minded all of a sudden," said Trixie. "I thought he was questioning me, which was a bit rude. What had started out as fun had become a career for him. He changed as soon as he went to Givenchy—he became a little bit pretentious. He also told me that Givenchy had told him that they didn't want him hanging out with certain types of people in Paris. I think that's why he couldn't wait to get back to London because in London he could do that. He told me he didn't like Paris, but he knew that he had to do the job."[39] Lee Copperwheat observed how fame began to change his friend's character. "When he got the fame he really began to struggle," he said. "He was around a lot of people who would do anything he said, which corrupted him a little. He would cause trouble and drama and really you had to question whether, on occasions, he really was your friend at all."[40]

McQueen's love of cocaine had also begun to intensify. By the mid-nineties, the drug in London's media, fashion and banking circles had become so widespread that its use had become normalized. "It's a post-rave, post-ecstasy culture," said *Loaded* editor James Brown at the time. "The toilet is the new boardroom. The toilet is the golf course where the deals get done."[41] "It wasn't just Lee, everyone was doing it," said Simon Costin, talking about cocaine. "It was rife. It was like someone having a cup of tea in the fashion industry. It was not unusual or shocking or surprising. But obviously I think if you're under that much pressure then yes, it does serve a purpose, it keeps you going."[42] Eric Lanuit, the press officer at Givenchy at the time, admitted to supplying McQueen with drugs. Lee "would call to ask for certain 'vitamin substances' to help him stay up all night and through the day of a fashion show," he said. "I'm not talking about Vitamin C, I am talking about cocaine."[43] Alice Smith remembers going to a party at Annabelle Neilson's London flat in Notting Hill with Lee and being alarmed by the effect the drug taking had on him. "He had taken a lot of cocaine already and Goldie was there with him in the loo," she said. "At the party he was straight-faced, not laughing, not enjoying himself. I went up to him and asked him if he was OK and he said he was fine, but he was really dismissive."[44]

That June, while in New York shooting the Givenchy fall ad campaign with Richard Avedon, McQueen heard rumors circulating within the fashion world that the couture house might sack him if he failed to deliver with his next collection. "I don't give a fuck, to be honest," he told Katherine Betts from American *Vogue*. "If they want to fire me, go ahead. Everybody knows that couture doesn't sell. I'm an intelligent designer. I know what I'm doing, for fuck's sake." Although he pretended not to care, Betts noticed tears beginning to well up in the designer's pale-blue eyes. "If they fire me from Givenchy, I can go back to London and get on with it. But I take offence for the people who work in the ateliers. Every day they're asking me, 'Are you gonna stay? Are you gonna stay?' And they want me to stay because otherwise they can't see the light at the end of the tunnel. If I leave they don't have a job or a pension or a fucking summer vacation!"[45]

When the *Sunday Times* ran a news story on 6 July 1997 head-lined "McQueen Chills Blood of the Fashion World," it seemed to many that McQueen might not have any choice in the matter. The newspaper alleged that the designer was under police investigation for using human body parts in his Givenchy collection *Eclect Dissect* to be presented at L'Université Paris Descartes medical school the next day. John Harlow, the arts correspondent, reported how McQueen had allegedly sewn "human bones, teeth and other body parts into his new clothes" and quoted one fashion insider as saying, "McQueen has gone too far—this is disgusting, uncivilized and rather juvenile." Harlow also wrote how Givenchy had moved the clothes to a secret location in order to shield them from photographers and also out of the reach of the local gendarmerie.[46] When Sibylle de Saint Phalle, the public relations executive at Givenchy, saw the story she became concerned at how it would affect McQueen. "He's so sensitive, this is really going to throw him off," she said. However, when she managed to contact the designer by phone McQueen was surprisingly unperturbed. "What a bunch of crap," he said, a neat summary of the baseless story for which the *Sunday Times* had to issue an apology. However, his reaction made Katherine Betts, who was shadowing him at the time, suspect that the story could have been a plant by his own office. "For all of his contempt for the press, McQueen knows how to grab headlines," she said.[47] Isabella Blow, herself a mistress of the dark art of public relations, could not have agreed more; in fact, McQueen's headline-grabbing antics had, she suggested, saved Givenchy. "I think he's already done a lot with the house because Givenchy has already had a lot of press," she said. "It's like, as Alexander says himself, taking a dinosaur out of the sea and I think in one season he's done that."[48]

In 1997, McQueen admitted how he had deliberately courted press attention by staging shows designed to shock. Referring back to his *Taxi Driver* collection at the Ritz in 1993, he talked about how one of his fellow designers "was sitting there and taking the piss because he was taking orders and I wasn't—but he didn't realize that

I had been in the game for so long and I knew what I was doing," he said. "I'd worked with Koji [Tatsuno] and seen how he had gone under, and I figured out that the way to get the best backers in the world, who are Italian, is to get the press and the identity first. Then you get the backer. Anyway, who's the one now earning half a million a year and who's the one who's still living in a dingy grotto?"[49]

Eclect Dissect was based around the idea of a Victorian doctor, an anatomist, who travels the world collecting the most beautiful women. After killing his victims he dismembers them in the laboratory and then reassembles them to form unsettling hybrids, figures which then come back to life to haunt their creator. "What you were seeing were the ghosts of all these various women from around the world," said Simon Costin. During the research process for this collection, Lee gathered together various visual references including "pictures of sutures, medical stitching, and facial plastic surgery." Simon worked from the anatomical drawings of Andreas Vesalius and together they spent hours cutting and collaging the images. "It was high Gothic, Poe meets Frankenstein meets Dr. Moreau," said Simon.[50] At either end of the catwalk, which consisted of a series of Persian carpets, Costin had installed two enormous cages containing ravens and crows, birds which in his dark fantasy fed off the flesh of the failed human experiments. "Five American dollars for the first eye those birds peck out," whispered a publisher of an American fashion magazine in the audience. "It's Tippi Hedren all over again." Isabella Blow, who came to the show dressed in a skintight outfit complete with collar and chain, declaimed, "I am my own dog."

Blow's declarations were cut short by "banshee screams" played over the sound system and the show started.[51] Katherine Betts commented on the excessive couplings of red Chantilly lace with chartreuse pony skin; Scotch tartan paired with Japanese embroidered satin; egret feathers with Spanish mantillas; jet beading mixed with leather and lace; leopard skin stitched into purple calf and human hair embroidered onto a velvet bolero. "The details, the fabrics, and the references of the creations they bore were so overwrought it was almost revolting," she said. Shalom Harlow looked like she had been cast as Leda and the Swan, "the neck of which was spiralling around her neck as if to choke her," while another model, who was dressed like a samurai complete with sword, "looked as if she'd slashed her own red lace dress down the front."[52] Yet the actress Demi Moore, who was in the audience, was thrilled by what she had just seen. "It was amazing—complete fantasy and illusion, as well as clothes that I would love to wear. Extraordinary elements of fun, grace and elegance were all fused together."[53]

The outlandish hairstyles were also something that had never been seen on a couture catwalk before. "Wound into wheels or piled into overgrown compost heaps or, in one case, coiled into a blonde ziggurat so tall it was hard for the woman to get her coif under a transom and into the back gallery," wrote Chip Brown in *New York* magazine. One straw hat comprised a birdcage, with a live songbird inside, while another "poor model had to navigate the route with her head and face completely cloaked in a red chador, though she seemed much more at ease than her comrade Honor Fraser, carrying a hooded falcon on a couture glove." Brown concluded that the imagery prompted a range of contradictory responses: "animality, power, helplessness, degradation and sovereignty, and otherwise suggests confusion in the categories of predator and prey."[54]

McQueen had experienced each of these states of being. He was at once the mad surgeon, dissecting the traditions of fashion and reconstructing the fragments to create a whole new look, and a victim, an object of abuse and exploitation who sometimes felt like he had come back from the dead. The feelings of disembodiment that occasionally threatened to destabilize him could only be held at bay for so long. His strategy for survival centered on replaying his deep-seated fears and fantasies relating to power and sex; each of his shows served as a cathartic purging of these feelings. Wasn't couture supposed to make women feel wonderful, not weird? asked Suzy Menkes in the *International Herald Tribune* the day after *Eclect Dissect*. Menkes, for once, had missed the point. McQueen did not produce these clothes for women; rather he created them for himself, as a rather public form of therapy. As such his shows can be read as the visual equivalent of fairy tales, a genre through which creator and consumer alike can express cultural anxieties and private desires. "I'm about what goes through people's minds, the stuff that people don't want to admit or face up to," he said. "The shows are about what's buried in people's psyches."[55]

After the show, Lee and Murray decided to escape the oppressive heat of Paris. Together with their former flatmate Mira Chai Hyde, they traveled to Pennan, on the coast of Aberdeenshire, where they rented a cottage. They lived simply, cooking meals and playing dominoes in the evenings. On 15 July 1997, while still in Scotland, they heard the news that Gianni Versace had been shot and killed. Six weeks later, on the morning of 31 August, the phone rang in the house in Coleman Fields; the couple were still in bed and so Murray leant over Lee to answer it. It was Joyce McQueen asking them whether they had seen the news. She simply told them to switch on the television and then hung up. Like millions of other people, Lee was left in a state of shock by the news of the death of Princess Diana in a car accident in Paris. He had told Murray that she was the only member of the royal family he would consider making a dress for. "When Diana died he cried. He was terribly heartbroken for days afterwards," remembers his sister Jacqui.[56]

To McQueen, death seemed not so much a distant stranger as an ever-present specter. "It is important to look at death because it is part of life," he said. "It is a sad thing, melancholic but romantic at the same time. It is the end of a cycle—everything has to end. The cycle of life is positive because it gives room for new things."[57]

Towards the end of 1997 the relationship between Lee and Murray began to deteriorate. "Givenchy started to weigh him down," said Murray. "He would go to Paris on his own and we would have arguments on the phone over nothing."[58]

Then in September, when Murray was away, Lee went to The End, a club in West Central Street, London, and met twenty-one-year-old Archie Reed. There was an instant attraction between them—Archie was blond, good-looking, had been married and had a daughter—and that night they went back to the house in Coleman Fields together. "I liked everything about him," said Archie. "We were from the East End of London and we spoke the same language, and knew the same people. There was never any bullshit, that's what we both liked. We quickly realized that we had met years before, when Lee had been working in Reflections, the bar in Stratford." The couple's relationship stretched over the course of the next twelve years, but it would be punctuated by long periods, often years, apart. Nevertheless, Archie believed he knew Lee better than most people. "He seemed to have so many different personalities—there was the old lady down the bingo; an old man that liked checking out the dirty old girls; the old tart; the rent boy; the little boy lost. But the Lee you would see out was not the Lee you would see at home, that little boy in his pyjamas watching *X Factor*, who was as sweet and as loving as could be."[59]

In December, Lee and Murray were invited to the premiere of *Titanic*, the film starring Kate Winslet, but they decided to go to a dinner hosted by Donatella Versace instead. "We had a massive argument before the dinner even started and left," said Murray. "I can't remember why or what happened, but I think it was because I wanted to see the film and he didn't. In the end we didn't see the film and we didn't have dinner with Donatella."[60]

Murray had stopped working at McQueen and had found it difficult to find another job; he had been overspending for some time and his overdraft amounted to more than his yearly salary. "I felt really low, I was missing Lee and upset that things weren't going as they had been," he said. One day they had a "massive screaming match on the phone"; Lee was in Paris and Murray at home in north London. "I took the biggest overdose of tablets I could lay my hands on," washed down with a lot of vodka and gin. "I took an overdose because I didn't think my life was worth anything at the time," he said. He remembers feeling spaced-out and nauseous, but then looked up to see Minter staring at him, a sight which prompted him to call for an ambulance. He was taken to Homerton Hospital where he had his stomach pumped. When Lee discovered what he had done "he was really upset and didn't want to speak to me," said Murray. "I came back, packed a bag and went straight to my parents' house in Scotland. I didn't talk to them, I went to my bedroom and shut the door." After a week in Scotland, Murray returned to London and moved his things out of the house in Coleman Fields. He went to stay at a friend's place in Camberwell. At the time he was so poor that he made a soup, eked out from a bag of frozen vegetables, last him a week. "I went from having everything to nothing," he said.[61]

Apart from when Lee sent Murray a card that read, "I hope you find what you are looking for," the couple had no contact for the next month or so.[62] Then, one night, McQueen rang Murray and told him that he missed him and wanted to see him. They started seeing one another again for a while—although Murray never moved back into Lee's house—but after a few months they decided that the relationship was over.

Years later, Murray felt irritated that people kept asking him why he still had "McQueen" tattooed on his arm. He talked to a designer friend about it who advised him to have it inked out with a black band. But then, after having it done, he felt that the image, a symbol of mourning, looked too depressing and asked a tattoo artist to lighten it by the addition of a Keith Haring design.

"I loved Lee more than anything else in the world and I would never have done anything to hurt him," said Murray. "He was my first love and he will be my only love. I was in it because of Lee, not Alexander, McQueen."[63]

CHAPTER NINE

He was the kind of daredevil that looks death and birth straight
in the eye.

—Björk

There was a moment, precisely seventeen minutes into *Untitled*, Lee's Spring/Summer 1998 show for his own label, when
McQueen secured his place as a contemporary artist of some note.
The audience of 2,000 people, who had gathered on the evening of
Sunday, 28 September 1997, at the Gatliff Road bus depot in Victoria, were intrigued as the loud club music that had accompanied
the first part of the show began to fade, and silence settled over the
brutal interior of the industrial building. Then the sound of inter-
mittent drops of rain was broadcast over the PA system, together
with a soulful refrain from Ann Peebles's "I Can't Stand the Rain,"
spliced together with the threatening deep bass notes of John Williams's theme from *Jaws*. The catwalk, a long transparent Perspex box
filled with water and lit underneath by ultraviolet light, started to
darken with black ink, oozing from an invisible source. By the time
the runway had turned black a yellow sleet of rain had started to fall
from above and as the models, all wearing white, walked forward
their clothes became soaked with water and their makeup and mascara ran down their faces.

Simon Costin, who designed the set of *Untitled* with McQueen,
regarded the show as a piece of installation art, and many others

agreed. "It's not just the clothes McQueen is good at, it's every-thing . . . the environment, the theatricality," said the photographer Mario Testino, who was in the audience, along with Janet Jackson, Demi Moore and Honor Fraser.[1] "The man's a creative genius," said Tommy Hilfiger, who watched with his wife and daughter.[2]

Of course, the clothes on display were extraordinary, "carved rather than cut from traditional tailoring fabrics, from pinstripe and Prince of Wales check, fused together to produce torso-skimming jackets."[3] There was a white muslin corset dress, its train dragging through the water, worn by Kate Moss. There were figure-hugging spiral dresses made from python skin, pinstripe jackets that revealed deep cowls at the back, finely tailored skirts and corsets worn by musclemen. And there was a suede bodice sliced into strips so as to reveal the breasts, worn by Stella Tennant. But there was something else at work, too. McQueen had commissioned a number of unset-tling additions, pieces of body sculpture that redefined the concept of the accessory. Jeweler Sarah Harmarnee made a number of har-nesses, fashioned from silver-plated metal, while McQueen's friend Shaun Leane constructed a spine corset made from aluminum. When Shaun initially heard Lee's idea he thought his friend had gone mad, but McQueen had been right—it could be done. "Sky's the limit," he would say.[4] But it was the accessories and the staging—particularly the juxtaposition of the Perspex tank filling with sinister ink and the nasty yellow rain that fell from the heavens—that lifted this event beyond the realms of a conventional fashion show.

In fact, in September 1997, *Untitled* would not have looked out of place within the hallowed confines of London's Royal Academy. Ten days before McQueen's show, the RA on Piccadilly opened the con-troversial *Sensation* exhibition—a display of contemporary art from the collection of Charles Saatchi. Works on show included Damien Hirst's *The Physical Impossibility of Death in the Mind of Someone Liv-ing* (the famous shark in formaldehyde); Marc Quinn's self-portrait of a frozen head made from pints of his own blood; Tracey Emin's tent called *Everyone I Have Ever Slept With 1963–1995*; Ron Mueck's

Dead Dad, an uncanny sculpture of the artist's father; the disturbing work of Jake and Dinos Chapman; and the most headline-grabbing of them all, *Myra*, Marcus Harvey's portrait of the serial killer Myra Hindley made from a child's handprints.

McQueen had initially wanted to call his show "Golden Showers" but the sponsor, American Express, who gave the designer £30,000 towards the reported £70,000 it cost to stage, objected to the risqué title. "Lee just got so angry with that," said Simon Costin. "He said to Steve Chivers [who was in charge of the lighting], 'I want that water to look like piss.'"[5] Although he and other designers—such as Lee's former boyfriend Andrew Groves, whose show that same day featured *Hellraiser*-style suits, an outfit that opened to reveal 500 live flies and, perhaps most prophetic of all, a hangman's noose—deliberately set out to shock, in McQueen's case that quest for sensation was balanced by a new maturity that thrilled the fashion critics. "His presentation late Sunday night was literally slick and entirely sophisticated," said *Women's Wear Daily*. "Sure, there were still a few theatrical moments, since it wouldn't be a McQueen show without them. But what he mainly produced was an immensely, totally wearable collection."[6]

McQueen's social life now straddled the worlds of fashion, art and celebrity. On 9 September, he had attended the launch of Damien Hirst's book *I Want to Spend the Rest of My Life Everywhere, with Everyone, One to One, Always, Forever, Now* at Quo Vadis, the restaurant the artist co-owned on Dean Street. Guests included Kylie Minogue, Keith Allen, Stephen Fry, Kate Moss, Robbie Williams, Bob Geldof and Malcolm McLaren. But he confessed that his social life was not as fun as it once was, in the days when he had hung out with his Old Compton Street friends. "I hate the circles I mix in now, I really hate them," he said. "The wankers you meet; the insular people you meet. I'm a great believer in honesty and I don't think you get that in fashion."[7] Certainly, A. A. Gill, the *Sunday Times* writer whose report on London Fashion Week was published the same day as McQueen's show, was scathing in his attack on the business. He described the circus of shows as a "thick shove and swelter of loathing." No other industry, he said, "is as swagged and encrusted with so much snide, bitter frustration and resentment, and with so many broken dreams and squandered promises. Here, for one whole week, you can find clothes made by men who hate women, women who hate women, and women who hate themselves."[8]

In private, Lee had started to talk to friends about the possibility of moving away from fashion, a yearning that he would continue to articulate until the very end of his life. Perhaps he would become a photojournalist and report from war zones, he said. Some friends thought he should concentrate on the contemporary art aspect of his shows and devote himself to making installation pieces or video art. In February 1997, McQueen had collaborated with Nick Knight on an image of the young Japanese/American model Devon Aoki for *Visionaire*, guest-edited by Rei Kawakubo. McQueen had dressed Devon in the same pink funnel-necked dress that Isabella Blow had worn for the *Vanity Fair* shoot, but this time he had gone one step further, styling her with one milky white eye and a huge safety pin through her forehead. After seeing the startling image, the London art dealer Anthony d'Offay got in touch with Knight and McQueen and asked them whether they wanted to work on an exhibition together at his gallery. The friends were intrigued by the idea, but rejected it because, they said, they wanted to stage an exhibition in New York. Björk also saw the futuristic image in *Visionaire* and commissioned McQueen to art-direct the cover for her album *Homogenic*, released in September 1997. The image, taken by Nick Knight, shows the Icelandic singer recast as an older sister of Devon Aoki, a stylized Samurai warrior who has returned from a tour of the globe. "I had ten kilos of hair on my head, and special contact lenses and a manicure that prevented me from eating with my fingers, and gaffer tape around my waist and high clogs so I couldn't walk easily," said Björk.[9]

McQueen and Björk shared many interests and obsessions, particularly a fascination with nature. "He was the kind of daredevil that looks death and birth straight in the eye," she said later. "Lee managed to connect not only with the civilized part of his culture but somehow channel beyond that a more primordial energy, which is probably where me and him met."[10] In 1998, McQueen would direct the video of Björk's single "Alarm Call," in which she was filmed floating on a raft in a jungle and living in close harmony with various exotic creatures such as crocodiles; in one shot she caresses a snake between her thighs. "I've done loads of collections based on man and machine and man and nature, but ultimately my work is always in some way directed by nature," McQueen told Björk in 2003. "It needs to connect with the earth. Things that are processed and reprocessed lose their substance."[11]

But dreams of escaping the fashion bubble for the world of pure art eluded Lee. He was simply too busy, he said, or there were too many people who depended on him. In reality, the gaps between his collections were so short that it was difficult for him to find time off. For instance, in the autumn of 1997 there were only two weeks between *Untitled* and his next haute couture show for Givenchy. On 22 October, McQueen won his second British Designer of the Year award, one he shared with John Galliano. Gossips speculated on why Galliano had not attended the ceremony at the Albert Hall. When Jasper Gerard of *The Times*' diary pages asked Galliano's office about this a spokesperson said that the designer was "busy in Paris." "Odd, then, that an acquaintance should have stumbled across him round the corner, drowning his sorrows at a local bar with the equally anti-social frock-maker Vivienne Westwood," said Gerard.[12]

Although it was reported that LVMH chief Bernard Arnault wanted to extend McQueen's two-year contract, the reviews in the press for Lee's Givenchy show that October were some of the worst of the designer's career. Brenda Polan in the *Financial Times* described the clothes as a mix between Dolly Parton at her most garish, the Folies Bergères and *Dynasty* done to excess. "His befringed, diamante-dotted, patent leather-trimmed body-flaunting could be construed as a bid to recruit the bereft customers of the late Gianni Versace," she said. "For these were clothes only rock-chicks, footballers' wives and exhibitionists with fat trust funds could love."[13]

It was easy for McQueen to laugh off the comments of eighty-eight-year-old Sir Hardy Amies, who wrote a piece in the *Spectator* attacking McQueen at Givenchy and Galliano at Dior. Their work was nothing less than "terrible," he said, and it was no wonder that reportedly their employees were in despair. "It is rumoured, not loudly, but everyone knows it, that the owners of these names don't really want couture business," he said. "They want to sell stockings and scent. They are prepared to spend a lot of money advertising their names and are glad of the publicity that catwalk shows can generate." Amies had also heard that many previously loyal customers of the two couture houses had started to shift their allegiance to Saint Laurent or Balmain. "If Givenchy and Dior continue with 'flash' designers, I fear this is where their customers will stay," he said.[14] Yet it was more difficult for McQueen to ignore the criticisms of someone like the *Sunday Times* fashion writer Colin McDowell, who hated the designer's latest look. "Crude colours, including searing orange, can be found on any provincial market stall," he wrote. "Fringed leather is a sempiternal horror story in cheap fashion chains." Not only did the collection fail to appeal to existing customers of Givenchy, but why would any woman who had money want to go out of her way to look so cheap? McDowell acknowledged that McQueen had enormous talent, but on this occasion it seemed as though he had worked himself into a dead end. And the worst of it was that "there seemed to be no new ideas."[15] In January 1998, just days before McQueen's next couture show, Hubert de Givenchy himself let it be known that he thought the designer's work at the house had been "a total disaster."[16]

In the run-up to his February show, *Joan*, for his own label, McQueen's office banned the *Sun* newspaper, together with a number of other tabloid newspapers and GMTV, from attending because apparently they represented "the wrong sort of audience." The news infuriated *Sun* columnist Jane Moore, who wrote of the fact that McQueen had come from working-class parents who regularly read her paper. "Their son is so far up his own bottom, I'm surprised he can still see daylight," she wrote. "Clothes are not works of art. They exist solely for the purpose of being worn . . . He is often appallingly rude to people, priding himself as the 'devil child' of the fashion world."[17]

McQueen, feeling stressed and under increased pressure to produce, also began to behave in a more tyrannical manner towards his staff. Simon Costin had already noticed the change in Lee's behavior in 1997. When they were in Paris the team would often go to the club Le Queen to relax after a long day's—and evening's—work. As McQueen became more famous so his treatment improved until eventually he and his staff were directed towards a roped-off VIP area. "Lee was quite shy, so that was quite nice for him, but it wasn't so much fun for us," said Simon. "That was the first time that it was becoming apparent that it was difficult for Lee to lead the sort of life he had led before," he said. Simon also remembers an incident, when McQueen was still with Murray, when after one of the Paris shows the team were whisked away to a private room in an upmarket hotel. Costin was enjoying a cuddle with his boyfriend when Murray, acting on McQueen's behalf, walked over and said to him, " 'Simon, that's not what's expected.' That's when I thought, 'Oh God, where's the rebel gone?' Lee started to be recognized and was pestered when we were out by people wanting work, or people just being sycophantic. He started to change in his dealings with other staff, people he'd known for a long time. I noticed that if anyone stepped out of line, you were brought up quite sharply. You'd go into the studio and ask, 'Where's so and so?' and they had gone. On the one level it was an incredibly intense experience, and the work was extraordinary, but all that comes with a cost. I suddenly realized that I didn't like it any more. I thought I was next to get the chop and so I wrote him a letter which outlined why it wasn't working any more, that he wanted me to go anyway, that I thought it was for the best—'but you are a bit of a nightmare.' Apparently, he was absolutely livid—'he can't talk to me like this,' was his attitude—and he read it out to everybody in the London studio. I didn't see him for years after that."[18]

Lee's friend Miguel Adrover also remembers times when McQueen would lose his temper, especially in the frenzied weeks leading up to a show. "Yes, he was a shy person, but at the same time he could be really vicious," he said. "Lee could be a crazy person with no feelings and sometimes he said, 'If you don't have it [a piece] finished for tomorrow you will get fired, bitch.'" Miguel would try and restore his friend's sense of perspective and force him to acknowledge that he wasn't the most important person in the universe. One time, when the two went on holiday to Majorca, Miguel took him around the village where he had grown up. He escorted him to the house of an old lady, dressed in black, who was sitting on the bench outside. Miguel asked the woman, "I have Alexander McQueen here—do you want to meet him?" "Who the fuck is this?" she replied. "And so I told him what she had told me and said, 'Not everyone knows you, they don't give a shit about you.'"

Lee decided to dedicate *Joan* to Miguel because, at that time, he felt particularly close to him. "We had this connection that he didn't have with many people," Miguel said. "He didn't trust many people—when you start to get fame and money you start to get a little paranoid."[19] Perhaps it was also McQueen's way of thanking his friend for looking after him on his visits to New York. Instead of staying in the room booked for him at a smart hotel, Lee preferred to spend time with Miguel at his grotty basement apartment on Third Street, between First and Second Avenues. People from the nearby blocks would regularly throw their trash down into the space between the buildings and although the flat had one window Miguel would never allow it to be opened as he was afraid the rats outside would spill into his home. Whenever it rained the apartment would flood and Miguel would have to make sure nothing was left on the floor. "But Lee loved this," said Miguel. "He was always in the search of real things and real friendship—authentic connections were really important to him. He associated the hotels with work."

Miguel served another function too: he would pay the rent boys ordered up by McQueen. "Lee was a really shy person and he thought that if he went out people would want to meet him for who he was in the public eye, not the real him." One day, after he had heard Lee complaining about this, Miguel gave him a booklet featuring a series of rent boys, their photographs and prices. "Lee would choose the one he wanted to spend time with, I would call them and they would come to the basement," said Miguel. "He would give me the money to pay them. I remember once, after he had finished, he shouted out to me, 'Sweetheart, can you make me a cup of tea?' "[20]

At the beginning of 1998 all Lee's attention was taken up with his new collection, *Joan*. The show, held on 25 February at the Gatliff Road bus depot, was inspired not only by Joan of Arc, who was burned at the stake in 1431, but also by an image of Agnès Sorel by the French artist Jean Fouquet. The two women had devoted themselves to the French king Charles VII—Joan as a self-sacrificial spiritual leader and Agnès as his mistress and mother of three illegitimate children. Both women had died serving him—Joan at the stake and Agnès, in 1450, after giving birth, a death which was later thought to have been a result of mercury poisoning. McQueen chose an image of Agnès from Fouquet's Melun Diptych, *Virgin and Child Surrounded by Angels*, painted around 1452, as the image for the show's glossy invitation. Fouquet portrayed the virgin (Agnès) wearing a dark-gray bodice that exposed her left breast, and with a high, pale forehead, showing a glimpse of a curled plait that sat just below her crown, an aesthetic that determined the look of McQueen's show. Although Lee—who had just dyed his hair blond—initially wanted to send the models out looking completely bald, the hair stylist Guido Palau thought this would be too severe. "I was not sure about that, so we agreed on a high hairline," he said. Many of the models' heads were covered with bald caps and draped with thin blond woven plaits, while their eyes were fitted with bloodred contact lenses, a look described by McQueen's makeup artist Val Garland as "Joan of Arc kidnapped by aliens."[21]

But the abiding image of the show, one that would be branded into the consciousness of those who watched it, was the finale. In this last scene a model wearing a breathtaking dress fashioned from red bugle beads and a red mask stepped onto the stage alone and was surrounded by a ring of fire. At that moment the anonymous female figure, wearing a bloodred dress and standing defiant on stage as the flames raged around her, became a symbol of the McQueen everywoman: resilient, strong, a survivor of unknown horrors. As McQueen progressed through life he had found himself drawn to a series of women who had endured physical, sexual or psychological torment and, as a fellow survivor of abuse himself, he felt he could understand them.

McQueen's latest muse was Annabelle Neilson, whom he had chosen to model in *Dante* and *Joan*. She had come from a wealthy background—her father was an investment and property adviser and her mother, a marchioness, a society interior designer—but she was far from conventional. She attended Cobham Hall in Kent but left school at sixteen without any O levels due to a combination of her dyslexia and her rebellious spirit; apparently she stayed in bed on the day of her exams. In 1995 she married Nat Rothschild, the hedge fund manager with a reported fortune of £270 million, but by the time Annabelle walked down the catwalk in *Joan* the marriage was in trouble and the couple divorced in 1998. It was reported that, as part of the generous divorce settlement, Annabelle had to give up using the Rothschild name and agree never to talk publicly about the marriage.

Isabella Blow had first introduced McQueen to the model-thin Annabelle. Isabella "was always shoving girls in his face, but he could tell I wasn't desperate to be a model," said Annabelle. "He took off my clothes, said he admired my filthy vocabulary, and agreed to dress me for a Paolo Roversi portrait. He also asked me to be in his show. I would have done anything he asked just to be around him. I found his energy magnetic."[22] McQueen made his first wedding dress for Annabelle, who had a more formal ceremony in London after her marriage to Nat Rothschild in Las Vegas in November 1995. "It's more difficult [than a runway collection]," said McQueen about designing a wedding dress, a creation that is "immortalized in photographs in a way that no other garment ever is."[23]

By 1998, the relationship between Lee and Isabella had started to change. "It's like vampires," said Isabella, trying to make light of the weakening bond between them, "you need somebody and then you don't need the drug any more."[24] John Maybury, who was friends with both Issie and Lee, described this as "a natural parting of the ways, but it would be a mistake to think that at any point he ceased to love her."[25]

Isabella was no longer the most important female friend in his life; that role had been taken over by Annabelle. "Isabella had scooped up what looked like this wounded bird and introduced her to Alexander," said Daphne Guinness, another close friend of both Isabella's and Lee's. "And the wounded bird turned into a bird that nudged everybody else out of the nest. Isabella wasn't at all competitive about her friends, and she never said it in a bad way, but she was disappointed in herself. She did say that that was the worst introduction she had ever made."[26]

Friends noticed the not-so-subtle shift in the dynamic between Lee and Isabella. "At times he could be dismissive of her and make fun of her," said BillyBoy*. "He treated her very badly and at times it was so gross I thought, 'How can he say that?' But there was a sort of psycho-sexual relationship between the two of them. She was completely enamoured of him and his work and I think he wanted to punish her. There was something deeply masochistic in his personality—that's why he always liked guys who treated him badly. I think by punishing her, he punished himself. Inside there was a certain cognitive dissonance—by hurting her he got a joy out of it, but at the same time he hurt himself."[27]

Isabella's husband, Detmar, remembers an occasion from May 1997 when McQueen had visited Hilles, along with a BBC film crew. The two men were sitting by themselves in the long room after supper, a fire blazed away in the hearth and Detmar was enjoying a cigar.

Then McQueen turned to him and said, "I'm the tycoon now, Detmar." "He wasn't laughing, he was saying I'm more powerful than you," Detmar recalls. The incident made him think of the scene in *Henry IV Part Two* where the King turns to Falstaff and says, "I know thee not, old man." The words made Detmar feel sad. "It was the end of a friendship as far as I was concerned," he said. "It was as though he meant to say, 'You're my slave now.' And I wasn't going to be his fucking slave. He was telling me the power was with him and not with me, but I never had any power anyway. Yet I knew Issie still loved him and she needed his clothes. She was addicted to his aesthetic."[28]

The day after the *Joan* show Lee took a car to Metro studios in the East End for a cover shoot with Nick Knight for *The Face* magazine. McQueen, as art director, wanted to cast himself as the Joan of Arc/ Agnès Sorel figure and re-create the look from the show, complete with bald head, a series of white plaits that draped over his head and face, red contact lenses and red eyeliner. Next to the published cover image of McQueen a caption read, "You're not going out like that." When asked to explain the significance of the photograph, McQueen wrote, "Deep inside of me I have no regrets of the way I portray myself to the General Public. I will face fear head on if necessary but would run from a fight if persuaded. The fire in my soul is for the love of one man but I do not forget my women whom I adore as they burn daily from Cheshire to Gloucester."[29] McQueen told the magazine how happy he had been with the collection—"it had a really good attitude," he said—and even his bosses from Givenchy thought it had been "a killer" (probably not their choice of words). He also revealed how a mysterious woman had contacted his office to inform them that she had left everything to him—"she thought I was the best thing that had happened to British fashion and she wanted me to have her savings," he said. It was not a "massive fortune" but it was enough for him "to start up a foundation in her name for upcoming fashion designers. That's what I'll do with the money; I want it to be helping out some of the young talent in Britain." (Although

McQueen put that idea on hold it was something he would eventually return to when he set up the charity Sarabande in 2007.) He also said that he slept a lot less than he used to because he had so many ideas spinning around in his head. After all, he only had two weeks before his Givenchy ready-to-wear show. "I'll probably wake up in the middle of the night tonight and already I'll be thinking about Givenchy," he said.[30]

In March 1998, McQueen presented a Givenchy collection that satisfied even his harshest critics. Brenda Polan, who had savaged his Givenchy show in October the previous year, said he had "toned down the gimmickry and employed his signature sharp tailoring to produce a strong, controlled collection which Hubert de Givenchy might have called his own."[31] In the front row of the show sat Kate Winslet, who was in Paris for a fitting with the designer for the dragonfly-embroidered gown that she would wear to the Oscars later that month—although she did not win best actress for *Titanic*, her outfit was considered "the coup of the night" and later that year she would marry her first husband dressed in McQueen.[32]

That April, back in London, Lee and his friend Shaun Leane went out in Soho for a few drinks. McQueen was in high spirits. The latest issue of *Visionaire* had just been released and it contained a photograph taken by him that Lee thought was hilarious. The "magazine," guest-edited by Tom Ford of Gucci, consisted of a black light box, like a "miniature coffin," and a series of twenty-four slides, including one shot by McQueen of an erect penis at the moment of ejaculation. "I was not surprised," said Ford at the time, "and I have not spoken to him about it. This was his vision of light."[33]

That night in Barcode, a gay bar in Archer Street, Lee spotted a man, like Murray, who was tall, thin and dark-haired. At the same moment, Richard Brett, who was then twenty-five, looked across the crowded bar and saw Lee, dressed in shorts and a short-sleeved checked shirt. Lee walked up to Richard and paid him a compliment about how great he thought he looked and the two started talking. "It was one of those magical moments where you have an instant attraction to someone and we just hit it off," said Richard. They talked for about an hour and a half and then the two men left separately. Over the course of the next few days, Richard kept thinking about the man he had met in Barcode, whom he recognized, and finally, after being persuaded by some friends at work, rang the office and spoke to one of Lee's assistants and left a message. McQueen rang back and they arranged to meet again. "I remember it was a beautiful May day and we took a cab and lay on Hampstead Heath for the afternoon," he said. "Then we went back to his house in Islington and then to a bar, the Edward, where we stayed until quite late in the evening. At the end of the night we went our separate ways." For Richard it was not love at first sight, more a gradual realization that he felt a deep connection to Lee. "He had an amazing energy about him," he said. "He was fun, he had an intense hearty laugh and I felt like this was going to be special."

That summer Richard Brett was working at a public relations agency in west London and during the day the couple would send affectionate fax messages to one another. Often, Lee would courier over to his new boyfriend enormous bunches of flowers; Richard remembers one that must have been at least four feet high and so big he was unable to take it home and it had to sit by his desk at work. Lee liked the fact that Richard did not seem to be particularly intimidated or impressed by the world of fashion and celebrity. In fact, his new boyfriend had quite a cynical attitude towards this superficially glamorous lifestyle, again something that helped them get along. "He knew that I saw him for who he really was, the genuine person," said Richard. "Other people on the gay scene probably wanted to be close to him for what he was rather than who he was. But I think we had a chemistry. We made each other laugh and probably, ultimately, that was what it was about."[34]

With each month McQueen's fame seemed to grow. In May 1998, American Express commissioned him to design a special limited-edition credit card and then, later that month, he was invited to attend a state banquet for the emperor and empress of Japan, along with a "full complement" of British royals, at Buckingham Palace.[35] However, at the last minute he decided not to go. "I just couldn't be bothered," he said.[36]

In June, an outfit McQueen had designed for the Billy doll—an anatomically correct gay doll designed by John McKitterick—went on display at the New Museum of Contemporary Art in New York. McKitterick had approached McQueen early on in the project and he was one of the first designers to deliver. "At that point he was so hot," said John. "And with his name we approached other designers [such as Paul Smith, Agnès B, Tommy Hilfiger, Calvin Klein and Christian Lacroix] to do it." The subsequent auction of the dolls, together with the design drawings, raised $425,000 for the AIDS charity LIFEbeat. McQueen had designed a bleached denim outfit for his Billy and it even featured a miniature copy of the koi tattoo that Lee had on his chest. "It was a bit like a mini me," said John, "apart from the fact that Billy didn't look anything like him."[37]

The following month, McQueen traveled with Richard Brett on Eurostar to Paris to prepare for the Givenchy couture show. It was then, in the frantic period in the run-up to the show, that Richard saw a different side to Lee. "He was very stressed and anxious and not particularly pleasant to be around," he said. "He also became very stressed about the reviews the next day; he really cared about what people thought about it. If he thought his show wasn't particularly good we would all spend a lot of time comforting him, telling him it was brilliant. Most of the reviews were good but occasionally there were bad ones and that really upset him."[38]

McQueen had chosen to stage the Givenchy show at the Cirque d'Hiver, which he had transformed into an Amazonian jungle complete with cascading water and lush greenery. On the night itself—19 July 1998—model Esther de Jong rode in on a white stallion and wore "nothing but a sheer white train scattered with exotic blooms." The theme of the collection centered on the image of "woman as victorious huntress."³⁹ Colin McDowell criticized the show for lacking focus—"he gave us a sampler of all the ideas that interest him," he said. McDowell could not make sense of the range of references— the Amazonian rain forest, the vision of a Lady Godiva–like figure riding in on a horse, a huntress with budgerigars hanging from her belt, bows and arrows hanging randomly from belts, faces painted red "and, to end it all, a bizarre bride in a dovetail dress."⁴⁰ Tamsin Blanchard of the *Independent* accused both McQueen and Galliano of staging overly theatrical shows and employing certain attention-grabbing techniques "which are now looking tired and repetitive."⁴¹

In Paris, McQueen also had to cope with the angry demonstrations of an animal rights group sponsored by Brigitte Bardot. The protesters traveled around the city in a red double-decker bus handing out leaflets to raise awareness of the use of fur and other animal by-products in the couture shows. Alexander McQueen was one of the worst offenders, they said. "This man is no better than a taxidermist," one protester complained, a comment that must have irked him.⁴²

That year McQueen acquired another pet dog, an English bull terrier from the Battersea rescue home, which he named Juice, "because that's what Mexicans say when they send dogs in for a kill," he said.⁴³ A photograph taken at the time shows him wearing pajamas and looking bleary-eyed, cuddling Minter with one arm and the puppy Juice, brown with white paws, hanging on to his shoulder. McQueen's brother Tony remembers a time when Lee was at the studio with Juice. "There was a lovely girl there and she told me that Juice had just weed on a dress, and she asked me to have a word with Lee about it," he said. "So I said to Lee, 'The dog has weed on the dress!' He said, 'Well, tell her [the assistant] to make another one then, the dog takes priority!'" Later, just after Lee had bought his parents a house in Hornchurch, he took the dogs there for a visit. Joyce and Ron told him not to let the dogs jump up onto the sofa, to which Lee replied, "Well, I paid for the house."⁴⁴

In August, Lee and Richard Brett went on holiday to Majorca.

Lee knew the island well because of the trips he had made there with his friend Miguel Adrover. (In 2006, after he had become even wealthier from his deal with Gucci, he would buy a luxurious villa near Santa Ponsa, on the southwest coast. After his death in 2010 it was valued at £1.735 million.) "It was great to see him away from London, somewhere he could relax for a few days," said Richard. "He was always happier and calmer away from the stresses of London or Paris."[45] But the more successful McQueen became, the more difficult he found it to enjoy his holidays and he would often return to London after only a couple of days.

On 17 September 1998, McQueen won an International Fashion Group award in New York. He started his acceptance speech with the words, "I'm so drunk I can barely even talk."[46] When BillyBoy* went for a night out with him he was always astounded by how much Lee could drink. "I couldn't keep up with him," he said. "He would down more alcohol during the period of my one drink than I could ever imagine drinking. He would drink five cocktails while I was still on my first one. He loved to get plastered. But the drug thing scared me. I was concerned because he was so completely out of it. It brought out a whole other person inside of him, like a demon trying to escape unleashed."[47]

"When I knew him Lee liked marijuana, cocaine and alcohol," said Miguel Adrover. "Lee could never have enough. I remember one day when we were going to bed he wanted to carry on, he was not listening to anybody. It was a vice, an addiction, because I think a lot of the time he was doing it [drugs and drink] and not enjoying it. But the drugs and the insecurity that came with them were connected with the business, the industry—fashion."[48]

Richard Brett did not like what cocaine did to his boyfriend. "It didn't lift him to a better place or make him happier," he said. "It took him to a dark place that was not particularly pleasant."[49]

Andrew Groves had become aware of his ex-boyfriend's cocaine use and although this was by no means the main inspiration for his own September 1998 show *Cocaine Nights*, a reworking of J. G. Ballard's dystopian novel, he was conscious that there were certain resonances between McQueen's drug habit and the collection. The catwalk had been decorated with a line of white powder and one of Groves's models wore a dress made out of razor blades. The *Sun* proclaimed it the "sickest fashion show of all time."[50] "I always said I held a mirror up to the front row and they didn't like what they saw," said Andrew. "They were put in an impossible situation where they had to give the show a bad review, otherwise they would be seen to condone drug use. Not my best career move."[51]

In contrast, however, McQueen's professional life could only be described as supercharged. His next few shows for his own label—particularly *No. 13*, *The Overlook* and *Voss*—were some of the most memorable of his career. He was in demand by Hollywood—he said he had just been asked to design the costumes for Lady Penelope for a proposed remake of *Thunderbirds*, a project that he turned down. "Give me *The Piano*, I might think about it," he said.[52] He was named best avant-garde designer of the year at the VH1 Fashion Awards in New York. Jefferson Hack, cofounder of *Dazed & Confused*, invited him to guest-edit the September issue of the magazine, an opportunity he seized. "He has always looked outside fashion," said Jefferson, "at film, photography, art and music for his inspiration, drawing from the avant-garde and the margins of contemporary culture before threading it into the mainstream."[53] McQueen told Helen Mirren, whom he interviewed for the magazine, that after he had made enough money from fashion he wanted to work as a journalist. Certainly, Lee had the right personality—he was curious and unshockable, had a prodigious memory, could sniff out a good story and thrived on controversy.

The most controversial feature in the issue focused on a subject close to McQueen's heart: the politics of appearance. As an overweight gay man, working within an industry that had a near-fascistic approach to physical appearance, McQueen had often been made to feel like a freak. Commentators and critics had mocked him for his weight: one went so far as to dub him not so much the *enfant terrible* of fashion as its *éléphant terrible*, while another said that, with his "blue eyes, downy puffs of facial hair, and an overbite flashing out of a narrow mouth, he resembles a walrus."[54]

Although McQueen did not pretend that he had suffered the kind of prejudice experienced by the eight men and women photographed for the magazine—each of them had a physical disability—at least he wanted to try and challenge "the mainstream concept of what is and isn't beautiful," something that was becoming "increasingly narrow—you have to be young, you should preferably be blond and, of course, pale-skinned." Working with Katy England and Nick Knight, McQueen matched the eight subjects with a number of different designers and, wherever possible, "clothes were made specifically for each individual in acknowledgement of the fact that, politics aside, people with disabilities have practical difficulties finding fashionable clothes." The resulting images were both radical and beautiful: Alison Lapper, her naked torso covered in fragments of colored light as styled by Hussein Chalayan; Mat Fraser wearing a golden waistcoat by Catherine Blades; and Aimee Mullins, the athlete and model, in a wooden fan jacket by Givenchy haute couture, a McQueen suede T-shirt, a crinoline frame hired from Angels and a pair of dirty prosthetic, doll-like legs that added to the dreamlike effect of the image. "I don't want people to think I'm beautiful in spite of my disability, but because of it," said Aimee, who posed topless for the cover of the magazine wearing a pair of high-tech prosthetic legs next to the cover line "Fashion-able?"[55]

On 27 September, Aimee Mullins—who was born without fibulas and who had the lower halves of her legs removed when she was one year old—opened McQueen's show *No. 13* at the Gatliff Road bus depot, London, striding onto the stage in a gesture of proud defiance. Lee had designed a pair of specially carved wooden legs for her that looked like "sexy high-heeled boots . . . Nobody knew they were fake, which was the beauty of the whole thing."[56] The highlight of *No. 13* came eighteen minutes into the show when model Shalom Harlow stood on a turntable and, as she revolved like a ballerina on a music box, tried to defend herself against the assault of two robots that sprayed her (and her stunning white bouffant dress) with yellow and black paint. The installation, a reworking of Rebecca Horn's 1988 work *Painting Machine*, can be seen as a tender tribute to Hitchcock's *Psycho*. As Shalom raised one hand, then another, to protect herself from the robots' approach, McQueen deliberately invoked the seminal shower scene in which Janet Leigh is stabbed to death by an unseen killer. Yet at the end of *No. 13* the model was left standing, covered not in blood but just paint, a symbol perhaps of McQueen's new optimism. After the finale, a happy and relaxed-looking McQueen came onto the stage with his two dogs and kissed his boyfriend Richard, who was sitting in the front row next to his mother, Joyce.

No. 13 won McQueen some of the best reviews of his career. The *Guardian* described it as "a fashion spectacle rich in imagery," while according to the *New York Times* the presentation of the "tailored frock coats with long tails worn over modified versions of his bumster pants, Grecian-draped jersey dresses à la Mme. Grès, delicate beauties in Battenburg lace tablecloth fabric, ruffled Chantilly laces and embroidered fish net," "skirts that resembled sandalwood fans" and "a garment with wings made of perforated slats" was a *tour de force*.[57] In France, however, McQueen faced accusations that he had exploited Aimee Mullins, a charge that was vehemently denied by both the designer and the model herself. "This notion that, because I am an amputee and have what people consider is a 'disability' I must be less capable, less confident, less intelligent and less competent to make a decision, that I must have been manipulated by Alexander McQueen, was so insulting," she said.[58]

Soon after *No. 13*, McQueen prepared to move home. He had become bored of his house in Coleman Fields, selling it for a £75,000 profit, and he wanted somewhere different. McQueen's new house—43 Hillmarton Road, near Caledonian Road tube station, which he bought in November 1998 for £620,000—looked quite ordinary from the outside, but at the back the previous owners had installed an enormous sash window that measured twenty feet high and eight feet wide, a theatrical touch that McQueen loved. Soon after having it refurbished by the architects Ferhan Azman and Joyce Owens— the same architects who had worked on Isabella Blow's house in Waterloo—Lee asked Richard Brett to move in with him. "Within six months Lee asked me to sort of marry him, in some kind of ceremony," said Richard. "I think it was some kind of security that he wanted. But I was too young, I wasn't ready."[59]

As well as dealing with accusations of exploiting Aimee Mullins and the stresses of moving home, McQueen also had to defend himself against a charge of plagiarism. The original case alleged that Lee had copied an off-the-shoulder white dress, as worn by Eva Herzigova in his first Givenchy haute couture collection in January 1997, from fashion student Trevor Merrell. Merrell's dress had been exhibited at a show on the Isle of Wight in June 1995, but disappeared soon after. When he saw a photograph of McQueen's design in the newspapers he could not believe it. "The dress looked just like mine," he told *The Times*. "I do not believe the similarities are coincidental. It would be truly remarkable. Eva Herzigova was even wearing an ancient Greek-style headdress, as was my model." In August 1997, the London College of Fashion student was granted legal aid to fight the alleged breach of copyright. "I have already been told I have a strong case—the comparisons between the dresses speak for themselves," he said. McQueen denied all allegations, saying that he had never met Trevor Merrell, nor had he seen any of his designs. "It is absurd to say that, because both dresses are white and have one shoulder, that one is based on another," said Trino Verkade, who ran McQueen's studio. "It wasn't the first design like that and it won't be the last. Are people going to start suing anyone who makes a strapless black dress because it's been done before?"[60] The news prompted one fashion editor to exclaim, "You might as well sue the Oracle of Delphi."[61]

The London listings magazine *Time Out* not only repeated Merrell's allegations but also printed the claims of another student who maintained that one of her fabric designs had been plagiarized by McQueen too. McQueen, with Givenchy, launched a successful legal bid to clear his name, and on 12 January 1999, the case went before a judge at the High Court on the Strand. Trevor Merrell admitted that his opinion of McQueen was "none too positive," but he still managed to see the comedic elements of the situation. He remembers the judge saying, "This is the High Court—IRA men come to this court—this is not the place for airy-fairy designers to argue about a lady's dress, we are talking about a lady's dress for goodness' sake!" Then, when McQueen's lawyers objected to Lee being referred to in such derogatory terms the judge replied, "Gentlemen, we are not talking about Leonardo da Vinci here!" "Everyone shut up after that," said Merrell.[62]

Nevertheless, the saga continued. In June 2000, Merrell, by then an art student at Goldsmiths, was forced to withdraw from his final collection a piece he had called *The Dress Wars Sofa*. This was a sofa covered in hand-printed fabric featuring newspaper stories about the case. "Alexander McQueen has written to the college threatening them with legal action if they allow my sofa to be shown in public," said Trevor at the time. "They've put the corporate bite on the college and I very much resent having my work repressed . . . The freedom of Goldsmiths is the freedom of artistic expression. It has always been associated with that. I do not have a vendetta against Alexander McQueen, though sometimes it has felt like he has one against me."[63]

CHAPTER TEN

It was like having a boyfriend that you know you have to break up
with, the only difference with this relationship was that I didn't feel
bad about doing it.

—*Lee McQueen on Givenchy*

I n the spring of 1999, Lee looked at himself in the mirror and was
not happy with what he saw. He was approaching his thirtieth
birthday and he knew that if he didn't do something about his weight
soon it could be too late. "It was something he talked about a lot and
I guess like many in the gay community, he was under pressure to
have the perfect physique," said Richard Brett.[1] Lee had tried going
to a gym, but he had found it boring and he never seemed to be able
to fit it into his busy schedule. What he needed was a quick fix and so
he booked himself into a private clinic in London's Harley Street that
specialized in cosmetic procedures. A few weeks after he turned thirty
he paid around £3,000 for a course of liposuction, where around
eight pounds of fat from his stomach and flanks was sucked out. The
treatment, which Detmar Blow likened to squeezing the toothpaste
out of a plastic tube, left him with extensive purple bruising across
his stomach.[2] "But he was very pleased with it, and it did make a difference to his belly and shape," said Richard.[3]

McQueen knew that, if he wanted to turn himself into a global
brand, he would have to become more "marketable" as a person. He
had his teeth fixed, employing the same celebrity dentist as Jerry Hall.

"Sometimes I would say to him, 'Oh fuck off, Jerry,'" said Archie Reed, "because his teeth were exactly like her teeth."[4] Slimming down was essential to this process. "Lee hated the way he looked," said Janet Street-Porter, the writer and broadcaster and a friend of McQueen's. "Designers like Ralph Lauren and Calvin Klein are all about looking good, and for them it is just as much about marketing themselves as the marketing of the clothes. In the fashion world there is this tyranny of people, like Tom Ford, who really work on their look. Poor old Lee would have thought, 'I'm in a glamorous world, but . . .'"[5] Although Lee was initially happy with his reduced girth—apart from joking that the puncture marks had left him with two extra navels—after a few months he realized that it was not the solution to his weight problem. "Liposuction is crap," he said in January 2000. "It doesn't work for men. It sucks all the fat cells up, but then they just get bigger."[6] It probably did not help that, after the liposuction, Lee continued to eat a diet rich in fat and carbohydrates. Andrew Groves recalls a story one of his friends told him about going out for a meal with Lee. "He was eating ice cream and saying that he could have whatever food he wanted because he had just had liposuction," he said.[7]

After the success of Lee's latest own-label collection *The Overlook*—which had been inspired by Stanley Kubrick's film *The Shining*—McQueen declared that he wanted to take a break from London and that his next show would be in New York. "The business has got to a stage where in order to expand fully in America we need to be there for one collection," he said. "We have the West and East Coast markets, but there's a whole continent in between for us to expand in."[8]

Before the New York show, scheduled for autumn 1999, McQueen had to prepare for his Givenchy collections (ready-to-wear in March and haute couture, inspired by the beheading of Lady Jane Grey, in July) and also oversee a selection of clothes from *Untitled* for the V&A's *Fashion in Motion* exhibition in June. Claire Wilcox, then the assistant curator of textiles and dress at the museum, wanted to display the work of McQueen, and other designers, as a live experience, turning the galleries into makeshift catwalks. "It's a very democratic process," she said. "People will be able to see designer clothes, shown from all angles and as they were intended to be worn by the designer. Very few of us would otherwise get to see that, apart from on TV."[9]

McQueen was also busy planning a move in London to new studio premises in Amwell Street, Clerkenwell, and the opening of his new shop in Conduit Street, W1, financed by the Japanese fashion company Onward Kashiyama. The designer had asked Azman Owens, the firm of architects that had refurbished his house in Hillmarton Road, to compete for the project. Ferhan Azman, a small but strong woman born in Turkey, remembers the first time she met McQueen. "His reputation reached us before we met him," she said. "I was scared—and it is difficult to scare me. But he was very polite, respectful and courteous. He came across as a very bright, intelligent man who knew what he wanted." At the first meeting about the store he told Ferhan and her business partner Joyce, an American architect, about his vision for the building and described to them his working methods. "I am not like Calvin Klein," he said, "I don't have a style"—a comment that Ferhan found intriguing. "You cannot pick up a jacket or a dress and say it's me," he said. "I cut. For a collection I come up with themes and I cut around them." He also told the architects that he had a passion for technology and that he wanted to see if they could incorporate a type of glass that changes from transparent to opaque. Initially, the two women were worried about the challenge—after all, they had seen the *Overlook* show and knew that he was not a conventional fashion designer. "What the fuck are we going to do?" said Joyce to Ferhan. "He's not Armani."[10]

The architects wanted to reflect the theatricality of McQueen's work in the design of the store and Lee adored what they came up with: a glass changing room that was clear before you entered but automatically turned opaque when it sensed movement; a display system constructed from stainless steel rods which resembled a giant piece of gym equipment; and a big glass vitrine at the entrance that could be filled with seasonal displays and which projected out into the street. McQueen would have liked this to have projected further, "as a bit of surrealism," he said, but the planning authorities at Westminster Council turned it down. "I wanted a shop that was interactive, with robots and stuff, so that people would learn something about the person behind the clothes," he said.[11] The store also contained a range of licensed products such as sunglasses, ties, scarves, footwear and watches, most of which had not been seen outside of Japan, and a range of objects that had featured in McQueen's shows, such as the prosthetic legs worn by Aimee Mullins in *No. 13*, as well as the portrait of the designer as Joan of Arc by Nick Knight.

Most of the design process went smoothly apart from two occasions when McQueen shouted at Ferhan. "I also heard he used to shout at his staff and throw things, but he never did that to us," she said. "McQueen was an outsider and you could feel it at all levels. He was moody and he was a very angry person. It felt like anything could happen."[12]

Janet Street-Porter, another woman who could hardly be described as timid, also remembers the feeling of anxiety with which she approached McQueen. "I thought he was terrifying—and everyone tells *me* I'm terrifying," she said. "The three most terrifying people I've met were Muriel Belcher [the legendary landlady of the Colony Room], Francis Bacon and Lee McQueen. They were all very similar and employed attack as a form of defence—they got in there first—so before you've got a sentence out they've got a put-down ready." When McQueen's Conduit Street store opened Janet bought five items, including a couple of suits, a brown skirt embroidered with a gold dragon and a brown coat. "Because his clothes were really tailored they looked great whatever size you were," she said. "His clothes weren't so much about sex as about power. When you wore them you knew you were in control, which is why they were great to wear to work." She thought some of the skirts he sold were so tight—at times they were like hobble skirts—that she found them difficult to walk in. "They reminded me of being a mod when I was fourteen," she said. "We had exactly those kind of skirts. Lee knew all that stuff; he was aware of tailoring not just because he had worked on Savile Row but because it was part of an English tradition." There was one outfit, however, that did not go down so well: a striped trouser suit that McQueen had sent over for her to wear for the premiere of Elton John and Tim Rice's *Aida* in New York in 2000. Janet was staying at the St. Regis Hotel with Elton and, after getting dressed in the trouser suit, which she wore with a pair of high platform shoes, she walked into Elton's suite. "I thought I looked quite striking but Sheila [Farebrother], Elton's mother, looked at me and said to Elton, 'What's Janet come as—a fucking deck chair?' That was before I had even left the room. I've never been able to wear it after that, and I couldn't sell it either."[13]

In September 1999, McQueen flew to America for his New York show in the midst of a tropical hurricane. The city was in chaos: parts of the subway system had been flooded, trees had been blown down, Bryant Park (housing the tents for New York Fashion Week) had closed, and there was even the threat that the overflowing sewage system would force manhole covers to shoot up into the sky, showering residents of Manhattan in effluence. Lee, of course, was in his element. "It's brilliant," he said, in the run-up to the show. "I've really brought London to America, haven't I? It's going to test the resolve of the British stiff upper lip and all that. It would take more than a bit of wind and rain to stop us."[14] Coincidentally, McQueen had already decided to fill the stage with water, a reworking of the idea that he had used in *Bellmer La Poupée*. The show—called *Eye* and held on 16 September at a West Side pier—was greeted with rave reviews, not so much for the clothes, "which didn't break any ground," according to Cathy Horyn of the *New York Times*,[15] but because of McQueen's sensational staging. "New York was a city waiting for the Big One," wrote Mimi Spencer, "but it turned out to be Alexander McQueen and not Hurricane Floyd that really shook up a storm."[16] The highlight of the show was the finale in which a number of ghostly shrouded figures seemed to float high above the stage in the darkened gloom. As strobe lights flickered it became clear that hundreds of sharp spikes (or were they missile heads?) had risen from the ground. The women, dressed in Arabian robes and burqas, and suspended from the roof by invisible wires, performed a beautiful aerial ballet above the deathly bed below. The image was both personal—the space above the spikes represented the realms of the spirit, a region in which Lee felt free from the dangers of the world—and political, as the show could be read as a prescient statement about the clash between the fundamentalist Islamic world and the values of the West, a conflict that resulted in the attacks of 9/11 in 2001. At the end of the show, Lee came onstage and, to the sound of Sharon Redd's "Can You Handle It," dropped his bleached jeans to reveal a pair of stars-and-stripes undershorts. From this closing gesture there was no doubting whose side McQueen was on.

On his return to London, on 20 September, McQueen attended a lavish party at Lancaster House hosted by Tony and Cherie Blair to mark the start of London Fashion Week. "You're not going to show me your underwear, are you?" asked the prime minister's wife when she met McQueen, a reference to his recent trouser-dropping on the catwalk in New York.[17] Later, the designer would describe her as "cheesy."[18] Tony Blair congratulated the guests, who included Nicole Farhi, Bruce Oldfield and Rifat Özbek, for both raising the profile of British fashion and contributing to the industry's economic success, a business that employed more than 300,000 people in the UK. "There are not many industries that can say they have trebled in size in just six years," he said.[19]

By that autumn, McQueen's relationship with Richard Brett had already entered its final stages. Earlier in the year, Lee had begged his boyfriend to move into the house in Hillmarton Road, but after about two months of sharing McQueen's house Richard had started to feel uncomfortable. "As soon as I'd moved in he became really controlling," he said. "I felt like I was losing all sense of my own identity. He also kept going on about having some kind of 'marriage' and I think my refusal made things worse. He thought I didn't want to do it because I didn't love him or like him enough and that caused issues in the end. So I moved out of the house and back into a shared flat in West Hampstead. Lee really struggled with relationships: he wanted partners he could control but he was attracted to people who were resistant to that. His positive side was almost addictive and incredibly good fun, but when he was in a dark place he was really difficult to deal with; it was exhausting and quite draining."

Richard also observed how the pressures of producing multiple collections each year began to take their toll. He learnt how to absent himself from the period in the run-up to the shows, when often McQueen would lash out and say hurtful things to him. "The fact that he was put on a pedestal made it worse because he couldn't just do a normal catwalk show, it had to be amazing," he said. "There was a part of him that wasn't suited to being in that world. He had some true friends, but there were people in his life who were really bad for him—I would call them the party set. They weren't healthy for him at all. I don't think he was suited to the excessive party lifestyle, as he was incredibly sensitive and quite a home boy. If you mix stress with drugs and add people who were a bad influence into the mix then it becomes really quite toxic."

In November 1999, McQueen sold the house in Hillmarton Road for £820,000, making a £200,000 profit, and moved into a rented flat in Shoreditch. The relationship between Lee and Richard was "fading" and McQueen told his boyfriend that he wanted to spend some time in New York. On 8 December, Lee attended the opening of the LVMH Tower, a skyscraper on East Fifty-Seventh Street. At the gala dinner, McQueen, dressed in a black suit and white shirt, sat next to the model Karen Elson and Elton John. Richard Brett was expecting Lee to return to London for the New Year, but during a telephone conversation it became obvious McQueen had other plans. "He said that he was going to be in New York for the New Year," recalls Richard. "I said, 'Well, it's Millennium Eve, so if we're not going to be together that doesn't bode well, does it?' And he said, 'No, I suppose not.' And that was it, that was the end."[20]

The real reason behind the split was that McQueen had already met someone else: Jay Massacret, a handsome twenty-two-year-old photography student born in Paris and raised in San Francisco. The pair met in a bar in Hoxton, where Jay was working part-time to earn some extra cash. "We exchanged little notes which we gave the cocktail waitress," recalls Jay, who is now a stylist.[21] Sebastian Pons was there at the first meeting between the two men. "Lee said to me, 'Oh my God, I can't believe he's into me,'" he remembers. "He also liked the fact that Jay did not know who he was. Lee's love life ruled him, always. If he was in a good mood with whoever he was dating everything seemed to run smoothly at the studio."[22]

By the autumn of 1999, Jay and Lee had reached such a level of intimacy that McQueen felt comfortable taking him to Hilles for the weekend. "We liked hanging out at home and cooking," said Jay. "He had this homey sort of vibe about him. I remember we had a joint Thanksgiving/Guy Fawkes' Night dinner. He had this huge laugh, and he was fun to be around. When I think of him now it's always his laugh that comes into my head." Although Lee had told Richard that he was spending the millennium in New York, the truth was that McQueen took his new boyfriend Jay to the Maldives.[23]

McQueen started the new millennium feeling happy and healthy—he had lost more than twenty pounds, an achievement that he said was a result of cutting out junk food and regularly ingesting chitosan, a dietary supplement that he bought from Harrods which he believed limited the absorption of fat. He returned from holiday feeling better than he had in months. "The eyes are clear, sparkling periwinkle against his tan," said one observer.[24]

On 16 January 2000, Lee staged his couture show in Paris for Givenchy, which featured a semi-naked Erin O'Connor lying on a plinth being dressed in a checked chiffon shirt and a beautifully tailored gray suit by an aged butler. Critics described the scene as "tender and romantic," and backstage McQueen told journalists that the show had been "all about restraint."[25] This stood in marked contrast to the show for his own label which he staged on 15 February at the derelict Gainsborough film studios in Hoxton, where Hitchcock had filmed *The Lady Vanishes.*

He named the show *Eshu,* after a deity from the Yoruba religion that originated in Africa. Eshu was a spirit that represented fortune and misfortune, a protector of travelers and also a personification of death. McQueen must have been particularly attracted to the god because, like the designer himself, Eshu reveled in dividing opinion. One story associated with the god features Eshu walking down a road wearing a hat, half of which was black, the other side red. Villagers standing on one side of the road could only see one color, those on the opposite the other color. As a result, the two groups argued over which perspective was the true one. Another version of the same story had the two sides killing each other over what they had seen, after which Eshu laughed and said, "Bringing strife is my greatest joy."

McQueen himself could be seen as an Eshu-like figure, a celebrator of the chaos and turmoil that he left in his wake. The day before the show an animal rights group had broken into the film studios and daubed a series of anti-fur slogans on the set—McQueen acknowledged that he used rabbit, broadtail and sheepskin in his collection, but maintained these were by-products of other industries. It had also been rumored that the protesters had tried to booby-trap the stage, an allegation that proved untrue but left hundreds of fashion critics and celebrities (including Helen Mirren, Björk, Ralph Fiennes, Francesca Annis, Sharleen Spiteri and Jade Jagger) standing outside in the drizzle as they waited in line to have their bags searched. Tracey Emin, who had been sent with photographer Juergen Teller to report on the collection for the first issue of the relaunched *Nova* magazine, wrote of how unsettled she felt by the experience—"Juergen says to me, 'You know, Tracey, there was something wrong with tonight.' 'Yeah,' I say, 'mate, there was nothing to celebrate—mate, there just wasn't any Love.'"[26]

The African theme split opinion like no other. While Mimi Spencer regarded the clothes as a dream—"the perfectly cut coat in creamy wool, with pinched shoulders and a placket-front (beautiful even though splattered with red earth); a leather dress, nicked a thousand times to let light through"[27]—other female commentators believed the show to be symbolic of a deep-seated misogyny that ran through

McQueen's work. Joanna Pitman in *The Times* wrote how the models looked as if "they had done a couple of rounds with Mike Tyson and then been kidnapped by Burmese guerillas and dressed up in local tribal gear. One tottered out trying to retain a shred of dignity while wearing a mouth brace that fixed her lips permanently open in a hideous grimace . . . This contraption was decorated with two six-inch metal fangs making the poor girl look like a demented wild boar."[28] Joan Smith, in the *Independent on Sunday*, attacked McQueen for the way, in her view, he debased and degraded women. She singled out imagery from his past shows, such as Debra Shaw in manacles in *Bellmer La Poupée* and the models in *Highland Rape*, who she thought looked like victims of sexual assault. However, she concentrated her ire on *Eshu*, particularly McQueen's decision to fit a model with a silver mouthpiece designed by Shaun Leane. "Vicious spikes framed her nose, the tips perilously near her eyes," she said. "What on earth was going through the mind of the man who designed it?"[29] But the most inflammatory response was one written by Brenda Polan in the *Daily Mail*, which carried the headline, "The Designer Who Hates Women." The writer saw McQueen as being representative of most male fashion designers, men who had an ambivalent love/hate attitude towards women. "It is an issue the industry refuses to explore because the designers in question are often the best and most creative," she said. Polan was at her most polemic—if not downright offensive—when she brought in the question of homosexuality. "They [the designers] are almost always gay and it is not hard to read into their work a combination of fear for women's bodies twinned with fascination and envy," she said. Photographs of the model wearing Leane's mouthpiece were accompanied by the caption "Insulting ideas: McQueen's designs seem to humiliate women."[30]

Of course, McQueen could have hit back, but to do so would have left him open to questions about the real source of the dark imagery that ran through his work: the psychological alignment he felt with his older sister, Janet. "Seeing me beaten up had a lasting effect on him," said Janet. "I don't want to sound as though I am pushing myself forwards, but Lee had this admiration for me. Because I was a bit of a mother to him he looked up to me. He might have seen through me what he could do for women, help make them stronger."[31] Lee used to call Janet "the wise one"; between them there was an unspoken bond, a knowledge that they had both suffered at the hands of the same man, but an awareness that they had survived. Once, when brother and sister were alone, Lee asked Janet a question that had been bothering him for some time. "Are you my mum?" he asked. "Of course not, Lee, no," she replied. "Are you sure you are not my mum?" he repeated. "No, Lee, I am not your mum," she said. "He thought that there was some sort of family secret that when I was fifteen I had had an illegitimate baby," said Janet.[32]

Isabella Blow viewed her friend Lee as something of a modern-day knight, a designer who had the ability to fashion clothes that served as sartorial force fields, suits and dresses and jackets that shielded people from the brutalities of the world. Her fantasy vision of McQueen had become a reality of sorts during a shoot, "The Dark Knight Returns," which she had styled for the August 1998 issue of *The Face*. Blow had dressed Lee in a suit of armor from the film *Excalibur* and had sent him into battle with a dirty and bloodied face, an imaginative reenactment that had been documented by the photographer Sean Ellis. Ellis had also been on hand to capture Isabella's birthday party in November 1998, where he shot her and McQueen playing with a giant vibrating dildo; he included the images in his book *365: A Year in Fashion*. "Issie had the most filthy tongue, a vulgar fishwife sense of humour, which made Alexander chortle, but which she kept away from me because I said I'm not interested in cocks and cunts," said Detmar. "Yet sometimes she made even McQueen blush."[33]

McQueen's quest to seek out fragile but strong women and clothe them in armor of his own making continued. "If you look at all their personalities, the world they live in, they are all out on a limb," he said of the women who inspired him. "They're not refined women like the women in a John Singer Sargent. They're like punks in their own world, individuals who don't fit in a mould."[34]

McQueen's muses often seemed fantastical, women who could have stepped from the pages of a fin de siècle novel, a Tennyson poem or a dark fairy tale. His latest, Daphne Guinness, a striking-looking woman with a "badger" streak of black in her peroxide hair, was described by one commentator as having the look of "a slightly deranged fairy invented by C. S. Lewis."[35] Her background was illustrious: she was the daughter of brewery and banking heir Jonathan Guinness and Suzanne Lisney, an artist and friend of Salvador Dalí and Man Ray; her paternal grandmother was Diana Mitford Mosley. Born in 1967, Daphne grew up in a world of aristocratic privilege and bohemian fantasy. The family moved between homes in Ireland, Warwickshire, Kensington Square and Cadaqués, Spain, where they owned a converted monastery. "I always wanted a piece of armour," she said. "When I was a child there were always suits of armour in our houses, and I wanted to be Joan of Arc."[36] From a young age she escaped into a self-created world of the imagination, constructing fantasies with each blink of an eye. "It was like a Spanish *Wuthering Heights*," she said of her time growing up in Cadaqués. "I would sort of wander around the hills, and I had all my little caves and things that I knew."[37] While at the family's estate in Warwickshire, she became aware that the coal pits in the county had closed and when she saw the rivers and streams running with red water she assumed that the earth was bleeding; in reality, the color was due to the iron oxide in the water. Then, when she was five, she suffered a traumatic attack when a family friend, Antony Baekeland, came looking for his mother, Barbara, the ex-wife of the Bakelite heir Leo Baekeland. "When I first saw him, I thought he'd come to tell me a story," said Daphne. "And then suddenly, out came the knife." Antony proceeded to drag her around the house, informing her that his mission in life was to kill all women, and that she would be his first victim. Although he did let her go, subsequently in November 1972, Baekeland went on to stab his mother to death and, after being released from prison in July 1980, he attacked his eighty-seven-year-old grandmother, too. "I remember the taste of blood in my mouth," said Daphne. "It was like being in a trance, and trying to reason with someone who is quite obviously not in their right mind was confusing."[38]

At nineteen, Daphne married the Greek shipping heir Spyros Niarchos and had three children with him. The couple divorced in 1999 and Daphne returned to live in London. "She had been in this jewelled Fabergé cage, which turned into a pressure cooker, and then she came out of it like Venus on the half shell," said her friend Robin Hurlstone.[39] Daphne had known Isabella Blow for most of her life—the latter's grandmother Lady Vera Delves Broughton had been the mistress of Daphne's great-grandfather Lord Moyne. In 1997, the two women met again at Claridge's at the ninetieth-birthday party of Daphne's relative Maureen, Marchioness of Dufferin and Ava. "It was white tie and tiara, and of course I didn't have a tiara, so I made one out of feathers and lots of black chiffon," she said. "Issie thought it was absolutely fantastic."[40]

Isabella had tried to persuade Daphne to get in touch with McQueen, but she had resisted; she was both shy and reluctant to be introduced to the designer with a feeling of expectation hanging in the air. She had bought a great many of his clothes from Givenchy and she was, she said, perfectly happy to know him solely through his work. "I also didn't want Isabella to think that I was another Annabelle [Neilson]," she said.

One day, as Daphne was crossing Leicester Square, she heard a voice behind her call out, "Oi—that's my coat you're wearing!" She turned around and saw the designer. "You're Alexander," she said, taking her lead from Isabella and calling him by his middle name. "Yeah, and you're the one who's always snubbing me," he replied. "Why don't you want to meet me?" The pair started laughing and took themselves off to the nearest pub, where they got "plastered." Daphne's first impressions of McQueen were of a man with bright blue eyes, who was kind, honest, and who had a good sense of humor. "And he was really clever, it was just oozing out of him," she said. With a reported divorce settlement of £20 million, together with her own money, Daphne had built up an enormous collection of haute couture and often she would lend McQueen items of clothing to examine more closely. "And he would send them back without linings because he wanted to take them apart and see how the seamstresses had worked," she said. The new friends shared a rebellious spirit—they talked about how they were naughty in class and how they had felt out of place as children. "If you look at me and my name you would think we were poles apart, but we were both sensitive and there was a lot of commiserating between us," she said. "He was kind of like a father figure to me, always trying to cheer me up because he thought I was making bad choices with men. He was extremely protective of me and furious when people were horrid to me. He was always the one talking me out of a tree. He was drawn to people who were wounded."

Daphne soon became concerned that her new friend was mixing with people who facilitated and encouraged his drug use. "Isabella was violently anti drugs, she thought they were very bad and very much disapproved of Alexander's drug taking," she said. "She thought they were for losers. If I could say one thing to Alexander now it would probably be a conversation about drugs and self-preservation."[41]

On 24 May 2000, McQueen and Annabelle Neilson attended a pool party at the Monte-Carlo Beach Hotel organized by Italian *Vogue* to celebrate the eightieth birthday of Helmut Newton. Guests at Lee's table included Naomi Campbell, Stella McCartney, Meg Mathews and John Galliano. "Theirs was by far the buzziest table at the party," said one source quoted in a newspaper. "They were loudly enjoying themselves and plainly up for some mischief. Galliano remarked how surreal the party was and decided to add to the theatrical atmosphere."[42] He and McQueen jumped into the pool, fully clothed, closely followed by Meg and Annabelle. When Meg climbed out of the water it was said that someone ripped her skirt from her waist, "leaving her to saunter off in a black thong," while Annabelle's sheer dress, which looked like a spider's web, became completely transparent. It was reported that the organizers of the party demanded full control of the photographs that were released to the press. "Those you didn't see would have beggared belief," said one witness.[43]

Despite all the debauchery there was a part of McQueen's mind that remained sharp and intensely focused. That night he had spotted in the crowd a man who he thought might have the power to change his life: Domenico De Sole, the CEO of the Gucci group and the suave rival to Bernard Arnault, McQueen's boss at LVMH. In April, McQueen had approached Marianne Tesler, the president of Givenchy, with the idea of selling them a stake in his own label. Apparently, neither Tesler nor Arnault was particularly enthusiastic about the idea—"They said, 'Yeah, yeah, yeah.' And nothing happened"—and so McQueen felt as though he would have to take his business elsewhere.[44] His interest was piqued when he heard that the Gucci group were going on a shopping spree—"There are good opportunities. There are companies out there that can be bought. But I do have a limit. I have $2.5 billion," De Sole had told *Time* magazine earlier in May.[45]

That night in Monte Carlo, McQueen walked up to De Sole, introduced himself and arranged to have his photograph taken with him, joking that he was tempted to send it to Arnault. "I thought to myself that this is my kind of guy," said De Sole, who suggested that they meet up in London.[46] Lee knew that he was playing a dangerous game—in 1999, Arnault had launched a takeover bid of Gucci as he stealthily acquired more than 20 percent of the company's outstanding shares and then offered £5.9 billion for the group. In order to defend itself from this form of attack, Gucci brought in "white knight" François Pinault, whose company Pinault-Printemps-Redoute (PPR) acquired a 42 percent stake in the group for £2 billion. So if Lee knew he was playing with fire, why do it? "It was like having a boyfriend that you know you have to break up with," McQueen said of his partnership with Givenchy, "the only difference with this relationship was that I didn't feel bad about doing it."[47]

• • •

By the spring of 2000, the relationship between Lee and Jay Massacret had run its course. "We just both went our separate ways," said Jay. "I was very young and he was the person he was. We didn't talk for a little bit and then we became friends again, and remained friends until he died."[48] Around this time, in a north London bar, McQueen met another man with whom he fell in love—twenty-three-year-old filmmaker George Forsyth. "Lee was a romantic, he was falling in love all the time," said his friend Miguel Adrover.[49]

George was the son of architect Alan Forsyth and his wife, Sandra. "I had no concept or interest in fashion really," said George. "We just got on really well from the very beginning. He was an East End boy, I'm a north London Jew. We could talk for hours. We courted for four weeks then, about five weeks after we met, we went out one Saturday night and I just didn't go home, ever."[50] George had ambitions to become an installation artist using video: one of his works involved filming men urinating and masturbating at a urinal. "George was lovely," said his friend Donald Urquhart, who knew him from before the time he started seeing Lee. "He was very inquisitive, always wanted to know more about culture. He had a good sense of humour and loved to have a laugh and was quite naughty."[51] Donald noticed how Lee's dress sense began to change as his new, younger boyfriend started to style him in his own image: a look centering on opulent casual wear, half bling, half "chav." "George was obsessed with trainers—he had dozens of pairs, usually very rare designer editions in a flashy style, often with thick, built-up soles to give him extra height," said Donald. The two young men stood out in Islington. "The Islington council estate look was then, as it is today, pale grey hoodie tops and trackie bottoms with a horizontal striped polo shirt from Gap," said Donald. "George and Lee were working the odd gold lamé trim, and over-exaggerated logos in fluorescent colours. Ibiza chic."[52]

George first realized his new boyfriend's level of celebrity and fame when he attended a *Vogue* party. As he and Lee, dressed in ripped jeans and trainers, walked down the Strand he recalled seeing flashes from a bank of photographers' cameras and hearing cries of "Alexander! Alexander!" "There was all the best drink, beautiful people," he said. "I remember him bringing over Naomi Campbell and Isabella Blow and Kate Moss and wanting to introduce me to them. That's when it really hit me how well-known he was. Until then I'd only met Lee, but there he was Alexander McQueen."[53]

On the surface it looked as though McQueen's world was one of hedonistic abandon. There were, according to George, parties every night; champagne receptions; an endless parade of ice sculptures; cocaine passed around on silver salvers; three-day-long drink and drug binges. Yet McQueen continued to work at a furious pace. In the spring of 2000, Lee announced that he would be soon launching McQueens, a denim collection, and a line of sunglasses. "What I want to do is make fashion fun again," he said. "At the moment, the beast is definitely stale."[54] He was also busy preparing a giant artwork, *Angel*, for the exhibition *La Beauté en Avignon*. McQueen had collaborated with Nick Knight to create the image of an angel's face from tens of thousands of different-colored maggots. The work, staged in a medieval church in the ancient town in southeastern France, was designed to be viewed from above and experienced while listening to a sound track recorded by Björk. "I'm not being big-headed, but I think what we've done for Avignon clears the fucking board with Tracey Emin," said McQueen at the time. "Turning maggots, the ugliest thing on earth, into a Madonna is better than listing the names of the blokes that I've fucked in my life."[55]

McQueen expected his employees to work at the same frenetic pace, and if they did not meet his exacting standards they would be insulted and humiliated. After five years with Lee, Sebastian Pons was feeling like he needed a change of scene. Working with McQueen had been a highly stimulating—but exhausting—experience. He also felt as though Lee sometimes took advantage of his goodwill, expecting him to walk his dogs and feed his fish when he was away from London. He also felt as though McQueen was not paying him enough for the hours that he put in and, because he did not have a company credit card, he would have to pay for his own travel to Paris and Italy and then claim the money back. "I told him, 'Lee, my numbers don't match,'" said Sebastian. If the two friends went out, Lee always wanted to take a taxi, and one day, after climbing out of the cab, McQueen snapped at Sebastian because he had been left to pay the fare. Sebastian told him that if it had been up to him he would never have taken a cab in the first place, preferring to travel by bus or tube. "He lost touch with how much things cost," he said. "I didn't have a bank account with endless money like him." The situation reached crisis point when McQueen suggested that they go shopping and the pair took a cab to Comme des Garçons. Lee spent £9,000 in just a few minutes on some clothes and a cashmere blanket that cost £3,000. "Later, I went round to his house to walk the dogs and I saw that he had given the blanket to his dogs to sleep on, and they had bitten it. I thought then this was too much."[56]

When Lee's friend Miguel Adrover offered Sebastian a better-paid job working for him in New York, Sebastian took it, a decision that resulted in the breakdown of two friendships. "Lee thought that I had betrayed him, which was not true," said Miguel. Adrover and McQueen never spoke again.[57] Lee told Sebastian that if he left the company he would never be allowed back; when he did leave, his place was taken by Sarah Burton.

In August, a month after presenting his Givenchy show at the Grande Arche de la Défense, which was decorated to look like a re-creation of a downtown New York loft party, McQueen was getting ready for his "wedding" to George Forsyth in Ibiza. The idea was born one night that summer when the couple had drinks in the Groucho Club with Kate Moss and Annabelle Neilson. Halfway through the evening one of the women asked George whether he would ever marry Lee. "Yeah, I would," he said. "Would you?" asked McQueen, after which George again replied, "Yeah." This was before civil partnerships or gay marriage became law in Britain, so they were talking about a ceremony rather than anything legally binding. The girls became immediately excited and in a few minutes had arranged everything: Annabelle wanted to be Lee's bridesmaid and Kate would be George's.

The foursome took a flight to Ibiza, where they rented a luxury villa. On the day of the ceremony, George and Lee were relaxing in the pool when the women told them to quickly get ready for their big day. At the door there were two Bentleys, one for Lee and Annabelle, the other for George and Kate. The cars whisked them down to the harbor, where they boarded a three-story motor yacht full of Lee's celebrity friends such as Sadie Frost and Jude Law, Patsy Kensit, Meg Mathews and Nellee Hooper. Annabelle had commissioned Shaun Leane to make two rings for the couple, each engraved with the words "George & Lee" and set with diamonds. A new-age priest performed the ceremony under a full moon, after which the guests ate lobster and drank their way through £20,000 of champagne. "There were no family," said George later. "It was all party people. I was nervous. I was sitting down at one point and Jude Law came up to me and said, 'You don't know anyone here, do you?' And I didn't. But afterwards Lee and I went down to the front, under the moonlight. It was a perfect night. It was romantic."[58]

The romance, however, did not last long. "The whole thing was a piss-take," said Archie Reed, Lee's long-term, on-and-off boyfriend. "It wasn't anything real, and anyone who said anything different would be lying. Lee only ever used George to wind me up—he was a nobody as far as he was concerned, just a pastime. Lee liked a bad boy and George wasn't that, even though he pretended to be."[59] The days spent in Ibiza following the wedding were apparently so debauched that Lee told friends he never wanted to see the Balearic party island ever again.

Friends witnessed how the relationship between Lee and George veered between ostentatious gestures of romance and base violence. Lee would take George to parties and openings—they were photographed together at the launch of the Burberry store in Bond Street on 7 September—he would send him 500 red roses, and on a whim he would organize a plane to take them to Paris for drinks, Spain for dinner and then Amsterdam for a night of clubbing. At the same time, "George was very badly beaten by Lee," said McQueen's friend Chris Bird.[60] "George and him used to fight a lot," said Janet Street-Porter.[61] "People think he's aggressive, but of course, the aggression comes from the vulnerability," said Elton John. "He does strike out, but that's all about insecurity."[62] Detmar Blow remembers an awkward dinner at Nobu with Elton John and David Furnish, and Tim Burton and his then girlfriend Lisa Marie. "Elton sensed that he was familiar with McQueen's demons and wanted to help," he said. "But McQueen was rude and churlish in response."[63]

As George and Lee spent more time together, the younger man gradually became aware that his new "husband" was a highly complex individual. "Everybody wanted to be with Lee," he said. "He was the hottest ticket in town. But I noticed that in the fashion world there were very few people who said, 'There's someone who needs looking after.'"[64] George was also a little startled to discover that McQueen had an unusual fetish. "Lee used to like to have athlete's foot and let it get into such a bad state that it became painful and very itchy," said Donald Urquhart. "He absolutely loved that sensation and enjoyed scratching between his toes, which George didn't get at all."[65] George told Donald that Lee "almost got off on it, it was almost like a sexual pleasure."[66]

McQueen explored the connections between pain and pleasure in his next show for his own label held on 26 September 2000 at the Gatliff Road bus depot. *Voss* was one of the highlights of McQueen's career, not so much a fashion show as a fully formed art installation that interrogated attitudes towards beauty and ugliness, sex and death, sanity and madness. Backstage, however, the atmosphere was far from gloomy. Kate Moss, a little piqued by having her head swathed in muslin, took hold of a bandage and wrapped it around hairstylist Guido Palau. "He did not like a taste of his own medicine," she said. "There is a picture in the office at McQueen of me and Lee cackling, laughing our heads off because I got him [Guido] back."[67]

Before the show started, the audience—which included some of the world's most beautiful women, including Gwyneth Paltrow, as well as dozens of style and fashion critics—were forced to look at themselves for an hour, their images reflected from the surface of an enormous rectangular box on the stage that had been constructed from surveillance glass. Finally, with many people in the audience already feeling distinctly uncomfortable, the models started to emerge. With their heads bandaged as if they had just undergone a mass lobotomy (or face-lift), the beautiful girls, unable to see out, paced up and down the catwalk, which was designed to look like a padded cell, and around a sinister darkened box that sat center stage.

The outfits themselves were both stunningly beautiful and deeply unsettling. There was a dress made from bloodred glass medical slides. Another dress had been constructed from razor-clam shells that Lee and George had found on a beach in Norfolk. There was a coat of purple and green silk woven with a thermal image of McQueen's face on the back. A startling Japanese-inspired jacket and trousers were made from pink and gray bird's-eye cloth and twinned with a hat the size of a small coffin embroidered with silk thread and real amaranth flowers. Finally there was an exquisite underdress of oystershells worn below a dress constructed from a nineteenth-century Japanese screen that Lee had found in the Clignancourt flea market in Paris and which had sat in his home until six months before the show. "The screen was so fragile that when we touched it, it crumbled," said Sarah Burton. "We fused it onto cotton so it wouldn't fall apart, then lined it with silk so it would hold its shape. The whole thing was done by hand. It was too delicate to put on a machine. Alexander did most of it himself. He didn't want any pleats or darts, he wanted it to be very flat, to show off the workmanship which is fantastic."[68]

The beauty of the clothes, however, was immediately challenged by the final image. As the last model walked from the set, a light started to burn inside the mysterious dark glass box and heavy breathing emanated from the PA system. The sides of the box opened and smashed to the ground to reveal a fat, naked woman in breathing apparatus together with hundreds of moths fluttering in the air, a reworking of Joel-Peter Witkin's 1983 photograph *Sanitarium*. "I am McQueen's pulsing mirror, fashion's greatest fear staring right back at them," wrote Michelle Olley, the model whom McQueen asked to strip off and don a gas mask, in her diary at the time. "I am the death of fashion. The death of beauty."[69]

The show represented McQueen's ambivalent attitude towards the fashion industry: while he still had the ability to imagine and make clothes of heart-stopping beauty, he felt there was something deeply toxic about the environment. The final image, as Michelle Olley recalls, was one that symbolized death. "Monsieur McQueen was cooking up a Big Momma Muerte finish," she wrote.[70] "I can't see myself staying in fashion," Lee told Nick Knight. "There is no substance to it any more. If you think about fashion through history, it was revolutionary. It's not revolutionary now." Did he not view his own work as revolutionary? Knight had asked. "No, I'm bored of trying. Bored of being an anarchist . . . With these big companies, it gets to a point where it means nothing . . . If I were God, I would stop fashion for five years."[71]

At this point, McQueen could have taken a step back and distanced himself from the unrelenting treadmill of producing collection after collection. His Givenchy contract was coming to an end in 2001; he said he didn't want to pursue dreams of greater wealth or fame; he had fulfilled many of the ambitions that he had harbored as a young man. And yet, when Isabella Blow telephoned him to tell him that Tom Ford wanted to talk about the possibility of Gucci buying a stake in his business, he seized the opportunity. He could not blame Ford's silken-tongued, Texan charm nor the suggestion, according to Isabella, that the creative director of Gucci found him attractive. After all, McQueen had started the process himself when he had introduced himself to Domenico De Sole in Monte Carlo. "I went for him [De Sole]," he said. "Some sort of arrangement with Gucci was on my mind."[72] Perhaps his motive was revenge? "I really think the reason he sold his share in his company to the Gucci group was really to stick two big fucking fingers up to Bernard Arnault," said Chris Bird.[73]

After a number of telephone calls that stretched throughout the summer of 2000, McQueen and Ford finally set a date to meet at the Ivy restaurant. "Tom would say, 'I'm going out to dinner with Alexander, and you can't come!'" said Richard Buckley, Tom's partner (now husband). "So I knew they were up to something." That October night at the Ivy, Lee and Tom sat and discussed their lives, everything apart from fashion. "We had Twiggy in front of us and Charles Saatchi behind us, and here we were, these two men sitting at this table, glowing," said McQueen. For his part Ford described McQueen as somewhat fierce-looking in photographs but a "marshmallow" in person—"adorable, charming and kind." The "poetic" quality of McQueen's work appealed to him. "He is a true artist, albeit an artist with a real commercial savvy," he said.[74]

McQueen, however, was far from malleable when it came to negotiations about how much he wanted for 51 percent of his company—or, rather, the three companies that he had set up, Paintgate, Autumnpaper and Blueswan. Figures quoted in the press at the time ranged from £54 million to £80 million, something of an exaggeration according to John Banks, his accountant. He remembers the series of clandestine meetings that went on, often in a room at the back of Brown's, in Mayfair. All business had to be done in an atmosphere of the utmost secrecy as "Gucci and Givenchy were at war," he said. "There was no question when it came to the amount of money Lee wanted; he had decided the figure. It was in the tens of millions of dollars, at the lower end. When we mentioned the amount I remember De Sole and James McArthur [then the executive vice president of Gucci group] had a sharp intake of breath, but he got the money: it went from $20 million, $30 million, until eventually the number was achieved."[75]

In addition to the money, De Sole and Ford guaranteed McQueen creative independence. What they expected in return was for him to transform himself into a brand. "The question I had to ask myself—

because it's my job—is does he really have the power and the talent to turn the Alexander McQueen label into a global brand?" said De Sole at the time. "I think he does; otherwise I could not have done the deal, basically."[76]

Gucci hoped to open ten flagship stores bearing McQueen's name around the world, plus a number of perfumes, accessories and spin-off ranges. "He'll soon have what we all want—a global empire," said Julien Macdonald, who took over from McQueen at Givenchy. "They will smarten his collar, straighten his tie and make his accessories conquer the world."[77]

On Saturday, 2 December, John Banks telephoned McQueen to congratulate him on the deal. Lee was in a car with a group of friends and John remembers hearing a great collective scream of joy coming down the line. "He was pretty deliriously happy," said John.[78] Lee and George returned to the flat and celebrated by sharing a bag of crisps washed down by a couple of Bacardi Breezers.

When the news of the super-deal was announced on 4 December the press went into overdrive; the story even made it into the pages of the *Sun*. "McQueen Move Fuels Fashion Feud," read the headline in the *Guardian*. "Gucci Embraces Bad Boy of Style McQueen," said *The Times*. A comment writer for the *Independent* examined McQueen's toxic time at Givenchy but hoped that the designer would be happier in his new role. "The partnership with Gucci will no doubt be full of sparks," the editorial said, "but at least it will not be deadly."[79]

CHAPTER ELEVEN

Lee was constantly searching for a state where he felt comfortable—peace was elusive.

—*Kerry Youmans*

One day towards the end of December 2000, Lee and George
were at home watching television. In the corner of the rented
East End flat stood an enormous Christmas tree covered in hundreds
of Swarovksi crystals taken from a £30,000 chandelier that McQueen
had bought from the Four Seasons hotel in Paris, and subsequently
dismantled. Lee was bored of watching nature programs on television and that night, as they sat through another documentary, he
turned to George and asked him if he wanted to go to Africa. Two
days later, the two men sat on the upper deck of a plane bound for
the continent—McQueen had booked the entire floor just for them.
Just forty-eight hours after that, the designer had had enough of the
dry landscape and the hours spent waiting to catch a glimpse of a
wild animal. He knew Naomi Campbell had a house on the coast
and chartered a private plane to see her. "We spent three days partying and taking drugs there—it was New Year," said George. "Naomi
didn't do any coke even though she was surrounded by people who
were."[1]

The deal with Gucci turned McQueen into a man with serious
money. George remembered flying with him to New York on a whim
to buy a few pieces of modern art; in one afternoon McQueen spent

£125,000 on a couple of Warhol prints, including one from the *Diamond Dust Shoes* series. "I just thought I wanted a bit of history," he said. "I was never a big fan of his. I only understood him when I read the diaries and then I felt like I could connect with him because the [fashion] industry is a pile of shit and he was very talented to recognize it before he died."[2]

In June 2001, McQueen paid £1.3 million for 11 Aberdeen Park, Islington, which he bought from his friend, hairstylist Guido Palau. Then, later that year, he bought his parents a house worth £275,000 in Rowan Walk, Hornchurch, Essex. Initially, Ron and Joyce were reluctant to leave the family home in Biggerstaff Road, Stratford. Ron liked fishing in the nearby River Lea, and Joyce liked the shopping center. "But after a couple of years they settled and realized they should have done it years before," said Janet McQueen.[3]

Lee was still unhappy with his appearance and asked Janet Street-Porter if he could have the number of her personal trainer. "He tried to work out with Lee but it was pointless," said Janet. "Lee was always coked out of his head or coming down from being coked out of his head, and doing loads of other drugs too. So my trainer said he couldn't work with him in case he had an accident or a heart attack while they were working out."[4] Still desperate to lose weight, McQueen paid thousands of pounds to have a gastric band fitted, a device that limited the amount of food that he could eat. The results were dramatic and he lost two stone in the first three months. "He was trying to conform, live up to a celebrity status, and it just didn't suit him," said Archie Reed.[5] "I always thought he looked better with a bit of weight," said his brother Tony.[6] But McQueen loved his new look—which he told journalists was a result of healthy eating and exercise, including yoga. "It's more to do with wanting to look in the mirror and think, 'God, I really fancy you,'" he told Harriet Quick in *Vogue*. "I was in this club in London and I was wired, but I went to chat myself up in the mirror—it was so funny. I thought, 'Oh, you're quite cute!' And it was me. Finally, I got there!"[7]

By the time McQueen appeared at the Rover British Fashion

Awards, on 20 February 2001 in Battersea Park, he had lost a great deal of the fat from around his middle; his face looked slimmer too. As he stepped up to receive the Designer of the Year award—he had beaten Julien Macdonald and Clements Ribeiro—McQueen seemed nervous and on edge; a pair of sunglasses that he refused to take off hid his shifty eyes. There was a reason why the designer felt so anxious: standing on the stage next to Condé Nast's Nicholas Coleridge, chairman of the British Fashion Council, was Prince Charles, the man whose suits McQueen had claimed he had secretly defaced all those years before. Although the encounter could have been an awkward one, Lee lightened the mood by joking about it. "It's kind of uncanny because I started off by making his Highness's suits at Anderson & Sheppard and now I'm getting an award from him," he said. "It's kind of really freaky"—at which point both the audience and the prince laughed. In the accompanying film about McQueen's work the designer talked about some of the pressures that he had experienced in the fashion industry, and how he had felt that he had needed to express this in his show *Voss*. "It's like an animal in a testing lab, being looked at and prodded at, a bit like fashion really," he said. "Fashion is a small world, [there is] a sinister side to it, a lot of voyeurism. Sometimes fashion can get so suffocating. It's a bit like a mental asylum sometimes."

That night, at the awards, Lee criticized the lack of support that designers received and claimed that "if it wasn't for Gucci I wouldn't be carrying on today,"[8] a point that he had already made on BBC2's *Newsnight* a couple of days before. "One minute you are having a drink in 10 Downing Street, the next minute someone grabs you to have your photo taken with Cherie Blair," he had said. "She hadn't said two words before she dragged me over for that picture. It's all fine and well, but you have to put your money where your mouth is."[9]

McQueen had had a particularly stressful start to 2001. He had hoped to work with Sam Taylor-Wood on an installation for the Givenchy couture show in January, but when LVMH heard about his deal with Gucci, it was reported, his bosses had pulled the plug on the project and, as a punishment of sorts, they had confined him to a "low-key, client-only showing in the Avenue George V salon."[10] Lee had also been hurt by some of the statements released by LVMH, particularly one announcement that outlined how, since the group had not backed his own company, it was "normal that Mr McQueen should seek financing for his tiny business." According to journalist Christa D'Souza: "Of all the press McQueen received after the deal, it was the word 'tiny' that most rankled."[11]

It was no surprise that he titled his next show for his own label *What a Merry-Go-Round*. The presentation, which took place on 21 February 2001, blended the sinister aspects of childhood (references included the character of the Child Catcher in *Chitty Chitty Bang Bang*, ventriloquists' dummies, models with faces made up like crazed clowns, creepy-looking dolls, the sound of children playing and an eight-horse carousel) with McQueen's undisguised distaste for the fashion industry. At one point, as Krzysztof Komeda's haunting lullaby from *Rosemary's Baby* played over the PA system, a model with a three-pointed wig and a clown face hobbled across the stage with a gold skeleton clasped to the hem of her skirt. "We show children clowns as if they're funny," he said after the show. "They're not. They're really scary. And the funfair was a metaphor for all that I've been through lately."[12] Although the show was well received—"the collection was a brilliantly balanced mix of masculine and feminine, ultra-romantic and brutally sharp," wrote Susannah Frankel[13]—later McQueen said that he believed that the spectacle had stolen the show, and "nobody remembers the clothes."[14]

Janet Street-Porter did not agree. Soon after the show, McQueen sent her a present of a long black leather coat with a train. The writer and broadcaster adored it, but wearing it did present her with several problems. "First of all it's very long and has a train and you have to be careful not to fall over it and look like a drunk," she said. The second issue had more to do with the coat's power to incite passions in those who came into contact with it. She remembers wearing it to an opening at the Tate and being followed around the gallery by a well-dressed, highly educated man in his early sixties. "He was an MP or a captain of industry wearing a very expensive suit," she said. "He came up to me and asked if he could have a word. 'I'll give you anything you want if you come round to my flat and stand there in that coat,' he said. I told him it wasn't going to happen. I also wore it to a wedding in Oxfordshire. I remember going round to a friend's house beforehand and she said, 'Fucking hell, are you wearing that coat?' I said that I was and she said, 'Well, I'm not coming, I can't compete.' That coat had a big effect on people, his best clothes were like that."[15]

On 13 March 2001, Lee and George attended the opening of the Pop Art exhibition at the Pompidou Centre. Three days later, McQueen showed his final collection for Givenchy, a rather muted affair held once again at the house salon on Avenue George V. The usual audience of 2,000 had been cut back to a mere eighty people, mostly just buyers. Photographers had been banned from the event and there were only a handful of fashion journalists present. "The show was based on the signatures he has honed . . . sleek masculine tailoring softened with dove gray and lilac colors and an exuberant frothiness in blouses and full layered skirts," said Suzy Menkes, writing in the *International Herald Tribune*. "McQueen pulled all that together with a wide corset cummerbund that was even moulded with the body's rib bones."[16]

That year, for his thirty-second birthday, McQueen had received a Joel-Peter Witkin photograph from Elton John. Lee had been collecting Witkin's work since 1997 and by 2003 he owned thirteen photographs. His collection included the triptych *Portraits from the Afterworld: Madame Daru, Monsieur David, Madame David* (three corpses with their heads cut open and brains exposed) and *A Day in the Country* (which seemed to show a white stallion about to mount a naked, older woman). "There are so many different ways that I look at Witkin," he said. "I don't find it extreme. I know it looks extreme to other people. But I don't just look at the dog with its stomach out or the faeces, I look at the whole thing and I find it poetic. It relates to my work." With the steady stream of money from Gucci, McQueen continued to build up his collection of art. He bought photographs by Mat Collishaw, Sam Taylor-Wood, Lee Miller, Bill Brandt and Marc Quinn, paintings by Cecily Brown and Francis Bacon, works by the Chapman brothers, and a piece made by British pop artist Allen Jones, which featured a sculpture of a woman dressed in a corset, suspenders, gloves and leather boots, her back supporting a glass table. "I'm not a money-minded person," he said. "I don't really look at the price tag. If it makes me happy and it makes me skint, then so be it. If I have to sell something when I'm fifty, then I will." One of his favorite paintings was *The Arnolfini Portrait*, Jan van Eyck's work of 1434 in the National Gallery, and he always wanted to buy a work by the fifteenth-century artist Hans Memling but assumed that he would never be able to afford it. "I'd love to buy a Lucian Freud," he said. "I think if I could, I'd commission him to paint me because he looks deeper than the surface. It's enough to spook you out. What he'd get from me would be psychosis."[17]

There were some friends, however, who began to worry about McQueen's taste in art. Lee told his friend Mira Chai Hyde that he had started to see orbs of light in his house. "I said, 'Well, no wonder, look at the art you have in the house, it's all about death,'" recalls Mira. She told him to get rid of the most disturbing pieces, including the Witkins, but he said, "They're worth a fortune." "Put them in storage or in your office, but don't have them where you live," said Mira. "I would tell Lee how to protect himself, how to visualize himself surrounded by white light."[18] Lee's gardener Brooke Baker also remembers being disturbed by the kind of images McQueen had started to collect. "Some of the art, like the enormous photograph of his bum hole that he had above his bed, was hilarious, but later he started to amass all these photographs that I thought must have brought him down and depressed him," she said. "There was a photograph of a shellshocked soldier and another of a decapitated woman who had been in a car accident."[19]

On 10 May, the designer introduced an hour-long question-and-answer session at the Barbican with Helmut Newton, an appearance designed to tie in with an exhibition of the photographer's work. McQueen regarded Newton, described as the "35mm Marquis de Sade" and a proponent of "porno chic," as something of a kindred spirit.[20] Newton, said McQueen, was "fascinated by powerful women, preoccupied with role play and crossing the divide between masculine and feminine," a description that could equally apply to McQueen himself. "It was good for me to know at the beginning of my career and at a time when I came in for so much criticism that I had a kindred spirit in such a respected name and for a photographer like Newton I would never need to explain myself," he said. "Newton's women look like if you tried to touch them they would try to bite your arm off, and perhaps not just your arm," a line that drew laughter from the audience. "He is interested as I am in the fine line between beauty and cruelty."[21] In turn, Newton described McQueen as a "true agent provocateur."[22]

McQueen's private life was as complicated as ever. His "marriage" to George had not worked out and that summer the relationship had deteriorated to such an extent that the couple were having violent arguments and neighbors near the house in Aberdeen Park often had to call the police. Lee started to see other men, one of whom was Ben Copperwheat, the cousin of his friend Lee Copperwheat. Ben had known McQueen since 1999, but after he graduated from the print design course at the Royal College of Art in the summer of 2001, the relationship between the two men became more intimate. "I found him to be really exciting, generous, caring, interesting, wild, dark with a lot of energy," Ben said.[23] "We used to go out partying and on one occasion I went back to his place and we fooled around. At the time he was still 'married' to George, but I'm not sure whether they were living together. Lee was pretty wild and he was partying more than anyone else I knew. He really liked to get completely out of it. I hung out with him about six or seven times. I remember after one time we had been taking some drug and I was completely out of it. I couldn't get to sleep for a day and a half afterwards." Ben is sober now—he found it easier to give up drink and drugs after he moved to New York in 2003. "The culture in London is a lot more prone to drinking and drugs," he said. "If he'd gone sober it might have saved him."[24] A few years later, the two men met in New York at an event, but Lee snubbed him. "He was cold and distant and it seemed he did that with a few friends, he pushed them away," Ben said.[25]

The relationship with George finally ended in August 2001. "Lee wasn't easy to get on with and George could really wind him up," said Donald Urquhart. "One would be really angry with the other. It was clash clash clash and eventually he was worn out."[26] According to Archie Reed, Lee discovered that George had stolen some gay porn films from the house. "George also wanted to borrow money to pay his mortgage and they split as he felt that George just wanted fame and money and not him," he said.[27] McQueen later expressed his sadness at the end of the relationship in a piece of fashion performance titled *The Bridegroom Stripped Bare*, which was filmed for Nick Knight's SHOWstudio as part of the *Transformer* season. A model with a white-painted face and wearing a white Yohji Yamamoto suit and white shirt stood on a white plinth in front of a white backdrop. Lee, with loud techno music blaring in the background, then began to hack at the suit, and with rope, a length of white fabric, a long white veil and a tin of white paint transformed the model into a bridegroom. His final touches were to tie his hands and feet with rope, add some bloodred tears onto the man's face, throw some more paint over his feet and stuff his tie into his mouth. "There were about twenty-five people there watching him, silently," remembers Nick Knight. "It was, I imagine, just like watching an artist like Yves Klein or Jackson Pollock doing their thing . . . There was a great sadness to it, I thought. I don't know how much of it was about Lee."[28]

A great deal, in fact, as the image expressed McQueen's sense of failed romance, betrayal and isolation. "He had issues with trust," said Archie Reed, who resumed his relationship with Lee. "He thought that everyone wanted him because of his fame. And we were never left alone for five minutes. I've got a notorious reputation for fighting and I can't begin to tell you the amount of people I beat up. Anyone he

A skinny Lee with model Kate Moss. She described him in the following terms: "Anarchist, fun, thin, controversial, friend, loyal, charismatic, innovative, dark, determined."

Lee with Annabelle Neilson at the Monte-Carlo Beach Hotel in May 2000.

Lee "was drawn to people who were wounded," said his friend Daphne Guinness.

Lee and Isabella Blow in 2005.

A frock coat with a barbed thorn pattern from McQueen's 1992 MA collection. He was fascinated by thorns—"They really represent me, they represent who I am," he said.

"Alexander McQueen's debut was a horror show," wrote Marion Hume in 1993 in the *Independent*.

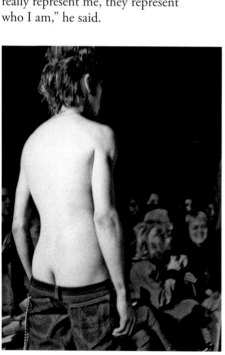

"I wanted to elongate the body, not just show the bum," McQueen said of the "bumsters."

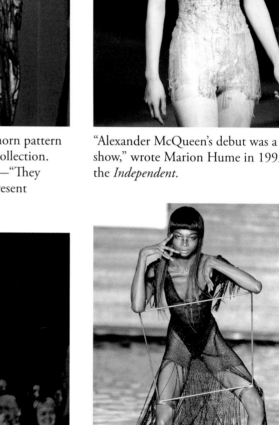

"When Debra Shaw walked contorted in a frame that image had nothing to do with slavery," McQueen said of *Bellmer La Poupée*. "It was the idea of the body reconstructed like a doll-like puppet."

"You can't come to Paris and compete with the Valentinos and the Chanels . . . and expect to win at twenty-seven," said Liz Tilberis, of McQueen's debut Givenchy show in January 1997.

Shalom Harlow in *No. 13*. As she revolved like a ballerina on a music box she tried to defend herself against the assault of two robots that sprayed her with yellow and black paint.

McQueen at the end of *Eye*, in New York, September 1999.

After *Eshu*, McQueen was attacked for being a misogynist.

"I am McQueen's pulsing mirror, fashion's greatest fear staring right back at them," wrote Michelle Olley, the model in *Voss*, set in an asylum. "I am the death of fashion. The death of beauty."

McQueen's show *In Memory of Elizabeth Howe, Salem, 1692,* held in March 2007, "was the start of him saying goodbye."

The models in *Horn of Plenty* looked like they had escaped the madhouse of *Voss* and had been let loose in a glorious fancy dress box that had once belonged to a French couturier.

When Lee started work on his collection *Plato's Atlantis,* he told his staff, "I don't want to look at any shapes, I don't want to reference anything, a picture, a drawing. I want it all to be new."

Lee with boyfriend Jay Massacret on holiday in the Maldives in early 2000.

McQueen with boyfriend Archie Reed.

Lee with his boyfriend and "husband" George Forsyth, whom he met in the spring of 2000.

Lee with his sister Janet, his first and greatest muse. He used to call her "the wise one" and between them there was an unspoken bond.

Lee with his parents in Claridge's, in October 2000, just before going to Buckingham Palace to accept his CBE.

Lee on the Isle of Skye, which he chose as his last resting place.

Lee with his mother, Joyce. In 2004 she had asked him
what was his most terrifying fear. "Dying before you," he replied.

The last public photograph of Lee, taken at Harry's Bar in Mayfair in February 2010. Tom Ford, pictured here with Annabelle Neilson, later "thought [that] Alexander had come to say goodbye."

Police stand outside McQueen's flat in Green Street, Mayfair, where he committed suicide on 11 February 2010, the day before his mother's funeral.

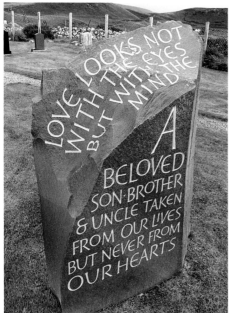

McQueen's grave on Skye stands on a windswept headland, looking out toward the sea. Inscribed on the green slate headstone are the words that he had had tattooed onto his right arm, "Love looks not with the eyes but with the mind."

went with I would just beat up. I would drag them out of clubs and I would knock their teeth down the back of their throats, and then I would go back in and finish my pint. Which he loved, by the way."[29]

After a holiday in the Mediterranean in the summer of 2001, McQueen returned to London refreshed and ready to put the finishing touches to his next collection, *The Dance of the Twisted Bull*, the first show for his own label under the auspices of the Gucci group. The show, held in Paris like all his future womenswear collections, featured variations on flamenco dresses and toreador suits, and seemed tame after the extremes of *Voss*. "I was thinking on a business level," said McQueen. "I did that collection because I was quite new to the label [Gucci] and needed to be more accessible. It wasn't so much about me, but the person who was buying it."[30]

McQueen was conscious of his new, more corporate responsibilities. Suzy Menkes remembers meeting him just before the Spanish-themed show and having a conversation with him about fonts and letterheads. "Is this the level I've come to?" he joked. He told Menkes of Gucci's plans for him: a 4,000-square-foot store in the Meatpacking District of New York which would open in 2002, and a further fifty shops worldwide; a fragrance; a menswear line; a small couture service for private clients; a range of footwear to be made by Bottega Veneta, also owned by the Gucci group; and an expansion of the offices in London. "There are a lot of meetings—there is a lot on the business side with opening shops and packaging," he said. "It was like starting all over again and sometimes it felt like two steps forward and twenty steps back. It's the same as any big conglomerate and multinational—there is red tape to get through. But I'm a strong force to be reckoned with. I play the game harder. I don't want to lose the essence of McQueen. I do think about selling goods. But I don't have to compromise my integrity." The distinguished fashion writer asked McQueen about how the bumsters had inspired a worldwide trend to wear trousers and pants slung low on the hips. How would he feel if he had been paid a dollar royalty for each pair sold? "I'd be a rich man now," he replied. "But then, I'm rich already!"[31] According to the *Sunday Times* Pay List, McQueen earned £5.75 million in 2001.

In order to mastermind McQueen's image, the company took on KCD, the New York–based public relations firm. KCD executive Kerry Youmans had already met McQueen a couple of years previously when he had been invited to dinner by a mutual friend in New York. "When he came into the office in Paris for that first meeting he said, 'I know you,'" recalls Kerry. "He didn't miss a thing. He could walk into a room and tell you what the woman was wearing on her feet across the room. He had an incredible memory. He had a huge reputation and I was a bit nervous because there was a volatility there, that he might be difficult and hard to please. But he made me feel very comfortable. That connection made our working relationship easier; he saw me as 'safe,' and then we became friends." Over the years the pair spent an increasing amount of time together: they went out to dinner; enjoyed holidays (which Lee would always cut short, often only staying forty-eight hours); and hit the clubs of New York, Ibiza and London. "He seemed in an everyday way like your great gay friend from the club," Kerry said. "He was a hilarious guy and had a wicked sense of humor. A lot of times it was a lot of fun to be around him. But then there was this other thing looming, this genius, and there was almost a disconnect. He had this inexplicable genius that was almost a gift from God, or a gift from something. With many designers there is a clear line from point of inspiration to final product. But he was totally unique. Where did that come from? How did he mash these things together? There was something unknowable in a way about his creativity."[32]

Twelve days after the Paris show, McQueen's work could be seen at the V&A, as part of the *Radical Fashion* exhibition highlighting the designs of Rei Kawakubo, Hussein Chalayan, Vivienne Westwood, Helmut Lang, Junya Watanabe, Azzedine Alaïa, Martin Margiela, Issey Miyake, Jean Paul Gaultier and Yohji Yamamoto. On show was McQueen's extraordinary dress from *Voss* constructed from hundreds of medical slides that had been painted red. "It took about a month and a half to make that dress," he said at the time of the exhibition. "The construction under the feather skirt is something else. It's like an eighteenth-century crinoline. It was the only thing that would stand the shape. Everything is sewn by hand." McQueen had used medical slides because he said he wanted to explore the image of the body's cells as seen under a microscope and he had painted them red because "there's blood beneath every layer of skin." Claire Wilcox, who curated that exhibition and *Alexander McQueen: Savage Beauty* at the V&A in 2015, remembers that the designer told her that "he thought there was passion in anger and that anger was a passion for him." "The experience of working with him on that show, for me as a curator, was extraordinary because I had never really realized that fashion had the potential to be so dark, but so beautiful at the same time."[33]

Radical Fashion opened just over a month after the terrorist attacks of September 2001. "It's a scary time," said McQueen just after 9/11. "But it will go down in history as a time of progression."[34] Yet McQueen did not lose his sense of humor. At the launch party of the exhibition he flirted with the former defense secretary Michael Portillo under the Chihuly chandelier that hangs in the museum. "If I'd been allowed to vote I'd have got him in," said McQueen, referring to his failed bid for the Tory leadership. "I've always fancied him."[35]

Towards the end of the autumn McQueen was contacted by the Hollywood actress Liv Tyler, whom he had met through Kate Moss. She wanted an outfit to wear for the premiere of *Lord of the Rings* on 10 December. Lee liked the fact that she was not a prima donna. "She's a nice down-to-earth girl," he said.[36] In addition to McQueen's tailoring skills, she liked his spark and bad-boy reputation. "Alexander almost beat up my boyfriend at that time, Joaquin Phoenix," said Liv, recalling an incident from five or so years previously. "He and Joaq had some beef or something. It was intense."[37] A few days before the premiere McQueen turned up at the Dorchester Hotel, where Liv was staying, for a fitting of the outfit that he had designed, a bright red trouser suit with a red lace, sleeveless top. Lee was not happy with the way the jacket fitted and began to attack it. "It felt as if I was in the hands of a true artist," she said. "I told him the shoulders felt a little tight, and out came an enormous pair of scissors. He started to snip away at the threads and then he just ripped the entire sleeve off. When I got the suit back it felt beautiful—it fitted perfectly. The jacket had millions of laces that tied around so my waist felt corseted in—I felt comfortable and sexy all night long."[38]

However, no matter how many stunning outfits he designed there was always a part of McQueen that needed to seek out other forms of creative expression. Throughout his career he was searching for a medium that would complement—or perhaps one day even replace—fashion design. "When we worked together he soaked up everything I did," said filmmaker John Maybury. "He loved the mechanisms of film-making and he was very hands-on. His intelligence was phenomenal; he would pick up information instantly, and it would have been very easy for him to sidestep into film or theatre."[39] For the September 2001 issue of *Dazed & Confused*, McQueen art-directed a shoot with the Bavarian-born photographer Norbert Schoerner. The images the two men conceived and executed were as disturbing as anything seen at *Apocalypse: Beauty and Horror in Contemporary Art*, the Royal Academy's exhibition of the previous year. There was a photograph of a naked woman wearing Chanel haute-couture, rose-colored silk shoes kneeling on a table, her back facing the rear end of a donkey. Another photograph showed a woman in a beautiful pale-pink corset standing in a pair of green waders which are being filled by what look like the urine streams of two men standing out of the frame. An enormous pile of food waste, mixed up with offal, pigs' heads and internal organs, and three naked boys lying amidst the rot appear in another picture. And, most disturbing of all, there is a shot of a hanging man, the lower part of his legs and feet covered with oil. "When American Express, McQueen's sponsors, saw the images they didn't want the brand to be connected with them," recalls Norbert.[40] Schoerner believed that McQueen had a "direct instinct for images" and described him as "more of an image-maker" than anything.[41] "There was a fierce quality about him, a visceral, to-the-point quality that was quite outstanding," he said. The photographer was impressed by McQueen's imagination, which he compared to a "gilded black heart, a heart of gold with a black centre."[42]

Lee claimed that he had drawn inspiration for the shoot from Pasolini's film *Salò*, but the real source was much more raw and personal. "It's just about human nature," he said. "Sometimes people take control for your own benefit, then it comes down to trust. But then sometimes people you trust will abuse that trust." He said that the imagery explored "how far you are prepared to let someone control a situation" and that the hanging man was "a person who is not in control." The shot of the naked youths rotting in a pile next to the pigs' heads expressed the inevitability of death and decay. "It doesn't matter if you're a man or a pig, we all end up on the scrap heap in the end," he said.[43]

McQueen's desire to escape himself appeared to be reaching addictive proportions. "Lee was constantly searching for a state where he felt comfortable," said his friend Kerry Youmans. "Peace was elusive."[44] On 14 November, McQueen attended the launch party of *Fable*—a magazine edited by Michelle Olley (the woman who had worn the breathing apparatus at the end of the *Voss* show). His old friend Eric Rose ran the door that night and remembers Lee turning up at the Cinnamon Club in Westminster "so off his fucking tits on cocaine." Eric told McQueen that he had better pull himself together because on the other side of the door were a bank of photographers. "He had a typewriter mouth and a hooker boy on his arm," he said. "Later that night I went to the Shadow Lounge—you can tell how long ago this was because that was when it was fun—and he was there with somebody else. I said, 'How did you get out?'—I was on the door the whole time. He said that he had got bored and had climbed out the fucking fire escape."[45]

At the end of 2001, Lee claimed that he wanted to scale down his party lifestyle. "I'm tired," he said. "I'm giving up all the drink and drugs and all that stuff." When journalist Maggie Davis questioned him on this, he responded, "I don't think you should forsake drinking and partying, but there comes a time in everyone's life when it just doesn't have the same effect any more, and you see there are better things in life than sleeping off a hangover."[46] Friends learnt to see through certain statements McQueen made in the press. In the same interview Lee told Maggie Davis that he had just passed his driving test; the truth was he never carried more than a provisional license and although he loved driving he always had to have an experienced driver in the car with him. Around this time his brother Tony McQueen went with him to buy a car, a VW Golf. Later he purchased two more vehicles: a Jeep, which he used to transport his dogs, and a Vauxhall Corsa, which Tony said he never saw move from outside his brother's house. "He asked me once to take the test for him," said Tony. "He couldn't be bothered to do it himself."[47]

McQueen often told journalists that he had decided to relinquish promiscuity in favor of monogamy, a declaration that had Kerry Youmans rolling his eyes in amazement. "He was always telling me that I needed to settle down and stop being such a slut," said Kerry. "It was good advice but maybe he was saying it to himself as much as to me. He and I were maybe similar in that way, in that we had a difficult time reconciling our lives as gay men with the idea of romantic love. And he had a difficult time trusting people."[48] Tony remembers having a conversation with his brother about his private life during which Lee turned to him and said, "Tony, there's so much shit out there. All they want is money." Tony was saddened to hear that Lee did not seem to have one partner with whom he could settle down. "I remember those words, 'There's so much shit out there,'" he said. "But in his life that was par for the course. I used to say to Lee, it's like playing with a loaded gun; in this day and age it's so dangerous."[49]

Lee's inclination towards promiscuity did not mean that he was not also prone to grand romantic gestures. One winter, after a heavy snowfall, Archie Reed lay in bed at his house in Totteridge Lane with a bad back. Lee rang asking him to come over, but Archie said he was unable to move because of his sciatica. McQueen refused to take no for an answer and said that he would send a helicopter over to pick him up. "I told him that would cost £150,000, and not to be so ridiculous," said Archie, who had a tattoo of the letters "L" for Lee and "A" for Alexander that snaked around his neck. Another tattoo, "Love Guidance Always," ran from his shoulders up to meet the initials. "He was highly passionate, on every level."[50]

McQueen's dark romantic spirit found full expression in his next Paris show, *Supercalifragilisticexpialidocious*, held on 9 March 2002 at La Conciergerie, the former prison where Marie Antoinette was held before she was executed by guillotine in 1793. The designer was fascinated by the history and costumes of the French Revolution and although he could not read French he loved looking through his copy of Charles Kunstler's 1943 illustrated book on the French queen. The show opened with an image straight from a fairy tale: a young girl wearing a mauve bonnet and cape leading two wolves through the dungeons. McQueen had asked film director Tim Burton, who shared his gothic sensibilities and who had designed the invite, to create the lighting for the show. "There were leather bras, contrived like harnesses and, often, conjoined to straps which delineated the torso and derriere, over satin French knickers and camisoles, but even these appeared graceful, not gratuitous," said Hilary Alexander in the *Daily Telegraph*.[51] Both the critics and the buyers thought that the show with its "whispered menace" had been a work of genius.[52] But there was one fashion outsider in the audience who had his doubts: respected war correspondent Anthony Loyd, who had been sent to report on Paris fashion week by *The Times* after Suzy Menkes had criticized the busy schedule for being "inhumane." Loyd observed that the wolves—which were in fact "hybrids," a cross between wolves and huskies—appeared to be doped, dazzled by the lights and scared of the crowd of people around them. But what made him more anxious was the sinister imagery of the show. "It looked like a misogynistic fantasy of warped sexual dawning and about as corrupt and twisted as anything I had seen that day," he wrote, "albeit entirely in keeping with a world dominated by the despotic chimera of eternal youth, power, sexuality and the tyranny of beauty."[53]

Loyd could have been describing the ritual of the annual Academy Awards ceremony in Los Angeles in which the world's most beautiful women aim to communicate and intensify the strength of their erotic capital by their appearance on the red carpet. That year Gwyneth Paltrow had chosen to wear a McQueen outfit similar to one worn by the Estonian model Carmen Kass in the show two weeks before, a shirt made from see-through black mesh and a skirt of black silk. The *Sun* criticized Paltrow for wearing nothing underneath this "tatty vest" and critics called the ensemble one of the worst Oscar dresses on display; later the actress admitted that she should have worn a bra.[54] McQueen, however, was pleased with the look; it gave him a thrill to see her wear something that exposed more than her vulnerabilities. "I like Gwyneth, she's a sweet girl, a typical American blond-haired, blue-eyed girl," he said. "Done well in the movie business. But I want to pull her apart and put her back together the way I see fit. I like to take people's characters out of themselves."[55]

At the beginning of May 2002, McQueen bought a two-bedroom cottage near the sea—the Old Granary, on Warren Lane, Fairlight, three miles east of Hastings. The property, on sale at £340,000, was small and simple, but it represented an escape from the pressures of work that Lee felt he so desperately needed. "I don't find inspiration there—it gives me peace of mind," he said. "Solitude, and a blank canvas to work from, instead of the distractions of the concrete jungle."[56] Often he would travel down to East Sussex with his dogs Minter and Juice on Fridays and return to London on Mondays. "He liked getting away from what can be perceived as the brutality and hardship of life," said Jacqui. "He loved walking along the beach with his dogs and being alone with his thoughts."[57]

Mira Chai Hyde remembers many visits to Fairlight to visit Lee, where she would cook him one of his favorite meals, chicken burritos using ingredients that she had bought in Los Angeles. Often the television would be tuned into cookery programs, which Lee liked to watch as he said it relaxed him (he could rustle up a mean Thai prawn curry, using plenty of lemongrass). "At the end of the day Lee yearned for a simpler way of living," said Jacqui. "He was very happy to eat beans on toast as well as fine food."[58] At work, Lee would often start his day with a bowlful of cornflakes, which he took with ice-cold milk, or toast and Marmite. In East Sussex, if guests had enjoyed a roast and there were leftovers he would take the food to the edge of the garden where it could be eaten by foxes. At night, when it was pitch-black, Lee would sometimes slip outside the cottage and suddenly appear at a window with a torch under his face to frighten and amuse unsuspecting guests. "There was a skein of humour running through everything he did," said Daphne Guinness.[59] The one thing that always made Janet McQueen laugh was when he would say, in a mock-pretentious tone, "It's not all about you, you know—it's all about ME!"[60] And his staff found it funny when he cleaned his ears with a pin.

Yet McQueen had earned the right to let his achievements go to his head a little. Joan Kaner, senior vice president and fashion director of US department store Neiman Marcus, said that McQueen had "reached his pinnacle,"[61] while *Vogue* called him "a creative god."[62] Over the course of six months, McQueen's office in Amwell Street had expanded over three floors and Lee had appointed a new CEO, Sue Whiteley, formerly the head of womenswear at Harvey Nichols. "We had to ask ourselves, 'What was our story going to be? How do you build a brand?'" said Sue. "Alexander McQueen had a very limited business in America. It was tiny. We realized there was a gap in the market. We could enter and have a unique voice."[63]

McQueen had appointed architect William Russell, who was married to a good friend of Trino Verkade's, to design his stores in New York and Tokyo, both of which opened in 2002, and on Bond Street, set to open the following year. "He asked me to create a new concept for his shops," said William. "He wanted a collaborative relationship, rather than someone imposing a look or a feel onto him." Russell had set out a program of six months in order to experiment and explore his ideas, but a space in Tokyo came up and the architect had to work to a deadline. He had been inspired by a recent trip to

Lalibela, in Ethiopia, where some of the buildings had been carved out of hillsides and cliff faces and, together with McQueen, he came up with the concept of a store hewn from a solid block of white material. "[McQueen] wanted to make a cave filled with light," he said.[64] Lee wanted all the stores to have an "ethereal" quality to them and the space in New York, on West Fourteenth Street in the Meatpacking District, referenced aliens and space travel. "I wanted something completely different, so I went for this spaceship-type feel like in *Close Encounters of the Third Kind*," he said, "where everything sort of levitates off the floor with this mother ship in the middle and all of these satellites sprouting from the top." One observer who visited the shop noted how the space had an "other-worldly" quality and how "burnished, carved busts hang throughout the store resembling floating corpses of sorts."[65]

There was something of the extraterrestrial about the image of McQueen photographed for the cover of the September issue of *The Face*. Shirtless and with his head shaved, he looked as though he had been sprayed with silver paint. During a question-and-answer interview the designer told journalist Chris Heath about his desire to push fashion into the future. He said that ideally he'd like to use liquid steel to forge a dress. "I can't, because it'd scald the person wearing it," he said. "Someone's got to live, or what's the point? But I've always wanted to construct clothes on a computer where you type in the measurements and the garment is weaved on the person as they stand there." The journalist asked McQueen a series of questions. What song did he play when he was sad? Anything by Mary J. Blige or Alicia Keys, he said. What was his favorite obscenity? "Cunt," he replied. "Because everyone hates it." How many times had he been in love? "Nearly twice," he said. Did he want a child? "Yeah, I'm going to try," he said. Why did he want one so much? "Because I deserve one." When did he feel most alone? "When I'm under stress, under pressure." When did he feel happiest? "When I'm in bed with someone I love," he said. Did he have any recurring dreams? "Snakes. Wriggling around my body. They're poisonous ones . . . Everywhere.

Between my legs. All over my body . . . I also have the dream where the room's closing in."[66]

Escape was the theme of McQueen's next show, *Irere*, held on 6 October 2002 in a sports stadium on the outskirts of Paris. Named after the Amazonian word for "transformation," the show took place in front of a screen measuring fifty feet by twenty feet, onto which was projected a film by John Maybury, whom McQueen had first met in the early to mid-nineties. "I would see him at various clubs in London and he was really funny, with always a snide comment about someone who was wanky or pretentious," said John, the director of *Love Is the Devil*, a film about Francis Bacon which McQueen loved. "When he asked me to come in I found it interesting to see him in this new context. He put out this slightly tough image; he was not your archetypal fashion person by any stretch of the imagination— there was nothing fluffy or frilly about him—and he had a fantastic sense of humour. He had this incredible clarity—he had a whole narrative in his mind—and we filmed the story of this shipwreck in a large water tank. During the shoot for the show, Lee was there, acting as co-director and art director. He wasn't hands-off in any way, and I don't mean that in a negative way. The model twisted and turned under water like a scene from a ballet and then this beautiful boy plunged in to rescue her. That sequence was incredibly romantic."[67]

The first shot in the film was taken from under water looking up towards the light, an image that McQueen may have remembered from his days with the synchronized-swimming club. McQueen had relived this experience at the end of an advertising shoot earlier that summer when, after Steven Klein had finished taking the photographs of a model in a tank of water, McQueen had jumped in fully clothed. The resulting portrait was published in *W* magazine. In the last years of his life, Lee also loved going away to the Maldives, where he enjoyed scuba diving. "Under water, I feel most at peace," he said.[68]

The spirit of the *Irere* show, full of vivid limes, bright oranges and startling chrome yellows—and featuring a chiffon dress in the colors of the rainbow—was undoubtedly optimistic and suggestive of the redemptive power of nature. And when McQueen, with newly dyed blond hair and wearing an exquisite white suit, appeared at the end of the show, observers noted how happy and healthy he looked. "He certainly was in a great place at that time," said John Maybury. "He was at the top of his game. Each piece was a sensational couture piece even though it was meant to be ready-to-wear. His enthusiasm and energy were like something you could warm your hands on. He was like an energy battery."[69] Susannah Frankel said of the collection, "Should a desert island ever be inhabited by such beauty, we might all wish to live there."[70]

One of the highlights of *Irere*—a piece that would become something of a fashion icon—was the so-called Oyster dress. This garment, made from hundreds of different layers of ivory silk and described by Metropolitan Museum curator Andrew Bolton as "almost like a *mille-feuille* pastry," reportedly cost almost £45,000. Sarah Burton recalls how Lee constructed the extraordinarily complex piece—"the top part of the dress is all fine boning and tulle, and the chiffon is all frayed and dishevelled on the top," she said. "The skirt is made out of hundreds and hundreds of circles of organza. Then, with a pen, what Lee did was he drew organic lines. And then all these circles were cut, joined together, and then applied in these lines along the skirt. So you created this organic, oyster-like effect."[71]

Culturally, McQueen occupied a curious position by this time as he attempted to bridge the gap between the sophisticated fashion scene and the mass market.

For example, after accepting a VH1 *Vogue* award in New York, McQueen traveled on to Las Vegas, where, on 1 November, he oversaw a catwalk show in a mall in front of 2,500 guests. Back in Britain, McQueen became involved in a row about which celebrities should wear his clothes. In October of that year, the television presenter Ulrika Jonsson had been photographed wearing an aubergine-colored, low-cut McQueen dress. "She didn't get it from us," snapped the designer, outlining how his office had not sent her the outfit to wear.[72] Jonsson was just one of a number of celebrities, including Victoria Beckham and Paris Hilton, whom the designer regarded as too uncool to wear McQueen. "If I dress someone, it's because I have a relationship with them—we are either friends or I am a fan of their work," he said.[73] McQueen believed it was perfectly possible to go global and still remain true to the aesthetics of the avant-garde. "If I can't keep honest then I'm not going to do it," he said.[74]

The end of 2002 and the beginning of 2003 was a time marked by a number of professional triumphs for McQueen. He had entered into a partnership with Savile Row tailors Huntsman to design a new collection of bespoke suits. Liv Tyler commissioned him to make a variation of the "Oyster" dress for the New York premiere of *Lord of the Rings: The Two Towers* in December and then a white empire-line gown for her wedding in April. *Scanners*, McQueen's Paris show in March 2003, received glowing reviews, particularly the sight of a model battling her way through a transparent wind tunnel wearing a hand-painted silk parachute dress. "Should Alexander McQueen ever tire of wearing a pincushion on his wrist, he might give movies a shot . . ." wrote Guy Trebay in the *New York Times*. "Mr. McQueen is a talent on an Orson Welles scale." Trebay noted that the invitation to the show—a grid showing sections of McQueen's brain taken by a CT scanner—suggested the designer's assertion that "surface is not everything."[75]

At the beginning of March, McQueen denied the rumors swirling around the fashion industry that he was next in line to take over from Tom Ford at Gucci, or that he would move to Yves Saint Laurent. "I'd rather kill myself," he said. "When I was at Givenchy I ended up designing fourteen collections a year, including stuff for my own house. It frazzled my mind. I'm never going back to that."[76]

On his thirty-fourth birthday, 17 March 2003, Lee launched his perfume Kingdom, and on 7 May he opened his new shop in Bond Street with a party attended by a host of celebrity friends. On 2 June the Council of Fashion Designers in America named him Best International Designer. "Anarchist, fun, thin, controversial, friend, loyal, charismatic, innovative, dark, determined," wrote Kate Moss in the brochure that was handed out at the award ceremony. "For McQueen . . . this was a moment in the sun," wrote Susannah Frankel in the *Independent*.[77] At a trunk show held at his New York store the same day, "the city's great and good" spent $1.2 million on clothes from the *Scanners* collection. Two weeks later, McQueen heard that the Queen had appointed him Commander of the British Empire. That summer, major refurbishment work started on the four-story house at 82 Cadogan Terrace, Hackney, which McQueen had bought the previous October for £700,000. "He bought the house because it was located on ley lines," said Archie Reed. McQueen spent £120,000 on a koi garden, designed by Brooke Baker, and hundreds of thousands more on the house. There was a steam room, a yoga room, a gym which he only used a couple of times and a large retractable skylight above the bed, "which he refused to open in case a bird crapped into the bedroom," said Archie.[78] There was also an aquarium that was installed in the wall dividing the bedroom from the bathroom. "If only those fish could talk," quipped one friend.

By his own admission, Lee had achieved far more than he had ever dreamed possible. But his season in the sun had been threatened by a shadow, the dark specter of the depression that had started to torment his friend Isabella Blow.

CHAPTER TWELVE

Joyce McQueen: "What is your most terrifying fear?"
Lee McQueen: "Dying before you."

The car slowed down and stopped outside the grand white building that looked a little like a castle from a fairy tale. Lee McQueen stepped out of the vehicle, followed by Philip Treacy, Shaun Leane and a fragile but well-dressed Isabella Blow. The four friends walked across the drive and into the Priory, the psychiatric hospital in Roehampton that had developed a reputation for treating the rich and famous. There, Isabella was questioned by doctors who then admitted her for treatment, a program that would necessitate a three-month stay, part of which was paid for by McQueen.

In the last few months, Isabella's lovable eccentricities—for instance, her habit of spelling out the address of her London home in Theed Street to taxi drivers with the words "T for tits, H for horny, E for erection" and so on—had started to mutate into a kind of mania.[1] At a lunch with a PR agent from Prada it was said that her breasts had escaped the constrictions of her corset and that she had remained seated throughout the meal without adjusting her outfit, simply letting her breasts remain on the table. At *Tatler*, where she worked as fashion director, she was running up huge bills: one shoot, which involved celebrities wearing Manolo Blahnik shoes, cost a reported £45,000, the entire annual budget of the fashion department. Her own personal spending had reached excessive levels, and she and Detmar were sued for £10,000 by a taxi firm. Friends said that if Isabella had been given a million pounds on Friday she would have blown it all by Monday morning.

Isabella and Detmar had been having problems in their marriage, there had been a number of failed IVF treatments, and Detmar's mother had been threatening to take their house, Hilles, away from them, a prospect that awakened old fears in Isabella. As a child she had been taken to live in what she called the gardener's cottage in the grounds of Doddington Park and she would spend hours gazing at the big house in the distance, which the family had been forced to leave because of dwindling resources. "People thought that Isabella was obsessed with fashion—and Isabella was very interested in fashion—but her obsession was Hilles," said Philip.[2] By January 2003, Isabella's behavior had become so erratic that Detmar filed for divorce; the fact that she had started to have an affair with an Italian hotelier—whom Detmar referred to as "the gondolier"—did not help their relationship. A holiday in Barbados did little to revive her spirits and she returned from the Caribbean feeling exhausted and on edge. She felt a failure on every level: she was ugly, she said, she worked hard but never had any money and she could not have children. "Detmar—I hear you're firing blanks," McQueen had said when he heard the news.[3]

Lee thought that part of Isabella's problem was her toxic relationship with her husband and he pleaded with her not to see Detmar. "When Issie and I separated he took her to the Priory and said whatever happens you're not going to see Detmar again," he said. "I thought that was wrong because Issie was very fragile and I knew without me she was going to crash."[4] At the hospital, Isabella befriended a young woman who called her "Miserabella," a girl who turned out to be the singer Lily Allen. Another patient told Issie that she was checking out of the hospital as it was too expensive and that she was going to book herself into Claridge's instead. Isabella was allowed out at weekends and she would often spend time with Philip Treacy and his boyfriend Stefan Bartlett at their house in Elizabeth Street. When the Priory discharged her in September, Isabella knew that she was far from well, and she had to take a course of medication that included lithium, which friends said turned her into something of a "zombie." She did not lose her zippy sense of humor altogether. She jokingly called her pills her "Marilyn Monroes" and told one journalist why she had always favored Alexander's clothes—"you can always fuck in McQueen," she said. "You just have to lift up the skirt."[5]

McQueen may have paid for Isabella's treatment at the Priory, but he found it difficult to cope with the reality of his friend's mental illness. Perhaps it would have been healthier for both of them if they could have severed contact altogether. Yet their relationship was powered by a strange codependency: Isabella was clearly addicted to McQueen's clothes, while Lee felt bonded to her almost as if she were a vision of a misshapen psychological twin or a distorted mirror image. "He was frightened of Issie's darkness, because he had it himself," said Detmar. "Alexander had his own demons. So he wouldn't go there, and I don't blame him. Issie was always trying to rebuild the early days, but that world had gone and they had moved on."[6]

In August 2003, McQueen rented a large villa in Ibiza with some friends, including Kerry Youmans and Sebastian Pons, who had made contact with Lee after not seeing him for three years. When Sebastian arrived at the luxurious house he discovered that there had been some kind of argument and Lee had locked himself in his room. Sebastian was already nervous at seeing his friend for the first time since they had parted company, and when he walked up the stairs and knocked on Lee's door he found himself shaking. When McQueen eventually opened the door Sebastian did not recognize him. "He wasn't the person I left in 2000 or the one I had met back in 1995," said Sebastian. "He was half the size I remember him, really pale and lost." The two men hugged and started talking. Sebastian asked him what had happened to his body, and Lee lifted up his shirt to reveal the scar from his gastric band surgery. The friends spent the next six or seven hours talking and catching up. McQueen asked him what he had been up to and when Sebastian told Lee that he had designed a collection ready for the New York season but that he had been let down by financing, he offered to lend him the £30,000 he needed to put on the show. McQueen's kind gesture touched Sebastian, as Lee had always told him that you should only give people one opportunity, not two or three; he realized then that the designer was breaking his own rules. Then, after a moment's silence, the conversation turned serious.

"On top of everything else I have the bug now," said Lee.

"What?" said Sebastian.

"Yeah, the fucking bitch passed it to me."

McQueen told his friend who he believed had infected him with the HIV virus. Lee felt too upset to continue the holiday and later that day Sebastian and Kerry drove him to the airport, where he took a flight back to London.[7] The designer sought treatment for the virus at the Royal Free Hospital in Hampstead and took a number of antiretroviral drugs to manage his condition. Lee told his family about his HIV diagnosis about five or six years before he died, and the news left them devastated.[8]

Although a positive status no longer meant premature death, as it had in the eighties when Lee had been discovering his sexual identity, there is no doubt that the news contributed to McQueen's mental-health problems and perhaps also his desire to escape reality through increased drug use. "He made a lot of drug dealers rich," said Archie Reed, who believed that McQueen regularly spent £600 a day on drugs. "He could do three collections in a day and half with cocaine—it opened up something in him. But it also took a piece of him away, and with that came the paranoia."[9] When he was with friends, Lee would often sing, "Paranoia will destroy ya," and although he meant it as a joke the statement proved to be a prophetic one.[10] Fashion designer Roland Mouret told Plum Sykes, "The thing about Alexander is that he loved the coming down from drugs because it was so dark and he carried on taking them not for the highs, but for the lows."[11]

Those who wore McQueen's clothes thrilled to his dark aesthetic, yet they had little idea of the legion of demons that haunted him.

That August, *Vogue* editor Alexandra Shulman, *Dazed & Confused*'s Rankin, Mark Rodol of Ministry of Sound and designer Ozwald Boateng singled out Alexander McQueen as the "coolest brand in the world," ahead of Bang & Olufsen, Agent Provocateur, the Tate Gallery and Ducati. On 25 September Lee won, once again, the Designer of the Year award. When Pamela Anderson presented the prize one commentator sitting in the audience at Old Billingsgate Market observed, "Just when we were beginning to think that the awards organizers could not possibly have picked anyone more inarticulate than the *Baywatch* Bombshell, up popped Alexander McQueen. His thank you for the British Designer of the Year award made Neanderthal Man sound like Sir John Gielgud."[12] Designer Jeff Banks criticized the result, believing that the award should have been given to Julien Macdonald. "Alexander McQueen's things are a bit like the Emperor's Clothes," he said. "In my opinion, they are totally unwearable and don't sell. He's funded by a big Italian company and was the 'in' thing to vote for."[13]

Yet comments like this were made redundant by the spectacle of McQueen's next show, *Deliverance*, held at the Salle Wagram, a former dance hall, on 12 October. Inspired by Sydney Pollack's 1969 film *They Shoot Horses, Don't They?*, the designer constructed the show around the theme of a dance marathon. The film, set in Depression-era Los Angeles, ends with an exhausted and depressed contestant, Gloria (played by Jane Fonda), begging her dance partner, Robert (Michael Sarrazin), to help shoot her, which he does. When the police question him, he replies, "They shoot horses, don't they?", a reference to an injured horse that he saw being killed when he was a boy. In McQueen's show, as a disembodied voice repeated the refrain, "They must keep moving, they must keep dancing at all times," over the PA system, the message was explicit, articulating as it did the pressures, both professional and personal, that McQueen felt he faced. "The show ended with the losers strung out, immobile or dead, wearing clothes rendered in patchwork or miserably, exquisitely torn up," said the *New York Times*.[14] The reaction from the audience was rapturous, yet Colin McDowell thought that the social realism of the dance marathon phenomenon sat at odds with the show's underlying capitalist intentions. To use this particular theme "as a vehicle for selling extremely expensive clothes seemed shocking to me," he said. "What next? The Holocaust? It's a marvellous opportunity to sell stripes, darling. Don't laugh: it could happen. The current fashion world is crude and insensitive enough to accept anything, as long as it comes with the right designer label."[15]

McQueen returned from Paris to London where on 15 October he coordinated a show at the Royal Albert Hall, which involved Björk performing her song "Bachelorette" as part of *Fashion Rocks*, in aid of the Prince's Trust. Then, on 29 October, and dressed in a kilt of McQueen tartan, Lee received his CBE from the Queen at Buckingham Palace. Some of the other guests, he said, sneered at his appearance, as if to say, "You're just a skinhead in a kilt," yet he was not immune from indulging in a little sartorial criticism himself;[16] he regarded Jamie Oliver, who had turned up in a Paul Smith suit and open-necked shirt to receive an MBE, as a little too dressed down. "I think Jamie should at least have worn a tie today," he said. "Whether ties are in or out, it just looks better."[17]

McQueen had always seen himself as a republican and had only agreed to accept the award because he knew it would make his parents proud. Before the ceremony Lee had told himself that he wasn't going to look into Her Majesty's eyes, but when the moment came he could not help himself. He later compared the encounter to falling in love. "And I looked into her eyes, it was like when you see someone across the room on a dancefloor and you think, 'Whoa!'" he said. She asked him how long he had been a fashion designer. "A few years, m'lady," he replied. "There was a simultaneous lock, and she started laughing, and I started laughing," he said. "It was obvious that she had her fair share of shit going on. I felt sorry for her. I've said a lot of stuff about the Queen in the past—she sits on her arse and she gets paid an awful lot of money for it—but for that instant I had a bit of compassion for her."[18]

266

McQueen was tired and hungover after the previous night's partying at Annabel's and Claridge's, but he gamely posed for photographs with his parents and then went with his family and a few friends, including Isabella, to the Mayfair hotel for lunch. Later, Lee gave his mother the CBE, and for a time she displayed the award proudly in her home, something that prompted his brother Tony to joke, "If I bring a brick home, will she put that up too?"[19]

At the beginning of November, Gucci chiefs Tom Ford and Domenico De Sole announced that they were stepping down from the company. A month later, Serge Weinberg, the chief executive of PPR (which in addition to Gucci owned Yves Saint Laurent, where Ford had been creative director), traveled from Paris to London for an appointment with McQueen to discuss the possibility of him taking over at YSL. But the designer decided to miss the meeting. "I just had a panic attack, I think," he said. According to Isabella, McQueen stayed in bed. "It could have been fear," she said at the time. Lee turned to her for advice, as she had always thought that YSL and McQueen would have made a perfect match. He told her about his concerns and how he did not want to abandon his own label or leave London. He looked at Karl Lagerfeld at Chanel and how the German-born designer had made a success of the French couture house at the expense of his own label. McQueen was of two minds about whether to accept it, but finally he turned down the offer. "I am such a fan of Saint Laurent that my heart would break if I damaged the house," he said. "It was a major decision not to take that job. I wanted to do it so badly." François-Henri Pinault, the son of PPR's founder, took the news quite well and discussed the possibility of Lee taking over at YSL at some future date when he had transformed his own label into a recognized brand. "But I need to be doing McQueen with my eyes shut," said Lee.[20]

McQueen loathed meetings with the "suits" of the fashion industry. Daphne Guinness remembers the three occasions when Lee had asked her along to a formal lunch with Pinault and his executives only for McQueen not to turn up. "François-Henri was very difficult, not exactly charm on a stick," she recalls. "I couldn't think of a thing to say." One day, Lee called Daphne in a panic. He had heard that PPR wanted 100 invitations to a show, meaning that some of his friends would have been unable to attend. Daphne telephoned François-Henri and told him that McQueen would not attend the event if this happened, a threat that resulted in the number of requests for invitations being reduced to five. Daphne rang Lee back and told him that she had "fixed it."[21]

At the beginning of December, McQueen started work on the installation of *Silent Light*, a Christmas tree made from 150,000 Swarovski crystals and designed with Tord Boontje, at the V&A. "It's inspired by when snow turns to ice," said McQueen.[22] The tree stood on a large turntable and as it slowly revolved it created an ethereal, magical effect. McQueen had long been fascinated by alternate states of consciousness, aliens and space travel (when he first interviewed Sarah Burton for her job he had asked her whether she believed in UFOs), and these themes were reflected in his show *Pantheon as Lecum*, held on 5 March 2004. A "cavernous" concert hall in north Paris had been transformed into an alien landing pad and the pale-faced models with particularly long, thin legs who stalked the circular runway looked like something from another planet. The music veered between electronic pop, Kate Bush's "Babooshka," and the themes from *Close Encounters of the Third Kind* and *Doctor Who*. "If that Tardis did exist, I'd be the first to buy one," McQueen said.[23]

Fifteen minutes into the show, the lights went down and onto the darkened stage stepped not so much a woman as a spectral form, a ghostly figure that drifted across the stage, her silvery, lampshade-like dress a vision of light illuminated by an LED necklace. Then, as the stage cleared, the music faded to be replaced by the sound of a heart monitor and the model Tiiu Kuik, wearing an hourglass-shaped gray lace ensemble, stepped forward into a circle of light. The heartbeat slowed until finally it flatlined; the model, bathed in a beam of light, raised her palms towards the sky and waited to be transported to the next dimension. The image articulated McQueen's desire for transcendence, for a state beyond his earthly existence.

During a mother-and-son question-and-answer session, published in the *Guardian* in April 2004, Joyce asked Lee about his most terrifying fear. "Dying before you," he replied. "Thank you, son," Joyce replied. Unknown to the outside world, both mother and son had potentially life-threatening conditions: Lee was HIV-positive, while Joyce had started to suffer from kidney failure, for which she received dialysis three times a week. "What makes you proud?" she asked him. "You," he replied. "Why?" she asked. McQueen was too moved to answer.

In the same interview, Joyce went on to ask Lee a series of questions: whom would he invite to a dream dinner party? "Elizabeth I . . . 'cause she's an anarchist," he said. If he could live and work as a designer in any era what would he choose? "Fifteenth-century Flemish, Netherlands," he said. "My favourite part of art. Because of the colours, because of the sympathetic way they approached life." What was the most breathtaking building he had ever seen? "The chapel of Notre Dame du Haut at Ronchamp by Le Corbusier," he replied. How would he have broken into the fashion industry if he had not trained on Savile Row? "I'd have slept my way there," he joked. If he lost his wealth tomorrow what would be the first thing he would do? "Sleep. I'd be pleased," he said.[24] Lee often felt exhausted not only by overwork, but also by a clutch of anxieties and stresses that left him feeling drained. One of his biggest worries was a concern for his personal safety, he said, which is why in May he bought a Rhodesian ridgeback as a guard dog. During one interview Lee told a journalist that he could not let the animal—Callum—into the room "because he'll bite you."[25] Sebastian Pons remembers that, during one holiday with Lee in Majorca, he had been so scared of the dog that he had been unable to use the bathroom in the middle of the night. "I opened my door to go to the bathroom and the dog was there, growling at me, so I had to open the window and pee out of it," he said.[26]

On 4 May, Lee hosted a party at Annabel's, the exclusive London nightclub, for the launch of Plum Sykes's novel *Bergdorf Blondes*. Fellow guests included Philip Treacy, India Jane Birley, Count Leopold von Bismarck, Arnaud Bamberger, Lucy Ferry, Countess Maya von Schoenburg, Matthew Williamson, Daphne Guinness and Isabella Blow. "I don't think he really liked going to parties unless he was on lots of drugs," said Plum. "If he was taking lots of drugs he would be more mean and vicious, but when he was healthy and going to the gym he would be delightful."[27] On 11 May, McQueen received an honorary doctorate from the University of the Arts London, along with other leading cultural figures such as Maggi Hambling, Jimmy Choo, Anthony Caro and Margaret Calvert. At the end of the month, McQueen heard the news that Isabella had reconciled with Detmar, a decision that forced him to break off contact with her for a few months. McQueen was also appalled when he heard that Detmar had endorsed a psychiatrist's recommendation that Isabella undergo electroconvulsive therapy to help shift her depression. "The electric shock treatment freaked everyone out, but it worked for Issie," said Detmar.[28] Suddenly, it seemed, for a while at least, that the old Issie had returned; the air of suicidal gloom had cleared and she was again "dynamic, spontaneous, positive thinking, charismatic and voluble," he said.[29]

On 3 June, McQueen staged *Black*, a retrospective catwalk show at Earl's Court of some of his most iconic designs. In addition to the fashion—items included black clothes from *Highland Rape*, *Dante*, *Supercalifragilisticexpialidocious* and *Voss*—there was a dance performance with Kate Moss and Michael Clark, and a charity auction. Items sold included a pair of black fishnet tights worn by Madonna; Christina Aguilera's black leather trousers; a photograph of Moss by Sam Taylor-Wood; and a collage by John Galliano. The proceeds went to the Terrence Higgins Trust. "I wish I was doing an original show in London, and one for more people," said McQueen of the event, his first London show in three years. "But from a business point of view there's no point showing in London—although from a vibe point of view there's every point."[30] At the after-show party, Kate Moss was photographed standing next to Naomi Campbell and Annabelle Neilson, who, according to one observer, "achieved the unthinkable and outshone her famous model friends by sparkling in one of his [McQueen's] green Givenchy vintage gowns."[31]

McQueen had also chosen Neilson to star in *Texist*, a film which documented Annabelle and a Swedish male model eating, sleeping, bathing, dressing and playing with their dog (a role taken by Juice). The idea, said McQueen, was "to capture and isolate a situation which might come across as banal but actually is what everyone's life is like." The film had had its premiere in Milan in January earlier that year to promote the relaunch of McQueen's menswear collection at the end of June in Italy's fashion capital. "I designed them for myself," he said of the sharply tailored clothes, which won him a *GQ* Designer of the Year award in September and a Menswear Designer of the Year award in November. "In the early days when I did menswear I made the mistake of designing things I thought people would want. I hardly wore any of it."[32]

McQueen spent the summer putting the finishing touches to the wedding dress that he had designed for his assistant Sarah to wear at her marriage in August to the photographer David Burton. Lee had taken inspiration from the "Oyster" dress in the *Irere* collection to make a gown described by *W* magazine as a "romantic English country confection."[33] Sarah Burton had always realized that although she loved the art and craftsmanship of making clothes she did not look like a self-constructed "fashion" person. "I'm not cool," she said. Neither was she, unlike McQueen, motivated by a near-pathological obsession with the macabre—the motto at her girls' school was "*Ad lucem*," towards the light. "I don't have that darkness," she said. "I'm not haunted or sad. I don't have that story in my youth." Burton would go on to take over the McQueen label after Lee's death and design the royal wedding dress for Kate Middleton's marriage to Prince William in 2011. "An instinctive, intelligent, imaginative young woman's wish for a beautiful wedding dress—or any kind of dress—is the most natural thing in the world," she said.[34]

McQueen had also been asked by his friend Plum Sykes to design her wedding dress for her upcoming marriage to the artist Damian

Loeb. But then, a few weeks after Lee had started work on the design, Loeb called off the wedding. Undeterred, McQueen told Plum that he would make her a dress anyway, a beautiful gown—which she wore to her sister's wedding—constructed from layers of corseting, metallic chocolate-brown silk and black and cream lace that he ripped up and dyed with tea. "It looked like a John Singer Sargent painting slightly torn up," she said.

When Plum became engaged to Toby Rowland, the son of businessman Tiny Rowland, McQueen offered to make her a dress for her wedding in March 2005. The process started with a meeting at the office in Amwell Street, where McQueen did a quick sketch to outline his ideas. The initial concept had been for an "inside-out" wedding dress, with all the luxury hidden on the inside of the garment. At one point, Plum suggested having a slightly more "trendy" design, but McQueen turned to her and said, "Plum, your wedding day is not about looking trendy, it is about looking absolutely immaculate." She also suggested having a bunch of red roses to hold, but again McQueen vetoed this idea. "If you have a bunch of coloured flowers it will distract from the dress," he said. "It has to be white." Plum remembers that he made the toile, or pattern, from paper taffeta instead of a cheaper toile fabric like cotton. "He came into the fittings with a black marker pen and marked where he wanted to cut, then got his scissors out and cut," she said. "I have never seen anyone else do that. He really was a sculptor in fabric." During one fitting, towards the end of the process, McQueen started adjusting the immaculate white dress with fingers still smeared in tomato ketchup from the McDonald's burger and chips that he had just eaten. "He really enjoyed making that dress," said Plum. "I remember I only paid for the cost of the fabric, otherwise it would have cost tens of thousands of pounds." The result was exquisite: a fairy-tale creation with a white satin corset and an eight-foot train covered in ruched silk net using a Victorian technique of gathering, with taffeta knife pleats that peeked out sharply from beneath. "I did invite him to the wedding, but I thought he probably wouldn't come," she said. "He wouldn't have wanted to sit through a wedding; he would have been totally bored. His scene was going out with some gay guys to really hectic gay nightclubs and getting absolutely smashed. There was a whole side to his life that people like me, and probably Issie, never saw. He kept the two sides of his life separate."[35]

At the beginning of September 2004, Lee, Archie and Isabella went to the V music festival with Archie's aunt Jacqueline. Before they left the house in Cadogan Terrace, Archie remembers, Lee did a few lines of cocaine and by the time they got to the festival, McQueen had started to show signs of anxiety. A photograph taken at the festival shows the designer looking ill at ease and blurry-eyed. Lee did not like the fact that Isabella had bonded so quickly with Jacqueline, who joked that she would teach her new friend a few tricks about how to attract and keep men. In fact, McQueen became so jealous that he would cut Jacqueline out of photographs. "He was also very jealous of my daughter," said Archie. When Archie went to see his daughter, Lee would bombard him with calls and messages until his boyfriend returned to the house. "He wanted me to stand up and shout out that I was Alexander McQueen's partner," he said. "But I just couldn't do that at the time because I didn't want my child bullied or to be affected by that."[36]

Back at work, the McQueen business was booming. In September 2004, Jonathan Akeroyd from Harrods was appointed the new CEO of the company, a man described by McQueen as "a really good CEO from the same side of the tracks."[37] Lee told his bosses that he would like to spend more time in New York and consequently Gucci arranged for him to have an office in its new building. On a whim, McQueen rented an expensive brownstone in the West Village for a year, "but was in it only for something like a week before he went back to London," said his friend Sue Stemp, whom he had employed to work for him in Manhattan.[38] "London drew him back; he realized he didn't want to be in New York," said Kerry Youmans. "It was a case of, 'What am I going to do to fill this hole?'"[39]

• • •

One of the reasons why McQueen felt he could not live in New York was because, in the autumn of 2004, he had met another man in London who he hoped would change his life. One night McQueen had gone to Barcode—the same gay bar in Soho where he had met his former boyfriend Richard Brett—and had started chatting to Glenn Andrew Teeuw, a handsome thirty-four-year-old Australian who had a shaved head and a handlebar moustache. After going to another bar for a drink, they made their way back to Lee's house in Hackney. "He took my number and then a week or so later he called," said Glenn, who worked in a bar at the time. "One night became two, became three, until I was living out of a suitcase at the end of his bed." The love affair started well: the pair enjoyed cooking, spending time together at the cottage in Fairlight—"he became a different person in the country," Glenn said—and walking by the sea with the dogs. "It was a whirlwind romance," he said. One weekend, Lee and Glenn went to a tattoo parlor in Hastings and had each other's initials inscribed onto their skin—McQueen had GAT in blue ink on the inside of his wrist and Glenn had LAM in red ink on the inside of his right arm.

It wasn't long, however, before McQueen's paranoia began to poison the relationship. Lee constantly questioned his new boyfriend's commitment to him and once, when he was away in New York, McQueen employed a private detective to trail Glenn. "Once that paranoia sets in, it is so destructive," said Glenn. "I remember once, soon after we started seeing one another, going to a party where there were the Chapman brothers and Vivienne Westwood. He took off and went home and when I got back to the house he turfed me out on to the street because he thought I had been checking out some guy." The relationship lasted three years, but there were often times when, in the middle of the night, Glenn would be thrown out. Months would go by when the pair would not see one another, but then they would be drawn inevitably back together. "It was incredibly volatile," said Glenn. "It was almost like an addiction. We couldn't leave one another alone, but it was attraction and destruction."

274

One day, Lee told Glenn that they were going shopping—he wanted his boyfriend to buy him a present. "He took me to Boucheron [the jeweler on New Bond Street] and he wanted me to buy him a diamond pinkie ring, which cost £2,500. He knew I had no money, and so I had to put it on my credit card," said Glenn. "The same thing happened when he had booked a holiday for us in Fiji. He told me that if I didn't pay for my part of the holiday—which cost £3,000—I wouldn't be able to go, and if I didn't go then that meant we were over. I racked up huge credit card debts during my time with him. For him it was a game, it was all about me proving my commitment and love for him."

The relationship was fueled by a shared love of drugs. "He hated the fashion world for introducing him to cocaine," said Glenn. The pair did the drug in McQueen's office while he was at work, sometimes when they were in restaurants having dinner, and at the house in Cadogan Terrace. There they would mix it with alcohol and strong sleeping pills, a cocktail that doctors believe is particularly toxic and dangerous. "We would be locked in the bedroom for two days at a time, it was craziness," said Glenn, who no longer touches drugs. "It was a way for him to escape."[40]

Despite McQueen's drug binges, his collections went from strength to strength, as he drew inspiration from the world of cinema. Peter Weir's 1975 film *Picnic at Hanging Rock*, about the real-life disappearance of a teacher and a number of girl pupils, influenced the "intense, knife-pleated and smocked tailoring and doll-like silhouettes" of *It's Only a Game* in Paris on 8 October 2004. The final part of the show, an elaborately choreographed human chess game, was a reference to a scene in *Harry Potter and the Philosopher's Stone*. (The show closed to the sound of "Suspicious Minds," a song which includes the line, "We can't go on together," another indication of McQueen's desire for escape.) References to aesthetically diverse films such as Patrice Chéreau's *La Reine Margot* and Mathieu Kassovitz's *La Haine* found expression in McQueen's menswear collection in Milan in January 2005. And Hitchcock's *The Man Who Knew Too Much* pro-

vided the title for McQueen's elegant show in March that year, a collection that also took inspiration from his films *Vertigo* and *Marnie*.
"You could almost see Doris Day, Kim Novak and Tippi Hedren in
McQueen's grey suits, which featured tight-fitting skirts and jackets
and accentuated the waist, or a short black coat with a gored back,"
wrote one fashion reporter.[41] In May 2005, McQueen announced
that he would design a range of sports shoes for Puma. One of the
trainers, which he called "My Left Foot Bound," included a cast of
the designer's left foot suspended in transparent rubber and visible
through the sole. "A bit Damien Hirst, isn't it?" he said. "Quite weird.
Nicey nicey just doesn't do it for me."[42] In July, he launched a range of
handbags, which included one named Novak, after the star of *Vertigo*.
Then in early 2006, McQueen announced that he would soon release
McQ, a more affordable range designed for a younger clientele. "The
new collection is a renegade version of the mainline," he said.[43]

Lee had always been drawn to rebels, anarchists and martyrs. In
July 2005, Radio 4's *Today* asked him to take part in the search for
Britain's greatest painting. McQueen nominated Paul Delaroche's
1833 work *The Execution of Lady Jane Grey*, a picture depicting the
nine-day queen in the moments before her beheading and which had
also inspired his Givenchy show in July 1999. He chose this particular work from the National Gallery, he said, because of the subject
matter of the painting. "It's just very imposing, very melancholic,
pretty much like my own personality," he said. "The painting shows
a blindfolded Jane about to be executed in one of the chambers of
the Tower of London. What lures me to this painting is the balance,
the colour. She is shown . . . almost like an angel, ethereal. She is in
white, in this duchess satin dress, but she stands tall even though she
is in her last moment . . . It's quite a tormented picture because you
want to jump into the picture and save her . . . It's just despicable, it
makes you grief-stricken as well for her. Personally, it's a form of ter-
rorism in itself by a government, so it's quite political for me, as well
as being a beautiful picture in itself."[44]

McQueen's protective instincts came to the fore a couple of

months later when, on 15 September 2005, the *Daily Mirror* ran a story on its cover titled "Cocaine Kate." The newspaper alleged that the thirty-one-year-old model Kate Moss had snorted five lines of the drug in forty minutes. Moss had been filmed by a secret camera at a recording studio in west London with her then boyfriend, Pete Doherty, front man of the band Babyshambles. In the weeks that followed, Moss was dropped as a model by Burberry, H&M and Chanel, losing millions of pounds in prospective earnings, and was criticized by the British press for being both a bad role model to teenage girls and an irresponsible mother. There were even reports that she could lose custody of her two-year-old daughter, Lila Grace, whose father is *Dazed & Confused* editor Jefferson Hack. Yet Kate Moss was never charged and McQueen was indignant at what he saw as a modern-day witch hunt. He made his feelings clear when he appeared on the catwalk at the end of his *Neptune* collection in October wearing a T-shirt emblazoned with the words "We Love You Kate." "She's not the first person in fashion to do cocaine, and she won't be the last," he said. "She's done more for London fashion than anyone else. Go to the newspapers and wipe their toilets. Fucking hell, you've got Columbia on your hands!"[45]

McQueen further expressed his support for Moss in his next show. On 3 March 2006, at the end of *Widows of Culloden*, she appeared as a hologram inside a glass pyramid, a beautiful specter swathed in an ethereal chiffon dress, shimmering like a mirage as John Williams's haunting theme from *Schindler's List* echoed around her. Moss later recalled how McQueen had first told her about the project. "He said, 'I've got this idea, I want you rising like a phoenix from a fire.'"[46] The film, shot by Baillie Walsh, served as a love letter to the model McQueen called "a female version of me."[47] Kerry Youmans remembers, soon after arriving at the venue, being asked by Lee whether he had seen the hologram. "When I said that I hadn't, he told me to come and sit with him," he said. "We sat and watched the hologram and it was so moving because he was so moved by it. And during the show itself I saw members of the audience in tears."[48]

The collection, inspired by an imaginative vision of the women left behind after the battle of Culloden, the final confrontation in the Jacobite Rising in Scotland in 1745, included a gown made entirely from pheasant feathers. Other clothes were made from McQueen tartan, and there was a model wearing a beautiful cream silk and lace dress with a pair of antlers sticking through a delicately embroidered lace veil on top of her head. McQueen was looking back to his own Scottish ancestry as narrated to him by his mother. "I wanted to start from the crux and the crux is my heritage," he said. "Fundamentally, the collection is luxurious, romantic but melancholic and austere at the same time. It was gentle but you could still feel the bite of the cold, the nip of the ice on the end of your nose."[49]

As Kate Moss danced and flickered in the film like a delicate white flame in a half-forgotten dream she became in Lee's eyes a ghost of all the women he had loved. McQueen dedicated the show to Isabella Blow, a friend he felt was slipping out of his hands and, like the hologram itself, passing into the realms of another world.

CHAPTER THIRTEEN

You are the sun, I am the moon.
—*from Neil Diamond's "Play Me,"*
featured in the McQueen show
La Dame Bleue

On 20 March 2006, after discharging herself from a psychiatric clinic in Surrey, Isabella Blow made the first of many suicide attempts. Earlier that evening Detmar had gone to a dinner in Notting Hill, followed by a screening at the Electric Cinema, and Isabella had remained at their flat in Eaton Square. There she took an overdose of pills and was only saved by the impromptu appearance of Philip Treacy and Stefan Bartlett. The men called an ambulance, which took her to St. Thomas's Hospital where Isabella had her stomach pumped. When Detmar arrived at the hospital, the doctor told him that Isabella had been sectioned and that she was suffering from classic symptoms of bipolar disorder.

In April, Isabella ordered a taxi to take her, courtesy of an account at Condé Nast where she worked, from Harrow-on-the-Hill, where she had been treated in a clinic, to Cheshire, where she'd grown up. "On the way she went to Broughton Church in Staffordshire and put flowers near her family vault where her father lay," said Detmar.[1] After checking into a hotel she took an overdose of paracetamol and then rang Philip to tell him what she had done and also about the Condé Nast driver, a piece of information that enabled her friend to trace her and save her once more. Again Isabella had her stomach pumped, but later that month, during a stay at Hilles, she disappeared. In the middle of the night Detmar heard that she had driven her car into the back of a Tesco lorry near Stroud. "I always hated Tesco's," she said later. To Detmar, and to anyone else who would listen, Isabella would repeat the phrase "I want to die. Let me die."[2] Although Isabella was taken back to the clinic in Harrow, one day she managed to escape and took a taxi to the elevated section of the A4 in Ealing, climbed over a barrier and prepared to throw herself off the overpass. At the last minute she changed her mind, but it was too late and, wearing a Prada coat and Prada shoes, she fell and broke her ankles and feet, shredding her fingernails in the process. Later, Isabella would joke that since she could no longer wear high heels there was little point in living. After being discharged from a hospital in Ealing, Isabella was admitted to the National Health Service–run Gordon Hospital in Victoria. "The conditions were just awful, it was like being in a Dickens novel," said Daphne Guinness. After an insurance policy ran out, Daphne and McQueen paid for a great deal of Isabella's treatment at the private Capio Nightingale in Marylebone. "But we didn't let her find out, as she would have hated the idea of charity," said Daphne.[3] There, psychiatrist Dr. Stephen Pereira, who would later treat McQueen, put Isabella on suicide watch and started treating her with a combination of medication, therapy and ECT.

American *Vogue* editor Anna Wintour arrived at the hospital with a present of Fracas, Isabella's perfume of choice, and Rupert Everett, who had returned from Milan, where he had covered the menswear shows for *Vanity Fair*, brought whitebait from a nearby fish and chip shop. Everett asked Isabella, whom he had known since the age of fifteen, why the collections made him feel so empty inside. "Money," she replied, before likening the treadmill of fashion shows to a fast-food restaurant. "You think you're watching beautiful people in wonderful clothes, but actually you're in a sausage grinder," she told him. "You forget who you are. You might have a luxury brand name written over your tits, but is that enough? In the end I was just a hat with lips, and that's not chic."[4]

While Isabella may have begun to think of herself as worthless, McQueen could still take satisfaction in his achievements and talents. On 1 May 2006, he attended the Costume Institute gala at the Met for the opening of *AngloMania: Tradition and Transgression in British Fashion*, an exhibition that featured a number of his designs, including the Union Jack frock coat that he had designed for David Bowie. That night Lee, dressed in a kilt made from McQueen tartan, accompanied Sarah Jessica Parker, his date for the evening, who wore a reworking of a dress from *Widows of Culloden* which included so much tartan that, according to one observer, "she looked like a cross between Flora MacDonald and a presentation box of Edinburgh shortbread."[5] From there, Lee flew to San Francisco to accept an honorary doctorate from the Academy of Art University, where his old friend Simon Ungless held the position of director of graduate fashion. He treated himself to a mud bath in the Napa Valley and a trip to the Sonoma Coast to see the surfers, but he was disappointed not to be able to dive with sharks; apparently it was the wrong season and the big fish were nowhere to be seen.

Back in Britain, McQueen busied himself with the design of his collection *Sarabande*, which he said had been inspired by a mix of Kubrick's 1975 film *Barry Lyndon*, the work of Goya and the Italian heiress and muse Luisa, Marchesa Casati Stampa di Soncino, particularly the portrait of her by the "master of swish," Giovanni Boldini. The show, held on 6 October 2006 at the Cirque d'Hiver in Paris, took its name from Handel's music, which accompanied it, a baroque piece played by a live chamber orchestra. As the show started, an enormous glass chandelier rose into the air, casting beautiful shadows onto the circular wooden catwalk below. "The effect was one of an eerie decaying grandeur," wrote one commentator.[6] In the finale to the show, a number of models appeared on the stage looking like walking Arcimboldo portraits, their bodies swollen by hundreds of flowers. But, as one model walked slowly around the catwalk, fresh flowers that had been frozen and attached to her dress started to melt and fall onto the floor, leaving a trail of beauty behind her. "Things rot," McQueen said. "It was all about decay. I used flowers because they die."[7]

McQueen still appeared to be the party boy about town. On 11 October he was invited to the opening night of the Frieze Art Fair in Regent's Park and later that month he was one of the guests at a masked ball at Strawberry Hill House, Twickenham, to honor Nick Knight. On 8 November, together with Daphne Guinness and Anna-belle Neilson, he attended *Vogue*'s ninetieth birthday party at the Serpentine, where it was rumored that Kate Moss had commissioned him to create a white and black lace dress for her upcoming marriage to Pete Doherty (a project that was never realized as the couple split in the summer of 2007). Yet, despite appearances, McQueen's mind was occupied with death and the afterlife. "The dark side to him was the next life," said Archie Reed. At night, Lee would sit in the dark with a camcorder hoping to capture glimpses of ghosts or spirits on film. He started to speak to a number of psychics over the phone, often using them to try and "spy" on Archie. One clairvoyant told McQueen that Archie did not like Fairlight, and that he found it too old-fashioned. In truth he loved visiting the cottage. When Archie came home from work Lee would confront him with a list of the places where he thought he had been and the men he had been seeing behind his back. All of it was nonsense, said Archie. One day, while browsing around Portobello Market, Archie came across a little doll without a face. "It had its arms above its head and if you put it against the wall it looked like a child crying," he said. "I gave it to him and said, 'That's you, a boy lost, with no face.'"[8]

Towards the end of 2006, Lee became increasingly fascinated by the Salem witch trials, a subject he wanted to take as the theme for his next collection. His mother had traced the Deane side of the family back to Elizabeth Howe, who had been accused of witchcraft by several girls in the Massachusetts village and who had been executed by hanging in July 1692. In December, McQueen traveled to Salem to research the history of what came to be known as witch hysteria, an episode in which twenty innocent people died. Accompanying Lee on the trip were his assistant Sarah Burton, fashion writer Sarah Mower, who had been commissioned by American *Vogue* to do a feature about the inspiration for the collection, and his American PR friend Kerry Youmans. "He seemed almost like an academic doing research," said Kerry. "He was very serious and focused. We went to libraries around Salem, he held the trial documents and each day he would ring his mum and tell her about what he had seen."[9] After a visit to the Salem Witch Museum, Lee drove to Topsfield, where he placed a bunch of flowers on the memorial stone to Elizabeth Howe and posed for a photograph. "Lee was wonderful company, he was very funny and quick," said Alison D'Amario, former director of education at the Salem Witch Museum. "He certainly didn't take himself seriously although he was serious about the fate of his ancestor and the other victims of the trials. A highlight of the day and an illustration of Lee's spirit occurred at the Old Burying Point in Salem. When the Salem witch trials' magistrate John Hathorne's grave was pointed out to him, he walked over to it and stamped on it—hard— in honor of Elizabeth Howe."[10]

McQueen's show *In Memory of Elizabeth Howe, Salem, 1692*— held on 2 March 2007 in a sports stadium on the outskirts of Paris— opened with a projected image of the pale faces of three young women and the sound of a voice whispering the words "I open my heart to you. I open my spirit to you. I open my body to you." The models paraded along the lines of a bloodred pentagram etched onto the black stage in front of a giant screen that showed a film, directed by McQueen, featuring locusts, owls, heads rotting into skulls, flames, blood and naked girls. Above the stage hung a forty-five-foot black inverted pyramid. The overall effect, of a fashion show conceived as a beautifully executed satanic ritual, was too much for many observers. When the editors of *Vogue* saw the collection they "thought it was too dark and they cancelled the feature [about the trip to Salem]," said Kerry. "His muse led him where it would and he didn't give a shit about American *Vogue* or the feature."[11] Bridget Foley of *W* magazine described it as a "study in vitriol expressed via fashion,"[12] while Archie Reed believed that the show "was the start of him saying goodbye."[13]

During the preparation for the show Lee received the news that his stylist Katy England had decided to leave McQueen because Kate Moss, recently commissioned to design a range of clothes for Topshop, had offered her a lucrative role at the high street chain. McQueen took the news badly and, for a time, felt angry at Moss for luring away one of his most trusted employees and friends. "Kate can come down, the bitch," he said to Archie, as he removed the photograph of Kate Moss from the wall in his office. "I went out on a limb for that girl, and she didn't even say thank you."[14]

In April 2007, Isabella invited McQueen to Hilles to stay for the weekend. She was in a delicate state, both mentally and physically, as she had recently been diagnosed with suspected ovarian cancer and would soon undergo surgery, but she wanted to make the visit particularly memorable for her old friend. In advance, she had taken the trouble to hang a photograph of McQueen in the great hall below a portrait of Detmar's grandfather by Augustus John. She had asked the cook to prepare a special menu for him, dishes that included a beetroot sorbet, a delicate anchovy and lemon mousse, followed by poached wild sea trout with saffron mash and salsa verde. But when McQueen arrived, with a couple of female friends, he proceeded to lock himself in his room. He refused all the food that had been prepared for him and just asked the cook for some cheddar cheese. "He was in bed coked out of his head," said Detmar. "And that was difficult for Issie. Everything was going wrong for her and it was sad that Alexander couldn't see that and pull himself together just a bit. So that must have been the last straw for her, I think."[15]

McQueen later gave an account of the visit in which he said he did have a three-hour talk with Isabella. "We were at peace with each other," he maintained, perhaps trying to convince himself. He told her that she looked good and, at one point in the conversation, said to her, "You're not talking about death—no, are you?" "No, no," she replied. "She really fucking shamboozled me, didn't she?" he said later. "She knew what she was doing . . . she had convinced me that she was fine, that she had come through the worst of it."[16]

Over the course of the next couple of weeks, Isabella sent a series of increasingly desperate e-mails to fashion critic Suzy Menkes, who had been invited down to Hilles the same weekend as McQueen but had been unable to go. "Issie did sound very alone and felt disappointed that Lee had let her down and that he had not given her any support," she said.[17]

On 5 May, while at Hilles, Isabella took a drink from a bottle of paraquat, the same weedkiller that Detmar's father had taken to commit suicide in 1977. Her sister Lavinia returned from shopping to find her vomiting in the bathroom; it was then that Issie told her that she had taken the poison. Lavinia telephoned Detmar, who told her to ring for an ambulance, which then took Isabella to hospital in Gloucester. She died there two days later; she was forty-eight. McQueen heard the news from his friend Shaun Leane while the two were taking a short break in Rome.

McQueen was left devastated. He flew back to Britain feeling so depressed and hollow that he immediately started to visit mediums in an attempt to contact Isabella. Sally Morgan, Princess Diana's former psychic, remembers McQueen coming to see her two days after Isabella's death. "When she [Isabella] went it was almost like he [had] lost an arm or a leg—it was peculiar," said Sally. The psychic told Lee that she had made contact with Issie, and claimed that he had been astounded by some of the things that she had related to him. "He was very troubled by her passing and the nature of it—the fact that she took her own life with poison," said Morgan. "He got great comfort from me being able to give him validation that she was talking to me."[18] When Lee returned home and told Archie Reed of his otherworldly encounter with Isabella he was initially skeptical. "I didn't want Sally Morgan to be feeding him bullshit and so I made an appointment to see her myself," said Archie. "She told me things that no one else could have known. She [Issie] was standing there next to me with bright red lipstick on—Issie always wore Chanel bright red lipstick. She said to me, 'Be careful,' because I think she could foresee what was going to happen."[19]

Detmar asked the milliner Philip Treacy to choose an outfit for Isabella to wear for her funeral, her last public appearance. Philip knew that Issie would want her old friend Alexander to make the decision and so he telephoned him and arranged to meet him at the Blows' flat in Eaton Square. There, the two friends, once rivals for Isabella's attention, selected a pale green McQueen kimono and a Treacy hat made from pheasant feathers in which she would be cremated. Lee also wanted to snip a lock of hair from Isabella's head, which he later incorporated into a ring for himself, but Philip felt he had to ask Isabella's sisters for permission.

On the day of the funeral, Philip and Lee, the latter dressed in his tartan, stopped off at the undertaker's to pay their last respects. McQueen, for all his obsession with death and its imagery, said that he had never seen a real corpse before. "Julia [Delves Broughton, Isabella's sister] told me that when Issie was being dressed, McQueen was just sobbing his eyes out," said Detmar.[20] At the funeral, held on 15 May at Gloucester Cathedral, Daphne Guinness remembers seeing McQueen looking broken. He cried uncontrollably throughout the service and left as soon as it was over. "He kept saying, 'I wish I had done more,' and I said, 'Alexander—what could you have done?'" she recalls.[21]

Lee told his friend BillyBoy* that he blamed himself for Isabella's death. "I must say I couldn't totally disagree with him because he was so cruel to her," said BillyBoy*. "He seemed to do things to hurt himself, like things he knew were wrong. He had total cognitive dissonance—one part of him was saying, 'I am going to put the screws on that bitch, I don't care any more, I don't need her any more,' and another, the more human side, realized that he was a monster."[22]

In Isabella's last addition to her will, which she wrote just before her death, she made a series of bequests to her friends, including Philip Treacy and Stefan Bartlett, but McQueen's name was notably absent from the list. Lee was surprised, as he had assumed that she would have left him her collection of McQueen clothes.

Isabella's death continued to haunt Lee. He placed a photograph of him with Issie on the coffee table in his sitting room and a further two portraits of his friend taken by Steven Meisel graced the wall. It seemed only fitting that his next show, *La Dame Bleue*, should serve as a tribute to his dead friend. The invitation, designed by fashion illustrator Richard Gray, showed Isabella as a Boudica figure riding in a chariot drawn by winged horses. "When we met to discuss the illustration *La Dame Bleue*, it was the last time I ever met Lee, so the memories of this are very poignant," said Richard, whose friendship with McQueen dated from the early nineties, when he had first met him in Comptons'. "Lee knew exactly how he wanted the illustration to look and spoke with precision about everything he wanted me to include in the drawing. He wanted me to draw Isabella with magnificent wings, wearing a specific McQueen dress and Philip Treacy hat, riding a chariot driven by winged horses in the sky. He seemed solemn and slightly subdued, and really wanted this to be something created with great consideration and care. This was obviously a very personal vision, to commemorate and to celebrate someone who meant so much to him, so the meeting and discussion were incredibly moving."[23]

Held on 5 October 2007, *La Dame Bleue* served as an elaborate visual epitaph for the woman whom McQueen thought of as a kind of second mother. She, in turn, had regarded him as something of a substitute son. "He's my child. I adore him," Isabella had once said about him.[24] As the fashion crowd took their seats at the Palais Omnisports in Paris that day they immediately felt the presence of Isabella; the organizers had filled the vast space with the scent of Fracas, Blow's favorite perfume. "For Blow's friends and colleagues the effect was as if her ghost was there with them," said one fashion critic.[25] The show opened with the image of a giant bird in flight made from blue neon lights, its enormous wings rising and falling above the entrance to the catwalk, a symbol of Isabella's spirit, free at last. McQueen's clothes for this collection celebrated not only Isabella's personality but her glorious physicality too: the models wore a series of outfits that exaggerated the hourglass shape, paying tribute to "the cantilevered cleavage and corsetted waist that dominated her silhouette."[26] At the end of the show, McQueen, wearing his tartan kilt and a Mickey Mouse sweatshirt, walked onto the stage with Philip Treacy.

This catwalk appearance was an emotional experience for Lee, intensified by the sound of Neil Diamond singing "Play Me." The song, which included the repeated words "You are the sun, I am the moon," highlighted the symbiotic nature of the relationship between Alexander and Isabella: the existence of one depended on the other. To some extent, McQueen had been created by Isabella, but as he became more confident and successful and her mental state degenerated, he tried to distance himself. Now that she had gone he felt like a planet out of kilter; her death, he said, had left a "big void" in his life.[27] Contact with psychics gave Lee a certain level of comfort—he needed to know, to feel certain, that her spirit rested in peace, that she didn't blame him—but he still felt uneasy. His psychiatrist, Dr. Stephen Pereira, said that McQueen had started to suffer from mixed anxiety and depressive disorder from 2007. Typical symptoms are low self-esteem, disturbed sleep, tiredness and lack of energy, feeling irritable, pessimistic or worried, while risk factors leading to the disorder include stress, trauma in childhood and living with a serious or chronic illness, all of which were experienced by McQueen. However, despite Pereira's best efforts, there had been "enormous difficulty in getting him to personally, physically come to appointments" with the psychiatrist.[28]

After *La Dame Bleue* show, Lee traveled to Kerala, India, with his boyfriend Glenn Teeuw. After a week in Kerala, Glenn returned to Australia for his grandmother's birthday and then went back to London, while McQueen flew to Bhutan to meet up with Shaun Leane. There, Lee immersed himself in Buddhism and learnt the basics of the religion. "It was on my suggestion that he went there," said Janet McQueen. "I knew someone from years ago who went and they said it was really humbling. I thought it would help him with his depression."[29] Many of Buddhism's central tenets—such as samsara (the continual repetitive cycle of birth and death), karma, rebirth, and dukkha (suffering or anxiety) and the path to liberation—not only enabled Lee to deal with the loss of Isabella but also ameliorated, for a time, his own dark thoughts and fears. Later, he visited the London Buddhist Centre in Bethnal Green, sometimes carried around a set of prayer beads and bought himself a number of classic Buddhist texts. He said the trip, which he described as a pilgrimage, had been "transformative."[30] In November 2007, on his return, McQueen took a taxi from Heathrow Airport to the Soho bar where Glenn worked, gave him a present of some Buddhist beads and told him that their relationship was over. "I knew that we couldn't carry on doing the same thing over and over, this perpetual backwards and forwards," said Glenn. "So we never spoke again—he was always changing his mobile number so I couldn't even text him—and I never saw him again. I felt a great deal had been left unresolved."[31]

That Christmas, McQueen went down to Fairlight with his sister Janet and on the morning of 25 December he lit a candle for Isabella. "From the day she passed away she was never far from his mind," said Janet.[32] "I learnt a lot from her death," said McQueen in the spring of 2008. "I learnt a lot about myself. [I learnt] that life is worth living."[33]

For a time, friends said, Lee seemed brighter, more optimistic. He could glimpse a future for himself—one that was positive—and he started to make plans. He was keen to move from Hackney and asked the architect Guy Morgan-Harris to help him find a new London flat or house. McQueen had known Guy, a handsome, well-spoken man who runs a boutique architectural practice with his wife, since 2006, when Lee's PA Kate Jones had recommended him. McQueen had needed some minor refurbishment work done to his house in Cadogan Terrace and from the first day they met, in the spring of that year, McQueen felt that he trusted him. "He was very sharp, witty and funny," Guy said. "He always kept you on your toes. Yet beneath that irreverent spirit was also a great deal of warmth." Guy had found him a stunning house in Montpelier Row, Twickenham, but Lee made it perfectly clear that living so far from central London was out of the question. The architect then saw an enormous flat in Whitehall Court, on the Embankment overlooking the Thames. Lee visited the property, priced at £4.25 million, on 1 February 2008 and was impressed by the view, the large living space (it had three interconnecting reception rooms) and the location; plus his old friend Paulita Sedgwick lived in the same portered block. Although it had a balcony that ran the length of the property Lee felt that life on the fourth floor of the building would not be suitable for his three dogs. McQueen, who by the end of 2008 had started to rent a luxurious flat at 7 Green Street, Mayfair, then became interested in a commercial building on Half Moon Court, Clerkenwell. The idea was to convert it into a home for him—complete with a roof garden for the dogs—plus a small gallery space in which to showcase his work. But McQueen finally decided that the building would be too close to his office.

Lee also had visions outside the capital, too. McQueen asked Guy to come up with plans to extend and renovate his small country cottage in Fairlight. In the end no major work was undertaken because he could not endure the thought of the disruption. One day Lee took Guy up to the fields behind the house, which commanded a sublime view of the bay, and told the architect that he would like him to build him a space-age home on the site. "He wanted a concrete tunnel under the ground which led to a lift that would take you up to the house, almost a James Bond villain's lair," said Guy. "It was going to be clad in aluminium so it looked like a spaceship that had just crashed into the hillside. However, the site was in an area of outstanding natural beauty and the likelihood of getting planning permission was something like 5 per cent. I will always remember him walking through that field, wearing his Mickey Mouse sweatshirt, looking happy and relaxed and really enthused about the project. He would have loved to have seen that materialize."[34]

McQueen's spirit of renewed hopefulness manifested itself in his February 2008 show, *The Girl Who Lived in the Tree*. He said that one day he had been down at his house in Fairlight when, while looking at the majestic elm tree in the garden, he had had a vision of a girl who lived in its branches. "She was a feral creature living in the tree," he said. "When she decided to descend to earth, she was transformed into a princess."[35] An enormous tree, swathed in fabric like a Christo and Jeanne-Claude installation, stood in the middle of the stage, its hue changing from icy blue to verdant green to bounteous yellow, a chromatic transformation that was reflected on the catwalk as the color of the clothes morphed from funereal black and deathly pale grays to virginal whites and royal reds. McQueen drew inspiration from both his time in India and Bhutan and photographs of Queen Elizabeth II as dressed by Norman Hartnell. The resulting look was a highly artificial concoction, a sweetened fairy-tale mix of the raj and royalty. "It was time to come out of the darkness and into the light," he said.[36] On the same day of his Paris show McQueen announced that his brand had turned a profit for the first time. "I was never in any doubt about the success of McQueen," he said.[37]

In March 2008, Lee flew out to Los Angeles to oversee the final changes to his new store, designed by William Russell, on Melrose Avenue. McQueen had commissioned Robert Bryce Muir to create a nine-foot-tall stainless steel sculpture of a man, called *Angel of the Americas*, which seemed to float in a dome above the store, making it visible from both the outside and the interior of the space. "It's anatomically correct," said McQueen, who likened his new store to a cathedral. Amy Winehouse had been booked to sing at the opening, but according to McQueen she canceled because of "visa problems."[38] The truth was much more complicated. McQueen had met the singer at a party in Chelsea which he had attended with his boyfriend Archie Reed. "But then they had a falling out, he said something about her, and she was livid," said Archie. Archie persuaded Lee to send her a dress worth £15,000 as an apology, but when she received it she threw it onto a barbecue in disgust.[39] "She also spat on one of his dresses at Selfridges which she had to pay for because she had soiled it," he said. "At first she refused, then she just said, 'Fine— but tell Alexander McQueen I ruined his dress.'"[40]

From LA, Lee flew to New York, where on 17 March he celebrated his thirty-ninth birthday at the Waverly Inn with a group of friends that included Trino Verkade, Sarah Burton, Annabelle Neilson, his former boyfriend Jay Massacret (who from 2006 McQueen employed as the stylist of his menswear shows), Kerry Youmans, actress Chloë Sevigny, Steven Klein and Sue Stemp. Photographs taken by Sue show Lee looking happy and relaxed, wearing a V-neck jumper, white shirt and tie, and sporting a goatee. Sue had first met Lee back in 1994, but the following year she moved from London to New York. When McQueen came to Manhattan he often met up with her. "I loved his boundless, uncompromising enthusiasm for something he was really into or interested in," she said. "He definitely had his demons and his difficulties, but I like to remember him laughing. Lee had a hysterically infectious, naughty laugh and I miss it."[41]

In April, McQueen heard that Gucci had agreed to his request for a pay rise: that year he would receive £10 million. Lee used part of that money to buy the house next door to 82 Cadogan Terrace so that his sister Janet, together with her daughter, Claire, and her five-month-old grandson, Tommy, would have a decent place to live. Janet moved into the house at the end of August and would often go round to her brother's house for dinner. They enjoyed visiting Columbia Road flower market and once he treated her to a weekend away at a spa near Badminton. "Lee was really generous and so I liked to treat us to a meal when we were out together," said Janet. "I know he appreciated someone not always expecting him to pick up the tab."[42]

One day, Lee was walking through Islington with Janet when he saw a giant stuffed polar bear standing on its hind legs in Get Stuffed, the specialist taxidermists on the Essex Road. He was so taken with it that he bought it and had it installed in his swish new offices on Clerkenwell Road. "The same day he also bought the head of a giraffe," said Janet. "I'm sure he would have checked that the animals had died from natural causes, as he hated cruelty to animals."[43]

In the summer of 2008, McQueen started work on *Natural Dis-Tinction, Un-Natural Selection*, his collection inspired by Darwin. "I was also interested in the Industrial Revolution because, to me, that was when the balance shifted, man became more powerful than nature and the damage really started," he said. "The collection is about looking at the world and seeing what we've done to it."[44] Lee asked his nephew Gary James McQueen to design the invitation using a lenticular image of his face which morphed into a skull (the same uncanny image would be later used on the cover of the Metropolitan Museum's exhibition catalogue *Savage Beauty*). "There may have been a subliminal message there, but Lee walked hand in hand with the macabre throughout his life," said Gary.[45]

The Paris show, held on 3 October in Le 104, a former mortuary near the Gare de l'Est, opened with the sound of animal noises. A host of stuffed animals from a Parisian taxidermist—a polar bear, an elephant, a panther, a giraffe and an armadillo—lined the catwalk. An image of a spinning earth was projected above the audience and then a parade of models walked forth covered in not so much clothes as second skins—a cape shaped like the fins of a giant manta ray, iridescent jumpsuits covered in Swarovski crystals, outfits that looked like walking Rorschach tests—giving the women the look of an alternative species, something that might have stepped from a space-age Noah's ark. The projected image changed into a single eyeball which stared down from the heavens and then, to add to the surreal effect, McQueen appeared onstage dressed as a rabbit, perhaps a reference to the 2001 film *Donnie Darko*, in which a figure dressed in a rabbit suit warned of the imminent end of the world. "I believe that we're in danger of killing the planet through greed," said McQueen. "Every species is fragile but animals are the underdogs while we are actually bringing about our own extinction—and theirs."[46]

On 6 November, Lee heard the news that his taxi-driver brother, Michael, who was then forty-eight, had suffered a massive heart attack while at Heathrow Airport in his cab. Michael had had to be taken to hospital by helicopter. "I had to be zapped four times," he said. Later, when Michael had recovered, Lee turned up at the hospital. "He sat on the bottom of the bed and asked, 'Did you see anything? Did you see the gates?' " recalls Michael. "He wanted to know whether I had seen anything on the other side, because I had died a couple of times." Michael laughed and told him to piss off.[47]

"The other side" became ever more alluring to McQueen. According to Archie, Lee started to research Marilyn Monroe's suicide on the Internet and read all the postmortem reports on her death. He gave his boyfriend a number of presents, including a Gucci box filled with cashmere jumpers and a vintage Cartier watch studded with diamonds. "That's to remember me by," Lee said. When Archie asked for details of where Lee was going, and why he was giving him keepsakes, McQueen remained silent.[48]

By the end of 2008, Lee and Archie Reed had decided to separate and at the beginning of the New Year, McQueen felt so lonely that he turned to the Internet for company. He was already an active member on the dating site Gaydar—for his profile picture he used a professional shot of him wearing combat trousers and a gray cardigan taken by Derrick Santini—and then in January he enlisted the services of escort and porn star Paul Stag. Lee asked Paul to come to his flat on Green Street, where he paid him £150 to £200 an hour for his services. "Drugs were involved, porn was involved, and probably somebody else in the room too, probably another escort—he was very much into groups," said Paul.

Paul did not recognize McQueen—he did not read the fashion press—and perhaps it was this that made Lee feel so comfortable with him. "He was masculine, and didn't fit into the fashion industry at all," said Paul. "If you didn't know him you'd think he was a successful car dealer or a scrap metal dealer." Over the course of the next three weeks, the couple saw each other twice or three times each week until eventually Paul asked Lee whether he would be interested in changing the nature of the relationship. From that point onwards the two men considered each other boyfriends, but Lee accepted the fact that Paul would need to carry on his work as an escort. Paul never touched drugs and sometimes found Lee's habit disconcerting. "For him, the drugs became second nature, like someone smoking a cigarette or having a gin and tonic," he said.[49] "I had heard that he was becoming more excessive," said Lee's sister Jacqui McQueen. "Since Issie's death, from what I gathered from the family, Lee changed and seemed to lead a fast and somewhat self-destructive existence. He had lost Issie and nothing would be the same."[50]

Some friends said that Lee had started to experiment with crystal meth, or "tina," a highly addictive drug particularly popular with promiscuous gay men who practice "chem sex." Fashion insider Matav Sinclair (a pseudonym) and Lee shared a sexual partner, a man who told Matav about the designer's fondness for crystal meth. In turn, Matav tried the drug for a week and for a few days he felt like a new world had unfolded before his eyes. Sex, and the pursuit of increasingly intensified erotic gratification, became the most important quest in his life. Then, after the sex and drugs binge was over, he was left feeling hollow and depressed. "Any inner goodness I had was spent and I felt so isolated and sad," said Matav. "It was the most scary thing I've ever done in my life. I've noticed since then that people who take 'tina' have these little dark button eyes, with no reflection, almost as if their eyes have died."[51]

McQueen knew by now that the world of fashion—with its relentless appetite for the new and its frenzied addiction to capturing the essence of the moment—did not make him happy. He told Sebastian Pons that, in retrospect, he should never have signed with Gucci. "But I cannot get out of it now," he said. "I have built my own prison."[52] He did begin to toy with the possibility of walking away from the multimillion-pound lifestyle to pursue a different course. He designed the costumes for *Eonnagata*, a contemporary dance piece directed by Robert Lepage about the eighteenth-century diplomat, spy and transvestite Chevalier d'Eon, which had its world premiere at Sadler's Wells in London in February 2009. He secured a place at the Slade School of Fine Art, flirted with the old idea of setting himself up as a photographer or heading his own design school, and even expressed a wish, to Paul Stag at least, of starting his own gay porn studio. Yet he felt powerless to pursue these latter options, fearful that if he stepped away from the brand he would harm the careers, and livelihoods, of countless employees.

Lee purged his feelings of frustration in the only way he knew how: by designing a new collection that attacked the fashion industry. McQueen said that he had been inspired by a work from his art collection—Hendrik Kerstens's photograph of his daughter Paula wearing a plastic bag on her head (a reworking of a painting by Vermeer), which was used as the image on the invitation to his show. *The Horn of Plenty*, staged on 10 March 2009 at the Palais Omnisports, Paris, served as a companion piece to *Voss*, the show set in an asylum. The models—with their pale, clown-like faces and exaggerated lips reminiscent of Leigh Bowery—looked like they had escaped the madhouse of *Voss* and had been let loose in a glorious fancy dress box that had once belonged to a French couturier. The clothes referenced Dior's New Look, Paul Poiret, Givenchy's little black dress, Matthew Bourne's *Swan Lake*, Cecil Beaton's designs for *My Fair Lady*, photographs by Irving Penn, and even McQueen's own previous designs. On their heads the models wore "hats" designed by Philip Treacy, utilizing plastic bags, tin cans, umbrellas and hubcaps. In the middle of the stage, its floor covered by broken mirrors, stood an enormous heap of what looked like rubbish, but on closer inspection was seen to contain a series of props from McQueen's previous collections. The statement was obvious. "The whole situation is such a cliché," the designer told Eric Wilson of the *New York Times*. "The turnover of fashion is just so quick and so throwaway, and I think that is a big part of the problem. There is no longevity."[53]

Sarah Burton recalls the sense of purpose with which Lee worked on the collection. "The second look in the show used traditional houndstooth that had been lacquered," she said. "Lee cut the jacket himself. He slashed it, cut an asymmetrical kimono sleeve, and took the collar off and recut it. He laid the piece of fabric on the floor and cut it to make just the right collar shape. It was incredible."[54]

The Horn of Plenty was also a reaction to the financial crash of 2008. "I'm always interested in depicting the age that we live in and this collection depicts the silliness of our age," McQueen told the journalist Susannah Frankel. "I think people will look back at it and know that we were living through a recession when I designed it, and we got to this point because of rampant, indiscriminate consumption."[55] In 2008, McQueen had contacted the photographer Nick Waplington and asked him if he would document *The Horn of Plenty* from its inception to final presentation. "I want it how you do it all dirty and nasty," he had said.[56] The designer told Waplington, whose work he had added to his art collection, that he wanted the resulting book to show his legacy. "Lee saw this collection as a kind of grand retrospective, a recycling of ideas from the last fifteen years of his production," said Nick.[57]

At the very end of *The Horn of Plenty*, which contained samples of music from previous McQueen shows as well as Marilyn Manson's "The Beautiful People," the sound of a heart monitor going into flatline was played over the PA system, just as it had at the end of *Voss* and *Pantheon as Lecum*. Immediately after a show it was normal for Lee to feel low, but this year it seemed more difficult for him to shake off the black specter of depression. His fortieth birthday was fast approaching, but on Friday, 13 March, he had made no plans to celebrate it. After the weekend he had changed his mind and called Shoreditch House, which set aside the top floor for him for Tuesday night. Guests on the night included singer Beth Ditto, Kate Moss and Stella McCartney. By coincidence, his former boyfriend Murray Arthur had turned up at the members' club in the East End only to find the space closed for a private party. As he was walking out he bumped into Lee, who was eating from a packet of sweets. Murray wished him happy birthday, they chatted for five minutes, and then

Lee walked back inside without inviting him to the event. Later that year, Murray invited McQueen to his own fortieth birthday party, a champagne reception for fifty at the George and Dragon pub in Shoreditch. "I got a reply from one of his secretaries saying thank you for the invitation but Alexander McQueen won't be attending your party," he recalls. "I was a bit hurt."[58]

In the spring of 2009, McQueen flew by private jet to Majorca for a holiday with Annabelle Neilson. The friends stayed at the house Lee had bought there, which by now had been refurbished to look like a copy of one of his London homes, complete with marble floors, glass partitions and a valuable collection of art and photography. Lee asked Sebastian Pons, who he knew to be on the island, to come and stay. Sebastian's father was dying—he realized that he could not stay long with Lee—but he felt as though his old friend needed him. One night, after Annabelle had gone to bed, the two men had a conversation on the terrace: they talked about the past, why Sebastian had felt the need to leave the company and McQueen's growing sense of claustrophobia and feelings of imprisonment. Lee showed Sebastian the ring that contained Isabella's hair; it was obvious that he still felt a certain level of guilt about the way he had treated her. "From the way he spoke he felt that he should have tried to be more helpful," Pons said.

Sebastian had noticed earlier in the day that McQueen had been reading a Buddhist text about death and dying, but what his friend told him next left him feeling shocked and disturbed.

"I've already designed my last collection," said Lee.

"What do you mean, your last collection?" asked Sebastian. "You mean your next collection?"

"No. My last collection. I have it in my head."

"What do you mean?" repeated Sebastian.

"In my last collection, I'm going to kill myself. I am going to end this."

McQueen then outlined how he planned to do it: he wanted to commit suicide during the show in full view of the audience. "He told me he would have a Perspex or glass box and in the middle of that another glass box," recalls Sebastian. "Then, towards the end of the show, he would come out from under the ground and shoot himself, so all his brains would drip down the glass."

It was almost too much for Sebastian to take in. McQueen then continued, telling his friend about how he had everything prepared. He had set up a charity, Sarabande, which he had formed back in 2007, to help people in need, including students at his old college, Central Saint Martins, and he had drawn up a will. "Another night [in Majorca], Lee asked me to see if there were any axes in the house," he went on. "He said, 'Can you go into the basement to see if you can find any?' I asked why and he told me he just needed them. I went down, but there were no axes and when I told him he said that I had to go and buy some. He said that I didn't understand, that he needed protection. That's why, he said, he had had to fly to Majorca on a private jet so he could bring his dog Callum. There were people who were after him, he said."

Sebastian was so worried about the state of his friend's mental health that he telephoned the McQueen office in London. He was told by a member of staff that the designer was fine, that there was nothing to be concerned about. "No, he is not fine, darling," he replied. "He is really messed up."[59]

Lee had perfected the art, often practiced by potential suicides, of appearing normal to the outside world. He returned to London to work on his menswear collection, due to be presented in Milan in June, and his next womenswear show, *Plato's Atlantis*. In April 2009, he met with Guy Morgan-Harris again to discuss the possibility of buying a new property, 17 Dunraven Street, a large ground- and lower-ground-floor flat in Mayfair valued at £2,525,000. "It was obvious that he seemed happy with the property, though it wasn't immediately clear that he was more serious about this one than others we had seen before," said Guy.[60] Certainly, there was nothing to suggest that Lee was anything but his normal, charming, funny self. Those closer to him, however, began to notice that he was behaving erratically. In the past, Joyce McQueen had become concerned about her son's increased drug use and, after a long talk, Lee had told his mother that he would try and quit. "He did stop, but only for six to eight weeks," said Janet.[61]

In the spring of 2009, Janet tried to talk to her brother about his drug use. "He was so erratic and perhaps I dealt with it the wrong way," she said. "When people take cocaine they can get quite nasty and there was no talking to him. I could not let him treat me like that, and obviously I retaliated, as I've got a bit of a temper as well."[62] In April, after the argument, Janet moved out of the neighboring house in Cadogan Terrace and brother and sister did not speak for a few months. McQueen had also fallen out with his other sister, Jacqui. "I was just waiting for Lee to come home," said Jacqui. "I didn't respect all the pretentiousness and shallowness of the fashion world and the front row. In that environment everyone wants to be your friend, but there was no one actually looking out for Lee McQueen."[63]

In May 2009, feeling alone and desperate, McQueen took an overdose, a cry for help that Janet believed was precipitated by the second anniversary of Isabella's death on 7 May. "I know how Lee's mind worked and he would have been beside himself," she said.[64] At the time, Janet knew nothing about the suicide attempt and learnt of it only later after her brother's death; McQueen's boyfriend, Paul Stag, was also ignorant. He did think, however, that McQueen was being placed under a ridiculous amount of pressure at work. "Lee was working these idiotic hours, getting up early, working all day and working deep into the evenings," he said.[65] Tony McQueen remembers that his brother would sometimes sleep on a bed in the office. "They talk about all this money he had—but he never went home," he said. "As soon as he'd got one collection out he'd have to start another."[66]

On 4 July 2009, Paul and Lee celebrated Gay Pride in London— Paul took part in one of the parades and later joined his boyfriend at Café Boheme in Soho. "By the time I got there he and his posse had been eating and drinking for four hours, obviously running a tab all afternoon," said Paul. "The bill came to something like £900, and I hated the way they let him pick up the bill. Lee had taken his Jeep into Soho and I had to drive it back. We went back to the flat, where he made me cheese on toast."[67] On 14 July, Lee went to see Lady Gaga at the Brixton Academy, and although he was not a great fan of her music, he must have recognized that the twenty-three-year-old singer from New York articulated similar concerns to his own: the pressures of fame, the dangers of celebrity, the pleasures of hedonistic abandon and the toxic interchange between sex and violence.

Meanwhile, McQueen's legal team were busy trying to finalize the details of his will. Lee had first drafted a will in 2008, and had made repeated versions of it over the course of the following year. By July 2009, the final version was ready for him to sign. "If Lee had not signed that will everything would have gone to my dad," said his sister Janet. The same month, Lee tried to kill himself again with an overdose of drugs. "Lee's mind in the year before he passed away was spiralling all over the place," said Janet.[68] As his drug use increased so did his feelings of anxiety, paranoia and depression. When he lost himself in one of his sex and drugs binges he stopped worrying about the fact that he was HIV-positive. "He was positive but he carried on having unprotected sex with guys on drugs," said Paul Stag.[69]

"He had HIV and was like, well, who cares?" recalls BillyBoy*. "I was a little bamboozled when he told me that. He had no responsibility to himself towards the end. I think he hated himself, sadly."[70]

Jane Hayward, a womenswear designer for the McQ diffusion line, remembers how the employees would tense up when they smelt smoke—a sign that McQueen (the only person who dared to flout the no-smoking rules in the office) was approaching. "People were apprehensive because he could have these mood swings," she said. "He'd also do these dawn raids, these early morning attacks when he would come and pounce." Staff feared that their work would be mauled and that they would be told to rework a whole line at the last minute. "At the same time he was disconnecting more and more, so he would go missing in action for days. There was a period when he didn't come in for three weeks."[71]

• • •

One of the things that kept Lee alive was the thought of what his suicide would do to his family, particularly his mother. In 2009, Joyce's kidney problems worsened and McQueen suspected that his mother did not have much time left. He made a decision to try and keep up appearances for her sake: he put his house in Cadogan Terrace on the market for £1.7 million (which he subsequently let), went through with the purchase of the flat in Dunraven Street and gave the go-ahead to Guy Morgan-Harris to start an elaborate program of refurbishment to turn the space into the kind of "world den" of his dreams.[72] He designed a wedding dress for his niece, Tony's daughter Michelle, gave an in-depth interview to Cathy Horyn of the *New York Times* and carried on socializing, regularly eating at Scott's in Mount Street, which now served as "his local canteen" for his nearby rented flat in Mayfair.[73] On 22 September, during the celebrations to mark the twenty-fifth anniversary of London Fashion Week, he went to a dinner hosted by *Vogue* and Net-a-Porter at Le Caprice to honor Nick Knight.

The other driving force in Lee's life at this time was his continuing desire to revolutionize fashion. Despite his frustrations with the system—the never-ending cycle of Autumn/Winter, Spring/Summer, menswear, accessories and so on—he still wanted to try and challenge himself. He was also conscious of his legacy and how he would be remembered—as far back as 2004 he had said, "I want to be the purveyor of a certain silhouette or a way of cutting, so that when I'm dead and gone people will know that the twenty-first century was started by Alexander McQueen."[74]

When Lee started work on his collection *Plato's Atlantis*—named after the mythological island first described by the Greek philosopher in the dialogue *Timaeus*, written around 360 BC—he told his staff, "I don't want to look at any shapes, I don't want to reference anything, a picture, a drawing. I want it all to be new."[75] Sarah Burton remembers that, one day in the design studio, he turned all the research boards around so that he and his team could only see pieces of printed fabric hanging on the wall. "And he was completely right, because he then created something new, without references," said Sarah.[76] The inspiration came from the sea—he loved diving and was a great fan of James Cameron's 1989 film *The Abyss*—and the murky depths of McQueen's subconscious. In Cameron's movie a search and rescue mission, looking for an American submarine that has disappeared in the Atlantic, discover a new species. McQueen, in *Plato's Atlantis*, imagined what that new species would be like: untouchable, statuesque women, raised a foot higher by "freakish" dome-shaped "armadillo" shoes, a reworking of a 1968 design by the artist Allen Jones.[77] Laura Craik, writing in the *Evening Standard*, likened them to "cloven hooves,"[78] while another fashion editor described them as "crab claws."[79] The collection served as a visualization of Darwinian progression in reverse. "We came from water and now, with the help of stem cell technology, we must go back to survive," said McQueen.[80]

Lee had experimented with the use of digital printing straight onto fabric in *Natural Dis-Tinction, Un-Natural Selection*, but in this collection he perfected the techniques. "Lee mastered how to weave, engineer and print any digital image onto a garment so that all the pattern pieces matched up with the design on every seam," said Sarah Burton. In total, there were thirty-six different prints, which were "circle-engineered" to the body. "By circle-engineered, I mean that the prints were based on a circle shape that sat in the middle of a bolt of fabric," said Sarah.[81]

Two robotic cameras on tracks filmed *Plato's Atlantis* and transmitted the event both onto a large screen—so that the audience caught glimpses of themselves—and live to the Internet via Nick Knight's website SHOWstudio. Half an hour before, Lady Gaga tweeted that her new single would make its debut during the show: the website recorded 30,000 hits in one second, causing it to crash. The title and lyrics of the song "Bad Romance"—about an addiction to toxic relationships—resonated with McQueen. In the video for the single, Gaga, playing a woman sold to the Russian mafia, wore a number of outfits from *Plato's Atlantis*, including the armadillo shoes. In the last year of Lee's life she became something of a McQueen muse. In May 2011, she told *Harper's Bazaar* that she felt as though McQueen wrote her song "Born This Way"—a paean to sexual diversity and difference—by channeling it through her. "I think he's up in heaven with fashion strings in his hands, marionetting away, planning this whole thing," she said. "I didn't even write the fucking song. He did!"[82]

That October, around the time of his last Paris show, Lee felt the need to get back in touch with his sister Janet. He said that he was sorry for the things that he had said. Janet told him not to be so silly, she was just pleased that he had phoned her. He asked her whether she would like to come down to stay with him in the cottage that Christmas, but unfortunately she had already booked a holiday. She also knew that her brother had a reputation for changing his mind at the last minute. "A couple of years before I had arranged a summer holiday with him and he ended up not coming," she said. "He was very much like that—if he was on a downer or if he didn't feel up to it he wouldn't want to socialize."[83]

Paul Stag noticed that by the autumn of 2009 Lee had started to retreat from life a little. Paul wanted to do more things with him away from the pleasure hub of the bedroom, but Lee seemed uninterested. "I do remember that he said that he was going to come out to the press about his HIV status," said Paul. "I thought that it was nobody else's business, but he felt he had to." Paul had been involved in an auction to raise funds for the Terrence Higgins Trust and, in November, Lee had promised to donate one of his dresses worth £10,000. "It was five in the morning and we were in bed with another guy, and both he and Lee were taking drugs," said Paul. "Lee said, 'I want you to fuck him,' but I had already come a couple of times. I told him I didn't want to do it—I was not on the clock here. He said, 'If you want that dress for the auction you fuck that guy now.' To me that was it and I just walked out."[84] The couple never saw each other again.

By the end of the year, McQueen felt isolated and vulnerable. In December, he agreed to meet Max Newsom and Nicola Brighton, who were in the process of writing a screenplay about Isabella Blow. McQueen spent the best part of the two-and-a-half-hour meeting sobbing his heart out, an encounter that left the filmmakers feeling shaken and disturbed.[85] Still, Lee kept a great deal of his grief to himself and there were many friends who only saw the façade and never suspected the depths of his depression. "He was very together, in great form," said the photographer Steven Klein, who had lunch with him in London over the Christmas period. "We made plans to do several new projects together."[86]

For New Year, Lee went to Val d'Isère, skiing with Annabelle Neilson and Jay Massacret; the friends stayed in a luxury chalet favored by Bono that had a spectacular view of the Olympic run. "Too much pine for me," said McQueen of the chalet. "You don't want to live in a sauna, do you?" In January, Lee traveled to Milan for his menswear show, which he said had been inspired by Sting, whom he described as "my ideal man, because he's a real man."[87]

He returned to London to find that his mother's health had worsened. "We all called Lee in the days before Mum passed away to tell him how bad she was and that he should come to see her," said Janet. "But he didn't want to come to the hospital. He was really struggling as he knew in his heart that these were probably Mum's final days."[88] The doctors had wanted Joyce to stay in hospital over Christmas 2009, but Joyce had other ideas. She loved a family Christmas and on 25 December she had got herself dressed and ready to leave. "The doctors refused and she was doing her nut," said Michael McQueen. "That was the only time I ever heard her effing and blinding, when she was sitting on the edge of the bed, complaining that the doctors wouldn't let her go home. That was the first time she had had a go at Lee, saying to him, 'You can eff off and all.' I went to see the doctors and they let her come home on condition that we brought her back after four hours. That was the happiest she had looked for ages."[89]

Joyce had prepared herself for death some time before and had written an extended letter in a notebook in which she listed certain possessions that she wished to bequeath to her children. She wanted Lee to have a Tiffany glass plate that he had bought for her, two Victorian paintings, six Spode plates that he had given her and two vegetable tureens. She also left him her first edition of *The Phillimore Atlas and Index of Parish Registers* and a first edition of a history of West Kingsdown, which listed some names of her Deane ancestors. Lastly, she gave him her collection of Jasperware by Wedgwood. She outlined that she wanted to be buried—not cremated—in Manor Park Cemetery and that she wished to be dressed in a high-necked nightdress, either in pink or white, which were the colors Ron liked on her. She wanted a spray of white lilies or roses on the coffin, but she did not want her children to pay for expensive wreaths, particularly not ones that read "Mum" or "Nan." "I have always thought I was one of the most luckiest mothers in the world to have such wonderful children," she wrote in the first few pages of the notebook. "I loved each and every one of you so much that sometimes I thought my heart would burst with happiness and pride. At the same time when things did not go right for you or you suffered in some way, I also felt your grief or despair and just wished I could wave a magic wand to put things right for everyone." She wrote of the love she still felt for Ron and outlined how she believed that she had gained strength of character and a sense of determination from him. They had had their troubles just like any other married couple, she said, but their strong love and devotion had always meant that they had managed to survive difficult times. "So I do not want any of you to grieve for me," she wrote. "Since my marriage I have had a wonderful life and was blessed with many happy memories. You have all given me so much love and happiness in my life, perhaps more than I deserve." She said that she had always tried to be a good mother, and that she wanted to tell all six of her children, together with her grandchildren, how much she loved them. "I wish you all peace and contentment for the rest of your lives, be happy, God Bless you All. Love as Always Mum," followed by six kisses.[90]

On 1 February, Lee turned up at a dinner hosted by *Vanity Fair*'s Graydon Carter in honor of Tom Ford, at Harry's Bar in Mayfair. He had previously turned down the invitation to celebrate the launch of Ford's film *A Single Man* and so the organizers were a little surprised to see him when he arrived unannounced with Annabelle Neilson. Tom Ford had a drink with McQueen at the bar and then returned to join his husband Richard Buckley and guests that included Valentino, Jay Jopling, Nicky Haslam, Colin Firth, Thandie Newton and Guy Ritchie, at the seated dinner. Later, Richard Buckley told the photographer Dafydd Jones, who took a series of images of the event for *Vanity Fair*, that he and Tom "thought Alexander had come to say goodbye."[91]

That same night, McQueen's family gathered around the hospital bed of Joyce, who was dying. The family did not know how much time she had left, and by eleven or twelve o'clock at night both Michael and Ron needed to return to their homes to take medication for their conditions. Janet volunteered to drive them back to get their tablets, leaving Tony alone with his mother. "So they've been gone for half an hour—it was about half past twelve at this point— and my mum started screaming," he said. "It was obvious she was in pain. I told them that they had best give her something because she was in real pain. And the nurse gave her some more morphine and she passed away in my arms." When Lee heard the news he was devastated; not only by the loss of his mother, but also by the prospect of what he knew he had to do.

The days that followed Joyce's death—on 2 February in Queen's Hospital, Romford, aged seventy-five—passed in something of a daze for the family, but Tony remembers Lee coming to their parents' house in Rowan Walk. "Lee was sitting on the settee and his head was down and he was obviously really upset," he said. Tony said to him, "It's all right, Lee." In response, Lee muttered, "Yeah." "And that was it—he said nothing to no one," said Tony. "He went away and I think the next day I got a phone call from him. He wanted to know what Mum had said [before she died]. And I said, 'She said she loves you and you're not to go and kill yourself now.' And then I didn't hear from him again."[92] A few days later, Jacqui recalls taking hold of her brother and cradling him in her arms and kissing him all over and telling him that she loved him. "He was lost," she said. "I was shocked that he allowed me to touch him, because he didn't know how to deal with being tactile. As he was leaving with his PA he stood at the doorway and gestured for me. I thought that's not like Lee because normally he says "Bye" and then he's gone. But I melted in his arms and he melted in my arms. He was like a child then."[93]

On 3 February, via his Twitter account, McQueen wrote, "I'm letting my followers know my mother passed away yesterday if it she had not me nor would you RIPmumxxxxxxxxxxxxxxxxxxxxxxxx . . ." A few moments later, he added, "But life must go on!!!!!!!!!!!!!!" On Sunday, 7 February, he wrote, "been a fucking awful week but my friends have been great but now i have to some how pull myself together and finish with the HELLS ANGELS & PROLIFIC DAE-MONS!!!!!!!!!!!!!!!!!!!!!!!!!!!!!!!," a reference to his latest collection. This was inspired by early Netherlandish artists such as Hans Memling, Hugo van der Goes and Hieronymus Bosch, Byzantine imagery, Grinling Gibbons and Jean Fouquet, whose *Virgin and Child Surrounded by Angels* Lee had used as a reference in *Joan*. However, McQueen could not face the thought of work and locked himself in his flat.

"A few days before he died he called me and I could tell that he had been taking drink and drugs," said Archie Reed. " 'My dog has been diagnosed with cancer and I have to make a choice about whether to put her to sleep.' " Archie felt annoyed by what he saw as Lee's self-centered attitude and, during the conversation, called him a "selfish cunt." "I've got my own problems to deal with, go and take a fucking sleeping pill," he told him. "I'll come around tomorrow, I'll cook dinner and we'll sort this out properly." He never heard from Lee again.[94]

Using small, subtle gestures, McQueen started to say his good-byes. On 8 February, he spoke to his nephew Gary James McQueen and asked him to create a gravestone for his mother that incorporated the design of an angel. "He said he wanted it to be uplifting," Gary said.[95] Then Lee phoned Janet and told her that he loved her. He gave Annabelle Neilson his wallet, explaining that he needed a new one, and a photograph of him with one of his dogs. On 9 February, at seven in the morning, he sent a tweet to Kerry Youmans, in a spirit of fun: "I'm here with my girl annie tinkerbell [Annabelle Neilson] wishing kerry the slag, happy birthday in NY, your [sic] 40 now girl time to slow it down we think."[96] The same day, he managed to drag himself into work, where he spoke to Trino Verkade about his mother's funeral. "Make it late," he had said, when Trino had asked him about the time he wanted a table at J. Sheekey's restaurant on the night of the funeral.[97] He also spoke to Janet again, telling her that he was going to make his mother an old-fashioned pink winceyette nightgown, which he would then have biked to the funeral home. He wrote a handwritten note to Kerry which said, "I want to thank you for always being a good friend to me. Love, Lee," which he sent by FedEx and which arrived in New York soon after the news of McQueen's death had broken.[98]

On 10 February Lee had dinner at Scott's with some members of his studio—"apparently he was very together at dinner," said Daphne Guinness[99]—and then he and Annabelle Neilson returned to his flat in Green Street. Lee had always promised Annabelle that he would never follow Isabella's suicide, "but who will ever know what was going on in his mind, what he was dealing with?" she wondered. Lee knew he could not bear to attend the funeral of his mother, which had been scheduled for 12 February. His much-loved dog Minter had been diagnosed with cancer. Death for him seemed like an escape, a blessed relief, a step towards the kind of thought-free existence that he had craved for so long. "I wonder now if things would have been different if I hadn't left that night, but a part of me knows that there is nothing anyone could have done to change anything," said Annabelle.[100]

In the early hours, and in a desperate state of mind, Lee took hold of a book, Wolfe von Lenkiewicz's *The Descent of Man*, and on the back cover wrote the words, "Please look after my dogs. Sorry,

I love you, Lee. PS Bury me at the church." He then started to use the Internet to research suicide methods. He tapped into the search engine Yahoo, "When someone slits their wrist how long does it take for them to die?" He would have read answers such as, "that's a carzy [*sic*] *** question but I've heard it takes 4 to 5 hours," "THIS IS A VERY SERIOUS MATTER. GOD BLESS YOU AND WHO EVER IS CUTTING THEIR WRIST!" and "It wouldn't make them die. It just leaves large gashes in their arms, which may turn into scars. Slitting your wrists isn't enough to kill you."[101]

The exact chronology of McQueen's actions that night is unclear, but there was no doubt of his intentions; this was no "cry for help." He took zopiclone, a prescription sleeping pill, and midazolam, a tranquilizer, both of which were found in his bloodstream, as well as a "significant" amount of cocaine. He tried to slit his wrists with a dagger in the en-suite shower room of the second bedroom; there, police found a chopping board together with a knife sharpener, a large kitchen knife and a meat cleaver. His family regarded this as completely out of character: Lee hated the sight of real blood and would scream in shock and distress if he so much as nipped his finger with a pair of scissors.[102] Then he tried to hang himself in the shower by using the cord of his dressing gown, but failed when the head buckled due to his weight. Finally, he removed the clothes from the guest bedroom closet, took his favorite brown leather belt, looped it around the rail and then used it to hang himself. As he died the scented candle that he had lit earlier continued to burn throughout the night.

AFTERWORD

The next morning, just before ten o'clock, the housekeepers Cesar and Marlene Garcia—a Colombian couple who had worked for McQueen for ten or so years—arrived at the flat in Green Street as usual. Cesar found the front door chained, but he managed to gain access through the utility room. Minter, Juice and Callum were in a state of distress, and he noticed that the flat was in more of a mess than normal. As he started to tidy up, Cesar made his way through into the guest bedroom, where he discovered McQueen's body hanging in the wardrobe. Cesar called McQueen's PA Kate Jones, who had just walked into the office and who could not take in the news. She drove around to Green Street, where she discovered the police and an ambulance. Meanwhile, Trino Verkade and Sarah Burton had taken a taxi to McQueen's flat and had stopped to pick up Shaun Leane, who had also been telephoned by Cesar. "As we walked toward the house there's a part of you that doesn't want to walk any further," said Shaun.[1]

McQueen's family were busy preparing for Joyce's funeral. Michael heard the news as he was picking up the glasses and cups for the wake from a hire shop. His sister Tracy called him and told him that something had happened to Lee and that he should go to his flat. "I was in my cab the night before, driving around Mayfair," he said. "I couldn't believe it."[2] Michael then had to break the news to his father, who on hearing about the suicide repeatedly said, "Why have you done this to me, Lee?"[3] Nobody could get in contact with Jacqui as she was on a treadmill in a gym, without her mobile phone. When she left the gym at midday and was told the news she broke down. "I was never informed that he had tried previously to take his

311

life even though others knew this and had kept it to themselves," she said. "I would never have left his side, but then again, with all the will in the world, he perhaps wouldn't have let me near him. But I will never know."[4]

Shaun Leane then telephoned Daphne Guinness, who was in New York with David LaChapelle, and told her about their friend's suicide. "It was the same telephone call as I got from Alexander when Isabella killed herself," said Daphne. "I couldn't fucking believe it—and the day before his mother's funeral."[5] Within minutes the news of McQueen's death started to be broadcast around the world, and the tributes began to pour in. "I admired him tremendously," said John Galliano. "He was a revolutionary. He will not be forgotten and it is an immense loss . . . Daring, original, stimulating, he understood how to be a fabulous British ambassador for fashion." Katharine Hamnett said that Lee was a "genius—what a tragic loss," while Domenico Dolce and Stefano Gabbana released a statement that read, "He has left an incomparable void in the world of fashion." Diane von Fürstenberg said, "It is so sad he was in such a state of despair. Such a great talent, such poetry, it is awful." François-Henri Pinault, CEO of PPR (which is now Kering, the majority shareholder of the McQueen label), declared that McQueen had been one of the greatest fashion designers of his generation. "Both a visionary and avant-garde, his creations were inspired by tradition and hypermodernity so that they were outside time," he said. Sarah Jessica Parker said, "I am still in shock and submerged in grief upon learning of the premature death of this gentle genius . . . The tiniest detail: inspired, original, whimsical, splendid, brilliant and gripping, that was Alexander McQueen. And there will be no other. What is even more distressing is that in spite of his success until now, be it creative, critical or commercial, his greatest success lay ahead of him . . . God accelerated Lee. It was a privilege for us to have known you. You will be indescribably missed."[6]

The news of Lee's death left McQueen's friends, lovers and colleagues in a collective state of shock. Alice Smith was in her office when her friend Katie Webb, who worked at the *Daily Telegraph*, telephoned her. "I was upset for him, but I was upset for fashion too," she said. "I remember thinking, 'What is fashion going to do without him?'"[7] Andrew Groves was in Salford, working as an external examiner, when a colleague told him. "It was incredibly sad, it didn't have to end like that," he said. "I thought it was his way of saying, 'Fuck you, you don't own me, I'm killing the brand.' I remember him saying years ago that if he died he wanted the label to die with him."[8] Archie Reed was not surprised by the news. "In my heart of hearts I knew that one day this would happen," he said. "The amount of times I would leave and go home and think to myself, 'Am I going to get a phone call? Is he going to go too far this time?'"[9] BillyBoy* was hosting a dinner party at his house in Switzerland when the news came through. He excused himself from the table and went to his bedroom, where he cried for hours. "I was angry, and felt wretched for weeks," he said.[10] Detmar Blow found out when he was contacted by a newspaper who asked him to write a piece. He was saddened, but not surprised. "I felt that Issie had got him and they would be together," he said. "They were soulmates. He wouldn't have done it had Issie or his mother been alive as it would have hurt them too much."[11]

Donald Urquhart was sitting in the garden of the Edward VI pub in Islington when George Forsyth came in, his face full of joy. It was obvious that he had not heard the news. "I really didn't know whether to tell him or not," said Donald. "It had been some years since they split up, but I knew sweet, big-hearted George would be devastated all the same. I took a deep breath and told him. He absolutely could not believe it . . . It is quite difficult for me to look back on that day and think that soon George Forsyth would be dead." George died, aged thirty-four, in London on 23 May 2010 from dihydrocodeine toxicity, which the coroner described as an accidental death. "It is almost as though I am watching scenes from some overwrought gothic melodrama, perhaps featuring Shelley and Byron at Lake Como," said Donald.[12] Lee's former tutor Louise Wilson was with fashion critic Sarah Mower, who had come into Central Saint

Martins to see a student show. "Sarah took the call and dropped the phone," said Louise. "She said, 'My God, Lee is dead.'"[13] That night Louise went on BBC Radio 3's *Night Waves* to talk about the importance of the designer. "It's an unimaginable loss to fashion worldwide because he was such a mentor and a visionary," said Louise, who on 16 May 2014 died in her sleep, aged fifty-two, when she was visiting her family in Scotland.[14]

Lee's friend Miguel Adrover had been working in Turkey and had just arrived home when he switched on CNN. "I saw him come out on a stretcher in a plastic body bag," he said.[15] Murray Arthur had traveled home to Scotland to visit his mother, who had been rushed into hospital with stomach cancer. He left the ward, walked downstairs to the canteen and switched his mobile phone on. There were dozens of missed calls and messages. He assumed that people were calling him about his mother. Then he listened to the voice mails, from friends asking him to call them. As he walked through the foyer he saw a television broadcasting images from outside McQueen's flat. "I remember walking to the front door of the hospital and falling to my knees and howling, really crying," he said. "For the rest of the day I was in silence. I could not contemplate what had happened."[16] In Majorca, Sebastian Pons logged onto the Internet where he saw the news, and then telephoned the McQueen studio in London and spoke to Kate Jones and Sarah Burton, who confirmed the worst. He remembers running from his home to his mother's house crying, "He's dead." Four days later he took a flight to London and visited the office. Sarah gave him a hug and she showed him Lee's desk and suggested he sit in his friend's chair. "And then I saw the collection that he had left, which to me looked like a version of purgatory, and it all made sense," he said.[17]

There were some people who blamed the fashion industry itself for McQueen's death. Journalist George Pitcher, writing in the *Daily Telegraph*, believed that fashion was nothing but a "chimera of a real industry, the absence of which would harm no one other than its self-serving catamites and courtesans. It is a disgusting place to make a living."[18] Designer Ben de Lisi said that fashion "is a horrible industry, rife with angst,"[19] while John Maybury stated, "I wouldn't wish success in fashion on my worst enemy—the demands it puts on people, the attention, the spotlight, is all so intense."[20]

On 12 February, the day of Joyce McQueen's funeral, Naomi Campbell and Daphne Guinness appeared as models at a benefit fashion show to raise funds for Haiti after the recent earthquake. Before the show started, the Duchess of York, Sarah Ferguson, paid tribute to the designer. "To Alexander McQueen, thank you," she said.[21] That morning, one of the fifteen catsuits Daphne had ordered from McQueen arrived and so she decided to wear that instead of the "pink confection" the organizers had planned for her. "I thought what would Alexander do and so I put some tulle around my head," she said. "I was already crying quite a lot, but I thought if I walked fast enough it would billow out. And it worked—you couldn't see the wet mascara."[22]

On 25 February, McQueen's funeral was held at St. Paul's Church, Knightsbridge. Janet, her son Gary, and Shaun Leane went to see Lee to pay their last respects. Gary placed a photograph of himself and his brother Paul when they were younger into the coffin, together with some rose petals. "I went in by myself and it was quite upsetting," he said. "I thought I could handle it, but I couldn't."[23] Tributes were read by Jacqui and her son Elliot, and Holly Chapman, McQueen's niece. Janet chose Elgar's "Nimrod," "a piece that Lee and myself enjoyed listening to—Lee always had Classic FM on," she said.[24] The service also included "Jerusalem," a hymn that had been sung at Joyce's funeral two weeks earlier, and the final song was Diana Ross singing "Remember Me."

On 28 April, an inquest held at Westminster Coroner's Court concluded, in the words of the coroner Dr. Paul Knapman, that McQueen had "killed himself while the balance of his mind was disturbed." The court reported the cause of death—asphyxia and hanging—and heard testimonies from the housekeeper Cesar Garcia and Dr. Stephen Pereira. "He certainly felt very pressured by his work, but it was a double-edged sword," said the psychiatrist. "He felt it was the only area of his life where he felt he had achieved something . . . He was a very secretive person. Over a period of time he had been let down by various friends who he felt were taking advantage of who he was. For that reason he was very guarded. He had been terribly let down in long-standing close relationships. He was very close to his mother. I think on top of the grief he felt there was that one link that had gone from his life and there was very little to live for."[25] The words presented a version of the truth, but by no means the whole picture.

Gucci had employed Jonathan Coad, who was then head of litigation at the specialist law firm Swan Turton and an expert in "reputation management," to help to restrain the reporting of McQueen's death. "Gucci were really good at putting everything in place to stop the press speaking to us," said McQueen's sister Janet. "We never really had a voice. Jonathan Coad said that there might be things at the inquest that would come out, and tried to warn us how bad it would be. But I wanted to be there for my brother."[26] From the court, Janet took the belt with which Lee had hanged himself, while Jacqui kept the rail, the last objects touched by their brother.

The police and the coroner maintained that Lee had died by his own hand, but McQueen's family had their suspicions. "Do we know that Lee committed suicide?" asked Ron, and both Janet and Jacqui have questioned the circumstances of their brother's suicide.[27] Considering the evidence—and McQueen's long-standing death wish—it seems highly unlikely that McQueen's death was anything but suicide. But the family feel that certain people could have done more to support Lee in his psychological troubles, and they have their suspicions about why more was not done.

McQueen died a rich man. Probate papers showed that his art collection had been valued at an estimated £1 million. His flat in Dunraven Street was worth £2.5 million, while other land and buildings he owned totaled £2,635,000. He owned £11,614,625 worth of shares. He had £193,290 in one bank account, £638,017 in another; £26,282 in a Euro account; £1,570,005 in a fixed account;

£27,688 in an Isa, and £30,000 in Premium Bonds. In his will, Lee left £100,000 each to four charities: the Terrence Higgins Trust, Battersea Dogs & Cats Home, the London Buddhist Centre and the Blue Cross. Lee gave the trustees £50,000 so they could administer the upkeep and maintenance of his three dogs; Marlene Garcia took Minter, Juice went to Annabelle Neilson, and Jacqui looked after Callum. He bequeathed £50,000 each to Marlene and Cesar Garcia, and the same sum to each of his nephews and nieces and his godson Thomas Alexander McQueen. He left £250,000 to each of his brothers and sisters, but the bulk of his net estate, which amounted to £16,036,500, went into a trust for his charity, Sarabande.

Since her brother's death Janet McQueen has had a long-running dispute with the trustees of the charity, particularly David Glick, a high-profile entertainment lawyer, and Gary Jackson, an accountant, men McQueen had appointed as executors of his will. "The executors may have behaved within the law but in our view they haven't behaved with compassion," Janet told the *Mail on Sunday*.[28] The family was upset that they did not have the opportunity to see Lee's Green Street flat or choose any mementoes to remember him by. Janet also wanted to know details of Sarabande's grants and bursaries, but she was told that the information was confidential. "I just wanted to know that his money was being spent wisely," she said.[29] Throughout the process the family maintained that they felt left out and overlooked. A typical communication was the solicitor's letter that Ron received on 2 November 2011 that gave him the details of the Big Yellow Self Storage unit, which contained the "personal effects of your late son which do not have monetary value."[30] Jacqui and Janet paid a visit to the storage unit on Wick Lane, Bow, an experience both of them found distressing; some of his clothes had been kept so long that they had been eaten by moths. Jacqui remembers holding a jumper that had once belonged to Lee and pressing it to her face; the sweater still smelt of her brother.[31]

• • •

On a misty day towards the end of May 2010, three months after McQueen's death, his close family gathered in Kilmuir Cemetery on the northern tip of the Isle of Skye to bury the cremated remains of their brother. He had given instructions that he should be buried on Skye, a place which both he and his mother connected with their family ancestry.

It was a small, private gathering attended by Lee's three sisters, Janet, Tracy and Jacqui, and his brother Tony. His other brother Michael was still recovering from his heart attack and his father, Ron, was too ill to travel (he was suffering from cancer and died in October 2012). Standing next to the grave, Lee's sisters and brother contemplated their sibling's extraordinary life and his untimely death. As a Scottish piper played, Tony, who had been charged with the task, knelt down and placed a black enameled urn containing Lee's ashes into the ground. The vicar said a prayer and then each family member dropped a handful of earth into the grave.

Since Lee's funeral his brothers and sisters have made repeated pilgrimages to the cemetery; in October 2011, after Callum's death, Jacqui took the dog's ashes to Skye and had them buried next to her brother.

McQueen's grave stands on a windswept headland, looking out towards the sea. Inscribed on the green slate headstone are the words that he had had tattooed onto his right arm, words that meant so much to him: "Love looks not with the eyes but with the mind." It was the one thing in the world, McQueen often said, that he knew to be true.

ACKNOWLEDGMENTS

This book could not have been written without the support and blessing of the McQueen family. Janet, Tony, Michael and Jacqui McQueen took the hard decision to allow a stranger into their lives. I must thank them for their patience and understanding during what must have been a difficult and emotional process. I would like to single out McQueen's first and greatest muse, his sister Janet, for special thanks. She took the brave step to disclose a family secret that affected both her and Lee. I interviewed her on multiple occasions and she answered dozens of queries by telephone and e-mail. I cannot thank her enough. I would also like to thank Janet's sons Gary James McQueen and Paul McQueen for sharing their memories of their much-loved uncle.

I must also thank the McQueen family for permission to reproduce excerpts from Joyce McQueen's unpublished history of the family and for the opportunity to use a range of unpublished photographs.

McQueen was not much of a letter writer and so this book was written not with the use of archival material but through interviews with the people who knew him. I must thank McQueen's boyfriends who helped me with the research: Murray Arthur, Richard Brett, Andrew Groves, Jay Massacret, Archie Reed, Paul Stag, and Glenn Andrew Teeuw.

I interviewed a wide range of people during the course of researching and writing the book and I would like to thank: Miguel Adrover, Linda Björg Árnadóttir, Carmen Artigas, Russell Atkins, Ferhan Azman, Brooke Baker, John Banks, Rebecca Barton, Nicola Bateman, Fleet Bigwood, BillyBoy*, Detmar Blow, Chris Bird, John Boddy,

ACKNOWLEDGMENTS

Rosemarie Bolger, Peter Bowes, Dr. Stephen Brogan, Fiona Cartledge, Adele Clough, Ben Copperwheat, Lee Copperwheat, Simon Costin, Liz Farrelly, Frank Franca, Lesley Goring, Richard Gray, Daphne Guinness, A. M. Hanson, Guy Morgan-Harris, Anna Harvey, Jane Hayward, Bobby Hillson, John Hitchcock, Marin Hopper, Mira Chai Hyde, Dafydd Jones, Ben de Lisi, John McKitterick, John Maybury, Jason Meakin, Suzy Menkes, Trevor Merrell, Réva Mivasagar, Max Newsom, Seta Niland, Mr. Pearl, Sebastian Pons, Janet Street-Porter, Dai Rees, Eric Rose, Norbert Schoerner, Alice Smith, Sue Stemp, Lise Strathdee, Plum Sykes, Koji Tatsuno, Stephen Todd, Derrick Tomlinson, Nicholas Townsend (Trixie), Simon Ungless, Donald Urquhart, Michelle Wade, Tania Wade, the late Professor Louise Wilson, and Kerry Youmans. Some interviewees wanted to remain anonymous, while one person I spoke to chose to use a pseudonym.

A large number of people provided leads and background information and I would like to thank: Yeana Ahn, Frans Ankoné, Oliver Azis, Kara Baker, Richard Benson, Andrew Bolton, Gavin Brown, Paula Byrne, Peter Close at Central Saint Martins (CSM), Nicholas Coleridge, Vanessa Cotton, Laura Craik, Alison D'Amario, Anne Deniau, Primrose Dixon, Paula Fitzherbert, Zoe Franklin, Natalie Gibson, Colin Glen, Hettie Harvey, Gavanndra Hodge, Liz Hoggard, Tina Jordan, James Kent, Jasmine Kharbanda, Pascale Lamche, Saskia Lamche, Stephanie Lilley, Gaby and Gary Lincoln, William Ling, Susan Lord, Debbie Lotmore at CSM, William Matthews at Gieves Hawkes, Colin McDowell, Shonagh Marshall, Marko Matysik, Princess Michael of Kent, Annabelle Neilson, Michelle Olley, Elinor Renfrew, Caroline Roux, Richard Royle, Angel Sedgwick, Alix Sharkey, Christopher Stocks, Joanna Sykes, Andrew Tanser, Sue Tilley, Katie Webb, Claire Wilcox at the V&A, Judy Willcocks at CSM.

A number of libraries proved invaluable during the course of the research. I would like to thank the staff of the libraries of Central Saint Martins, the London College of Fashion and the British Library. The British Library's Oral History of Photography project, held in the Sound Archive, provided some useful background information on colleagues who worked with McQueen, especially an in-depth interview with Nick Knight.

For use of the photographs in the book I would like to thank, in addition to the McQueen family: Miguel Adrover, Murray Arthur, Rebecca Barton, BBC Photo Library, Rosemarie Bolger, Peter Bowes, Richard Brett, Camera Press, Claridge's, Jeremy Deller, Getty Images, A. M. Hanson, Mira Chai Hyde, Dafydd Jones, Jay Massacret, Archie Reed, Rex Features, and Derrick Tomlinson.

I have consulted a number of broadcast sources, including: *British Style Genius*, BBC, October 2008; "Cutting Up Rough" (*The Works*), BBC, 1997; *McQueen and I*, More4, 25 February 2011; *The Clothes Show*, BBC1, 26 January 1997.

I have also referred to a wide range of newspaper and magazine reports, all of which are referenced in the notes. However, I would like to single out the following journalists and writers for their work: Hilary Alexander, Lisa Armstrong, Lynn Barber, Katherine Betts, Alex Bilmes, Tamsin Blanchard, Hamish Bowles, Grace Bradberry, Jess Cartner-Morley, Vassi Chamberlain, Laura Collins, Maggie Davis, Godfrey Deeny, Christa D'Souza, Edward Enninful, Bridget Foley, Susannah Frankel, Chris Heath, Cathy Horyn, Marion Hume, David Kamp, Rebecca Lowthorpe, Colin McDowell, Lisa Markwell, Rebecca Mead, Suzy Menkes, Sarah Mower, Samantha Murray Greenway, Andrew O'Hagan, Harriet Quick, Melanie Rickey, Alix Sharkey, James Sherwood, Ingrid Sischy, David James Smith, Mimi Spencer, Stephen Todd, Judith Thurman, Lorna V, Iain R. Webb, and Eric Wilson.

Thanks are also due to Andrew Bolton, curator of the Met's wonderful 2011 show and editor of *Alexander McQueen: Savage Beauty*, Metropolitan Museum of Art, New York (Yale University Press), and Judith Watt, whose book *Alexander McQueen: The Life and the Legacy* (Harper Design, London and New York) provided a useful overview of the designer's career.

At Simon & Schuster UK I would like to thank my editor, Abigail Bergstrom; Mike Jones (who commissioned the book but has moved on to pastures new); copy editor Lindsay Davies; Sarah Birdsey; Olivia Morris; Hannah Corbett; Elinor Fewster; at Scribner, Roz Lippel, my US editor; Jason Heuer, who designed the jacket; Ashley Gilliam, Scribner publishing manager; Isolde Sauer, production editor. And thank you to all the staff in London and New York for their support and enthusiasm.

Clare Alexander, my agent and friend, has been with me from day one. This book would not have been written without her. I would also like to thank all the staff of Aitken Alexander, particularly Lesley Thorne and Sally Riley.

Lastly, I must thank—as always—my parents, my friends and Marcus Field.

ALEXANDER McQUEEN
WOMENSWEAR
COLLECTIONS 1992–2010

To see all of McQueen's shows, apart from *Jack the Ripper*, *Taxi Driver* and *Supercalifragilisticexpialidocious*, go to: http://www.gainsburyandwhiting.com/fashionshow/

Saint Martins MA Graduate collection, *Jack the Ripper Stalks His Victims*, 1992
Taxi Driver, Autumn/Winter 1993
Nihilism, Spring/Summer 1994
Bheansidhe (Banshee), Autumn/Winter 1994
The Birds, Spring/Summer 1995
Highland Rape, Autumn/Winter 1995
The Hunger, Spring/Summer 1996
Dante, Autumn/Winter 1996
Bellmer La Poupée, Spring/Summer 1997
It's a Jungle Out There, Autumn/Winter 1997
Untitled, Spring/Summer 1998
Joan, Autumn/Winter 1998
No. 13, Spring/Summer 1999
The Overlook, Autumn/Winter 1999
Eye, Spring/Summer 2000
Eshu, Autumn/Winter 2000
Voss, Spring/Summer 2001
What a Merry-Go-Round, Autumn/Winter 2001

The Dance of the Twisted Bull, Spring/Summer 2002
Supercalifragilisticexpialidocious, Autumn/Winter 2002
Irere, Spring/Summer 2003
Scanners, Autumn/Winter 2003
Deliverance, Spring/Summer 2004
Pantheon as Lecum, Autumn/Winter 2004
It's Only a Game, Spring/Summer 2005
The Man Who Knew Too Much, Autumn/Winter 2005
Neptune, Spring/Summer 2006
The Widows of Culloden, Autumn/Winter 2006
Sarabande, Spring/Summer 2007
In Memory of Elizabeth Howe, Salem, 1692, Autumn/Winter 2007
La Dame Bleue, Spring/Summer 2008
The Girl Who Lived in the Tree, Autumn/Winter 2008
Natural Dis-Tinction, Un-Natural Selection, Spring/Summer 2009
The Horn of Plenty, Autumn/Winter 2009
Plato's Atlantis, Spring/Summer 2010

NOTES

INTRODUCTION

1 "Remembering a Renegade Designer," Cathy Horyn, *New York Times*, 20 September 2010.
2 "Crazy for a Piece of the Fashion Action," Lisa Markwell, *Independent*, 22 September 2010.
3 Alexander McQueen obituary, Imogen Fox, *Guardian*, 11 February 2010.
4 "An Enigma Remembered," *Economist*, 12 November 2012.
5 "The Real McQueen," Susannah Frankel, American *Harper's Bazaar*, April 2007.
6 *Alexander McQueen: Savage Beauty*, Metropolitan Museum of Art, New York (New Haven: Yale University Press, 2011), 26.
7 "Memories of McQueen, a Brave Heart," Hilary Alexander, *Daily Telegraph*, 21 September 2010.
8 *The Great Fashion Designers*, Brenda Polan, Roger Tredre (Oxford, New York: Berg, 2009), 244.
9 Interview with Jacqui McQueen, 8 April 2014.
10 Reverend Canon Giles Fraser, *A Service of Thanksgiving to Celebrate the Life of Lee Alexander McQueen CBE*, Monday, 20 September 2010, 5.
11 Interview with Andrew Groves, 24 April 2013.
12 Interview with Alice Smith, 7 May 2013.
13 Interview with Andrew Groves, 24 April 2013.
14 "The Real McQueen," Susannah Frankel, op. cit.
15 *Savage Beauty*, 12.
16 "Fashion World Gathers to Celebrate Alexander McQueen," Alistair Foster and Miranda Bryant, *Evening Standard*, 20 September 2010.
17 "Stars Pay Tribute to 'Genius' Alexander McQueen at Memorial Service," PA, *Independent*, 20 September 2010.
18 *Numéro*, December 2007.
19 "Alexander McQueen's Haunting World," Robin Givhan, *Newsweek*, 18 April 2011.
20 Interview with Janet Street-Porter, 16 April 2013.
21 *Harper's Bazaar*, April 2007.
22 "Stars Pay Tribute," PA, op. cit.
23 "Memories of McQueen," Hilary Alexander, op. cit.
24 Interview with Alice Smith, 7 May 2013.

NOTES

25 "The Savage and the Romantic," Suzy Menkes, *New York Times*, 20 September 2010.

26 Interview with Murray Arthur, 21 November 2013.

27 "Remembering a Renegade Designer," Cathy Horyn, op. cit.

28 Interview with Archie Reed, 25 May 2013.

29 "General Lee," Cathy Horyn, *T Magazine, New York Times*, 11 September 2009.

30 *Numéro*, December 2007.

31 "General Lee," Cathy Horyn, op. cit.

32 Interview with Andrew Groves, 24 April 2013.

33 "All Hail McQueen," Lorna V, *Time Out*, 24 September–1 October 1997.

34 "Tears for Alexander the Great, Stars Turn Out for McQueen," Damien Fletcher, *Daily Mirror*, 21 September 2010.

35 "Catwalk Stars Celebrate the Brutal Candour of a Tormented Virtuoso," Lisa Armstrong, *The Times*, 21 September 2010.

36 "McQueen: The Interview," Alex Bilmes, *GQ*, May 2004.

37 *Harper's & Queen*, April 2003.

38 "Killer McQueen," Harriet Quick, British *Vogue*, October 2002.

39 "Dressed to Thrill," Judith Thurman, *New Yorker*, 16 May 2011.

40 "An Enigma Remembered," *Economist*, 12 November 2012.

41 "Alexander McQueen's Last Collection Unveiled on Paris Catwalk," Jess Cartner-Morley, *Guardian*, 9 March 2010.

42 Quoted in *McQueen and I*, More4, 25 February 2011.

43 "Lean, Mean McQueen," Vassi Chamberlain, *Tatler*, February 2004.

44 *Dazed & Confused*, September 1998.

45 *Guardian*, 19 September 2005.

46 "Radical Fashion," Tamsin Blanchard, *Observer Magazine*, 7 October 2001.

47 "Lean, Mean McQueen," Vassi Chamberlain, op. cit.

CHAPTER ONE

1 Interview with Michael McQueen, 7 November 2013.

2 Interview with Tony McQueen, 20 October 2013.

3 "A Brief History of Cane Hill, The Cult of Cane Hill," Simon Cornwell, 2002, http://www.simoncornwell.com/urbex/projects/ch/index.htm.

4 *CR5 Magazine*, Simon Cornwell, February 2013, reprinted on http://www.simoncornwell.com/urbex/projects/ch/ps/tunnels1.htm.

5 Personality Questionnaire, Cane Hill Hospital, http://www.simoncornwell.com/urbex/projects/ch/doc1/personal1.htm.

6 Interview with Michael McQueen, 7 November 2013.

7 Interview with Janet McQueen, 17 September 2013.

8 Interview with Tony McQueen, 20 October 2013.

9 Ibid.

10 Record Your Own Family, Joyce B. McQueen, unpublished manuscript, copyright the McQueen family.

11 Interview with Jacqui McQueen, 8 April 2014.

12 Interview with Tony McQueen, 20 October 2013.

13 "The Real McQueen," Alix Sharkey, *Guardian*, 6 July 1996.

14 Interview with Alice Smith, 7 May 2013.

15 "Fashion's Hard Case," Richard Heller, *Forbes*, 16 September 2002.

16 Interview with Janet McQueen, 17 September 2013.

17 Interview with Jacqui McQueen, 29 August 2013.

18 Interview with Tony McQueen, 20 October 2013.

19 Interview with Peter Bowes, 11 December 2013.

20 Interview with Alice Smith, 7 May 2013.

21 Interview with Murray Arthur, 21 November 2013.

22 "'Meeting the Queen Was Like Falling in Love,'" *Guardian*, 20 April 2004.

23 McQueen: The History of a Clan, Joyce B. McQueen, 1992, unpublished manuscript, copyright the McQueen family.

24 Ibid.

25 Ibid.

26 Ibid.

27 Ibid.

28 Report of Dr. Thomas Bond, quoted in *The Ultimate Jack the Ripper Sourcebook: An Illustrated Encyclopedia*, Stewart Evans and Keith Skinner (London: Constable and Robinson, 2001), 345–7.

29 McQueen: The History of a Clan.

30 Record Your Own Family.

31 Ibid.

32 Interview with Michael McQueen, 7 November 2013.

33 McQueen: The History of a Clan.

34 "Alexander McQueen, The Final Interview," Godfrey Deeny, Australian *Harper's Bazaar*, April 2010.

35 Record Your Own Family.

36 Ibid.

37 Interview with Jacqui McQueen, 29 August 2013.

38 Interview with Michael McQueen, 7 November 2013.

39 "Lean, Mean McQueen," Vassi Chamberlain, *Tatler*, February 2004.

40 McQueen: The History of a Clan.

41 Interview with Tony McQueen, 20 October 2013.

42 Interview with Jacqui McQueen, 29 August 2013.

43 McQueen: The History of a Clan.

44 Will book, Joyce B. McQueen, unpublished, copyright the McQueen family.

45 "'Meeting the Queen Was Like Falling in Love,'" *Guardian*, 20 April 2004.

46 Deane family tree, Joyce B. Deane, unpublished, copyright the McQueen family.

47 Record Your Own Family.

48 *The Cuckoo's Nest*, Ron S. King (Raleigh, NC: Lulu Enterprises, 2010), 125.

49 Interview with Peter Bowes, 11 December 2013.

50 "Emperor of Bare Bottoms," Lynn Barber, *Observer*, 15 December 1996.

NOTES

51 "Alexander McQueen," Chris Heath, *The Face*, September 2002.

52 Interview with Janet McQueen, 30 April 2014.

53 Interview with Rebecca Barton, 1 February 2014.

54 Interview with Andrew Groves, 24 April 2013.

55 Interview with Richard Brett, 16 July 2013.

56 Interview with Detmar Blow, 26 June 2013.

57 Interview with BillyBoy*, 8 August 2013.

58 Interview with Janet McQueen, 16 January 2014.

59 "The Real McQueen," Susannah Frankel, *Independent Fashion Magazine*, Autumn/ Winter 1999.

60 "Macabre McQueen," Katherine Betts, American *Vogue*, October 1997.

61 "I Am the Resurrection," Tony Marcus, *i-D*, September 1998.

62 Interview with Peter Bowes, 11 December 2013.

63 Lee McQueen, School Report, December 1980, courtesy of the McQueen family.

64 Ibid.

65 Ibid.

66 Lee McQueen, School Report, March 1982, courtesy of the McQueen family.

67 Lee McQueen, School Reports, December 1980 and March 1982, courtesy of the McQueen family.

68 "The Real McQueen," Susannah Frankel, op. cit.

69 Interview with Jason Meakin, 11 February 2014.

70 "The Real McQueen," Alix Sharkey, op. cit.

71 Interview with Peter Bowes, 11 December 2013.

72 Ibid.

73 "The Real McQueen," Susannah Frankel, op. cit.

74 "Lean, Mean McQueen," Vassi Chamberlain, op. cit.

75 Joyce McQueen, McQueen family photo album.

76 Interview with Russell Atkins, 11 March 2014.

77 Interview with Jason Meakin, 11 February 2014.

78 "i-Q," Alexander McQueen, *i-D*, February 1996.

79 Interview with Jason Meakin, 11 February 2014.

80 Interview with Peter Bowes, 11 December 2013.

81 Interview with Jason Meakin, 11 February 2014.

82 Ibid.

83 Interview with Peter Bowes, 11 December 2013.

84 "Emperor of Bare Bottoms," Lynn Barber, op. cit.

85 Interview with Peter Bowes, 11 December 2013.

86 Ibid.

87 Andrew Bolton quoted in "Alexander McQueen: 'He Sewed Anger into his Clothes,'" Sarah Mower, *Daily Telegraph*, 17 April 2011.

88 Interview with Janet McQueen, 16 January 2014.

89 "Dressed to Thrill," Judith Thurman, *New Yorker*, 16 May 2011.

90 Interview with John Maybury, 15 September 2014.

91 "Lean, Mean McQueen," Vassi Chamberlain, op. cit.

92 Alexander McQueen on *Rhona Cameron Show*, quoted in *McQueen and I*, More4.
93 "Emperor of Bare Bottoms," Lynn Barber, op. cit.

CHAPTER TWO

1   "A Man of Darkness and Dreams," Ingrid Sischy, *Vanity Fair*, April 2010.
2   "The Real McQueen," Susannah Frankel, *Independent Fashion Magazine*, Autumn/ Winter 1999.
3   "Emperor of Bare Bottoms," Lynn Barber, *Observer*, 15 December 1996.
4   Interview with Janet McQueen, 17 September 2013.
5   *McDowell's Directory of Twentieth Century Fashion*, Colin McDowell (London: Frederick Muller, first published 1984, revised edition 1987), 9.
6   Ibid., 15.
7   Interview with Gary James McQueen, 11 June 2013.
8   Interview with Paul McQueen, 17 September 2013.
9   Interview with Janet McQueen, 17 September 2013.
10 "The Real McQueen," Alix Sharkey, *Guardian*, 6 July 1996.
11 Joyce McQueen, speaking in 1997, quoted in *McQueen and I*, More4.
12 "The Real McQueen," Susannah Frankel, op. cit.
13 "A Style Is Born," David Kamp, *Vanity Fair*, November 2011.
14 Interview with John Hitchcock, 17 April 2013.
15 "Emperor of Bare Bottoms," Lynn Barber, op. cit.
16 Interview with John Hitchcock, 17 April 2013.
17 "Emperor of Bare Bottoms," Lynn Barber, op. cit.
18 Interview with Derrick Tomlinson, 17 April 2013.
19 Interview with John Hitchcock, 17 April 2013.
20 Interview with Rosemarie Bolger, 24 May 2013.
21 "Emperor of Bare Bottoms," Lynn Barber, op. cit.
22 *Frank Skinner Show*, quoted in *McQueen and I*, More4.
23 Interview with John Hitchcock, 17 April 2013.
24 Interview with Rosemarie Bolger, 24 May 2013.
25 "Alexander McQueen's Sarah Burton on Life after Lee," Shaun Phillips, *The Times*, 24 October 2012.
26 Interview with Jacqui McQueen, 29 August 2013.
27 Interview with Andrew Groves, 24 April 2013.
28 Interview with John Hitchcock, 17 April 2013.
29 "Emperor of Bare Bottoms," Lynn Barber, op. cit.
30 "Cutting Up Rough," *The Works*, BBC, 1997.
31 "Emperor of Bare Bottoms," Lynn Barber, op. cit.
32 Interview with Andrew Groves, 24 April 2013.
33 "Emperor of Bare Bottoms," Lynn Barber, op. cit.
34 Interview with Andrew Groves, 24 April 2013.
35 Interview with Archie Reed, 25 May 2013.

36 "Emperor of Bare Bottoms," Lynn Barber, op. cit.

37 "Prototypes from the Perimeters," Roger Tredre, *Independent*, 17 July 1993.

38 "The Real McQueen," Susannah Frankel, op. cit.

39 Interview with Koji Tatsuno, 14 September 2014.

40 *Frocking Life, Searching for Elsa Schiaparelli*, BillyBoy* (Delémont, Switzerland: Foundation Tanagra).

41 Tom Tredway in *Biography, Identity and the Modern Interior*, ed. Anne Massey and Penny Sparke (Farnham, UK: Ashgate Publishing Limited), 98.

42 *Shocking Life*, Elsa Schiaparelli (London: J. M. Dent & Sons, 1954), 17.

43 E-mail from BillyBoy* to AW, 13 October 2014.

44 Interview with BillyBoy*, 8 August 2013.

45 BillyBoy* interview, Predrag Pajdic, *The Pandorian*, August 2010.

46 Interview with BillyBoy*, 8 August 2013.

47 *The Pandorian*, August 2010.

48 Ibid.

49 Interview with BillyBoy*, 8 August 2013.

50 Lee McQueen, excerpt from *My American Life: In One Era, Out the Other, An Autobiography*, BillyBoy*, fierth.com.

51 E-mail from BillyBoy* to AW, 3 March 2014.

52 Interview with BillyBoy*, 8 August 2013.

53 Interview with John McKitterick, 1 April 2014.

54 "The Real McQueen," Susannah Frankel, op. cit.

55 *McDowell's Directory of Twentieth Century Fashion*, 295.

56 "An Italian Takes Paris," Frank DeCaro, *Newsday*, 20 March 1989.

57 "With Striking Fashions, Gigli Reaches New Heights," Bernadine Morris, *New York Times*, 17 September 1989.

58 "The Real McQueen," Susannah Frankel, op. cit.

59 E-mail from Lise Strathdee to AW, 6 May 2014, copyright Lise Strathdee.

60 "Alexander McQueen," Katie Webb, Infotainment, *Sky Magazine*, March 1993.

61 E-mail from Lise Strathdee to AW, 6 May 2014.

62 Interview with John McKitterick, 1 April 2014.

63 "Romeo, Romeo: The Monk of Milan," Michael Gross, *New York*, 5 December 1988.

64 Interview with Carmen Artigas, 6 April 2014.

65 E-mail from Lise Strathdee to AW, 6 May 2014.

66 Interview with Simon Ungless, 24 January 2014.

67 Interview with Carmen Artigas, 6 April 2014.

68 Ibid.

69 "Romeo, Romeo," Michael Gross, op. cit.

70 "The Real McQueen," Susannah Frankel, op. cit.

71 E-mail from Lise Strathdee to AW, 6 May 2014.

72 "Cutting Up Rough," BBC.

CHAPTER THREE

1 "I Taught Them a Lesson," James Sherwood, *Independent*, 19 February 2007.
2 Interview with Bobby Hillson, 11 December 2013.
3 "I Taught Them a Lesson," James Sherwood, op. cit.
4 Interview with Bobby Hillson, 11 December 2013.
5 "I Taught Them a Lesson," James Sherwood, op. cit.
6 Interview with Bobby Hillson, 11 December 2013.
7 Interview with Janet McQueen, 16 January 2014.
8 *British Style Genius*, BBC, October 2008.
9 Interview with Professor Louise Wilson, 14 May 2014.
10 "Central Saint Martins Fashion College Bids Farewell to Charing Cross Road," Tamsin Blanchard, *Daily Telegraph*, 24 June 2011.
11 "No Rules Britannia!," Hamish Bowles, American *Vogue*, May 2006.
12 Interview with Professor Louise Wilson, 14 May 2014.
13 Interview with Simon Ungless, 24 January 2014.
14 Interview with Rebecca Barton, 1 February 2014.
15 E-mail from Rebecca Barton to AW, 3 February 2014.
16 E-mail from Rebecca Barton to AW, 2 February 2014.
17 Interview with Adele Clough, 28 May 2014.
18 Interview with Tony McQueen, 20 October 2013.
19 Interview with Réva Mivasagar, 31 January 2014.
20 E-mail from Réva Mivasagar to AW, 28 May 2014.
21 Interview with Professor Louise Wilson, 14 May 2014.
22 Interview with Bobby Hillson, 11 December 2013.
23 Interview with Rebecca Barton, 1 February 2014.
24 Interview with Simon Ungless, 24 January 2014.
25 Interview with Réva Mivasagar, 31 January 2014.
26 E-mail from Réva Mivasagar to AW, 28 May 2014; interview with Réva Mivasagar, 31 January 2014.
27 Interview with Frank Franca, 14 June 2013.
28 Interview with Eric Rose, 18 July 2013.
29 Interview with Rebecca Barton, 1 February 2014.
30 Interview with Tania Wade, 21 July 2014.
31 "Inside London: The Groupie," Marion Hume, American *Vogue*, January 1997.
32 Interview with Rebecca Barton, 1 February 2014.
33 Interview with Adele Clough, 28 May 2014.
34 "The Fashion Stars of Central Saint Martins," Johnny Davis, *Observer Magazine*, 7 February 2010.
35 Interview with Professor Louise Wilson, 14 May 2014.
36 Interview with Réva Mivasagar, 31 January 2014.
37 Interview with Adele Clough, 28 May 2014.
38 Interview with Bobby Hillson, 11 December 2013.

39   Interview with Rebecca Barton, 1 February 2014.
40   Interview with Réva Mivasagar, 31 January 2014.
41   Interview with Simon Ungless, 24 January 2014.
42   Interview with Simon Costin, 15 April 2013.
43   Press Notes, Saint Martins MA Graduate Show 1992.
44   Interview with John McKitterick, 1 April 2014.
45   Interview with Simon Ungless, 24 January 2014.
46   "Cutting Up Rough," *The Works*, BBC, 1997.
47   Interview with Professor Louise Wilson, 14 May 2014.
48   "All Hail McQueen," Lorna V, *Time Out*, 24 September–1 October 1997.
49   Interview with Réva Mivasagar, 31 January 2014.
50   Interview with Lesley Goring, 29 May 2014.
51   Interview with Bobby Hillson, 11 December 2013.
52   Interview with Rebecca Barton, 1 February 2014.
53   "Cutting Up Rough," BBC.
54   Interview with Rebecca Barton, 1 February 2014.

CHAPTER FOUR

1   *McQueen and I*, More4.
2   "The Mad Muse of Waterloo," Larissa MacFarquhar, *New Yorker*, 19 March 2001.
3   "A Blow to Accuracy," Rachel Cooke, *Observer Review*, 3 October 2010.
4   Interview with Réva Mivasagar, 31 January 2014.
5   "Hail McQueen," Bridget Foley, *W Magazine*, June 2008.
6   "A Blow to Accuracy," Rachel Cooke, op. cit.
7   *Blow by Blow: The Story of Isabella Blow*, Detmar Blow with Tom Sykes (London: HarperCollins, 2010), 6.
8   Ibid., 4.
9   Ibid., 1.
10   "The Mad Muse of Waterloo," Larissa MacFarquhar, op. cit.
11   *Blow by Blow*, 42.
12   Interview with Detmar Blow, 26 June 2013.
13   Interview with Réva Mivasagar, 31 January 2014.
14   "The Real McQueen," Alix Sharkey, *Guardian*, 6 July 1996.
15   Interview with John McKitterick, 1 April 2014.
16   "Kinky Gerlinky," *The Word*, Channel 4, https://www.youtube.com/ watch?v= GAhqlcwxVYA.
17   Ibid.
18   Interview with Réva Mivasagar, 31 January 2014.
19   Christopher Hussey in *Country Life*, 7 and 14 September 1940, quoted in "A Family's Idyll on the Hill," Clive Aslet, *Country Life*, 1 February 2012.
20   *Isabella Blow: A Life in Fashion*, Lauren Goldstein Crowe (London: Quartet Books, 2011), 111.

21 Interview with Detmar Blow, 26 June 2013.

22 "A Family's Idyll on the Hill," Clive Aslet, op. cit.

23 Interview with Detmar Blow, 26 June 2013.

24 *Blow by Blow*, 158.

25 Interview with Detmar Blow, 26 June 2013.

26 *Isabella Blow: A Life in Fashion*, 130.

27 "Isabella Blow on Alexander McQueen," Maggie Davis, *Time Out*, 13 September 2005.

28 E-mail from Réva Mivasagar to AW, 28 May 2014.

29 Interview with Réva Mivasagar, 31 January 2014.

30 E-mail from Réva Mivasagar to AW, 28 May 2014.

31 Interview with Réva Mivasagar, 31 January 2014.

32 Ibid.

33 Interview with Simon Ungless, 24 January 2014.

34 Ibid.

35 *The One Hundred and Twenty Days of Sodom*, Marquis de Sade (London: Arrow Books, 1990), 184.

36 "Bowie & McQueen," *Dazed & Confused*, November 1996.

37 Interview with Chris Bird, 4 September 2013.

38 *Fashion at the Edge: Spectacle, Modernity and Deathliness*, Caroline Evans (New Haven and London: Yale University Press, 2009), 152–3.

39 Interviews with Chris Bird, 4 September, 16 September 2013.

40 Interview with Alice Smith, 7 May 2013.

41 Interview with Anna Harvey, 23 April 2014.

42 Interview with Chris Bird, 16 September 2013.

43 "Alexander McQueen," Katie Webb, Infotainment, *Sky Magazine*, March 1993.

44 "All Hail McQueen," Lorna V, *Time Out*, 24 September–1 October 1997.

45 "The Real McQueen," Lucinda Alford, *Observer*, 21 March 1993.

46 "Fashion Stars Who Won't Wear Britain," Roger Tredre, *Independent on Sunday*, 28 February 1993.

47 Interview with Lee Copperwheat, 4 July 2014.

48 "Catwalk Capital," Sarah Mower, *Guardian*, 30 August 2009.

49 "Shaping Up," Nilgin Yusuf, *Sunday Times*, 7 March 1993.

50 "The Real McQueen," Lucinda Alford, op. cit.

51 Interview with Janet McQueen, 17 September 2013.

52 "Something to Show for Themselves," Iain R. Webb, *The Times*, 8 March 1993.

53 E-mail from Simon Ungless to AW, 18 June 2014.

54 Interview with Alice Smith, 7 May 2013.

55 Interview with Tania Wade, 21 July 2014.

56 Interview with Michelle Wade, 6 November 2013.

NOTES

CHAPTER FIVE

1 "McQueen's Theatre of Cruelty," Marion Hume, *Independent*, 21 October 1993.
2 *Draper's Record*, original review of show, reprinted in *Draper's Record*, 20 February 2010.
3 "McQueen's Theatre of Cruelty," Marion Hume, op. cit.
4 "Great British Fashion," Edward Enninful, *i-D*, October 1993.
5 "Great British Fashion," Avril Mair, *i-D*, October 1993.
6 Interviews with Fleet Bigwood, 23 June, 25 June 2014.
7 Interview with Marin Hopper, 7 August 2014.
8 Interview with Bobby Hillson, 11 December 2013.
9 "Cool Britannia: Fashion's Fickle Eye Is Fixed on London," *The Times*, 26 September 1996.
10 *Alexander McQueen: The Life and the Legacy*, Judith Watt (New York: Harper Design, 2013), 63–4.
11 "The Real McQueen," Alix Sharkey, *Guardian*, 6 July 1996.
12 Interview with Seta Niland, 12 June 2013.
13 Interview with Chris Bird, 16 September 2013.
14 "Neo-Riemannian Theory and the Analysis of Pop-Rock Music," Guy Capuzzo, *Music Theory Spectrum* 26, no. 2 (Fall 2004): 177–99.
15 Interview with Seta Niland, 12 June 2013.
16 Interview with Alice Smith, 7 May 2013.
17 Interview with Michael McQueen, 7 November 2013.
18 Interview with Seta Niland, 12 June 2013.
19 "Madonna's Magician," Michael Gross, *New York*, 12 October 1992.
20 Ibid.
21 Interview with Plum Sykes, 30 August 2013.
22 "Conflicting Conviction," Samantha Murray Greenway, *Dazed & Confused*, September 1994.
23 "New Kid on the Block," Kathryn Samuel, *Daily Telegraph*, 24 February 1994.
24 "All Hail McQueen," Lorna V, *Time Out*, 24 September–1 October 1997.
25 "Punk: On the Runway," SHOWstudio, Rebecca Lowthorpe, http://show studio.com/project/punk_on_the_runway/rebecca_lowthorpe.
26 Interview with John Maybury, 15 September 2014.
27 "Alexander McQueen," Mark C. O'Flaherty, *The Pink Paper*, April 1994.
28 "Talent Pool," Adrian Clark, *Fashion Weekly*, 3 March 1994.
29 "McQueening It," Mimi Spencer, *Vogue*, June 1994.
30 "Alexander McQueen," Mark C. O'Flaherty, op. cit.
31 Interview with Plum Sykes, 30 August 2013.
32 Interview with Andrew Groves, 24 April 2013.
33 Interview with Eric Rose, 18 July 2013.
34 Interview with Dai Rees, 18 September 2013.
35 Interview with Nicholas Townsend/Trixie, 24 May 2013.

36 Interview with Eric Rose, 31 July 2013.

37 Interview with Nicholas Townsend/Trixie, 24 May 2013.

38 "Paulita Sedgwick: Rancher, Actress and Independent Film-maker," Charles Darwent, *Independent*, 29 January 2010.

39 Interview with Frank Franca, 14 June 2013.

40 Interview with Nicholas Townsend/Trixie, 24 May 2013.

41 Interview with Frank Franca, 14 June 2013.

42 Interview with Nicholas Townsend/Trixie, 24 May 2013.

43 "Lee McQueen" by Donald Urquhart, e-mail to AW, 23 October 2013.

44 Interview with BillyBoy*, 8 August 2013.

45 Interview with Miguel Adrover, 13 August 2013.

46 "Down the Runways," Ingrid Sischy, *New Yorker*, 2 May 1994.

47 Ibid.

48 "Conflicting Conviction," Samantha Murray Greenway, op. cit.

49 Interview with Andrew Groves, 24 April 2013.

50 "Forever England," Susannah Frankel, *Independent*, 8 September 2001.

51 "The Court of McQueen," Rebecca Lowthorpe, *Observer Life*, 23 February 1997.

52 "England's Glory," Melanie Rickey, *Independent*, 28 February 1997.

53 "England Rules OK," Nick Foulkes, *Evening Standard*, 26 September 1997.

54 "Forever England," Susannah Frankel, op. cit.

55 "England Rules OK," Nick Foulkes, op. cit.

56 "Forever England," Susannah Frankel, op. cit.

57 "England Rules OK," Nick Foulkes, op. cit.

58 Interview with Nicholas Townsend/Trixie, 24 May 2013.

59 "Conflicting Conviction," Samantha Murray Greenway, op. cit.

60 Interview with Andrew Groves, 24 April 2013.

61 E-mail from Mr. Pearl to AW, 12 October 2014.

62 Interview with Alice Smith, 7 May 2013.

63 "Lee McQueen" by Donald Urquhart, e-mail to AW, 23 October 2013.

64 Interview with Plum Sykes, 30 August 2013.

65 "Alexander McQueen 1969–2010," Hamish Bowles, American *Vogue*, April 2010.

66 "Avant-Garde Designer of the Year, Alexander McQueen," Hamish Bowles, American *Vogue*, December 1999.

67 "Alexander McQueen 1969–2010," Hamish Bowles, op. cit.

68 "In London, Designers Are All Grown-Up," Amy M. Spindler, *New York Times*, 11 October 1994.

69 "Conflicting Conviction," Samantha Murray Greenway, op. cit.

70 Interview with Seta Niland, 12 June 2013.

CHAPTER SIX

1 "Life as a Look," Hilton Als, *New Yorker*, 30 March 1998.

2 E-mail from Nicola Bateman to AW, 24 July 2014.

3 Interview with A. M. Hanson, 2 July 2014.

4 E-mail from Stephen Brogan to AW, 3 July 2014.

5 "Life as a Look," Hilton Als, op. cit.

6 Ibid.

7 Ibid.

8 Leigh Bowery, Diary, quoted in *Leigh Bowery: The Life and Times of an Icon*, Sue Tilley (London: Hodder & Stoughton, 1997), 97.

9 *Leigh Bowery*, 100.

10 "Life as a Look," Hilton Als, op. cit.

11 "Lee McQueen" by Donald Urquhart, e-mail to AW, 23 October 2013.

12 "Drama McQueen," Rob Tannenbaum, *Details*, June 1997.

13 Interview with Nicholas Townsend/Trixie, 24 May 2013.

14 Interview with Fiona Cartledge, 7 August 2013.

15 E-mail from A. M. Hanson to AW, 3 July 2014.

16 Interview with Nicholas Townsend/Trixie, 24 May 2013.

17 Interview with Detmar Blow, 26 June 2013.

18 Interview with Anna Harvey, 23 April 2014.

19 "Fashion: A Little Bit of What You Fancy," Marion Hume and Tamsin Blanchard, *Independent*, 17 March 1995.

20 "Shock Treatment," Colin McDowell, *Sunday Times Style*, 17 March 1996.

21 "Boy Done Good," Colin McDowell, Richard Woods, Simon Gage, *Sunday Times*, 10 December 2000.

22 "Emperor of Bare Bottoms," Lynn Barber, *Observer*, 15 December 1996.

23 Interview with John Boddy, 28 January 2014.

24 Interview with Andrew Groves, 24 April 2013.

25 E-mail from Andrew Groves, 13 October 2014.

26 Interview with Andrew Groves, 24 April 2013.

27 Interview with Nicholas Townsend/Trixie, 24 May 2013.

28 Interview with Chris Bird, 16 September 2013.

29 "McQueen of England," Ashley Heath, *The Face*, November 1996.

30 Interview with Andrew Groves, 24 April 2013.

31 Interview with John McKitterick, 1 April 2014.

32 Interview with Adele Clough, 28 May 2014.

33 Interview with Alice Smith, 7 May 2013.

34 *Balancing Acts: Commerce Versus Creativity*, ICA video, 1995.

35 *Lucky Kunst: The Rise and Fall of Young British Art*, Gregor Muir (London: Aurum, 2009), 168.

36 "Where Have all the Cool People Gone?," Jess Cartner-Morley, *Guardian*, 21 November 2003.

37 *Lucky Kunst*, 155.

38 Interview with Mira Chai Hyde, 16 May 2014.

39 Interview with Andrew Groves, 24 April 2013.

40 Interview with Mira Chai Hyde, 16 May 2014.

41 Interview with Sebastian Pons, 20 August 2014.

42 "Wings of Desire," Susannah Frankel, *Guardian Weekend*, 25 January 1997.

43 "Alexander the Great," Judy Rumbold, *Vogue* supplement, August 1996.

44 Interview with Suzy Menkes, 13 June 2014.

45 "Simply Cool for Summer," Iain R. Webb, *The Times*, 25 October 1995.

46 "Divided We Rule," Colin McDowell, *Sunday Times*, 29 October 1995.

47 "Alexander the Great," Judy Rumbold, op. cit.

48 Interview with Simon Ungless, 24 January 2014.

49 E-mail from Liz Farrelly to AW, 25 November 2013.

50 E-mail from Linda Björg Árnadóttir to AW, 4 July 2014.

51 Interview with Janet McQueen, 17 September 2013.

52 "i-Q," Alexander McQueen, *i-D*, February 1996.

53 "Fabric of Society," Paula Reed, *Sunday Times Style*, 3 March 1996.

54 Interview with Chris Bird, 16 September 2013.

55 Interview with Chris Bird, 16 September 2013.

56 Interview with Mira Chai Hyde, 16 May 2014.

57 "Out of the Crypt and on to the Catwalk," Tamsin Blanchard, *Independent*, 5 March 1996.

58 *Sunday Telegraph Magazine*, 22 September 1996.

59 "All Hail McQueen," Lorna V, *Time Out*, 24 September–1 October 1997.

60 Interview with Simon Ungless, 24 January 2014.

61 "In London, Blueblood Meets Hot Blood," Amy M. Spindler, *New York Times*, 5 March 1996.

62 "The Macabre and the Poetic," Suzy Menkes, *International Herald Tribune*, 5 March 1996.

63 Interview with Andrew Groves, 24 April 2013.

64 "Shock Treatment," Colin McDowell, *Sunday Times Style*, 17 March 1996.

65 "Alexander the Great," Judy Rumbold, op. cit.

66 "Shock Treatment," Colin McDowell, op. cit.

67 "Dullsville," Guy Trebay, *New York*, 15 April 1996.

68 Ibid.

69 "The McQueen of England," *Women's Wear Daily*, 28 March 1996.

70 Interview with Andrew Groves, 24 April 2013.

71 "Alexander McQueen Meets Helen Mirren," *Dazed & Confused*, September 1998.

72 Interview with Marin Hopper, 7 August 2014.

73 "The McQueen of England," *Women's Wear Daily*, op. cit.

CHAPTER SEVEN

1 Interview with Murray Arthur, 21 November 2013.

2 Postcard from Lee McQueen to Murray Arthur, 1996, courtesy of Murray Arthur.

3 "Drama McQueen," Rob Tannenbaum, *Details*, June 1997.

4 Interview with Murray Arthur, 21 November 2013.

5 Interview with Mira Chai Hyde, 16 May 2014.

6 Interview with Murray Arthur, 21 November 2013.

7 "Cutting Up Rough," *The Works*, BBC, 1997.

8 Ibid.

9 "Isabella Blow on Alexander McQueen," Maggie Davis, *Time Out*, 13 September 2005.

10 *Blow by Blow: The Story of Isabella Blow*, Detmar Blow with Tom Sykes (London: HarperCollins, 2010), 157.

11 Interview with Murray Arthur, 21 November 2013.

12 "All Hail McQueen," Lorna V, *Time Out*, 24 September–1 October 1997.

13 Lee McQueen Twitter account, 1 February, reproduced in "Alexander McQueen's Twitter Revealed Troubled Mind," Nick Collins, *Daily Telegraph*, 12 February 2010.

14 Interview with Dai Rees, 18 September 2013, e-mail from Dai Rees to AW, 7 July 2014.

15 Interview with Simon Costin, 15 April 2013.

16 Interview with Sarah Burton, Susannah Frankel, *AnOther*, Spring/Summer 2012.

17 "Alexander McQueen's Sarah Burton on Life After Lee," Shaun Phillips, *The Times*, 24 October 2012.

18 "Betraying Convention," Liz Farrelly, *Design Week*, 3 October 1996.

19 Nick Knight, Oral History of British Photography, British Library.

20 "McQueen of England," Ashley Heath, *The Face*, November 1996.

21 Ibid.

22 Nick Knight, Oral History of British Photography, British Library.

23 "London Rules Again," Iain R. Webb, *The Times*, 2 October 1996.

24 "All Hail McQueen," Lorna V, op. cit.

25 "Charity Attack on Designer," *Independent*, 2 October 1996.

26 "London Rules Again," Iain R. Webb, op. cit.

27 "British Thrills and Frills and Stateside Buzz—It's Called Symbiosis," Tamsin Blanchard, *Independent*, 1 October 1996.

28 "Will This Be Dior's New Look?—She Denies It of Course," *Independent*, 14 August 1996.

29 "French Fashion Has Designs on Britons," Grace Bradberry, *The Times*, 9 October 1996.

30 "Will This Be Dior's New Look?", *Independent*, op. cit.

31 *McDowell's Directory of Twentieth Century Fashion*, 148.

32 "If Galliano Goes to Dior, Will Alexander McQueen Go to Givenchy?," Constance C. R. White, *New York Times*, 24 September 1996.

33 *Alexander McQueen: Savage Beauty*, Metropolitan Museum of Art, New York (New Haven: Yale University Press, 2011), 226.

34 Interview with Andrew Groves, 24 April 2013.

35 Interview with Murray Arthur, 21 November 2013.

36 Interview with John Banks, 1 July 2014.

37 "I'm Not Having Bumsters on George V," Hilary Alexander, *Daily Telegraph*, 14 October 1996.

38 *Blow by Blow*, 173.
39 "Blowing In," *The Times*, 1 November 1996.
40 E-mail from John Banks to AW, 4 July 2014.
41 *Blow by Blow*, 173.
42 *McQueen and I*, More4.
43 Interview with Detmar Blow, 26 June 2013.
44 Isabella Blow interview, Lydia Slater, *Daily Telegraph*, quoted in *Blow by Blow*, 175.
45 Interview with John Maybury, 15 September 2014.
46 Interview with Daphne Guinness, 10 December 2013.
47 "Bull in a Fashion Shop," Susannah Frankel, *Guardian*, 15 October 1996.
48 Interview with Murray Arthur, 21 November 2013.
49 "From Rebel to Royalty as McQueen Is Crowned King of Fashion," Angela Buttolph, *Evening Standard*, 23 October 1996.
50 "Low Cut—Diary," PHS, *The Times*, 24 October 1996.
51 "Cutting at Central Saint Martins," *Independent on Sunday*, Ideal Home, 3 November 1996, reproduced in *Alexander McQueen: The Life and the Legacy*, 109.
52 "McQueen and Country," Christa D'Souza, *Observer Magazine*, 4 April 2001, originally published in *Talk Magazine*, March 2001.
53 "Alexander McQueen's Final Bow," Cathy Horyn, *New York Times*, 3 April 2010.
54 "The Court of McQueen," Rebecca Lowthorpe, *Observer Life*, 23 February 1997.
55 Interview with Murray Arthur, 21 November 2013.
56 *McQueen and I*, More4.
57 "Ideal Homes, Alexander McQueen," Rosanna Greenstreet, *Independent on Sunday*, 3 November 1996.
58 Interview with Mira Chai Hyde, 16 May 2014.
59 *McQueen and I*, More4.
60 "England Rules OK," Nick Foulkes, *Evening Standard*, 26 September 1997.
61 *Savage Beauty*, 226.
62 Interview with Simon Ungless, 24 January 2014.
63 "I'm Not Having Bumsters on George V," Hilary Alexander, op. cit.
64 *McQueen and I*, More4.
65 Interview with Murray Arthur, 21 November 2013.
66 "The Court of McQueen," Rebecca Lowthorpe, *Observer Life*, 23 February 1997.
67 *Love Looks Not with the Eyes: Thirteen Years with Lee Alexander McQueen*, Anne Deniau (New York: Abrams, 2012), 13.
68 "Backstage McQueen: Q and A with Anne Deniau," Eric Wilson, *New York Times*, 7 September 2012.
69 *Love Looks Not with the Eyes*, 15.
70 Ibid.
71 *McQueen and I*, More4.
72 Interview with Murray Arthur, 21 November 2013.
73 *Blow by Blow*, 175.
74 *McQueen and I*, More4.

NOTES

75 "Postcard from London: Gear," Hilton Als, *New Yorker*, 17 March 1997.

76 Liz Tilberis, *The Clothes Show*, BBC1, 26 January 1997.

77 "Paris Match," Colin McDowell, *Sunday Times*, 26 January 1997.

78 Diary, Kate Muir, *The Times*, 8 March 1997.

79 "Postcard from London: Gear," Hilton Als, op. cit.

80 "Wings of Desire," Susannah Frankel, *Guardian Weekend*, 25 January 1997.

81 "Postcard from London: Gear," Hilton Als, op. cit.

CHAPTER EIGHT

1 "London Swings! Again!," David Kamp, *Vanity Fair*, March 1997.

2 "London Reigns," Stryker McGuire, *Newsweek*, 4 November 1996.

3 "This Time I've Come to Bury Cool Britannia," Stryker McGuire, *Observer Review*, 29 March 2009.

4 E-mail from Detmar Blow to AW, 17 July 2014.

5 *Blow by Blow: The Story of Isabella Blow*, Detmar Blow with Tom Sykes (London: HarperCollins, 2010), 25–6.

6 E-mail from Detmar Blow to AW, 17 July 2014.

7 "Alexander McQueen and Issie Blow, You Will Be Missed," David Kamp, *Vanity Fair* blog, 11 February 2010.

8 "London Swings! Again!," David Kamp, op. cit.

9 "Alexander McQueen and Issie Blow," David Kamp, op. cit.

10 "London Swings! Again!," David Kamp, op. cit.

11 Interview with Murray Arthur, 21 November 2013.

12 Interview with Mira Chai Hyde, 16 May 2014.

13 Ibid.

14 E-mail from Stephen Todd to AW, 8 June 2013.

15 "The Importance of Being English," Stephen Todd, *Blueprint*, March 1997.

16 "Rock Steady," John Harlow and Olga Craig, *Sunday Times*, 9 February 1997.

17 "Cutting Up Rough," *The Works*, BBC, 1997.

18 "Drama McQueen," Rob Tannenbaum, *Details*, June 1997.

19 Ibid.

20 "England's Glory," Melanie Rickey, *Independent*, 28 February 1997.

21 "Cutting Up Rough," BBC.

22 "McQueen's Vision of Urban Chaos," Grace Bradberry, *The Times*, 28 February 1997.

23 "Cutting Up Rough," BBC.

24 Ibid.

25 "Alexander: The Great is Back in Britain," Mimi Spencer, *Evening Standard*, 28 February 1997.

26 "McQueen's Vision of Urban Chaos," Grace Bradberry, op. cit.

27 "London Has More Buzz Than Swing," Tamsin Blanchard, *Independent*, 5 March 1997.

28 "The Inspiring Truth about the Self-Styled Yob of Fashion," Richard Pendlebury, *Daily Mail*, 30 January 1997.

29 Interview with Janet McQueen, 12 September 2014.

30 "Chanel and Givenchy Traditions," Amy M. Spindler, *New York Times*, 14 March 1997.

31 "Do You Think It's Me," Colin McDowell, *Sunday Times*, 23 March 1997.

32 Ibid.

33 "Oh, Malone!," Carole Malone, *Sunday Mirror*, 16 March 1997.

34 "Conflicting Conviction," Samantha Murray Greenway, *Dazed & Confused*, September 1994.

35 Interview with Murray Arthur, 21 November 2013.

36 *Love Looks Not with the Eyes: Thirteen Years with Lee Alexander McQueen*, Anne Deniau (New York: Abrams, 2012), 16.

37 "Macabre McQueen," Katherine Betts, American *Vogue*, October 1997.

38 Interview with Murray Arthur, 21 November 2013.

39 Interview with Nicholas Townsend/Trixie, 24 May 2013.

40 Interview with Lee Copperwheat, 4 July 2014.

41 "London Swings! Again!," David Kamp, op. cit.

42 Interview with Simon Costin, 15 April 2013.

43 *McQueen and I*, More4.

44 Interview with Alice Smith, 7 May 2013.

45 "Macabre McQueen," Katherine Betts, op. cit.

46 "McQueen Chills Blood of the Fashion World," John Harlow, *Sunday Times*, 6 July 1997.

47 "Macabre McQueen," Katherine Betts, op. cit.

48 "Cutting Up Rough," BBC.

49 "Go On My Son," Nick Compton, *Sunday Times*, 12 October 1997.

50 Interview with Simon Costin, 15 April 2013.

51 "The Kids Are All Right," Chip Brown, *New York*, 25 August 1997.

52 "Macabre McQueen," Katherine Betts, op. cit.

53 "Fur and Feathers Fly for McQueen Triumph," Heath Brown, *The Times*, 8 July 1997.

54 "The Kids Are All Right," Chip Brown, op. cit.

55 "All Hail McQueen," Lorna V, *Time Out*, 24 September–1 October 1997.

56 Interview with Jacqui McQueen, 29 August 2013.

57 *Alexander McQueen: Savage Beauty*, Metropolitan Museum of Art, New York (New Haven: Yale University Press, 2011), 73.

58 Interview with Murray Arthur, 21 November 2013.

59 Interview with Archie Reed, 25 May 2013.

60 E-mail from Murray Arthur, 25 July 2014.

61 Interview with Murray Arthur, 21 November 2013.

62 Postcard from Lee McQueen to Murray Arthur, undated, courtesy of Murray Arthur.

63 Interview with Murray Arthur, 21 November 2013.

CHAPTER NINE

1 "McQueen Takes London by Storm," Melanie Rickey, *Independent*, 29 September 1997.

2 "Splash Hit," *Women's Wear Daily*, 30 September 1997.

3 "McQueen Reigns as the King," Mimi Spencer, *Evening Standard*, 29 September 1997.

4 *Love Looks Not with the Eyes: Thirteen Years with Lee Alexander McQueen*, Anne Deniau (New York: Abrams, 2012), 15.

5 Interview with Simon Costin, 15 April 2013.

6 "Splash Hit," *Women's Wear Daily*, op. cit.

7 "The King of Yob Couture," *Sunday Telegraph*, 28 September 1997.

8 "It's a Stitch-Up," A. A. Gill, *Sunday Times*, 28 September 1997.

9 "Warrior Björk," Greg Kot, *Chicago Tribune*, 15 May 1998.

10 "Lee McQueen by Björk," GQ.com, 28 September 2010.

11 Alexander McQueen interviewed by Björk, *Index Magazine*, 2003.

12 "Cut Dead," Jasper Gerard, *The Times*, 24 October 1997.

13 "Hard to See the Frills for the Froth," Brenda Polan, *Financial Times*, 18 October 1997.

14 "Catwalk Culprits," Sir Hardy Amies, *The Spectator*, 1 November 1997.

15 "Vain Glorious," Colin McDowell, *Sunday Times*, 26 October 1997.

16 "Shocks Fade as McQueen Goes Fishing for Applause," Grace Bradberry, *The Times*, 19 January 1998.

17 "His Majesty McQueen is a King-Size Yawn," Jane Moore, *Sun*, 5 March 1998.

18 Interview with Simon Costin, 15 April 2013.

19 Interview with Miguel Adrover, 13 August 2013.

20 Interview with Miguel Adrover, 4 August 2014.

21 "To Hell and Back," Emma Moore, *Sunday Times*, 15 March 1998.

22 "Annabelle Neilson Remembers Alexander McQueen," *Harper's Bazaar*, April 2011.

23 "The Runway Bride," Meenal Mistry, *W*, June 2006.

24 "Isabella Blow on Alexander McQueen," *Time Out*, Maggie Davis, 13 September 2005.

25 Interview with John Maybury, 15 September 2014.

26 Interview with Daphne Guinness, 10 December 2013.

27 Interview with BillyBoy*, 8 August 2013.

28 Interview with Detmar Blow, 26 June 2013.

29 "Alexander McQueen on Joan," *The Face*, April 1998.

30 "The Killer Queen," *The Face*, April 1998.

31 "Fashion: The Revamp by 'Yoof' Pays Off," Brenda Polan, *Financial Times*, 14 March 1998.

32 "The Oscars: And the Best-Dressed Actress Award Goes to . . . ," Melanie Rickey, *Independent*, 25 March 1998.

33 "The Most Exclusive Fashion Magazine in the World," Grace Bradberry, *The Times*, 8 April 1998.

34 Interview with Richard Brett, 16 July 2013.

35 "A Diet of Fashion Without Victims," Alan Hamilton, *The Times*, 27 May 1998.

36 "McQueen and Country," Christa D'Souza, *Observer Magazine*, 4 March 2001.

37 Interview with John McKitterick, 1 April 2014.

38 Interview with Richard Brett, 16 July 2013.

39 "Fashion That Goes to the Head," Susannah Frankel, *Guardian*, 20 July 1998.

40 "Fantasy League," Colin McDowell, *Sunday Times*, 2 August 1998.

41 "Haute Couture: The Sublime to the Ridiculous," Tamsin Blanchard, *Independent*, 22 July 1998.

42 "Inside Paris," Kirsty Lang, *Sunday Times*, 26 July 1998.

43 "Mr Letterhead: McQueen Shows a Corporate Side," Suzy Menkes, *International Herald Tribune*, 18 September 2001.

44 Interview with Tony McQueen, 20 October 2013.

45 Interview with Richard Brett, 16 July 2013.

46 "Pandora," *Independent*, 22 September 1998.

47 Interview with BillyBoy*, 8 August 2013.

48 Interview with Miguel Adrover, 13 August 2013.

49 Interview with Richard Brett, 16 July 2013.

50 "Sickest Fashion Show of All Time," Catherine Westwood, *Sun*, 30 September 1998.

51 E-mail from Andrew Groves to AW, 27 July 2014.

52 "Alexander McQueen Meets Helen Mirren," *Dazed & Confused*, September 1998.

53 Editor's Letter, Jefferson Hack, *Dazed & Confused*, September 1998.

54 "Drama McQueen," Rob Tannenbaum, *Details*, June 1997.

55 "Access-Able," Alexander McQueen, *Dazed & Confused*, September 1998.

56 "'Barbie Girl' Steps Out in Style," Melanie Rickey, *Independent*, 28 September 1998.

57 "In London, Indulging in a Bit of Creativity," Anne-Marie Schiro, *New York Times*, 29 September 1998.

58 "Oxygen," *Independent on Sunday*, 29 November 1998.

59 Interview with Richard Brett, 16 July 2013.

60 "Designer Wins Legal Aid for Fashion Fight," Mark Henderson, *The Times*, 5 August 1997.

61 Arts Diary, Kathleen Wyatt, *The Times*, 15 May 2000.

62 E-mail from Trevor Merrell to AW, 21 January 2014.

63 "College Drops Sofa Exhibit after McQueen Legal Threat," Katie Nicholl, *Daily Telegraph*, 10 June 2000.

CHAPTER TEN

1 E-mail from Richard Brett to AW, 2 August 2014.

2 Interview with Detmar Blow, 26 June 2013.

3 E-mail from Richard Brett to AW, 2 August 2014.

4 Interview with Archie Reed, 25 May 2013.

5 Interview with Janet Street-Porter, 16 April 2013.

6 "McQueen's Back, and He's Dynamite," Lisa Armstrong, *The Times*, 31 January 2000.

7 Interview with Andrew Groves, 24 April 2013.

8 "McQueen True to His Promise with Best Yet," Lisa Armstrong, *The Times*, 24 February 1999.

9 "Fashion: Art of Poise," Susannah Frankel, *Independent*, 9 June 1999.

10 Interview with Ferhan Azman, 17 April 2013.

11 "Shop of the New," Marcus Field, *Independent on Sunday*, 5 December 1999.

12 Interview with Ferhan Azman, 17 April 2013.

13 Interview with Janet Street-Porter, 16 April 2013.

14 "Backstage with the McQueen of New York," Simon Mills, *Evening Standard*, 20 September 1999.

15 "McQueen's Audacity, Beene's Impishness," Cathy Horyn, *New York Times*, 18 September 1999.

16 "Hurricane McQueen Shakes Up New York," Mimi Spencer, *Evening Standard*, 17 September 1999.

17 "Cherie Dares to Blair for Designer Set," Avril Groom, *Daily Record*, 21 September 1999.

18 "McQueen and Country," *Observer Magazine*, 4 March 2001.

19 "McQueen Comes to the Aid of the Fashion Party," Lisa Armstrong, *The Times*, 21 September 1999.

20 Interview with Richard Brett, 16 July 2013.

21 Interview with Jay Massacret, 22 October 2014.

22 Interview with Sebastian Pons, 20 August 2014.

23 Interview with Jay Massacret, 22 October 2014.

24 "McQueen's Back, and He's Dynamite," Lisa Armstrong, op. cit.

25 "McQueen Puts on the Style, with a Touch of Refinement and Romance," Susannah Frankel, *Independent*, 17 January 2000.

26 "Who: Tracey Emin, Juergen Teller, What: Alexander McQueen Collection Autumn/Winter 2000, Where: Gainsborough Film Studios, London N1," *Nova*, June 2000.

27 "McQueen's Inferno," Mimi Spencer, *Evening Standard*, 16 February 2000.

28 "It's Time to Give These Fashion Freaks the Bum's Rush," Joanna Pitman, *The Times*, 17 February 2000.

29 "Degradation Dressed Up as Joke," Joan Smith, *Independent on Sunday*, February 2000.

30 "The Designer Who Hates Women," Brenda Polan, *Daily Mail*, 17 February 2000.

31 Interview with Janet McQueen, 16 January 2014.

32 Interview with Janet McQueen, 17 September 2013.

33 Interview with Detmar Blow, 26 June 2013.

NOTES

34 "Lean, Mean McQueen," Vassi Chamberlain, *Tatler*, February 2004.

35 "Precarious Beauty," Rebecca Mead, *New Yorker*, 26 September 2011.

36 "The Heiress's Old Clothes," Vanessa Friedman, *Financial Times*, 19 April 2008.

37 "Precarious Beauty," Rebecca Mead, op. cit.

38 "Daphne Guinness's Glove Story," Sheryl Garratt, *Daily Telegraph*, 25 June 2011.

39 "Precarious Beauty," Rebecca Mead, op. cit.

40 Ibid.

41 Interview with Daphne Guinness, 10 December 2013.

42 "Water Swell Party," Rick Fulton, *Daily Record*, 26 May 2000.

43 "Moment Noel Knew the Game Was Up," James Scott, *Daily Record*, 7 September 2000.

44 "McQueen and Country," Christa D'Souza, *Observer Magazine*, 4 March 2001.

45 "Battle Deluxe," Karl Taro Greenfield, *Time*, 8 May 2000.

46 "Fashion's Hard Case," Richard Heller, *Forbes*, 16 September 2002.

47 "McQueen and Country," Christa D'Souza, op. cit.

48 Interview with Jay Massacret, 22 October 2014.

49 Interview with Miguel Adrover, 4 August 2014.

50 "Alexander McQueen's Ex-Partner Throws a Disturbing Light on the 'Hangers-On' Who Lionised Him, but Who Never Truly Knew Him," Laura Collins, *Daily Mail*, 14 February 2010.

51 Interview with Donald Urquhart, 30 October 2013.

52 Donald Urquhart, e-mail to AW, 23 October 2013.

53 "Alexander McQueen's Ex-Partner," Laura Collins, op. cit.

54 "McQueen Branches Out," *Women's Wear Daily*, 27 April 2000.

55 "McQueen Meets Knight," *i-D*, July 2000.

56 Interview with Sebastian Pons, 20 August 2014.

57 Interview with Miguel Adrover, 13 August 2013.

58 "Alexander McQueen's Ex-Partner," Laura Collins, op. cit.

59 Interview with Archie Reed, 25 May 2013.

60 Interview with Chris Bird, 16 September 2013.

61 Interview with Janet Street-Porter, 16 April 2013.

62 "McQueen and Country," Christa D'Souza, op. cit.

63 E-mail from Detmar Blow to AW, 17 August 2014.

64 "Alexander McQueen's Ex-Partner," Laura Collins, op. cit.

65 Donald Urquhart, e-mail to AW, 23 October 2013.

66 Interview with Donald Urquhart, 30 October 2013.

67 "Kate Moss," *Subjective*, SHOWstudio, http://showstudio.com/project/subjective/kate_moss_for_alexander_mcqueen_a_w_06.

68 "McQueen: The Diary of a Dress," Susannah Frankel, *Independent*, 25 October 2000.

69 Michelle Olley, Diary Entry, 26 September 2000, http://blog.metmuseum. org/alexandermcqueen/michelle-olley-voss-diary/.

70 Ibid.

71 "McQueen Meets Knight," *i-D*, July 2000.

72 "Fashion's Hard Case," Richard Heller, op. cit.

73 Interview with Chris Bird, 16 September 2013.

74 "McQueen and Country," Christa D'Souza, op. cit.

75 Interview with John Banks, 1 July 2014.

76 "McQueen and Country," Christa D'Souza, op. cit.

77 "Boy Done Good," Colin McDowell, Richard Woods, Simon Gage, *Sunday Times*, 10 December 2000.

78 Interview with John Banks, 1 July 2014.

79 "Bagged," *Independent*, 5 December 2000.

CHAPTER ELEVEN

1 "Alexander McQueen's Ex-Partner Throws a Disturbing Light on the 'Hangers-On' Who Lionised Him, but Who Never Truly Knew Him," Laura Collins, *Daily Mail*, 14 February 2010.

2 "'I Know It Looks Extreme to Other People. I Don't Find It Extreme,'" Marcus Field, *Art Review*, September 2003.

3 Interview with Janet McQueen, 12 September 2014.

4 Interview with Janet Street-Porter, 16 April 2013.

5 Interview with Archie Reed, 25 May 2013.

6 Interview with Tony McQueen, 20 October 2013.

7 "Killer McQueen," Harriet Quick, *Vogue*, October 2002.

8 "Brit Style," *British Fashion Awards*, BBC2, 21 February 2001.

9 "Designer in Blast at Cherie," Simon Mowbray, *Daily Mirror*, 17 February 2001.

10 "The Paris Shuffle," Hamish Bowles, American *Vogue*, April 2001.

11 "McQueen and Country," Christa D'Souza, *Observer*, 4 March 2001.

12 "Dark Talent Who Conjures Fun from the Sinister," Lisa Armstrong, *The Times*, 22 February 2001.

13 "McQueen's Magic Roundabout Brings Fantasy to London's Fashionistas," Susannah Frankel, *Independent*, 22 February 2001.

14 "Clever Is Better Than Beautiful," Lisa Armstrong, *The Times*, 31 May 2004.

15 Interview with Janet Street-Porter, 16 April 2013.

16 "A Farewell from McQueen," *International Herald Tribune*, 20 March 2001.

17 "'I Know It Looks Extreme,'" Marcus Field, op. cit.

18 Interview with Mira Chai Hyde, 16 May 2014.

19 Interview with Brooke Baker, 1 September 2014.

20 "Helmut Newton, Master of the Camera, Dies in Crash," Oliver Poole, *Daily Telegraph*, 24 January 2004.

21 "Face to Face, Helmut Newton in Conversation," *The Barbican*, 10 May 2001.

22 "Helmut Newton: A Perverse Romantic," Lindsay Baker, *Guardian*, 5 May 2001.

23 E-mail from Ben Copperwheat to AW, 20 June 2014.

24 Interview with Ben Copperwheat, 2 July 2014.

25 E-mail from Ben Copperwheat to AW, 20 June 2014.

26 Interview with Donald Urquhart, 30 October 2013.

27 E-mail from Archie Reed to AW, 13 August 2014.

28 "Show Stoppers," Susannah Frankel, *Independent on Sunday*, 29 September 2002.

29 Interview with Archie Reed, 25 May 2013.

30 "The Boy Is Back in Town," Maggie Davis, *ES Magazine*, 4 January 2002.

31 "Mr Letterhead: McQueen Shows a Corporate Side," Suzy Menkes, *International Herald Tribune*, 18 September 2001.

32 Interview with Kerry Youmans, 30 April 2014.

33 *Last Word*, BBC Radio 4, 12 February 2010.

34 "Radical Fashion," Tamsin Blanchard, *Observer*, 7 October 2001.

35 "Fashion Guru McQueen Has Designs On," *Daily Express*, 19 October 2001.

36 "The Boy Is Back in Town," Maggie Davis, op. cit.

37 "Alexander the Great," Ariel Levy, *New York*, 25 August 2002.

38 "Killer McQueen," Harriet Quick, *Vogue*, October 2002.

39 Interview with John Maybury, 15 September 2014.

40 Interview with Norbert Schoerner, 18 August 2014.

41 "Paint It Black," Susannah Frankel, *Independent Magazine*, 11 August 2001.

42 Interview with Norbert Schoerner, 18 August 2014.

43 "Paint It Black," Susannah Frankel, op. cit.

44 Interview with Kerry Youmans, 30 April 2014.

45 Interview with Eric Rose, 18 July 2013.

46 "The Boy Is Back in Town," Maggie Davis, op. cit.

47 Interview with Tony McQueen, 20 October 2013.

48 Interview with Kerry Youmans, 30 April 2014.

49 Interview with Tony McQueen, 20 October 2013.

50 Interview with Archie Reed, 25 May 2013.

51 "McQueen Stands and Delivers," Hilary Alexander, *Daily Telegraph*, 11 March 2002.

52 "Paris Style: Age of Elegance," Jess Cartner-Morley, *Guardian*, 15 March 2002.

53 "Front Row v Front Line," Anthony Loyd, *The Times*, 12 March 2002.

54 "Oscar Losers," Fatima Bholah, *Sun*, 26 March 2002.

55 "McQueen and Country," Christa D'Souza, op. cit.

56 " 'Meeting the Queen Was Like Falling in Love,' " *Guardian*, 20 April 2004.

57 Interview with Jacqui McQueen, 29 August 2013.

58 Interview with Jacqui McQueen, 29 August 2013.

59 Interview with Daphne Guinness, 10 December 2013.

60 Interview with Janet McQueen, 16 January 2014.

61 "McQueen Stands and Delivers," Hilary Alexander, op. cit.

62 "Killer McQueen," Harriet Quick, op. cit.

63 "Britain's New Queen of Fashion," Chris Blackhurst, *Evening Standard*, 2 March 2011.

64 "Ten Years with Lee," William Russell, Pentagram video, http://new.pentagram.com/2012/12/ten-years-with-alexander-mcqueen/.

65 "McQueen's Space Odyssey," Anamaria Wilson, *Women's Wear Daily*, 1 August 2002.

66 "Alexander McQueen," Chris Heath, *The Face*, September 2002.

67 Interview with John Maybury, 15 September 2014.

68 "Killer McQueen," Harriet Quick, op. cit.

69 Interview with John Maybury, 15 September 2014.

70 "McQueen's Parisian Love Story," Susannah Frankel, *Independent*, 7 October 2002.

71 "Oyster Dress," *Irere*, *Savage Beauty*, Metropolitan Museum, http://blog.met museum.org/alexandermcqueen/oyster-dress-irere.

72 "Go to Gucci . . . I'd Rather Die," Lisa Armstrong, *The Times*, 3 March 2003.

73 "How the West Coast Was Won—McQueen in LA," James Collard, *The Times*, 7 February 2004.

74 "Go to Gucci . . . ," Lisa Armstrong, op. cit.

75 Fashion Diary, Guy Trebay, *New York Times*, 11 March 2003.

76 "Go to Gucci . . . ," Lisa Armstrong, op. cit.

77 "McQueen Is Gifted Enough to Persuade Women to Take Risk," Susannah Frankel, *Independent*, 12 June 2003.

78 Interview with Archie Reed, 25 May 2013.

CHAPTER TWELVE

1 "Fashion Victim: Isabella Blow," David James Smith, *Sunday Times*, 12 August 2007.

2 *Blow by Blow: The Story of Isabella Blow*, Detmar Blow with Tom Sykes (London: HarperCollins, 2010), 223.

3 *Blow by Blow*, 162.

4 Interview with Detmar Blow, 26 June 2013.

5 "McQueen: The Interview," Alex Bilmes, *GQ*, May 2004.

6 Interview with Detmar Blow, 26 June 2013.

7 Interview with Sebastian Pons, 20 August 2014.

8 Interview with Janet McQueen, 12 September 2014.

9 Interview with Archie Reed, 25 May 2013.

10 Interview with Sebastian Pons, 20 August 2014.

11 Interview with Plum Sykes, 30 August 2013.

12 "Mwaah! Mwaah! I'm a Dedicated Follower of Fashion," Jeff Randall, *Sunday Telegraph*, 28 September 2003.

13 "Stella Gets Dressed Down by Banks," Kathryn Spencer, Julie Carpenter, Kate Bohdanowicz, *Daily Express*, 29 September 2003.

14 "At This Dance, McQueen's the Last Man Standing," Ginia Bellafante, *New York Times*, 13 October 2003.

15 "Paris Fashion Report," Colin McDowell, *Sunday Times*, 26 October 2003.

16 "Day & Night," Kathryn Spencer, Julie Carpenter, Kate Bohdanowicz, *Daily Express*, 15 January 2004.

17 "Oliver, MBE, Fails to Invest in a Tie," Alan Hamilton, *The Times*, 30 October 2003.

18 "'Meeting the Queen Was Like Falling in Love,'" *Guardian*, 20 April 2004.

19 Interview with Janet McQueen, 12 September 2014.

20 "Sticking with London, and Himself," Cathy Horyn, *New York Times*, 2 March 2004.

21 Interview with Daphne Guinness, 10 December 2013.

22 "Crystal Gazing McQueen Branches Out for V&A," Charlie Porter, *Guardian*, 16 December 2003.

23 "McQueen: The Interview," Alex Bilmes, op. cit.

24 "'Meeting the Queen Was Like Falling in Love,'" *Guardian*, op. cit.

25 "The Real McQueen," Susannah Frankel, American *Harper's Bazaar*, April 2007.

26 Interview with Sebastian Pons, 20 August 2014.

27 Interview with Plum Sykes, 30 August 2013.

28 Interview with Detmar Blow, 26 June 2013.

29 *Blow by Blow*, 234.

30 "The Old Black McQueen in London for Charity," Jess Cartner-Morley, *Guardian*, 4 June 2004.

31 "Annabelle Neilson," *Evening Standard*, 18 June 2004.

32 "McQueen: The Interview," Alex Bilmes, op. cit.

33 "The Runway Bride," Meenal Mistry, *W*, June 2006.

34 "The Genius Next Door," Andrew O'Hagan, *T Magazine*, *New York Times*, 22 August 2014.

35 Interview with Plum Sykes, 30 August 2013.

36 Interview with Archie Reed, 25 May 2013.

37 "Hail McQueen," Bridget Foley, *W*, June 2008.

38 Interview with Sue Stemp, 21 August 2014.

39 Interview with Kerry Youmans, 30 April 2014.

40 Interview with Glenn Andrew Teeuw, 13 October 2014.

41 "Paris Fashion Week: McQueen's Vamps and Secretaries for Next Winter," Dominique Ageorges, Agence France Presse, 4 March 2005.

42 "Boy Done Good," Jess Cartner-Morley, *Guardian*, 19 September 2005.

43 "Renegade Luxury Is Born as McQueen Courts Youth Market," Hilary Alexander, *Daily Telegraph*, 10 February 2006.

44 "Alexander McQueen on *The Execution of Lady Jane Grey*," *Today*, BBC Radio 4, http://www.bbc.co.uk/radio4/today/vote/greatestpainting/index.shtml.

45 *Elle* magazine interview, quoted in *Alexander McQueen: The Life and the Legacy*, Judith Watt (New York: Harper Design, 2013), 228.

46 "Kate Moss," *Subjective*, SHOWstudio, http://showstudio.com/project/subjective/kate_moss_for_alexander_mcqueen_a_w_06.

47 "Scorn of 'Stitch Bitch' Alexander McQueen . . . Designer Who Dressed (and Dissed!) the A-list," Wendy Leigh, *Mail on Sunday*, 27 July 2014.

48 Interview with Kerry Youmans, 30 April 2014.

49 *Alexander McQueen: Savage Beauty*, Metropolitan Museum of Art, New York (New Haven: Yale University Press, 2011), 25.

NOTES

CHAPTER THIRTEEN

1 *Blow by Blow: The Story of Isabella Blow*, Detmar Blow with Tom Sykes (London: HarperCollins, 2010), 243.
2 *Blow by Blow*, 246.
3 Interview with Daphne Guinness, 10 December 2013.
4 "Lips Together, Knees Apart," Rupert Everett, *Vanity Fair*, September 2006.
5 "NY UK," Valentine Low, *Evening Standard*, 2 May 2006.
6 "McQueen's Tailoring Wins Wearability War," Imogen Fox, *Guardian*, 7 October 2006.
7 "The Real McQueen," Susannah Frankel, American *Harper's Bazaar*, April 2007.
8 Interview with Archie Reed, 25 May 2013.
9 Interview with Kerry Youmans, 30 April 2014.
10 E-mail from Alison D'Amario, 9 September 2014.
11 Interview with Kerry Youmans, 30 April 2014.
12 "Hail McQueen," Bridget Foley, *W*, June 2008.
13 Interview with Archie Reed, 25 May 2013.
14 "Scorn of 'Stich Bitch' Alexander McQueen . . . Designer Who Dressed (and Dissed!) the A-list," Wendy Leigh, *Mail on Sunday*, 27 July 2014.
15 Interview with Detmar Blow, 26 June 2013.
16 "Hail McQueen," Bridget Foley, op. cit.
17 Interview with Suzy Menkes, 13 June 2014.
18 "Alexander McQueen: Psychic Search That Haunted Star," *Daily Express*, 15 February 2010.
19 Interview with Archie Reed, 25 May 2013.
20 Interview with Detmar Blow, 26 June 2013.
21 Interview with Daphne Guinness, 10 December 2013.
22 Interview with BillyBoy*, 8 August 2013.
23 E-mail from Richard Gray to AW, 11 September 2014.
24 "Scorn of 'Stitch Bitch,'" Wendy Leigh, op. cit.
25 "Fashion Scents McQueen's Perfumed Tribute to Late Muse," Jess Cartner-Morley, *Guardian*, 6 October 2007.
26 Ibid.
27 "Hail McQueen," Bridget Foley, op. cit.
28 "Alexander McQueen Hanged Himself after Taking Drugs," Sam Jones, *Guardian*, 28 April 2010.
29 E-mail from Janet McQueen to AW, 8 September 2014.
30 "Hail McQueen," Bridget Foley, op. cit.
31 Interview with Glenn Andrew Teeuw, 13 October 2014.
32 E-mail from Janet McQueen to AW, 2 September 2014.
33 "Hail McQueen," Bridget Foley, op. cit.
34 Interview with Guy Morgan-Harris, 30 July 2013.
35 "Collections Report," Susannah Frankel, *AnOther Magazine*, S/S 2008.

36 "Hail McQueen," Bridget Foley, op. cit.

37 "Lagerfeld's Seamless Twist on Classic Chanel," *Guardian Unlimited*, 29 February 2008.

38 "Alexander Has No Designs on Paris," Kathryn Spencer with Lizzie Catt, Claudia Goulder and Catherine Boyle, *Daily Express*, 8 April 2008.

39 Interview with Archie Reed, 25 May 2013.

40 "Amy Threw a £15,000 Dress from Alexander McQueen on the Barbecue," Katie Nicholl, *Mail on Sunday*, 7 August 2011.

41 E-mail from Sue Stemp to AW, 14 August 2013.

42 E-mail from Janet McQueen to AW, 9 September 2014.

43 Interview with Janet McQueen, 16 January 2014.

44 "Natural Beauty," Susannah Frankel, *Independent*, 6 April 2009.

45 E-mail from Gary James McQueen to AW, 9 September 2014.

46 "Exotic Creatures: McQueen's Bid to Save the Planet," Jess Cartner-Morley, *Guardian*, 4 October 2008.

47 Interview with Michael McQueen, 7 November 2013.

48 "Scorn of 'Stich Bitch,'" Wendy Leigh, op. cit.

49 Interview with Paul Stag, 24 April 2013.

50 Interview with Jacqui McQueen, 8 April 2014.

51 Interview with Matav Sinclair, 27 May 2013.

52 Interview with Sebastian Pons, 19 August 2014.

53 "McQueen Leaves Fashion in Ruins," Eric Wilson, *New York Times*, 12 March 2009.

54 *Alexander McQueen: Savage Beauty*, Metropolitan Museum of Art, New York (New Haven: Yale University Press, 2011), 227.

55 *Alexander McQueen: Working Process*, photographs by Nick Waplington, foreword by Susannah Frankel (Bologna: Damiani, 2013), 1.

56 "The Outsider," Rachel Newsome, *Ponystep*, 21 January 2012.

57 *Alexander McQueen: Working Process*, 5.

58 Interview with Murray Arthur, 21 November 2013.

59 Interview with Sebastian Pons, 19 August 2014.

60 E-mail from Guy Morgan-Harris to AW, 27 February 2014.

61 Interview with Janet McQueen, 2 October 2013.

62 Interview with Janet McQueen, 16 January 2014.

63 Interview with Jacqui McQueen, 29 August 2013.

64 Interview with Janet McQueen, 17 September 2013.

65 Interview with Paul Stag, 24 April 2013.

66 Interview with Tony McQueen, 20 October 2013.

67 Interview with Paul Stag, 24 April 2013.

68 Interview with Janet McQueen, 16 January 2014.

69 Interview with Paul Stag, 24 April 2013.

70 Interview with BillyBoy*, 8 August 2013.

71 Interview with Jane Hayward, 16 April 2013.

72 "Hail McQueen," Bridget Foley, op. cit.

73 "General Lee," Cathy Horyn, *New York Times*, 13 September 2009.

74 "As Tom Ford Bows Out, a Tiff over Star Power," Cathy Horyn, *New York Times*, 8 March 2004.

75 "An Interview with Sarah Burton by Tim Blanks," *Savage Beauty*, 229.

76 Ibid.

77 "Alexander McQueen's Last Collection Unveiled on Paris Catwalk," *Guardian Unlimited*, 9 March 2010.

78 "McQueen of the Jungle Prints and Towering Heels," Laura Craik, *Evening Standard*, 7 October 2009.

79 "Going Gaga over 'Unwearable' Shoes," *Observer*, 15 November 2009.

80 Alexander McQueen Show Notes, Spring/Summer 2010, Susannah Frankel.

81 *Savage Beauty*, 230.

82 "Lady Gaga: The Interview," Derek Blasberg, *Harper's Bazaar*, May 2011.

83 Interview with Janet McQueen, 16 January 2014.

84 Interview with Paul Stag, 24 April 2013.

85 Interview with Max Newsom, 19 July 2013.

86 "A Man of Darkness and Dreams," Ingrid Sischy, *Vanity Fair*, April 2010.

87 "Alexander McQueen: The Final Interview," Godfrey Deeny, Australian *Harper's Bazaar*, April 2010.

88 E-mail from Janet McQueen to AW, 16 September 2014.

89 Interview with Michael McQueen, 7 November 2013.

90 "To All My Children," Joyce McQueen, courtesy of McQueen family archive.

91 Interview with Dafydd Jones, 31 July 2014.

92 Interview with Tony McQueen, 20 October 2013.

93 Interview with Jacqui McQueen, 29 August 2013.

94 Interview with Archie Reed, 25 May 2013.

95 Interview with Gary James McQueen, 11 June 2013.

96 "Alexander McQueen's Twitter Revealed Troubled Mind," Nick Collins, *Daily Telegraph*, 12 February 2010.

97 "Alexander McQueen's Final Bow," Cathy Horyn, *New York Times*, 3 April 2010.

98 Interview with Kerry Youmans, 30 April 2014.

99 Interview with Daphne Guinness, 10 December 2013.

100 "Annabelle Neilson Remembers Alexander McQueen," Annabelle Neilson, *Harper's Bazaar*, May 2010.

101 https://answers.yahoo.com/question/index?qid=20070221133728AAJGbds.

102 Interview with Janet McQueen, 16 January 2014.

AFTERWORD

1 "Alexander McQueen's Final Bow," Cathy Horyn, *New York Times*, 3 April 2010.

2 Interview with Michael McQueen, 7 November 2013.

3 "The Lonely Suicide of Alexander McQueen . . . and Family's Anger at Mystery of £16m Legacy," Claudia Joseph, *Mail on Sunday*, 24 November 2013.

4 Interview with Jacqui McQueen, 8 April 2014.

5 Interview with Daphne Guinness, 10 December 2013.

6 "L'Officiel, Alexander McQueen Le génie provocateur," *Tributes and Testimonies,* ed. Patrick Cabasset, February 2010.

7 Interview with Alice Smith, 7 May 2013.

8 Interview with Andrew Groves, 24 April 2013.

9 Interview with Archie Reed, 25 May 2013.

10 Interview with BillyBoy*, 8 August 2013.

11 Interview with Detmar Blow, 26 June 2013.

12 "Lee McQueen" by Donald Urquhart, e-mail to AW, 23 October 2013.

13 Interview with Louise Wilson, 14 May 2014.

14 *Night Waves*, BBC Radio 3, 11 February 2010.

15 Interview with Miguel Adrover, 13 August 2013.

16 Interview with Murray Arthur, 21 November 2013.

17 Interview with Sebastian Pons, 19 August 2014.

18 "It's Sad That Alexander McQueen Has Died, but 'Fashionistas' Are Just Freaks: There I've Said It," George Pitcher, *Daily Telegraph*, 15 February 2010.

19 Interview with Ben de Lisi, 31 July 2013.

20 Interview with John Maybury, 15 September 2014.

21 "Naomi Campbell Hosts Haiti Show That Mourns McQueen," Christine Kearney, *Independent*, 13 February 2010.

22 Interview with Daphne Guinness, 10 December 2013.

23 Interview with Gary James McQueen, 11 June 2013.

24 E-mail from Janet McQueen to AW, 17 September 2014.

25 "Alexander McQueen Hanged Himself after Taking Drugs," Sam Jones, *Guardian*, 28 April 2010.

26 Interview with Janet McQueen, 17 September 2013.

27 Interview with Janet McQueen, 12 September 2014.

28 "The Lonely Suicide of Alexander McQueen," Claudia Joseph, op. cit.

29 Ibid.

30 Letter from Richard Day to Ronald McQueen, 2 November 2011, McQueen family papers.

31 Interview with Jacqui McQueen, 29 August 2013.

PHOTOGRAPHY CREDITS

INDEX

INDEX

INDEX

ABOUT THE AUTHOR

Andrew Wilson is a journalist who has written for the *Guardian*, the *Daily Mail*, the *Daily Telegraph* and the *Observer*. He is the author of the critically acclaimed *Beautiful Shadow: A Life of Patricia Highsmith*, the novel *The Lying Tongue*, *Harold Robbins: The Man Who Invented Sex*, *Shadow of the Titanic* and *Mad Girl's Love Song: Sylvia Plath and Life Before Ted*.